The Modern Rhyming Dictionary

The Modern Rhyming Dictionary

How To Write Lyrics

Including a practical guide to lyric
writing for songwriters and poets

Gene Lees

*To the memory
of Johnny Mercer*

Sonnet

Music is a strange and useless thing.
It doesn't offer cover from the storm.
It doesn't, really, ease the sting
of living, or nourish us, or keep us warm.

And men expend their lives in search of sound,
learning how to juggle bits of noise,
and by their swift illusions to confound
the heart with fleeting and evasive joys.

Yet I am full of quaking gratitude
that this exalted folly still exists,
that in an age of cold computer mood,
a piper still can whistle in the mists.
His notes are pebbles falling into time.
How sweetly mad it is, and how sublime.

— Gene Lees

FOREWORD

In wandering through Bartlett's *Familiar Quotations,* we came across this, written by one R.L. Sharpe in 1890:

Each is given a bag of tools,
A shapeless mass,
A book of rules;
And each must make,
Ere life is flown,
A stumbling block
Or a stepping stone.

This book of rhymes, this bag of tools (hardly a shapeless mass) contains highly polished stepping stones that can assist both the amateur and professional lyric writer across what may sometimes seem a great divide.

In addition to being a dictionary of rhymes, organized in a new and more logical way, it is a primer on the art and craft of lyric writing. Gene Lees has not only written some perfectly wonderful lyrics, but in the chapter on General Principles preceding the dictionary itself, he offers perhaps the most scholarly, most complete treatise on the art of marrying language to music. As distinct from poetry, he analyzes the exacting task of lyric writers in not only writing words that fit the music but give singers a chance to make effortlessly beautiful sounds. He makes clear that the rules that govern the craft are not arbitrary. Lyrics that observe the natural rhythms and accents of speech are a pleasure to sing. Pure rhymes are a pleasure to hear. All practical and reasonable requirements. Reason and rhyme have always been a great combination.

If there exists a stigma against the use of a rhyming dictionary, it may help to know that every lyric writer worth his or her salt, even the best, like Alan Jay Lerner and Stephen Sondheim, acknowledge its occasional use. True, after years of rhyming, you may have most of it in your head. But that *one* rhyme that eludes you at a particular moment might be the one that you need, *le mot juste.*

This book is dedicated to the memory of Johnny Mercer. Coupled with a study of this master's lyrics, Gene Lees has given the experienced as well as neophyte writer (composers too might benefit from its opening chapters) all the tools necessary to brave "the long, solitary, often frustrating, but ultimately very rewarding task of writing lyrics."

—Alan and Marilyn Bergman

CONTENTS

HOW TO WRITE LYRICS

THE DICTIONARY

How To Write Lyrics

1.

SOME GENERAL PRINCIPLES

"It is," Hilaire Belloc once wrote, "the best of all trades to make songs, and the second best to sing them."

As one who has been privileged for some years to make his living doing both, I concur. Singing is more fun. Writing is more work. But the writing of a perfect song gives its creator an inexpressible pleasure, one that is heightened by the thought that others, hearing it later, will perhaps derive a pleasure from it, too. A friend of mine described seeing Harold Arlen stop still in La Guardia Airport when one of his melodies came over the sound system. A look of puzzled wonder filled his face. And the crowd moved on around him, no one among them knowing him but many and perhaps most of them knowing the song.

In the French lyrics of "L'âme des poètes" ("The Soul of Poets"), the great Charles Trenet wrote: "Long after the poets have disappeared, their songs still run in the streets. Sometimes a singer will change a word or a phrase or, forgetting a line entirely, substitute *da-da-dum da-da-dum*. Will the song play on a phonograph by the water in the spring?" he asks. "Will it lull a baby to sleep?"

We never know, when we write a song—at least those of us who are fortunate enough to do so professionally, with a reasonable hope of its exposure to the public—where it will end up. My friend Johnny Mandel, who wrote (among many superb melodies) one of the most recorded songs in history, "The Shadow of Your Smile," quipped one day, "I do very well in elevators."

It is commonplace for songwriters to be told by a new acquaintance that he or she fell in love or had a great romance or got married to the accompaniment of one of their songs. I usually make some such joke as, "I hope you won't hold me responsible." But this is only to hide an embarrassed pleasure. Therein lies one of the subtlest thrills of song-writing, particularly lyric writing: the totality of the communication. People memorize your thoughts. Playwrights and novelists rarely have that experience.

But at the time you are actually doing the writing, which is a lonely business—all writing is lonely—the chief thrill is that of craftsmanship, in and of and for itself. Boris Vian, the French novelist and lyricist who died all too young, said once in an interview that he was more proud of his lyrics than of his novels. The lyric is the most exquisitely difficult literary form of them all. It is much more difficult to write lyrics *well* than it is to write poetry. If the poet wants to spring his rhythms to express a thought, if he wants to insert an extra syllable, he usually can do so without violating the integrity of the line. Even within the discipline of the iambic pentameter in which Shakespeare wrote his plays, he had the liberty to shift the stresses within the lines when it suited his purposes, a liberty the lyricist does not have—not, that is, if he is practicing the craft at its highest levels. You will, of course, encounter only too many examples of the craft practiced at a lower level.

It is best to write the melody first, for reasons we will discuss later. But then the lyricist, fitting his words to it, must work within rigid restrictions. To be sure, he may on occasion ask the composer with whom he is collaborating for two eighth notes in place of a quarter, or ask him to remove a pick-up note. But circumstances that permit this are comparatively few, and, what is more, it becomes a point of pride with a really skilled lyricist *not* to tamper with the melody.

I am not talking about those writers who so often will jam leventy-seventeen-syllables-into-a-line that should have only a few, simply because they lack the discipline and skill to find a more graceful solution to the problem, a solution that leaves the melody undistorted. I am talking about a man like Tom Adair, whose taste, sensitivity, and craftsmanship are manifest in such lyrics as "Everything Happens to Me," "In the Blue of Evening," "There's No You," "Let's Get Away from It All," "The Night We Called It a Day," and "Violets for Your Furs."

The craft of lyric writing has declined in America in the latter part of the twentieth century. One of the major causes of this decline is the rise of the record industry and Top 40 radio as the dominant forces in American musical life. In the 1940s, the record industry was a small one, and a mere adjunct to American music. It recorded those stars who had been created by other media, including network radio, the movies, and the theater. The quality of American popular music rose to a level it had never achieved before and may never reach again.

A generation that has grown up since the advent of television cannot imagine the part network radio played in American life, the force it exerted for musical enlightenment. Network radio's treatment of music bore no resemblance to that of contemporary local radio. It gave the United States a cornucopia of musical riches, from Grand Ol' Opry to grand opera, from Woody Herman to Arturo Toscanini. And it was "live," not recorded music. The networks paid orchestras and solo musicians and singers, providing employment for countless performers. Many local radio stations even generated their own live music. Records didn't make stars. Stars made records. And radio made the stars.

Television came into prominence in the late 1940s and early 1950s. The networks, finding TV more profitable (and more glamorous to their advertisers), let their national radio programming fall into desuetude. Local radio stations, no longer able to depend on high-quality programs emanating from New York, Chicago, and Los Angeles, perforce relied more and more on records for their program content. And the record industry, which was expanding rapidly as the post-war bumper crop of

4

babies reached puberty and began buying their product, was more and more dependent on "air-play" to sell that product. Meantime, radio had discovered the so-called Top 40 format, playing only a very few songs each week—some stations as few as fifteen—and all of them designed to appeal to the limited and inexperienced perception of adolescents. An inevitable constriction of American taste set in.

Radio has no interest in music. It is in the advertising business. The record industry has no interest in music. It is in the business of selling pieces of plastic. It is a gigantic machine, almost entirely owned now by international conglomerates, whose only purpose is to accrue profits. It is indifferent to what is on its plastic discs, except insofar as it induces the undiscriminating to buy them. It virtually ignores the discriminating audience because the undiscriminating are so much more numerous. That they are so numerous may be attributed to several factors, although the schools must bear some of the blame. The teaching of English has declined sadly—disastrously, some would say. It is not only that our communications complex, which includes both the school system and the mass media, has produced a generation of lyricists who are only rudimentarily literate; it has created an audience of millions who would not recognize the excellent on encountering it.

One purpose of this book is to help define the excellent in lyric writing. The book will tell you nothing whatever about how to make money in the music business. There are other books devoted to that subject, although some of them seem directed more toward making their authors money that making you money.

The principles herein described apply to all kinds of lyrics, from country-and-western lyrics, some of which are very good, to Broadway show lyrics, some of which are very bad. In general, however, the highest standard of lyric writing has been set by the theater, and I would recommend that any beginner make a study of Broadway musical scores, particularly the older ones.

Every artist begins by imitating the masters—or at least he does if he has any brains. Eventually, one begins to understand what the masters did, and why, and grasps the technique itself. If the aspirant artist has what is generally called talent, he will begin to do fresh and personal work, and it will be said of that work that is has a style. If he has no talent and remains derivative, he will at least, through the imitation of good models, produce competent work and will do no great harm to the art. Perhaps there is no such thing as talent. Perhaps what we call talent is an unquenchable curiosity about how things are done or made, coupled with a dogged patience about becoming adept in the application of the principles thus uncovered. Or, inverting the thought, we might say that everyone has talent, but not everyone has the determination and patience to develop it. The beginning place in that process is the study of the work of the masters.

5

Indeed, to ignore the work of one's predecessors is to waste a lot of time discovering for yourself what others have already learned. A man would be a fool to try to "invent" counterpoint when he can look to Bach to see how it is done.

When Queen Victoria complained to William Gladstone that there were not many good preachers, he said, "Ma'am, there are not many good *any*thing."

There have been only a few truly great lyricists in modern English. Most of them have been American, which is puzzling, when you consider how much more literate and expressive English speech usually is than American. Nonetheless, the best lyricists all owe a debt, direct or indirect, to an English lyricist, William S. Gilbert, of the Gilbert and Sullivan team. "We all come from Gilbert," Johnny Mercer used to say.

In his introduction to Alec Wilder's book *American Popular Song: The Great Innovators, 1900-1950* (published by Oxford University Press in 1972 and far and away the most important book ever written about American popular music), James T. Maher wrote, "Could it be then that what really distinguishes musical theater from Tin Pan Alley is the discipline of a tradition that permits freedom of innovation while exacting, in return, that rare and peculiar eloquence which only theater music can yield, an exaction few have truly met?

"One writing in the theater lives with that tradition, with its freedom and its penalties. Puccini, far off, Lehár in the middle distance, and Jerome Kern, Irving Berlin, George Gershwin, Richard Rodgers, Arthur Schwartz, and Harold Arlen close at hand are *listening*. (So, too, are P. G. Wodehouse, Lorenz Hart, Cole Porter, Oscar Hammerstein II, Ira Gershwin, Dorothy Fields, and John Mercer.) The newest songwriter in the theater must answer to them, for they are the measure of what he does. Throughout his career, he must stand up against the formidable witness of their best work. And he cannot wish them away for they have instructed the communal ear—their songs are part of the unconscious reflex of the common memory."

The models I would recommend to any aspiring lyricist are Cole Porter, Howard Dietz, Lorenz Hart, Dorothy Fields, Sheldon Harnick, Alan Jay Lerner, E. Y. Harburg, Frank Loesser, and Irving Berlin. One should also look into the satiric lyrics of Tom Lehrer, many of which are to be found on records. They are superb, and very funny.

There are other lyricists, in and out of the theater, such as Carolyn Leigh, who have done fine work, but the quantity of it is less. Jake Thackray, an English songwriter whose melodies are fresh and interesting and whose lyrics are works of utter virtuosity, is not well known in America, although he has made many records in England.

If I were asked to pick what I thought were the two best scores ever written for American musical theater, I would unhesitatingly name *Guys and Dolls* by Frank Loesser and *My Fair Lady* by Lerner and Loewe.

You can learn an enormous amount about lyric writing from these scores.

My Fair Lady may, in fact, be the most perfectly crafted musical in American history, much of the credit for which must go to Alan Jay Lerner, who wrote the book from Shaw's play, *Pygmalion*, as well as the lyrics. Certainly the lyrics are the best to be found in any one show. Every one of them is a masterpiece. Fortunately, the score is still available on records, and likely to remain so.

Perhaps the best lyricist of all was Johnny Mercer. Although he wrote seven musicals for the theater, Mercer produced the larger body of his work for films and recordings. Paul Weston, the composer and arranger who worked extensively with Mercer, said, "John did more things well than any other lyricist. John had genius." I agree with Weston, and go farther in the sense that I believe John was one of the great lyric poets in history. And he achieved that within the strict and confining discipline of songwriting.

Although lyrics should be heard rather than read to be appreciated, there is a useful book by Lehman Engel titled *Their Words Are Music* (Crown, New York, 1973) in which many of the finest theater lyrics are printed. They are deftly and accurately analyzed by Engel, himself a Broadway conductor.

There is no book that I have seen, other than the one you have in your hand, that deals directly and specifically and only with the craft of lyric writing, although there are a number of books that will assure you that anybody can write a song and get rich in the music business.

Nor is there another rhyming dictionary designed to meet the special and specific needs of the lyricist. The two best-known rhyming dictionaries are *New Rhyming Dictionary and Poet's Handbook* by Burges Johnson (Harper and Row) and *The Complete Rhyming Dictionary: The Essential Handbook for Poets and Songwriters* by Clement Wood (Doubleday, 1936). Johnson's "new" dictionary was published in 1931. Both books contain essays on the techniques of poetry, but not one word on how to write a lyric, despite the title of the latter volume.

The compilations of rhymes are indeed exhaustive. But they are too undiscriminating to be of quick and efficient assistance to the lyricist. And they are not organized along phonetic lines, like the present volume, which is, to the best of my knowledge, the only one of its kind. Indeed, this dictionary is the result of my own experience as a songwriter: the principles of its organization grew out of need. If someone had written it years ago, it would have saved me an enormous amount of work.

The professional lyricist will perhaps be familiar with all the principles set forth in the chapters on technique. Still, he or she may derive a certain pleasure from a discussion of principles most of us had to discover for ourselves and rarely talk about. These chapters are nonetheless designed primarily for the beginning songwriter.

The dictionary is intended for the beginner and professional alike.

2.
ABOUT RHYME

Is rhyme necessary to lyric writing? A poem does not have to rhyme, and, strictly speaking, a lyric does not either. "Moonlight in Vermont," one of the loveliest of American songs, does not rhyme. I wrote a song with Lalo Schifrin called "The Right to Love," which has been recorded by many singers, not one of whom seems to have noticed that the lyric is not written in rhyme.

But rhyming seems to be a natural thing. Children make up rhymes to amuse themselves. There is a peculiar pleasure we get from rhyming, perhaps because of the musical effect established by the recurrence of sounds. And rhyming is a powerful mnemonic device. In the long epic poems of earlier cultures, in eras when reading and writing were rare skills, anticipation of the rhyme helped the narrator to remember his lines.

These two factors alone, the musical effect and the reinforcement of memory that rhyme provides, make it a useful device. There is a third: the very search for a rhyme, as Goethe noted, leads the mind in fresh directions of exploration—though it can lead it to clichés such as *moon* and *June* if the writer is lazy. Most of the lyrics of the past have been written in rhyme and undoubtedly most of those in the future will be as well.

There are two basic types of rhyme, known as masculine and feminine. The terms derive from the Latin languages and their genders. English is the only European language that does not apply genders to words. French, Spanish, Italian, and the other Latin languages recognize words as masculine or feminine.

As the term is used in poetry and lyric writing, masculine rhymes are those of one syllable, such as *lone* and *own*. *Alone* also constitutes a masculine rhyme, since the first syllable is unstressed; the stress falls on the single final syllable.

Feminine rhymes are those of two syllables with (and this is very important) the stress on the first of them, e.g., *FEA-ther* and *WHE-ther*, or in the case of two-word feminine rhymes, *MISS you* and *KISS you*. A two-syllable word, such as *in-DULGE*, would not function as a feminine rhyme, since the accent is, as it is in *alone*, on the final syllable. It would function as a masculine, rhyming with *BULGE* and *di-VULGE*.

There are three-syllable rhymes, such as *hurried by* and *worried by* and four-syllable rhymes. They have no specific technical names; lyricists call them, sensibly enough, three-rhymes and four-rhymes.

Two-syllable or feminine rhymes should be perfect. But there is a certain amount of latitude inherent in three-rhymes and four-rhymes.

In "I Won't Dance" Dorothy Fields rhymed "bumped on the shore" with "stumped on the floor." Does the fact that the consonants beginning *shore* and *floor* do not match make the rhyme imperfect? Not really. There is another way to look at these lines. *Bumped* and *stumped* form a quite correct masculine rhyme, and so do *shore* and *floor*. Thus, we have perfect masculine rhymes alternating in an ABAB pattern, if you want to look at it that way—or an imperfect four, if you want to look at it another.

Alan Jay Lerner used a five-rhyme in the release of "On the Street Where You Live"—"And oh, the *towering feeling*," which is followed by "the over*powering feeling*," which gives us a perfect five-rhyme. And, incidentally, because of the *oh* sound in both lines, Lerner very nearly pulled off a seven-rhyme. His craftsmanship is never obtrusively clever: such lines occur as if they were natural and spontaneous expressions.

When you get into these compound rhymes, then, you have a certain amount of flexibility to play with the patterns of sound. Not so with the simpler masculine and feminine rhymes, wherein an improper match is as jarring to the sensitive ear as an out-of-tune note.

The two-syllable rhymes present particular problems to anyone writing lyrics in English, because ours is a strongly stressed language, unlike French. If a composer presents you with a melodic phrase that ends with a *DAH-dum*, followed by another that ends with a *DAH-dum*, one is compelled to use a feminine rhyme, such as *NA-tion* and *in-FLA-tion*. You cannot use *PY-rex* and *WIN-dex*, which I heard, in fact, in a college lyric, because the stress in each word is on the first syllable, and the first syllables do not match.

English is not rich in feminine rhymes—nor in rhymes generally, compared with French, Spanish, Portuguese, or Italian. In Italian, almost everything seems to rhyme.

One of the most conspicuous examples of the poverty of rhyme in English will be found in the word *love*, which makes the problem positively excruciating, since most songs are love songs. There are only four true rhymes for the word—*above, dove, glove,* and *shove*. Since in America we are inclined to mispronounce *of* (which should rhyme with *suave*) as *uv*, it can be used as a fifth rhyme. It is a bit of a cheat, but one that custom has made acceptable, leading, alas, to innumerable lines about the various things that someone is *dreaming of*. And of course there are in the collective body of our lyrics more *stars above* than are to be found in the Hayden Planetarium.

Rhyming dictionaries may include *fox-glove* and *turtle-dove* as rhymes for *love*, but in the first place, these are merely words compounded of two already on that pathetic little list, and in the second place, they do not rhyme properly with *love*. *Fox-glove* must function as a feminine rhyme, because of the stress on the first syllable. It would thus rhyme with some such synthetic term as *box-glove*. As for *turtle-dove*, it isn't of much use—quite aside from its lavender-scented archaicism—unless you happen to be writing a song about a girl named Myrtle Dove. As for *dove* itself, nobody besides W. C. Fields has shown much inclination to call anyone that since the 1890s.

I once found a way, somewhat to my own surprise, to use *shove* in a lyric. Written to music by Antonio Carlos Jobim and called "This Happy Madness," it ended:

> *The gods are laughing far above.*
> *One of them gave a little shove.*
> *and I fell gaily, gladly, madly into love.*©

Glove is not often used as a rhyme. It turns up in "Misty"—"I don't know...my hat from my glove." In "People Will Say We're in Love," Oscar Hammerstein wrote: "Give me my rose and my glove." For years, I did not understand the line. A lady eventually told me that it was, in the era in which the song is set (it is from the musical *Oklahoma!*), the custom of a gentleman to pilfer a rose and a glove from the object of his ardor as an earnest of his affection. I have only that lady's word for it that this petty larceny does (or did) have this poetic meaning, and I still consider the Hammerstein line awkward and obscure. On the other hand, Alan Jay Lerner used this rhyme with wit. flair, and naturalism in "I'm an Ordinary Man."

> *You want to talk of Keats or Milton;*
> *she only wants to talk of love.*
> *You go to see a play or ballet*
> *and spend it searching for her glove.*

The scarcity of rhymes for *love* makes the task of writing a love song in English much more difficult than it is in French, which has more than forty rhymes for *amour*. These include *faubourg* (the *g* is mute), which means *suburb; tambour,* which means *drum; carrefour,* which means *crossroads*; and *jour*, which means *day*. Thus you could write, "My heart is beating like a drum because we have come to a crossroads of our love in the suburbs," without encountering a rhyming problem.

Or consider the word *mouth*. It has only one rhyme, *south*, and Cole Porter took care of that one forever with:

> *I love the eyes, the arms, the mouth of you,*
> *the east, west, north, and the south of you.*

(That is a three-rhyme, by the way, let us note in passing.)

In Portuguese, *heart* rhymes with *guitar* and *song*—*coracão, violão,* and *cancão*. They seem like fresh rhymes to anyone first encountering

Brazilian songs, but after you have heard the hundred-and-thirty-third variant on "the feeling I have in my heart as I play you a song on my guitar," you begin to yawn over that pattern, too.

Some years ago, when I was translating some of Charles Aznavour's songs from French into English, we fell into a discussion about the comparative richness of rhyme in French, of which I was envious. "Yes," he said, "but in practice, we end up using the same rhymes over and over, just as you do in English. The trick is to find a fresh way to get to them."

There are few fresh rhymes in English, certainly not one-syllable or masculine rhymes. Occasionally, something unexpected is encountered in a feminine rhyme, as in the lyric by Howard Dietz for "That's Entertainment." Describing Shakespeare's *Hamlet*, he wrote:

> *... where a ghost and a prince meet,*
> *and everybody ends in mincemeat.*

In "Mountain Greenery," Lorenz Hart attached the ending of one word to the beginning of another to achieve a rhyme for *greenery*:

> *Beans could get no keener re-*
> *ception*
> *in a beanery...*

This kind of extremely clever, conspicuous, and calculatedly synthetic rhyme will usually be found effective only in humorous songs, however. In a ballad, such cleverness would tend to overshadow the emotional content.

The problem of the well-worn rhyme is that it usually sets the listener up to expect the next line. He half knows what it is going to be. The trick, as Aznavour points out, is to fool him by your unexpected approach to the anticipated rhyme. The lyrics of a trite writer are predictable. Those of the ingenious and inventive one are not.

Though *love* and those other four (or five) words present us with the most depleted set of rhymes in the English language, there is no way, when you hear Lerner's line, "She only wants to talk of love," to predict that he is going for something as fresh and funny and universally understandable as "spend it searching for her glove." The very sense of anticipation that the word *love* sets up, and then the unexpected use of one of its few rhymes, adds to the elements of surprise and charm.

You will rarely, however, find so astute a use of those four (or five) rhymes. It is therefore advisable to avoid altogether, if possible, using the word *love* at the end of a line, or any other rhyme point. As a matter of fact, if you can avoid its use altogether in a love song, you will probably find that the song has been rendered more subtle and original.

but there is in it a considerable truth. The writer should never fall so in love with a line that he will not abandon it for the sake of the larger effect. Never interrupt the mass for the detail.

There is a phenomenon we can refer to as the usable false rhyme.

The ear seems to accept a similarity between *m* and *n*, as in *pain* and *game, known* and *home*. These rhymes should be avoided if possible, but you can sneak them by and get away with it. It's a cheat, but it works.

Another cheat you can get away with is the rhyming of a singular with a plural. *Lamps* and *camp* cannot be considered a perfect rhyme because the *s* is missing from *camp*. I nonetheless used that cheat in "Quiet nights of quiet stars, quiet chords from my guitar..." The rhyme could easily have been perfected with "quiet chords from soft guitars" or some such. But I wanted to create an image of two persons alone, and of a very personal and direct musical communication. Therefore, I did not want some anonymous background strummers intruding on the intimacy. And so I sacrificed the perfect rhyme for the better image. It bothered me, incidentally, until I discovered that Shakespeare on occasion used the same cheat.

There are, in fact, many false rhymes. In the song "Nancy with the Laughing Face," *summer* is rhymed with *from 'er.* Shakespeare used that one, too. It is, nonetheless, a pretty bad rhyme. The omission of the *h* is less disturbing than the unnatural stress occurring in *FROM her.* The natural stress would be *from HER.* Thus *SUM-mer* and *from 'ER* constitutes not only a false rhyme but a forced one as well.

The lyricist should avoid inverted or otherwise peculiar word orders in seeking to set up a rhyme. The practice was common in nineteenth century poetry, which is one reason I for one dislike much nineteenth century poetry. The practice apparently was still acceptable in 1930s American songwriting. Lorenz Hart wrote a song called "You're Nearer." It is quite lovely, but it contains a flaw.

It begins:

> *You're nearer than my head is to my pillow,*
> *nearer than the wind is to the willow.*

A little farther along, these lines occur:

> *You're nearer than the ivy to the wall is,*
> *nearer than the winter to the fall is...*

Hart needed feminine rhymes, and found them in *pillow* and *willow.* But the effect of *wall is* and *fall is* is awkward, because of the unnatural order of the words, and it seriously mars the song.

All we have discussed so far about acceptable and natural rhyme applies to songs making serious statements—in general, the ballads. The

14

picture alters completely when the intent is to be humorous. In humorous songs, almost anything goes, including peculiar word orders and outrageous false rhymes. Indeed, sometimes the more outrageous the rhyme, the funnier the effect.

In "Manhattan", Lorenz Hart rhymed *spoil* and *goil,* because that's the way they pronounce *girl* in Brooklyn — although the rhyme slightly bothers me because, as I have noted elsewhere, in Brooklyn they might also pronounce *spoil* as *sperl.* (I once met an otherwise cultivated New Yorker who said that he was in the business of *"poifume erls".)* Still elsewhere in the song, Hart was able to build an internal rhyme on *onyx* and *Bronx,* because many native New Yorkers do indeed (or did in Hart's time; I haven't heard that pronunciation in years) refer to the *Bronnix.*

In "Bob White", Johnny Mercer rhymed *jackdaw* with *back door,* and when Johnny sang it, it worked perfectly: In his Georgia accent the two do indeed rhyme. In Mercer's humorous songs, indeed, you will find an absolute treasury of these odd, tongue-in-cheek rhymes.

Howard Dietz, one of the most brilliant of all American lyricists, wrote a song called "Rhode Island Is Famous for You," which begins with perfectly correct rhymes, proceeds through false rhymes such as "Kansas gets bonanzas from the grain," and goes on to some outrageous distortions, puns, and mispronunciations, all of them quite funny in context:

> *Pencils come from Pennsylvania,*
> *vests from Vest Virginia,*
> *and tents from Tentessee.*
> *They know mink*
> *where they grow mink*
> *in Wyomink.*
> *A camp chair*
> *in New Hampchair,*
> *that's for me.*
> *And minnows come from Minnesota.*
> *Coats come from Dakota.*
> *But why should you be blue?*
> *For you,*
> *you come from Rhode Island.*
> *Don't let them ride Rhode Island*
> *—it's famous for you.*

In a Broadway musical, one might use all sorts of false and bent pronunciations, depending on whether a given character came from

Lancashire, London, Glasgow, Tennessee, Texas, or Alabama—to say nothing of Brooklyn, where a character might be made to rhyme fencing *foils* with dancing *goils*. But no, come to think of it, that wouldn't work. In Brooklyn, *foils* would be pronounced *ferls*!

These are areas in which the lyricist must use his intelligence, judgment, and pride of craft. Purity of rhyme is desirable, preferable, and sometimes downright necessary in a song that makes a sober statement. The rules can be bent discreetly. And in humor, anything goes—except bad writing.

4.

VOWELS, CONSONANTS, AND SINGING

There are twenty-six letters in the English alphabet. This is hideously inadequate.

We have no letter for the *th* sound of *thing,* no letter for the different *th* sound in *weather.* (And we have no need for that *a* in *weather,* either— or, pardon, ither.) Yet the letter *c* is quite useless, since its two functions are covered by *k* and *s.* So is *x,* whose functions are handled quite nicely thank you by *ks* and *gz,* as in *boks* and *egzaktly.* If we took the unemployed *c* and *x* and assigned them to new jobs, we might talk and write about *cings* and *xe wexer* instead of things and the weather. We might invert the letter *v* (after all, an *n* is an inverted *u*) for use as the *ch* in *chop.* But after that, we would have to start introducing new letters into our alphabet to specify the *sh* of *shop* and a good many other sounds that we at present spell in various clumsy ways. It has been estimated that the institution of a proper English phonetic alphabet would shorten every book by at least twenty-five percent, substantially reduce printing costs, increase everyone's reading speed, and shorten enormously the time it takes a child to learn to read. We have no way of knowing to what extent it would reduce the appalling illiteracy rate of the United States, since we do not know how many children fall behind in "reading skills," as contemporary bureaucrats quaintly call reading, simply because they become discouraged by a stupid system—which, in some cases, may actually constitute proof of intelligence.

If we have so long resisted the metric system of weights and measures, which a child can learn in a week if not an afternoon, and have clung to a ponderously complicated and archaic system that takes a year or two to teach to a class (at great expense to the taxpayer, let us note), I do not think we will soon reform our spelling. And so we are stuck with it.

And under that system, we are taught that there are five vowels, *a, e, i, o,* and *u,* which any fool knows is not true, since we have the sounds heard in *bat, bate; beet, bet; bite, bit; boat, bought; boot, but.* These are called the long and short forms of these vowels, but clearly, we have there ten different vowel sounds, each of which deserves a letter of its own. In addition, we combine certain of these letters to designate still more vowel sounds: *ou* and *ow* as in *proud cow;* and *oi* or *oy* as in *soiled boy,* which gets us up to twelve. There is, in addition, what is called the neutral vowel, which is more or less like the *u* in *but,* but not quite. Nobody much says *a book;* most of us refer to *uh book.* What is more, we do not even use these combinations consistently. We do not know whether to spell long sibilant of *his* tends to fuse with the first *s* of *surcease*, whose final *s* then fuses with the first *s* of *success*.

We can see what happened. Shakespeare was taken with the visual resemblance between *surcease* and *success*—there is no other conceivable reason for using them together—and, in a sudden attack of the clevers, lost the will to reject the phrase, which is too cute by half. Here we see the wisdom of Dickens' admonition that when you write a line you particularly like, you should strike it out. Shakespeare obviously liked that phrase, and he did not follow Dickens' advice, possibly because Dickens hadn't been born yet. But then, as Horace Walpole (who also hadn't been born yet) observed, "One of the greatest geniuses that ever existed, Shakespeare, undoubtedly wanted taste."

The *s* presents a problem only in overuse, as in an alliteration. As for whatever reservations recording engineers may have toward it, I am reminded of what Sinatra told his engineer on that session when the latter asked him to stand farther from the orchestra, since their proximity was creating a separation difficulty. "That's *your* problem," Sinatra said pleasantly. And so it is with the letter *s*. That's *their* problem. It is, after all, the letter we use to form the plural in English.

If the prejudice against *s* is largely unjustified, there is one that is not: that against the plosive consonant *p* and the softer, voiced form of it, *b*. If you observe how you enunciate them, holding your fingertips before your lips, you will note that either letter releases a little burst of air. That burst of air can strongly affect the element in a microphone, and the distorted sound thus produced goes onto the tape, thence onto the record. The sound will actually rattle the speakers in your phonograph, producing an odd sort of *whoof*. The letters *t* and *d* can do the same, though to a lesser extent, and sometimes even the aspirated *h*. But *p* and *b* are the most treacherous in the recording studio. Clearly, the lyricist cannot be expected to eliminate from his vocabulary such words as *baby, lullaby,* and *poem*. But he should know about this problem. Whereas alliterations with the semivowels, such as "merry month of May," can be attractive and useful, alliterations such as the famous "Peter Piper picked a peck of pickled peppers" would drive a singer and recording engineer to distraction. Incidentally, good singers learn how to pronounce the *p* without popping it. It's quite a little trick.

Up to this point, we have been discussing preferences, the process of selection—esthetic discrimination, if you will. The next "rule," however, comes close to being a strict prohibition. Consider again the smeared *esses* in "his surcease success."

Do not, if it can possibly be avoided, begin a word with the same consonant that ended the preceding word. One awkward example of this can be found in the phrase "tallest tree." The singer has a choice between enunciating *talles' tree* or *tallest* (pause) *tree*, which makes the phrasing artificial, though it is the better solution to the problem. (Sinatra, whose meticulous enunciation is one of the secrets of his genius as a singer, did precisely that.)

The problem is minor with the semivowels—*dream maiden*, for example, or *pale lily*. But it is deadly with hard consonants: *black cat, dead dog, Rob Brown, rap party,* and so forth. It is even desirable to avoid collisions of similar voiced and unvoiced consonants—*b* with *p, d* with *t, f* with *v*. If you wrote *of vendors*, it would be hard to tell whether the words were *of vendors, a vendor's,* or *offenders. Rob Brown* sounds like *raw brown*

In passing, it should be noted that this consideration applies, though nowhere so stringently as in lyrics, to all forms of writing intended to be heard—whether for television, radio, or the stage. Indeed, I believe it is a good principle to follow even in writing for print. Its observance produces more fluid and attractive prose, since the inner ear detects it. Its violation produces a clumsy effect even to someone reading silently.

Clusters of consonants, even if they are dissimilar, can cause problems. The sound of *t* followed by that of *l* produces an ugly little click, as in the words *gently* and *softly*. This does not occur in *gentle*, since we in fact separate the sounds in the pronunciation *gentul*.

When "Quiet Nights of Quiet Stars" was first published, someone changed it to "Quiet Nights and Quiet Stars," to the detriment of both the imagery and the singability of the line. This is an example of insensitivity to sound and ignorance of the mechanics of singing. Note the clumsiness of motion caused by *and quiet*. Compare this with the flow of the *f* into the *qu* when *of quiet* is used.

If this seems like excessive concern with detail, let me assure you that it is not. The failure to make an almost microscopic examination of sound and the mechanics of singing is one of the major shortcomings of the average lyricist. Johnny Mercer was deeply sensitive to sound and the problems of singing, no doubt because he was a capable singer.

One can learn a great deal about the use of the vowels and consonants by examining two of Mercer's lyrics, "I Remember You" and "I Thought About You."

The most singable and attractive of the vowels, as we have noted, are the *oo* and *oh* sounds. In the first of these lyrics, Mercer uses both of them for his rhymes. The *oo* sound, amazingly, is used all the way through the song.

I remember you.
You're the one
who made my dreams come true
a few
kisses ago.

F dropping to C-sharp and rising to D, it would mean a minor worry. If the last tone fell a little, and was extended melodically, it would be an expression of compassion for someone's bad fortune. If, on the other hand, the last note went up, it might be said by a wide-eyed child on being given the bicycle he has wanted for so long. The French make amazingly versatile use of that expression, and its meaning is determined entirely by musical pitches.

Stephen Sondheim's musical, *Company,* opens with the orchestra playing a falling minor third. The chorus begins to sing it—and it is the name of the show's protagonist, Bobby. We usually pronounce the name Bobby in the general area of a falling minor third.

Consider the expression "peek-a-boo." It is usually said to babies in one of two ways. If you said it with "peek-a" on one note and "boo" a fourth below it (F-F-C, for example), the baby would be amused. But somehow it is even funnier if you expand the melody, and make it C-A-F— a rising sixth and a falling major third.

That, incidentally, is the melody of the old nursery song beginning, "Baby-bye, see the fly." And it is, in fact, the second inversion of a major triad, a very stable chord unless the context acts to make it otherwise.

Now let us see what happens if we apply these intervals to another expression—for example, "Put it back." Let's use the "Baby-bye" melody, except that "put it" remains on the bottom note, and "ba-ack" is used as a descending glissando from the sixth to the fourth. This is the way you might say it to a little boy caught with his hand in a cookie jar just before dinner. It has a teasing, joking tone to it.

But now change the melody. Say "Put it" on one note and "back" a fifth below it, and it takes on a world-weary sound, as if to say, "How long do I have to put up with your tricks?"

Now say "Put it back" with all three words on the same note and the effect is threatening and even sinister.

It is not my intention to suggest that one must be a fully developed musician to be a good lyricist. (In fact, I doubt that most musicians have noticed that *Oh-oh* is often a falling tritone.) But I do wish to make the point that our speech is musical, it is intervallic—and indeed more "tonal" than is generally supposed. I will resist speculating whether the public has for so long shown a great indifference to twelve-tone or serial music because our speech is itself inherently tonal. Nor will I ponder at length on the possibility that speech grew out of intervallic emotional cries, and that music therefore precedes language.

But I do wish to make the point that a good lyricist should be highly sensitive to intervals, whether he knows their names or not.

One will hear superficially clever lyrics that do not somehow work with the music. The reason will be found to be, in many cases, that they do not accord comfortably with the intervals and inflections of the melody. This is particularly true in jazz lyrics, many of which are hideous and downright ludicrous, to say nothing of pretentious and silly.

But consider the exquisite sensitivity with which Alan Jay Lerner's "I've Grown Accustomed to Her Face" accords with the music phrase, fitting it as perfectly as sand in a bottle. One would say these words approximately as they are sung in that song. One cannot imagine the phrase with any other melodic line.

It is advisable, when setting out to write lyrics for a melody, to listen and listen and listen to it until its intervals and contours almost begin to suggest words to you. And, of course, one should listen to the shifting moods created by the melody's harmonic sequences.

The fitting of words to musical intervals is another factor that makes lyric writing a more exacting task than writing poetry. In traditional poetry, a given metrical structure is established and used, along with a specific rhyme scheme. Within that structure, the poet has comparative freedom. The control of inflection is nowhere near as strict as it is in good lyric writing, nor is there the same concern about what vowels "sing well" and what do not. In so-called modern poetry, the poet has even greater freedom since there often is no rhyme at all nor is there even a metric structure. It becomes difficult to draw the line between prose and poetry.

Lyrics have, as a rule, nothing whatever to do with the metrics of poetry, with occasional exceptions. Lyrics are written according to the phrasings of music; they are not written in stanzas, but (usually) in eight-bar units. Within a given eight-bar unit, the melody may call for four, five, six, or more lines of lyric. An exception that should be mentioned immediately is the blues, which is written in three four-bar phrases (totaling twelve bars) and in iambic pentameter, which is the classical rhythm of Shakespeare's plays. Blues lyrics are extremely easy to write.

The very obvious question arises: If it is that difficult to fit lyrics to music, why not write the lyrics first and fit the music to them? It is, in fact, often advisable to do so with comedic songs, wherein the words are usually more important than the music and the sole purpose of the exercise is to provoke laughter. It rarely works in ballads. A very few composers have shown a peculiar knack for writing lovely melodies to lyrics. Most composers do not write well in that way. This has been my experience, and that of Johnny Mercer and everyone else with whom I have discussed the matter. In general, composers confronted with existing lyrics tend to write rather dry and academic melodies that do indeed fit the lyric mechanically but somehow fail to achieve any distinguishing musical color or even to evoke the mood of the lyrics. Even Cole Porter, who was not only a very clever lyricist but a superior composer as well, wrote music first. Or to be more precise, he would establish the title of his song, write the music, and then complete the lyric.

This is a good practice whether you are both lyricist and composer or whether you as lyricist are working in collaboration with a composer in the joint creation of a song.

Sometimes in the course of such a collaboration, the composer will try to induce you to write the lyrics first. Refuse. Flatly. Stand there and be adamant about it. If you do write the lyrics first, you will be inclined — for the sake of creating some sort of order in your work — to use the metrics of poetry which, as we have discussed, have little to do with the character of music. The composer will then do all sorts of arbitrary and peculiar things to solve the problems created by the words, probably feel quite proud of what he has done, as if he had filled in all the squares of *The New York Times* crossword puzzle, and wait smilingly for your praise. You will know that his music is lousy and will not have the heart to tell him so. Apparently good lyricists are more sensitive to the intervals and inflections of music than composers are to those of speech. Only a few of them in history have had the knack of taking lyrics off the page and setting them in soaring, rather than pedestrian, melodies. Richard Rodgers, for one, was quite good at it.

If the composer wants a departure point, find it for him: the title. The title is the center of a song. But having found it, tell the composer he's on his own. Let him finish the melody, then leave you alone to finish the lyric.

None of the foregoing applies to the blues. The blues have a more or less invariable structure. Yet that structure can be used in a careless and loose-wristed way. If you omit a syllable here and there and add a syllable somewhere else, it doesn't seem to undermine this enduring and sturdy form. You need only one rhyme per stanza, and you not only can repeat a line, you *should* repeat the first line if you are going to write a true blues.

The meter, as we have noted, is known: it is iambic pentameter. An iamb is a foot of poetry consisting of two syllables, the first weak and the second strong: *ba-DUM*. And, as the word pentameter makes clear, there are five such feet in each line, so that a line of iambic pentameter contains ten syllables, stressed as follows:

ba-DUM ba-DUM ba-DUM ba-DUM ba-DUM

The opening line of Shakespeare's "Sonnet XXIX" is:

When in disgrace with fortune and men's eyes

This perfectly fits one line of a blues melody. A famous line of blues lyric (and note that it contains *two* weak beats instead of one at the beginning) is:

Don't the moon look lonesome shining through the trees?

In the blues, it is customary to repeat the entire first line. Thus, the lyric becomes:

Don't the moon look lonesome shining through the trees?
Don't the moon look lonesome shining through the trees?
Don't your arms feel empty when your baby packs up to leave?

(Note that *leave* is a false rhyme for *trees*.)

Once you know the structure, you can make up blues lyrics all day:

My best friend left and took my chick away.
My best friend left and took my chick away
I'm in debt to him more than I can can ever say.

Except in the case of carefully written instrumental blues in jazz, the melodic structure of a blues is variable, to say the least, and a great blues singer will do weird and wonderful things to it, anyway. So relax.

The problems arise when you deal with a specific melody. Contrary to the layman's impression, the fewer the notes in the melody, the more difficult it is to fit with lyrics—for many of the notes will require long vowels that sustain well.

If it is desirable to fit short vowels to short notes, long vowels to long notes, it is absolutely necessary to fit unstressed syllables to unstressed notes, stressed syllables to stressed notes. (Again, exceptions will be found in comic songs, where sometimes the very mispronunciation of a word can elicit laughs.) That you will hear this rule violated is neither here nor there: the violations constitute bad writing. Good lyricists *never* take this liberty. Indeed, stressing the wrong *syl-LAB-le* can alter meaning. A buggy is something drawn by a horse; a *bug-GEE* is presumably someone suffering from a wiretap.

A few years ago, with composer Roger Kellaway, I was called on to write a disco song for a scene in a movie. Purity of grammar and polished craftsmanship would have been quite inappropriate, and so, to give the song an authentically ignorant feeling, I violated this rule in these lines:

Baby, I'm so crazy about you.
I tell you, I don't know what's happ'nin' to me.
I can't imagine livin' without you.
I tell you, you're some kinda new myster-REE.

Mystery, of course, rhymes correctly with *history,* not with *me.* The way I used it in that song was deliberately awkward, in imitation of an effect all too common in contemporary popular music. On the other hand, I used the word as a masculine rhyme in a way that was not awkward in "Song of the Jet":

31

...city of love and mysteries.
Fasten seat belts. No smoking please.©

The difference lay in the character of the melodic line: the stress was not that strong on the last syllable.

You will discover that under certain melodic conditions, these very slight distortions of pronunciation will not offend the ear. You can never use a two-syllable word whose normal stress is on the first syllable in such a manner, only a three-syllable word whose second syllable is weak. And it will not always work even then.

A more detailed analysis of the way words fit music is possible. Downbeats, for example, always take stressed syllables; pick-up notes always take unstressed syllables. In point of fact, no lyricist, even one who is himself a composer, ever works in so consciously mechanical a fashion. Simply listen carefully to the melody and fit unstressed syllables to unstressed notes, stressed syllables to stressed notes.

Can you fit one syllable to two or more notes? Yes, and it is often done—too often, nowadays. I consider it a bad practice, in most instances, one that results from lack of discipline on the part of the lyricist, if he is writing to a melody, or on the part of the composer, if he is setting a lyric.

Its most serious fault is that it hinders or prevents the immediate understanding of the word being sung. The holding of one syllable—one vowel of a syllable, in practice—through two or more notes is known as a melisma. In the golden age of American lyric writing—the 1920s, 30s, 40s, and 50s in the theater—the practice virtually disappeared. You will encounter few examples of the use of melisma in the work of Lorenz Hart, Cole Porter, Oscar Hammerstein, Howard Dietz, Johnny Mercer, or any of the other classic lyricists. Lionel Bart, the English composer and lyricist, used one in *Oliver,* in the song "Where Is Love?" The word *where* is spread over five notes, to awkward effect. Bart could easily have solved the problem by writing "Someone tell me: where is love?" or something of that ilk. If he found that solution unacceptable, he should have written something else.

Every professional songwriter knows that the worst example of a mismatching of words and music is "The Star-Spangled Banner." Not only does it contain some very strange pairings of strong syllables to weak or unstressed notes ("THE bombs bursting in air"), but it is a squirming string of melismas from beginning to end. The opening syllable is a melisma. "Oh-oh say can you see.." Then occurs the glorious mismatch: "In the twilight's last gleaMING." Later comes: "Oh say does tha-at star-spangled ba-a-nu-ur ye-et way-ave o'er the la-and of the free..."

Let's consider that awkward mismatch, "THE bombs bursting in air," in which the stress is on "THE." Substitute the phrase "swallows high in the air," and you will find you have a perfect fit for the melody. And instead of "twilight's last gleaMING," use "twilight's crimson glare." For "o'er the la-and of the free," substitute "o'er the nation of the free," and we find we are cleaning up a bad lyric to a melody that is not easy to sing under any condition.

That so famously clumsy a song should have been made the national anthem of the United States, when the magnificent "America the Beautiful," whose words and music match perfectly, was the available and better-loved alternative, is one of life's minor mysteries. The song does have one value, however: it will stand forever as a shining example of how not to write one.

Melismas are common in opera, which may be one reason Americans prefer their homegrown musicals. Our musical theater, our substitute for opera, has never embraced melismatic singing and writing. Melisma occurs in much country-and-western music and in so-called contemporary folk music, which is really a commercial pop music. Indeed, many of the true folk songs, the gorgeous ones, use the melisma little or not at all. The moving "Shenandoah" contains one, on the word *a-away,* and somehow it seems just right.

One man, one vote: that is the principle of democracy. One syllable, one note: that is the principle of skilled songwriting.

6.
FORMS, PATTERNS AND ANALYSIS

The most common length of American songs (and those of many other countries) is thirty-two measures, or bars, as musicians are more likely to call them. If you are not a musician and are inclined to panic at mention of musical technicalities, be not discouraged: some of our finest lyricists have been unable to read music. For that matter, some of our very finest composers, including the prolific Irving Berlin, have been unable to read music. (That is no reason, of course, for anyone to take a quiet pride in ignorance. Some of our worst composers cannot read music either.) But it is helpful if you can count bars, and it is really quite easy to do.

Most American popular music is in four-four time. Some of it is in three-four time, particularly in the country-and-western field. Just tap your foot to the rhythm and count the beats: one-two-three-four. That's one bar. To continue the count and keep track of it, count: one-two-three-four, two-two-three-four, three-two-three-four, four-two-three-four, and so on. In waltz time, you count one-two-three, two-two-three, three-two-three, and so on.

Music is made up, for the most part, of two-, four-, and eight-measure units. The normal length for the full melodic line of a popular song is eight. (There are odd-numbered phrases, such as seven, nine, and eleven bars, but one encounters them rarely.)

Most songs that you will encounter comprise thirty-two bars, made up of four eight-bar units. There are longer forms. "Begin the Beguine" is a surprising one hundred and eight bars long; "Desafinado," a Jobim tune that I translated into English as "Off Key," is sixty-eight. But the norm is thirty-two. Sometimes a four-bar extension, called a tag, will be added to the end for dramatic effect and to give the song a more complete feeling.

In the standard thirty-two bar tune, an eight-bar melody is played, then repeated. Then a new eight-bar melody is heard, one that has—or should have—a melodic or harmonic relationship to the first melody (which is called the front strain). But the mood of it is usually different. This variant section is called the release, or bridge (even the French call it the *pont* of the song), presumably because it functions as a bridge between the front strain and the last section of the song, which is usually the front strain repeated for a third and final time, with or without a tag. Jerome Kern's "Smoke Gets in Your Eyes" is a magnificent and classic example of this form.

If the first section is called the A melody and the release is the B melody, we have the standard AABA form of song. It has become so common that we are prone to forget that it did not come into general use in American popular music until the 1920s. It is by no means the only form in wide use. George Gershwin was partial to the ABAB form, and his wonderful "A Foggy Day" (which has the further distinction of one of Ira Gershwin's best lyrics) actually has an ABABC form, since the protracted tag really introduces a new melodic element. The *rondeau* form, French in origin and little-used in America, can be very effective. One form of the *rondeau* is AABACADA.

While it is usual to repeat one of the eight-bar units, the front strain, it is not necessary, strictly speaking. Publishers used to think so, and would pound on composers to write that way, along with imposing on lyricists such foolish formulae as: the title must be repeated three times in the song. One of the finest of American songs, and one of the most widely performed, does not have one full melodic repeat: "Stardust." The "Flora Dora Chorus" ("Tell Me, Pretty Maiden, Are There Any More at Home Like You?") does not contain one repeat, nor even a hint of a repeat. And this quite sophisticated structure came early in this century. Audiences apparently had no trouble understanding or accepting it. The form of "Indiana" is ABAC.

So it will be seen that, while the AABA form is common, a song may, in fact, have any one of several forms. And the first job of the lyricist is to find out what that is, for it will—or should—affect the mood, as well as the structure, of the lyric.

If a lyricist is working with a composer, the latter will usually give him a cassette recording of the tune. He should listen to it not only until he knows it but until he can't forget it. He should soak in it.

Once he has been given the tune, the lyricist may want the composer to go away and leave him alone. It usually takes far less time to write a melody than to write a lyric, and it is disconcerting to have somebody impatiently waiting for results when the lyricist's need is to think slowly, painstakingly, and, one hopes, deeply. Sometimes composer and lyricist will want to work together, and there is the advantage that the lyricist can say, "Play the release again—very slowly." Only occasionally will a song come quickly. Howard Dietz and Arthur Schwartz wrote "That's Entertainment," words and music—all three sparklingly witty, cleverly rhymed choruses—in one hour flat.

Once you have determined the overall form of the tune, you will next break it down in terms of where the rhymes should fall. This is usually fairly obvious.

Perhaps the melody will go:

Something something DA-dum,
something something DA-dum.

35

7.
IDEAS AND OTHER DILEMMAS

There are two questions that every songwriter encounters in interviews.

One of them is: Which comes first, the words or the music? The answer, as we have seen, is that both approaches are used, depending on the circumstances. But if the song is to have a truly melodic nature, the music should come first.

The other question is: Where do you get your ideas? And the answer to that one is: Wherever you can find them. And the search is often a desperate one.

Finding melodies is no problem, even if you're not a composer. John Mercer, who wrote some very good melodies as well as lyrics. said to me once, "I think writing music takes more talent, but writing lyrics takes more courage." I can sit around by the hour, writing tunes that I think are pretty, or dramatic, or amusing. Finding lyrics for them, even for my own tunes, is not easy. "All art," wrote Walter Pater, "constantly aspires towards the condition of music." Pater meant, I presume, that writers and other artists envy the musician the abstraction of his work: he fiddles around with sounds, putting them together in different ways, like a child playing with colored blocks, until he finds an arrangement of them that pleases him. The writer must find a subject, a story to tell, and that's the hard part. Once you have acquired a certain basic knowledge of harmony and its relationship to melody (and such knowledge can be acquired in six months by a dull person, three by a smart one), it is easy to write melodies. Some individuals will show more imagination in their writing, more flair, something subtly different and fresh. But the *technique* of it is easy. Everybody and his brother (and nowadays his sister as well) knows the II-V-I and I-VI-II-V chord sequences, including guitar-players who play them all the time and don't know what it is that they're playing. But a lyric requires a specific and concrete *idea,* and, if he loves the art, the lyricist will demand that it be a fresh one.

Once a lyricist is established and has a reputation (and getting there is *not* half the fun), he will number among his acquaintances many trained professional composers, some of whom will from time to time ask him to write lyrics for their music. In addition, it seems that every musician in the world is a closet composer, and he has several tunes at home which, he assures you, are just great, and he can get the song to Frank Sinatra or Jack Jones or Waldo Oxcart or whoever is big at the moment. Saxophone players, drummers, trumpet players, kazooists, castanet virtuosos, Cuban percussionists, and sometimes even their wives (although musicians' wives are more prone to think they are lyricists) seem to have these innumerable melodies in drawers that would really make it if only someone, namely you, would put lyrics to them. The tone of voice conveys unmistakably that melody writing is a strange and wonderful gift, while just about anybody can toss off a lyric. After all, it's only words. After a few years of this curious combination of pressure and condescension, the professional lyricist becomes gun-shy, inclined to flee screaming into the night whenever, at a party, he hears those deadly words, "There's this tune I've written that…"

Mercer used to try, without much success, to avoid hearing tunes brought to him by friends. "If I can't come up with an idea in a few days, they get mad at me, and I lose a friend," he said. This from a man who turned out 1500 published lyrics during a thirty-five-year career, which works out to more than forty songs a year. "You get tired," he said to me once, "of being everybody's lyric boy."

It is probably a good idea for a lyricist to keep a notebook of song ideas. This may work for you. It never did for me, and I abandoned the practice. Any given situation for which I had to write a song, in a film or wherever, never seemed to have anything to do with those dandy little titles in my book; or else none of those titles would fit the melody with which I was confronted.

There is one useful trick that Mercer, and others, have used to good effect—sometimes brilliant effect. Take some ordinary, everyday expression, such as "Guess Who I Saw Today," and use it as a song title. The expression may be a catchword of current slang, or one of the older clichés of the language, but in the hands of a master lyricist, it can take on startling freshness and originality, yet retain the advantage of general familiarity. Cole Porter was partial to this approach, and out of everyday expressions, he built such songs as "Just One of Those Things," "Well, Did You Ever!," "Wouldn't It Be Fun?," "Use Your Imagination," "Look What I Found," "I Get a Kick Out of You," "Anything Goes," "Where Have You Been?," "Between You and Me," "From This Moment On," and "It's All Right with Me," some of which are among the finest songs in the American literature.

Mercer used the device to give us "Something Tells Me," "In a Moment of Weakness," "Wait and See," "Oh, You Kid," "Seeing's Believing," "Great Guns," "Any Place I Hang My Hat Is Home," "Too Marvelous for Words," "Jeepers Creepers," "Fools Rush In (Where Angels Fear to Tread)," "If You Build a Better Mousetrap," "Out of This World," "Something's Gotta Give," "You Can't Run Away from It," "If I Had My Druthers," and "Two of a Kind."

There are songs, by various composers, called "You Said It," "As Long as I Live," "Fancy Meeting You," "It's All in the Game," "I Should Care," "You'll Never Know," and many more that embody everyday expressions. The device works only if the lyricist does indeed do something fresh with such an expression. If not, the song may be as trite as the title. Another possibility is the resurrection of old and forgotten (or even not-so-forgotten) song titles. You cannot copyright a title.

On the other hand, why should anyone be able to copyright a common expression such as "Anything Goes"? There must be dozens of songs titled "I Love You." I know at least three songs titled "All Through the Night." If being derivative doesn't bother you, you can plow through lists of song titles and use them to your heart's content.

Most of the time, however, the lyricist with a job to do, a melody to find words for, and a deadline, will simply sweat in the search for a good idea. Roger Kellaway and I had to do a song for a television movie. He gave me a melody that had a two-note motif that meant I would have to find feminine rhymes throughout. The song had to catch the character of a foolish girl who runs from one affair to another. Roger offered to change the tune, to make my job easier, but I thought it was too fresh, too good, to be discarded or tampered with. After two weeks of searching for an idea, I gave up and went fishing with a friend. Our boat was rolling gently on a swell a mile or so off Anacapa Island. The sun glinted off the serene, smooth, Pacific waters. Some seals swam around the boat, turning gracefully, looking up at us, sleek and carefree. I turned to my friend and asked, "What day is it, by the way?"

"Sunday," he said. "Is it important?"

"No," I said, "not really. And anyway..." I pointed to the seals "...I guess to them, the days have no names."

A lightbulb went on over my head, as in the comic strips. "That's it!" I said. "That's the title of the song!"

The song, I saw, would be about the days of the girl's life. I remembered that she was always meeting one of her lovers on Friday afternoons. By nightfall, the song was finished:

Remember how we met one Monday,
fell in love by Sunday,
and how slow the days would go
until our crazy fun days?

All those lazy Fridays
that you said were my days
were my flying-high days.
I thought they could
go on and on and on

till one day,
you were gone forever.
And since then, I've put
the pieces of my life together.

I have friends to play with,
friends to spend a day with,
but I have no taste for the game.

The weeks are all the same
shade of blue
and the days have no names
without you.

There are two cheats in that song—*games* and *name, forever* and *together*— and one grammatical error, deliberately made. I surrendered to common colloquial practice for the sake of a rhyme where I wanted one. If the grammar were pure, the word would be "slowly" instead of *slow.* I could have covered the melody by writing "and how slowly days would go..." I preferred "and how slow the days would go." It nailed the idea down better, and it fit the character of the girl.

Songwriting often requires such compromises. When Mercer was writing the title song for the film *The Americanization of Emily* (the finely made melody is by Johnny Mandel), he faced the fact that there is no rhyme for Emily. So instead of using a rhyme at the end, he utilized a kind of unfolding sound pattern: "As my eyes visualize a family, they see dreamily Emily too."

Oscar Hammerstein disliked the word "divine" at the end of "All the Things You Are," in the lines "and someday I'll know that moment divine when all the things you are, are mine." He vowed that he would, before his life was over, find an ending to the song he liked better. He never did.

The lyricist who has an assignment, a melody, a deadline, and a worried look on his face will often be offered suggestions by family and friends. They're usually useless, and so often have I growled, "That doesn't rhyme with anything," that my wife insists she is going to have it engraved on my tombstone.

However, suggestions should not be dismissed lightly. Some years ago, a woman named Sadie Vimmerstedt wrote to Mercer, telling him of something she'd heard someone say. Mercer wrote "I Wanna Be Around (to Pick Up the Pieces)" from that suggestion, got one of his biggest hits, and shared the royalties with Mrs. Vimmerstedt.

Professionals, in fact, often get suggestions or even complete lyrics in the mail. They are rarely as good as Mrs. Vimmerstedt's, and some are hilarious.

Usually, however, professionals will not look at lyrics that are sent to them. The reason is that if one should, even years later, write a song that bears the most remote and accidental resemblance (such as containing some such highly original line as "I love you") to a song submitted to him by an amateur, he can find himself in a lawsuit. Cole Porter once had

43

to defend himself in such a suit. He won it, but at a considerable cost in legal fees, to say nothing of wasted time.

It is unfortunate that you cannot teach taste. It may be possible to acquire it—certainly, it is possible to refine it—but you cannot teach it, particularly to someone who does not wish to have it, or, more precisely, who is satisfied with his or her taste just as it is. A really gifted artist may spend a lifetime improving his taste. "Taste," according to an old French maxim, "is the result of a thousand distastes."

One can, in fact, teach only the underlying mechanical skills of any art or craft. It is possible, to be sure, to be a craftsman without being an artist. But it is not possible to be an artist without being a craftsman. Once he or she has acquired the skills, the craftsman-cum-artist is faced with a permanent search for ideas *that are good enough*. Mercer would often lay a lyric aside for months, then look at it and, if he felt it wasn't up to standard, simply throw it out.

The lyricist should avoid self-pity at any price, whether he is writing a song about his own feelings or about some fictional character in a musical. Self-pity is boring. It reminds one always of the barroom drunk, so brilliantly characterized and satirized by Mercer in "One for My Baby," pulling your shoulder and telling you his troubles.

Indirect expression of emotion is usually more effective than direct, and less risky. It is better to describe bare trees in an autumn rain than offer a catalogue of miseries. Because songs deal for the most part with love (and there is nothing wrong with that; love is the central theme of most of the world's literature), there is always a danger of being excessively sentimental. A song can slip over the edge into pathos and, finally, the downright ludicrous.

The worst piece of advice ever given to writers is that you should only write out of your experience. This instruction seems to have come chiefly from Ernest Hemingway, who was incapable of doing anything else. But other writers are not so limited. Shakespeare did not have to commit a murder in order to create Macbeth as a character. A good writer can become in his imagination another human being, just as a good actor can. And sometimes it seems to me that the most vivid fiction is created precisely when the writer is working with invented characters and situations. For the writer must convince himself of the veracity of the story, and in the process convinces the audience as well.

In working on a theater musical, the writer is confronted with fictional characters whose emotions he must express in specific situations in the plot. If you are simply writing a song, it is wise to invent the fictional character who is "singing" it about a moment or an experience in his or her life. This will make the song vivid and real. A far better piece of advice to writers than Hemingway's came from F. Scott Fitgerald: "Begin with an individual and before you know it you have created a type; begin with a type, and you find that you have created—nothing."

In other words, don't generalize, particularize. Don't tell your listener that life is happy, or sad. Show it. Prove it. Illustrate it.

Finally, sing the lyrics that you write—and those of the lyricists you admire. The final test of a lyric is its singability. You may find you want to change a word, because for some obscure reason it comes out of the mouth awkwardly. There is no better training for lyric writing than singing. I have never known a good lyricist who didn't at least enjoy singing, even if he or she was not expert at it. In point of fact, the best composers of vocal melodies like to sing, and all of them that I have known sing their melodies while composing them, rather than work them out on the piano. Those who do not compose in the throat, as it were, but on the piano, tend to write pianistic and unsingable songs.

Above all, the lyricist needs patience to keep searching for that elusive better idea. Keep turning over all the possibilities for words that fit that line, that phrase, of the music until you find that certain something that illuminates you from within and makes you say, "That's it! That's what I was looking for!" This can take days, but one should not cheat the song or oneself by seizing on the first idea, the first shop-worn rhyme that turns up.

It is quite true the Johnny Mercer wrote the lyrics for "Days of Wine and Roses" in five minutes, and for "Autumn Leaves" in about fifteen. But "Skylark" took him a year. That should console and encourage all of us in the long, solitary, often frustrating, but ultimately very rewarding task of writing lyrics.

8.

THE WORDS YOU CHOOSE

It is common for teachers of writing to advise students to use small words. There is of course no special virtue in their being small, and often-particularly in prose-the only perfect word may be polysyllabic. At times the only truly accurate word may even be obscure, as in a reference to a gibbous moon. There is no other word for this condition, and if your reader has to look it up, so be it: you have enlarged that person's vocabulary. But a somewhat different situation obtains in poetry and lyrics, wherein small words often will be found more effective. They are more emotional, and the reason for that lies fairly far back in history, at the very foundation of what we now call the English language.

The English language is a hybrid, composed of Germanic and French elements. The words in either language trace back to Sanskrit and a language that preceded it, known as Indo-European. The word snow may seem to have little, if any, relationship to German *snee,* Spanish *nieve,* Portuguese *neve,* and the French *neige.* They all derive from the Indo-European *sneigh,* distorted by time and use and descent. Language is constantly changing. We dropped the *d* out of Wednesday, and are well on our way leaving the first *r* out of February.

But English as we know it began to form after a specific date, 1066, which is the year the Norman French under the bastard William, Duke of Normandy— who soon saw to it that he be called William the Conqueror—defeated King Harold at the Battle of Hastings and installed himself as the ruler of England. Both groups of contestants were Vikings, but those led by William had been living in France in what is now called Normandy and had taken on the French language.

When William had installed himself as ruler of England, French was automatically the language of the court and the ruling class. The older Germanic language, which we refer to (not entirely accurately) as Anglo-Saxon, became the language of the conquered, the underclasses, the peasantry.

For nearly 300 years, from the time of the Norman conquest until 1362, legal proceedings in England were in French. And so to this day, in England and Australia and Canada, the vocabulary of the law was almost entirely French, excepting Latin technical terms such as *sine die* and *nollo contendere,* and thus it remains: *tort, appeal, justice, jurisprudence, arraignment, verdict, illegal.*

But though the common people learned a certain amount of French—they had no choice—they did not forget their own Anglo-Saxon.

And this led to the curious double vocabulary of modern English. When the peasants were raising animals in the field, the beasts were known by their Germanic names, swine or pig, cow, calf, and sheep, but when they reached the table of the Norman rulers, the meats took on the French names, *porc, boeuf, veal,* and *mouton,* which is where we get our modern words for them. We still call the animals by one name, the meats by another.

Polite ladies and teachers caution the young not to use certain words because they are "not nice" without having any idea why they are not nice. They are "not nice" for no other reason than that they are, or sound like, or seem like, Anglo-Saxon words, still perceived as the language of the coarse and lowly. For example, to avoid the use of the word *belly,* which derives from Anglo-Saxon *belg,* polite people say *stomach,* which is wrong, since the stomach is an internal organ of digestion. But *stomach* derives from the French name for that organ, *estomac,* and therefore seems more genteel (from French gentil). We feel that a promenade has more "class" than a mere walk. And in English the verb *to promenade* carries a connotation of conspicuous display and self-conscious posturing. Nice people don't *sweat,* they *perspire.* An *odor (odeur)* is less offensive than a *smell.* It is far more elegant to *recline* than to *lie down,* to *retire* rather than *go to bed,* to *dine* than *eat.*

You will notice that the words we refer to as profanity are Anglo-Saxon. The same words are used in jokes, for in both cases, cursing or jesting, the function of the words is to shock, to give one a sort of auditory slap in the face. There is, in all languages, a link between "profanity" and "joking," because each requires the use of the forbidden to achieve its effects.

On thoughtful examination of the double vocabulary of English, the very thing that makes it one of the richest languages in the world, you will find that there are subtle differences between the so-called synonyms. Indeed, it has been said that there are no synonyms in the English language, and this is true, for each of the similar words has a subtle connotation of its own.

The flow of French into English has continued until this day; and to the great irritation of French purists, a comparable flow of English into French has been accelerating for the last fifty years.

While the first influence was Norman French, Central French later penetrated the language. Thus we find in English many words we have imported from those two forms of French, including *catch* from Norman French, *chase* from Central French. The w of the former is replaced by a *g* in the latter: *warden* and *guardian, warranty* and *guarantee, wage* and *gage, reward* and *regard.* English preserves many traces of the evolution of the French language that French itself does not. These include words imported twice, both before and after French dropped an *s* and replaced it with a circumflex accent over the vowel—*hostel* and *hôtel,* for example.

Because the French were the aristocracy, even now things French seem chic (although the French have taken to saying smart) and we import French terminology insatiably, adding to the English vocabulary such words as *couturier, coiffeur, chemise, culotte, chef, maître d'hôtel* (now assimilated to the point of the truncated "mater dee"), *hors d'œuvre, cuisine, à la mode, à la carte, au gratin, au jus,* and *table d'hôte,* reflecting our profound admiration for French food and fashions. So great was French pioneering in the field of flight that its vocabulary is still extensively French—*aviation, aviator, aileron, fusillage, nacelle, dirigible.*

English continued to borrow from Latin words that had already entered it in their French forms, giving us such pairs as *blame* and *blaspheme, chance* and *cadence, count* and *compute, dainty* and *dignity, fealty* and *fidelity, frail* and *fragile, poor* and *pauper, spice* and *species, strait* and *strict, sure* and *secure.*

Roughly half the English language is French or else derives from Latin words also used in French. The other half derives from Anglo-Saxon or Old Norse. The words that derive from Anglo-Saxon seem earthier and more immediate than those from French, as in the pairs *freedom–liberty, friendship–amity, hatred–enmity, truth–verity, lying–mendacity, domicile–home.* Consider your own response to those two French words *hostel* and *hotel* and that Anglo-Saxon word *inn.* An inn seems older, more intimate, cozier, than a hotel, with good plain food and a fire. The words for basic things and concepts tend to derive from Anglo-Saxon: *heaven, earth, hell, love, hate, life, death, beginning, end, morning, night, day, month, year, heat, cold, way, path, meadow, stream.* But we use French or Latin (or sometimes Greek) words to cope with and express abstractions, and our scientific vocabulary is almost entirely Latin or Greek.

When we use a French word instead of the Anglo-Saxon, it has an effect of intellectuality and detachment. English contains the French word *crépuscule* but it does not have the emotional and evocative power of *dusk, twilight, sunset* and *sundown.*

When he was being witty, Cole Porter urged in "I've Got You Under My Skin" that you use your mentality (from French *mentalité*), wake up to reality (from French *réalité*). But when he wanted a lyric to be touching and poignant, such as "In the Still of the Night," he used, almost exclusively, short Anglo-Saxon words because of their evocative power: *gaze, moon, flight, thoughts, still, chill, rim of the hill, love.*

It has been said that we whose primary language is English speak Anglo-Saxon until the age of three and then begin learning French. From that age onward, by some deep intuition, we use the old language for matters of the heart and things of the earth and things close to home, and French to soar into imaginative abstraction. A child first learns words like *hand, foot, arm, leg, mouth, smoke, burn, feel, touch, rain, sun, moon, sleep, wake, love, fish, kiss, sky, stars.*

It is only later the he entertains such abstractions as nation, inflation, infatuation, superstition, liberty, confidence, assurance. Ever after, the simple Anglo-Saxon words one learns during the dawning of consciousness will have far the more powerful effect.

That is the value of such words, to the lyricist and the poet and for that matter any writer. They are of the home, of the hearth, of the earth, of the soul, of the heart.

Good Anglo-Saxon words all.

French may have it all over us for rhymes (and a few other things).

But we have the richer vocabulary.

9.

TATTERED STANDARDS

Steve Allen, best known as one of the most literate comedians of the late twentieth century, less known as a songwriter (his songs include "Impossible" and "This Could Be the Start of Something Big"), wrote a letter to the magazine *Performing Songwriter.* It read:

> I happened to see the feature on page 79 of the May '99 issue concerning the subject of rhyme, but I'm puzzled by something in the text.
>
> In the first two lines of the sample lyric, *frayed* and *cafe* are given as rhymes. Naturally, having been conditioned in the true rhymes of Lorenz Hart, Alan J. Lerner, Johnny Mercer, Ira Gershwin, and other master craftsmen of the lyric-writing art I do not understand how words that have nothing in common except the same basic vowel sound can be referred to as rhymes. The next couplet presents the same problem. The two words spoke and petticoats are represented as rhymes when in fact they are not.
>
> There was a time, and not terribly many years ago, when rhyming of this sort was considered a mark of amateurishness or carelessness. But perhaps when all my attention was diverted to a thousand-and-one elsewheres, the rules of the lyric-writing game have been changed. I note that at one place in the explanatory text the writer refers to "imperfect rhymes."
>
> There is a great deal more to the craft of lyric writing, needless to say, than rhyming. But for centuries both poets and song lyricists have at least agreed on the definition of the word *rhyme.* As regards today's rules, I would appreciate it if you would explain them to me.

It wasn't so much that the rules of the game had changed. Worse, they had been largely abandoned. For these last several decades, mediocrity has been not only accepted but celebrated, because it is, and always has been, far more common than excellence. In an age of mass consumerism, the record industry and all the facets of the music business have perforce put out what they could find in plenty rather than the rare and exceptional. The reason for this cultural development is discussed with eerie prescience in De Tocqueville's *Democracy in America.* Further insight, for anyone interested, can be gained from Ortega y Gassett's *The Revolt of the Masses.* Art of high quality takes time and exacting standards to produce, and requires an "audience" with taste and money to fund its making. In a mass age, this is not feasible. The merchants of entertainment need lots of people, not a few with excellent taste, and they elected to inspire and distribute abysmal trash and simply *call it* art. This esthetic gerrymandering, whereby three-chord guitar players became known as "composers" and the worst possible scratch-throated singers became "artists," altered the esthetics of society.

The public-relations experts of the record industry invented a remarkably effective simple device to discredit any expectation of excellence: they coined a term, referring to that demand as *elitism,* suggesting that those who clung to them were somehow anti-democratic, if not downright fascistic. This campaign began in the 1950s.

It is a mistake, of course, to think that bad popular music began in that decade. There has always been bad popular music. And the excellence of so much of the song of the 1920s, '30s, '40s, and '50s must be considered an aberration in the general evolution of popular cultural. "How Much Is that Doggy in the Window" and novelties such as "Mairzy Doats" predate the '50s. But during that period of about thirty-five years, from roughly 1920 to 1955, a certain element of American popular song rose to the level of art music. Those who are nostalgic for that time assume that all the songs were good. They weren't. But at least there was a general perception in the society as a whole that the songs of, among others, Kern and Rodgers and their literate lyricists, deserved a respect that the general run of trash did not.

With the '50s, however, and with the growing power of the record company publicists, the line was erased, and Grammy awards were given to abominable songs and singers. The record industry had a vested interest in lowering standards, and it did. But it was considerably helped by television.

Back in 1950s, a cigarette advertising campaign used the slogan "Winston tastes good like a cigarette should." Grammarians groaned, and some editorial writers asked what effect this would have on the English language. The sentence should of course have been "Winston tastes good, as a cigarette should." Such television usages, coupled with those increasingly common in popular music, had their inevitable effect. A generation of journalists devoid of any sense of grammatical nicety—they had probably never had to parse a sentence in their school days—moved up the corporate ladder to become editors incapable of correcting the reporters coming up behind them. And so it was that, at last, on the cover of the July 5, 1999, issue of *Time* magazine, the Winston heritage came to full journalistic flower in the headline *Cruise and Kidman Like You've Never Seen Them.*

The word almost has *almost* disappeared, replaced in television journalism by *most,* which of course means a majority. The first *r* has largely disappeared from *February,* and *nuclear* is widely pronounced *nook-you-lur;* even Jimmy Carter said it that way, and he commanded a nuclear submarine. Trying to be correct, people say "to him and I" instead of "to him and me," never having learned the difference between subject and object. The dislocated adverb *hopefully* has become almost universal in American usage, and now has metastasized to England and elsewhere. Its example led to the equally improper *thankfully. Venue,* which has a very precise meaning as the locale of a crime, and the jurisdiction of the trial resulting from it, has come to mean any location whatever, including rock-and-roll nightclubs. One is forced, to be sure, to the admission that some of the performances therein held might be defined as crimes.

The most ominous development concomitant to the rise of bad songwriting lies in the sly shifting of definitions and the honors showered on the makers of the meretricious. If we have a generation of editors who cannot correct bad writing, we have had now nearly three generations of listeners who cannot detect it in the song form.

The pop music world is big business—very big business, a multi-billion dollar business. It is not about art, it is about money.

Because of its pervasive presence in our culture, inevitably courses in songwriting have been established in our schools and universities. I know of no instance of a first-rate professional lyricist teaching a regular credit course in his specialty. The courses given horrify the skilled professionals who now and then monitor them. To justify the slipshod usage endemic in modern pop songwriting, some new terms have been introduced to define (read: *justify)* contemporary practices. One of these is "slant rhymes," meaning those almost-rhymes that those who understand the craft abhor.

Some of these courses are taught by academics, but the academics rarely know much about the craft of writing lyrics. An outstanding exception is Philip Furia, an English professor whose book *The Poets of Tin Pan Alley* (Oxford University Press) is probably the finest treatise on the subject ever written; it belongs on the bookshelf of every songwriter, accomplished or aspirant.

In the rarefied academic world of dictionary formulation, there are two kinds of dictionary, called prescriptive and descriptive. Prescriptive dictionaries tell you how words should be used. Descriptive dictionaries deal with and in effect celebrate actual practice. Without question, the misuse of *hopefully, thankfully, venue,* and the abominable *arguably,* will find themselves included in descriptive dictionaries.

The English language is in trouble, and not only in America: its decline is noted by older writers and journalists in Canada, England, and other English-speaking countries. But this deterioration is not limited to our own language. It is going on, according to colleagues with whom I have discussed it, even in Swedish, and certainly in French. Urbane literacy used to be one of the glories of French cinema. Now of course, crude language in endlessly redundant use is as much a part of French film as it is of American. Films of the literacy of *All About Eve* (a smash hit in its time) are not likely to be made now. Television is one of the chief culprits, without question. But the effect of an inferior popular music and the poor use of language therein on the people who write and produce and appear on television has to be taken into account.

We are all the losers.

If, a few years ago, you saw the Ken Burns series of documentaries on the Civil War, you were probably struck, as many viewers were, by the gracious literacy of the letters quoted in the narrative, letters by common soldiers, who had come to the horrors of war from farms and homesteads and a simple agrarian life. The letters of soldiers today could not even approach the precise and elegant eloquence that was apparently common then.

A few years ago, I was asked to give a master class on songwriting at the New School in New York. I discussed many of the principles of writing described in this book, then asked for questions. The questions from these young people were lively, and for the most part thoughtful. Then one young woman asked, "How do you get into the songwriting business?" The answer slipped out of me almost without thought, and it made this rather large assemblage of students gasp. I said, "You start by forgetting everything I just taught you." For success in the contemporary pop music has nothing to do with the quality and merit of one's work. You don't have to know that it is correct to say that you do well, instead of that you do good. Such distinctions have been lost. But if you want to write well, instead of good, the principles are there to be learned.

10.
HOW TO USE THE RHYMING DICTIONARY

The first known rhyming dictionary of the English language was published in England in 1775 by John Walker, an ex-schoolmaster. Walker had no intention of writing a rhyming dictionary: his book was called *The Critical Pronouncing Dictionary*, and it was intended as a guide to the spelling and pronunciation of the English language. Walker considered that its potential use for rhyming was the least of its values. But poets soon discovered that its words were grouped in patterns of rhyme, and generations of them used it for precisely that purpose. Lord Byron, for one, used it.

You do not use a rhyming dictionary because you are incapable of thinking up a rhyme. To find a rhyme, you simply take your rhyming sound and go through the alphabet, attaching the different consonants in sequence, and eliminating those words that do not exist: bat, cat, *dat*, fat, *gat*, hat, *jat*, *lat*, mat, and so forth. When you have done that, you repeat the process with compound consonants: chat, *crat*, *clat*, and the rest. It is a mechanical process, not an artistic one. So is consulting a rhyming dictionary. And the dictionary, in fact, saves you time.

But a rhyming dictionary has other values. The conscientious lyricist wants to be sure he has considered *all* the possibilities for a rhyme when he finally commits a line to paper. He wants to feel secure in the knowledge that he has not settled for some second-best image or idea. And the dictionary permits him to see quickly what those possibilities are. Sometimes it will suggest a better idea or line than the one he had vaguely in mind—even a startlingly fresh and original one, if he gets lucky. And, at other times, it may reveal that a line he has already written has so few rhyming possibilities that he had better abandon it now, rather than invest further work and worry in an idea that is not going to lead to a good rhyme.

Above and beyond these immediate practical uses, the dictionary has a broader value. The very process of browsing in it enriches one's familiarity with rhyme. It makes you a better craftsman.

This dictionary is deliberately designed *not* to be exhaustive—and exhausting.

There are, according to the Burges Johnson dictionary, 1035 words that rhyme with *nation*. According to the Wood dictionary, published five years later, there are 1377, which just goes to show how quickly a bad trend can develop. Among them are *arcuation, etiolation, hariolation,*

53

pronation, and *recusation.* I cannot imagine anyone wanting to use these words in a song, or anywhere else, for that matter. Anyone who has a taste for such words is probably already working for the government, not writing songs. I have therefore omitted a great many obscure, pretentious, unpronounceable, and certainly unsingable words. A good writer, particularly a good writer of songs, seeks out those words that express thoughts most directly, simply, vividly, and immediately. The vocabulary included in the present dictionary is, nonetheless, extensive. Who knows what you might have to write? I know a young lady who makes a very good living writing satiric lyrics for various professional and business meetings and conventions.

This dictionary differs radically from other rhyming dictionaries in the way in which it is organized. The common complaint against some of the other available rhyming dictionaries is that they are confusing. Some use diacritical markings to indicate how a given vowel is pronounced, markings that only a few specialists understand. Others are somewhat arbitrary in the placement of words.

This dictionary is designed to be, insofar as it is possible, self-explanatory. But as a friend of mine says, "When all else fails, read the instructions." Herewith the instructions:

The dictionary is divided into three basic sections: MASCULINE OR ONE-SYLLABLE RHYMES, FEMININE OR TWO-SYLLABLE RHYMES, and THREE-SYLLABLE RHYMES.

These sections in turn are divided into five sections, according to the sequence of the vowels in the alphabet: **A, E, I, O, U.**

The various ways the vowels are pronounced are designated by commonplace phonetic spellings. If you want the words that rhyme with *bay,* you will find them under **A**: the words that rhyme with *hurrah* under **A (AH).**

This dictionary also differs from others in the English language in that there are subgroupings according to the consonant that begins *the final syllable of the word*—or the group of syllables, in the two- and three-rhyme sections.

You will therefore not find *disarray* under D in the **A** section but under R in the **A** section. Look up *ray* and under it you will find *Monterey* and *manta ray,* as well. *Ricochet* is under *shay.*

Phonetic spellings—not the "normal" spellings of English—are used. You will find *ampersand* under *sand.* But you will find *partisan* not under *san* but under *(zan).* Where no true word exists in English to conform to the needed phonetic syllable, I have enclosed the syllable in parentheses, as in the case of *(zan).*

This grouping of words makes it possible to skim the rhymes very quickly. But it has a further value: the words within these subgroups should not be used as rhymes with each other. *Bazaar* forms not a rhyme but an identity with *czar.* Look for a rhyme for *czar* among other words in the **AR** group.

Some words function as nouns and verbs, adjectives and nouns, or verbs and adjectives. Sometimes one form will work as a rhyme while the other will not. The verb *deliberate* rhymes with *straight;* the adjective *deliberate* does not.

Some words are marked *(n)* to indicate that only the noun form works as a rhyme. Others are marked *(v)* to indicate that only the verb should be used or *(a)* to indicate that only the adjective should be used. Still others are marked *(i)* for imperfect.

As we noted in Chapter V, under certain circumstances, three-syllable words can be used in rhyme with one-syllable words, *providing that* the second syllable is weak. *PHO-to-graph,* for example, can under the right melodic conditions be used as a rhyme for *laugh.* It is a matter of delicate judgment and tasteful handling. These imperfect rhymes, so-called for lack of a better term, marked *(i)* in the dictionary, will be used nicely by the skilled and conscientious lyricist, awkwardly by the careless one.

The same principles that govern the ordering of words in the masculine rhyme section operate in the two-rhyme and three-rhyme sections. You would look up *reckon* under **EK-on.** Only *beckon* rhymes with it in the present tense, but in its past tense, *second* also rhymes with it.

Plural and past-tense forms are not listed unless the addition of the *s* or *d* causes another syllable to be added to the pronunciation. *Watch* is a one-syllable word, and so is *watched,* which is actually pronounced *wocht.* On the other hand, *taste* is a one-syllable word and so is *tastes.* But *tasted* is a two-syllable word, and will be found among the feminine rhymes under **A-sted.**

Compound forms, including negatives, will be found immediately following the root form of the word, as in

tasted
untasted

Go strictly by the pronunciation of a given word, not the spelling. *Caught* will be found under **OT.**

Because *d* is a soft *t,* terminal *t* usually will form a rhyme with the past tense of words that resemble it but for the *t.* For example, there is no difference in pronunciation between *paste* and *paced, chaste* and *chased. Craft* rhymes correctly with *laughed, passed* with *last.* Caution: it doesn't always work. Consider *canned* and *cant, panned* and *pant.* Hints for the use of past-tense rhymes with words ending in *t* are offered in the book.

Conventional rhyming dictionaries do not include multiple-word rhymes. This one does. To be sure, it would be impossible to list all such rhymes, but at the ends of certain groups of rhymes, suggestions are made for the formation of still more of them. In humor, one might form a four-rhyme of *euthanasia* and *truth in Asia.* Presumably everyone who has ever tried a hand at writing lyrics has discovered that *in it,* in the course of normal American speech and because of the neutral vowel, forms a dreary little rhyme with *minute.* Many of these compound rhymes have been worked to exhaustion, but others have not, and it is to the end of creating fresh ones that suggestions for their pursuit have been offered.

There is still another way that this rhyming dictionary differs from others. Popular music, whether at its highest level in theater or at its lowest level in the commercial record industry, uses the vernacular in ways and to an extent that poetry does not. Vernacular rhymes are not included in standard rhyming dictionaries. They are in this one. *Spoken,* in the vernacular and by virtue of the neutral vowel in the second syllable, rhymes with *jokin'*. In many accents of England, as well as those of America, the *g* is unsounded in the present participle. Perhaps in fifty years it will have disappeared altogether. There will be no loss of clarity in meaning, and our rhymes will be enriched. (And the sooner we drop the *m* in *whom,* the better. "Between who?" Hamlet says to Polonius.)

The letter *r* occupies a curious position among consonants. It has fallen silent in much of the American south, though not in New Orleans, as well as New England, and in many areas of England itself. (In many parts of England, the aspirated *h* might as well not exist, either.) Lancashire coalminers and Kentucky coalminers alike, Oxford dons and Boston Brahmins, Cockney musicians and Georgia politicians, Vermont farmers and Carolina housewives, all treat the letter *r* in a manner that is cavalier, to put it mildly. Nor does the omission have anything to do with class: the rich and the poor, the educated and uneducated, have simply stricken the letter from the language. Indeed, in England, its firm pronunciation is limited to a few pockets of adamantine Celtic resistance, such as Ireland and Cornwall, where they pronounce the *harrrd arrrrr*. This hard *r* is considered the norm of American speech, but as we have noted, it is honored more in the breach than the enunciation, as one readily notices in *Noo Yock*. Oddly and interestingly, in all these regional accents, the letter goes unpronounced in different ways. Someone from Cambridge, England, might ask a garage attendant to *pock my caw,* while someone from Cambridge, Massachusetts, would ask him to *pack my ca'*.

To compound this interest, well-trained singers usually have been taught to avoid stressing the letter, for the sake of a pretty enunciation — and it is true that if the letter is overpronounced, the effect is *rrratherrr harrsh*. Singers tend to deal with *stahs* and *guitahs*.

Consequently, there are many words ending in *r* that rhyme in regional dialects with words ending in vowels. In northern Florida, the name of the state tends to rhyme with *corridor,* and an Alabaman visiting the Louvre would no doubt pause to *ponduh* the *Gioconda*.

I have given some suggestions for these rhymes in the dictionary, designating them *U.S. southern,* since southerners have most conspicuously excised the letter from their speech. But, in fact, these rhymes would work in humorous songs and theatrical characterizations using all sorts of accents from all over the English-speaking world. These regional variants are great fun to explore.

But clearly, a total catalogue of such regional lingual eccentricities would run to many volumes, seriously compromising the intent of this book to be concise and readily useful. Therefore standard neutral American pronunciations, if any, are used throughout, which brings us into modest conflict with our more fastidious English brethren, who would not rhyme *autumn* (one of the loveliest words in our language, by the way) with *bottom.* Most of us in America would, and in a Broadway musical you might have a countrified character rhyme it with *taught 'em.*

I thought it inadvisable to include given names in the dictionary, since they are of limited use, except where they have taken on secondary meanings such as *Jerry* for *German,* or where they are of sufficient fame— *Lincoln,* for example—that they might well be used symbolically in a song. I am sure you will be able to think of many more.

One final point: wherever you are referred to another rhyme elsewhere in the book, the page number is given. This has never been done in a rhyming dictionary, and it should save all of us many hours of floundering.

I wish you serendipitous browsing.

Words That Do Not Rhyme

Laymen seem to think that it is an odd and remarkable thing that there is no rhyme for *orange*. There are hundreds of words in the English language which rhyme with nothing. *Nothing* itself rhymes with nothing. *Mistress* does not rhyme with *distress*. Roger Miller in fact wrote a funny song using words that have no rhymes.

Many words have only a few rhymes. *Realty* has only one rhyme, *fealty*.

To save you a lot of time and futile searching, here is a list of a few more words that have no true, one-word, pure rhymes, although sometimes one can work one up in slang (*jivey* for *ivy,* for example) and by distortion (*toss-up* for *gossip*).

You may well add many other words that lack rhymes to the list.

abbess	bagpipe	chartreuse	deceitful
aberrant	ballot	chemist	different
absence	bargain	cherub	dolor
absent	beloved	civic	donkey
accent	bestowal	cockeyed	druggist
access	bilge	cockney	dulcet
accomplish	bishop	coffin	
acrid	bogus	coinage	eastward
adage	boscage	comfort	ebon
adornment	breadth	common	edict
advent	broadcast	consummate	emblem
alacrity	budget	costly	employee
alarum	buffet	crotchet	envy
allegiance	bulb	cuckold	evening
almost		cuckoo	every
alum	cabbage	cudgel	exhaustion
ambush	cactus	culprit	exit
anal	cadence	cusp	
angel	cadre	cutlass	faithful
anthem	camphor	cyclone	falsehood
April	capstan	cypress	fanfare
ardent	captious		fathom
arrant	carotid	dainty	film
aspic	censure	damage	filthy
assassin	challenge	dampen	foible
August	chaos	darkness	folklore
axle	charcoal	deafen	fondle

forger
fortress
foundry
fragment
frailty
frosty
fullness
furnace

gadget
gala
gallop
gallstone
gambol
gauntlet
gleeful
goodness
gorgeous
gospel
gossip

hairpin
halo
handsome
haply
happen
hardly
hatchway
havoc
heron
homage
homely
hoodlum
hostage
hostel
hostess
hostile
humbug
humdrum
hundred
hungry

incense
infant

irony
item
ivy

jackass
jasmine
joyful
joyous
judgment
junior

kinsman
kitchen

language
legend
lethargic
license
lilac
liniment
loathsome
lozenge
luggage

madcap
magpie
mama
mandate
mangrove
manhood
margin
market
mastiff
maudlin
method
mischief
modern
moldy
molten
monarch
monster
monstrous
month
morbid

niblick
nitric
noisy
nosedive
nosegay

obese
object
oblige
ogler
ogre
okra
olive
omelet
open
orange
orchid
ornate
ostrich
oval
ozone

padlock
pamphlet
pedant
piebald
placard
plaintiff
platform
plinth
polka
portent
portrait
postage
postern
postmark
potash
poverty
practice
primrose
princess
proboscis
profile
prosper

proverb
provincial
psychic
purchase
puss
pussy
putrid
pygmy

quagmire
quatrain

rainbow
ramrod
rapine
rebellious
refuge
regent
reindeer
reluctant
reproachful
respite
roguish
rouge
rumba

sabbath
sacred
safest
sarcasm
satire
sausage
scarcely
scoundrel
sculptor
secret
sedative
segue
serpent
shamrock
shapely
shindig
shortage
shorten

signal	swarthy	vampire	zebra
sinful	sylph	vengeance	
siren	syzygy	vertical	
snowstorm		victim	*Also:*
sofa		villain	
softest	tablet	violin	eighth
softly	tactful	violinist	eightieth
sojourn	tadpole	viviparous	
solace	taffrail	volcano	fifth
soldier	tailspin	voltage	fiftieth
soreness	target	vulgar	fortieth
species	tidied		
sportsman	tinsel	wakeful	
squirrel	toady	wanton	hundred
stagnant	tombstone	warfare	hundredth
stalactite	topaz	warlock	
stalagmite	torment	wasp	ninetieth
stalwart	torpor	watchword	ninth
statue	torture	weapon	
strangely	tramway	weirdly	seventieth
stubborn	tribune	welfare	sixth
substance	trinket	westward	sixtieth
sudden	tumbril	whoopee	
sudsy	turbine	window	tenth
sugar	tyranny	woeful	thirteen
sulphur		wolf	Thursday
sultan		wolves	twelfth
sundry	vaguest	woman	twentieth
sunrise	valiant	wooden	
sunset	valve	wounded	Wednesday

Masculine
Rhymes

A

A
eh?
bay
  obey
    disobey
brae
bray
cay
  decay
Kay
  bouquet
  sobriquet
  tourniquet
clay
day
  holiday
  lack-a-day
  Lady Day
  midday
  today
  yesterday
  Christmas Day, etc.
dray
fay
fey
flay
  soufflé
fray
  affray
  defray
gay
  distingué
gray
hay
jay
  bluejay (i)
lay
  allay
  belay
  delay
  Mandalay
  mislay
  overlay

underlay
waylay
May
may
  come-what-may
  dismay
  résumé
nay
née
  matinee
  pince-nez
neigh
pay
  coupé
  overpay
  prepay
  repay
  toupee
  underpay
)lay
  interplay
  overplay
  replay (v)
  underplay
ray
  array
    disarray
  hooray
  manta ray
  moiré
  Monterey
  x-ray, etc.
say
  assay (v)
  essay (v)
  gainsay
  naysay
  yeasay
(scay)
  Biscay
  risqué
shay
  ricochet

sachet
sashay
slay
sleigh
spay
splay
  display
spray
stay
  outstay
  overstay
stray
  astray
sway
  asway
they
tray
  betray
  portray
trey
way
  away
  Broadway (i)
  halfway
  midway
  Milky Way
weigh
  aweigh
  habitué
whey
(vey)
  convey
  purvey
  survey (v)
  inveigh
  oi vay (Yiddish)
yea
(zay)
  exposé
  José
    San Jose
  rosé
(zhay)

negligée
protégé

A (AH)
ah
bah
bra
claw
éclat
ha
  ha-ha
Ma
Pa
  papa
paw
  pawpaw (*i*)
Ra
rah
  hurrah
raw
shah
spa
(zah)
  huzzah
(*see* **O (AH)**, *page 110*)

AB
blab
cab
crab
dab
drab
gab
grab
jab
lab
nab
scab
slab
stab
tab

AB (OB)
squab
swab
(*see* **OB**, *page 110*)

ACH
batch
catch
  recatch
hatch
latch
  unlatch
match
  rematch
patch
  dispatch
  repatch
scratch
snatch
(tatch)
  attach
  detach
thatch

ACH (OCH)
watch
(*see* **OCH**, *page 111*)

AD (AID)
blade
braid
  upbraid
  abrade
brayed
cade
  arcade
  barricade
  blockade
  brocade
  cavalcade
  cockade
  stockade
fade
frayed
  afraid
    unafraid
(gade)
  brigade
  renegade
glade
grade

centigrade
degrade
downgrade (*i*)
retrograde
upgrade (*i*)
hayed
laid
  inlaid
  overlaid
  accolade
  fusillade
made
  pomade
  remade
  self-made
  unmade
maid
  dismayed
neighed
  cannonade
  colonnade
  esplanade
  grenade
  harlequinade
  lemonade
  marinade
  promenade
  serenade
paid
  overpaid
  postpaid
  prepaid
  repaid
    unrepaid
  escapade
raid
  charade
  masquerade
  parade
  tirade
(sade)
  crusade
shade
spade
staid
suede

dissuade
persuade
trade
(vade)
  evade
  invade
  pervade
(played, etc.)

AD (ADD)
ad
add
bad
  Hyderabad
bade
  forebade
brad
cad
chad
clad
  unclad
  autumn-clad
  ivy-clad
  winter-clad, etc. (i)
dad
  Trinidad (i)
fad
gad
  egad
glad
grad
  Leningrad
  Petrograd
  Stalingrad, etc.
  undergrad
had
lad
mad
pad
plaid
sad
shad
(yad)
  naiad (i)
  olympiad

AD (ODD)
(fod)
  guffawed
(lod)
  roulade
nod
  promenade
rod
  charade
  hurrahed
sod
  facade
wad
(*see* **OD,** *page 111*)

ADZ
adz
scads
(adds, etc.)

AF (AIF)
chafe
safe
  unsafe
strafe
waif

AFF
calf
chaff
graph
  chronograph (i)
  cinematograph (i)
  lithograph (i)
  monograph (i)
  pantograph (i)
  paragraph (i)
  phonograph (i)
  photograph (i)
  polygraph (i)
  telegraph (i)
raff
  carafe
  giraffe
  riffraff (i)
staff

staph
strafe
(taff)
  cenotaph
  epitaph

AFT
aft
(baft)
  abaft
craft
  handicraft (i)
  witchcraft (i), etc.
daft
draft
  overdraft
draught
graft
haft
raft
shaft
(chaffed, etc.)

AG (AIG)
Hague
plague
vague

AG
bag
brag
crag
drag
flag
gag
hag
jag
lag
mag
nag
rag
sag
scrag
shag
slag
snag

stag
swag
tag
wag

AJ (AIJ)
age
  Stone Age (*i*)
  over age (*i*)
  under age (*i*)
cage
  encage
  uncage
gage
  engage
    disengage
gauge
page
  rampage (*v*)
sage
stage
  downstage
  upstage
(suage)
  assuage
wage

AJ
badge
cadge
hadj *(Arabic)*

AK (AIK)
ache
  headache (*i*)
  heartache (*i*)
bake
brake
break
cake
drake
fake
flake
jake
make
  remake

unmake (*i*)
(pake)
  opaque
quake
earthquake
rake
sake
  forsake
  keepsake
shake
sheikh
slake
snake
stake
  mistake
steak
take
  overtake
  partake
  undertake
wake
  awake

AK
back
  aback
black
(brack)
  amphibrach
  bric-a-brac
clack
  clickety-clack
claque
hack
jack
lack
  Cadillac
knack
  almanac
pack
plaque
quack
rack
wrack
sack
shack

slack
snack
stack
  haystack(*i*)
tack
  attack
    counterattack
track
WAAC
whack
yack
yak
  cardiac
  demoniac
  hypochondriac
  kayak(*i*)
  maniac
    dipsomaniac
    egomaniac
    kleptomaniac
    monomaniac, etc.
  Nyack (*i*)
  Pontiac
  zodiac

AKS
ax
(fax)
  Halifax
lax
  relax
  parallax
pax
sacks
Saks (Fifth Ave.)
sax
slacks
wax
(attacks, etc.)

AKT
act
  counteract
  enact
    reenact
  overact

react
transact
underact
fact
(fract)
diffract
refract
pact
compact (*v*)
impact (*v*)
racked
cataract
(stract)
abstract
distract
tact
intact
tract
attract
contract (*v*)
detract
protract
subtract
(zact)
exact
(attacked, etc.)

AL (AIL)
ail
ale
bail
bale
Braille
dale
fail
flail
frail
gale
regale
grail
hail
hale
exhale
inhale
jail
kail

mail
blackmail (*i*)
male
female (*i*)
nail
pail
pale
empale
impale
rail
derail
sail
assail
outsail
wassail (*i*)
sale
scale
shale
snail
stale
tail
cocktail (*i*)
curtail
detail
entail
they'll
vail
avail
prevail
veil
unveil
wail
bewail
whale

AL
Cal
tropicale
gal
(nal)
canal
pal
râle (*French*)
chorale
morale
shall

AL (OL)
ball, etc.
(*see* **OL (ALL),** *page 114*

AM (AIM)
aim
blame
came
became
overcame
claim
acclaim
declaim
disclaim
exclaim
proclaim
reclaim
fame
defame
flame
enflame
inflame
frame
game
lame
maim
name
misname
rename
same
shame
tame
untame

AM
am
cam
clam
cram
dam
Amsterdam (*i*)
Rotterdam (*i*)
damn
madame
dram
flam

flim-flam
(fram)
  diaphragm
gam
gram
  anagram (*i*)
  cryptogram (*i*)
  epigram (*i*)
  monogram (*i*)
  telegram (*i*), etc.
ham
  Birmingham (*i*)
  Effingham (*i*), etc.
jam
jamb
lam
lamb
ma'am
pram
ram
scram
sham
slam
swam
tram
yam

AM (OM)
balm, etc.
(*see* **OM**, *page 115*)

AMP
amp
camp
  decamp
  encamp
champ
clamp
cramp
damp
lamp
ramp
scamp
stamp
tamp
tramp

vamp
  revamp

AMP (OMP)
swamp
(*see* **OMP**, *page 115*)

AN (AIN)
bane
  urbane
brain
  featherbrain (*i*)
  scatterbrain (*i*), etc.
Cain
  cocaine
cane
  hurricane
  sugar cane
chain
  unchain
crane
Dane
  disdain
  ordain
    foreordain
deign
drain
fain
  profane
feign
(frain)
  refrain
gain
  again
  regain
grain
  engrain
  ingrain
  migraine (*i*)
lain
  chamberlain (*i*)
  chatelaine (*i*)
lane
  lovers' lane, etc.
main
  domain

legerdemain
remain
mane
  germane
  humane
Maine
  chow mein
(nane)
  inane
pain
  campaign
  champagne
pane
  counterpane (*i*)
  frangipane
  propane
  windowpane
plain
  complain
  explain
plane
  airplane
  astral plane
  hydroplane
rain
  April rain, etc.
  arraign
  moraine
reign
rein
sane
  insane
slain
Spain
sprain
stain
  abstain
  bestain
  sustain
strain
  constrain
  restrain
swain
tain
  appertain
  ascertain

attain
contain
detain
entertain
maintain
obtain
pertain
retain
thane
train
  entrain
twain
  Mark Twain
vain
vane
vein
wane

AN
ban
bran
can
  pecan
clan
fan
flan
gan
  began
man
  superman (*i*)
  talisman (*i*)
  unman (*i*)
pan
  flash in the pan
  Japan
plan
ran
  also ran
  outran
  overran
scan
span
  spick-and-span
tan
  rattan
than

van
  divan
  pavane
(zan)
  courtesan (*i*)
  partisan (*i*)

AN (ON)
swan
wan
(*see* **ON**, *page 116,*

ANCH
blanch
branch
(lanch)
  avalanche
ranch

ANCH (ONCH)
haunch
launch
paunch
stanch
staunch

AND
and
band
  contraband
  disband
brand
canned
  Samarcand
grand
  Rio Grande
hand
  first-hand
  overhand, (*i*)
  second-hand
  underhand (*i*)
  unhand
land
  fairyland (*i*)
  fatherland (*i*)
  lotus land (*i*)

motherland (*i*)
overland (*i*)
wonderland (*i*) etc.
manned
  command
  countermand
  demand
  remand
  reprimand
panned
  expand
sand
  ampersand
stand
  candy stand
  music stand, etc.
  understand
  withstand
(planned, etc.)

AND (OND)
wand
(*see* **OND**, *page 117*)

ANG
bang
  shebang
bhang
clang
dang
fang
pang
rang
  boomerang (*i*)
  harangue
  meringue
sang
slang
sprang
tang
  orangutang (*i*)

ANJ (AINJ)
change
  exchange
grange

mange
range
　arrange
　　disarrange
　　rearrange
　derange
strange
　estrange

ANK
bank
　embank
　mountebank (*i*)
blank
clank
crank
dank
drank
flank
　outflank
frank
hank
plank
prank
rank
　outrank
sank
shank
shrank
spank
stank
tank
thank
yank
Yank

ANKS
(lanks)
　phalanx (*i*)
Manx
(banks, etc.)

ANS
chance
　bechance
　perchance

dance
France
(ganse)
　extravagance
glance
hanse
　enhance
lance
manse
　romance
(nance)
　assonance (*i*)
　dissonance (*i*)
　dominance (*i*)
　finance
prance
(skance)
　askance
(spanse)
　expanse
stance
　circumstance
trance
　entrance (*v*)
(vanse)
　advance
(ants, etc.)

ANT (AINT)
ain't
faint
feint
paint
　repaint
plaint
　complaint
quaint
　acquaint
saint
(straint)
　constraint
　restraint
taint
'tain't

ANT
ant
aunt
brant
cant
　decant
can't
chant
　enchant
　　disenchant
(dant)
　commandant
(fant)
　sycophant
grant
pant
plant
　implant
　replant
　transplant
rant
scant
　descant
shan't
slant
(tant)
　extant

AP (AIP)
ape
cape
crape
drape
gape
　agape
grape
jape
nape
rape
scape
　escape
　cityscape
　landscape
　seascape, etc.
shape
　reshape
tape

AP

cap
  foolscap (*i*)
  handicap (*i*)
  kneecap (*i*)
chap
clap
flap
gap
hap
  mishap
lap
  dewlap (*i*)
  overlap
Lapp
map
nap
knap
pap
rap
wrap
  unwrap
sap
scrap
slap
snap
strap
tap
trap
  claptrap (*i*)
  entrap
yap
zap

AP (OP)

swap
(*see* **OP,** *page 118*)

APS (AIPS)

(napse)
  jackanapes
traipse
(apes, etc.)

APS

apse
craps
haps
  perhaps
lapse
  collapse
  elapse
(caps, etc.)

APT

apt
(dapt)
  adapt
rapt
  enrapt
(capped, etc.)

AR (AIR)

air
  midair
heir
bare
  threadbare (*i*)
bear
  forbear (*v*)
blare
care
chair
Clare
  declare
  éclair
dare
fair
  affair
  unfair
fare
  thoroughfare
flair
glare
hair
hare
lair
mare
  mal de mer (*French*)
  nightmare (*i*)

(naire)
  billionaire
  commissionaire
  concessionaire
  debonair
  legionaire
  millionaire
ne'er
pair
  impair
  repair
    disrepair
pare
  compare
  prepare
pear
prayer
rare
scare
snare
spare
  despair
square
  four-square (*i*)
stair
stare
  outstare
swear
  forswear
tear
  solitaire
their
there
ware
  aware
    unaware
wear
  ready-to-wear
  underwear
where
  anywhere
  elsewhere
  everywhere
  somewhere
(yare)
  Pierre

AR
are
bar
  debar
  disbar
car
char
far
  afar
gar
  cigar
(guar)
  jaguar
jar
  ajar
(lar)
  funicular
mar
(nar)
  canard
par
Saar
  hussar
scar
spar
star
(strar)
  registrar
tar
  avatar
  guitar
(vyar)
  caviar (*i*)
(zar)
  bazaar
  bizarre
Czar

ARB
barb
garb

ARCH
arch

larch
march
parch
starch

ARD (AIRD)
laird
(cared, etc.)

ARD
bard
  bombard
card
  discard
chard
guard
  avant-garde
  en garde
  on guard
  regard
    disregard
hard
lard
  foulard
nard
  canard
  spikenard
pard
shard
tarred
  petard
  retard
yard
(barred, etc.)

ARJ
barge
charge
  discharge
  overcharge
  undercharge
large
  enlarge
marge

ARK
arc
ark
bark
  debark
  embark
    disembark
barque
clerk (*English*)
dark
hark
lark
mark
  remark
narc
nark (*English*)
park
sark
shark
spark
stark
(vark)
  aardvark
(yark)
  patriarch

ARL
Arles
carl
gnarl
marl
snarl
  ensnarl

ARM
arm
  disarm
  forearm
charm
farm
harm
(larm)
  alarm

ARN (AIRN)
bairn
cairn

ARN
barn
darn
Marne (*River*)
tarn
yarn

ARP
carp
harp
scarp
sharp

ARS
farce
parse
sparse

ARSH
harsh
marsh

ART
art
cart
chart
dart
hart
heart
  sweetheart
mart
part
  apart
  counterpart
  depart
  impart
smart
start
  upstart (*i*)
tart

ARV
carve
starve

AS (AIS)
ace
base
  abase
  debase
bass
brace
  embrace
case
  encase
  in case
chase
  steeplechase (*i*)
face
  deface
  efface
grace
  disgrace
lace
  interlace (*i*)
  unlace
mace
pace
  apace
place
  commonplace
  displace
  misplace
  replace
  resting place
plaice
race
  erase
space
Thrace
trace
  retrace

AS (ASS)
ass
bass
brass
class
  middle class
  working class, etc.
crass

(frass)
  sassafras
gas
glass
  hourglass
  isinglass
  looking-glass
grass
lass
  alas
mass
  amass
  en masse
pass
  overpass
  surpass
(rass)
  harass
  morass
Tass
  demitasse

ASH
ash
bash
  abash
    calabash (*i*)
brash
cash
clash
crash
dash
  balderdash
fash
flash
gash
hash
  rehash
lash
mash
Nash
gnash
pash
plash
rash
sash

slash
smash
splash
stash
  mustache
thrash
trash

ASH (OSH)
quash
wash
(see **OSH,** page 121)

ASK
ask
bask
Basque
cask
casque
flask
mask
  unmask
masque
task

ASP
asp
clasp
  unclasp
gasp
grasp
hasp
rasp

AST (AIST)
baste
  .ambaste
chaste
faced
  freckle-faced
  hatchet-faced,etc.
haste
paste
taste
  aftertaste (i)
  distaste

foretaste (i)
waist
waste
(braced, etc.)

AST
blast
cast
  forecast (v)
  overcast
  recast
caste
(clast)
  iconoclast
fast
gassed
  aghast
  flabbergast (i)
last
  outlast
mast
past
  repast (i)
(trast)
  contrast
vast
  avast
(classed, etc.)

AT (AIT)
ate
eight
bait
  crow bait (i), etc
bate
  abate
  celibate
  debate
  exacerbate
  incubate
  reprobate
(brate)
  celebrate
(cate)
  abdicate

adjudicate
advocate (v)
authenticate
certificate (i)
communicate
  excommunicate
complicate
dedicate
deprecate
domesticate
duplicate (v)
educate
equivocate
eradicate
extricate
fabricate
implicate
imprecate
inculcate
intoxicate
locate
  dislocate
lubricate
placate
pontificate
prevaricate
prognosticate
reciprocate
rusticate
suffocate
supplicate
vacate
vindicate
crate
  consecrate
    reconsecrate
  desecrate
  execrate
krait
date
  accommodate
  candidate
  consolidate
  elucidate
  intimidate
  liquidate

sedate
validate
　invalidate
hate
late
　accumulate
　ambulate
　　perambulate
　　somnambulate
　annihilate
　articulate (*v*)
　assimilate
　calculate
　capitulate
　　recapitulate
　circulate
　coagulate
　congratulate
　copulate
　desolate (*v*)
　dilate
　ejaculate
　elate
　emulate
　flagellate
　formulate
　gesticulate
　granulate
　immolate
　inoculate
　insulate
　interpolate
　isolate
　manipulate
　matriculate
　modulate
　oscillate
　osculate
　percolate
　populate
　　depopulate
　postulate
　　expostulate
　regulate
　relate
　　correlate

scintillate
simulate
　dissimulate
speculate
stimulate
stipulate
tabulate
titillate
translate
triangulate
undulate
vacillate
ventilate
violate
　inviolate
mate
　amalgamate
　animate
　　inanimate
　consummate (*v*)
　decimate
　estimate
　intimate (*v*)
　sublimate
　ultimate (*i*)
Nate
　abominate
　alienate
　assassinate
　contaminate
　criminate
　　discriminate
　　incriminate
　　recriminate
　culminate
　designate
　detonate
　dominate
　　predominate
　donate
　eliminate
　emanate
　fascinate
　fulminate
　germinate
　hibernate

illuminate
impersonate
innate
marinate
nominate
　denominate
ordinate
　coordinate
　inordinate
　subordinate
originate
ornate
procrastinate
rejuvenate
ruminate
seminate
　disseminate
　inseminate
terminate
　exterminate
pate
　constipate
　dissipate
　emancipate
　exculpate
　participate
　syncopate
plait
plate
　contemplate
　armor plate
　nickel plate
　silver plate, etc.
prate
(quate)
　equate
rate
　accelerate
　adulterate
　agglomerate
　ameliorate
　aspirate
　asseverate
　berate
　collaborate
　　elaborate (*v*)

78

commemorate
commiserate
corroborate
decorate
deteriorate
evaporate
exonerate
expectorate
generate
  degenerate (v)
  regenerate
incarcerate
incinerate
incorporate
invigorate
irate
lacerate
liberate
  deliberate (v)
moderate (v)
narrate
obliterate
operate
  cooperate
orate
overrate
pastorate (i)
perforate
protectorate
recuperate
reiterate
remunerate
reverberate
saturate
second-rate, etc.
separate
tolerate
ulcerate
underrate
venerate
vituperate
sate
  compensate
  tergiversate
skate
  confiscate

slate
  legislate
spate
state
  devastate
  estate
  overstate
  reinstate
  understate
straight
  demonstrate
  frustrate
  illustrate
  magistrate
  orchestrate
  penetrate
  remonstrate
strait
Tate
  agitate
  amputate
  annotate
  cogitate
  debilitate
  decapitate
  dictate
  facilitate
  gravitate
  hesitate
  imitate
  incapacitate
  irritate
  levitate
  meditate
    premeditate
  militate
  necessitate
  palpitate
  precipitate
  regurgitate
  rehabilitate
  resuscitate
  rotate
  vegetate
trait

arbitrate
concentrate
perpetrate
(vate)
  aggravate
  captivate
  cultivate
  elevate
  excavate
  innovate
    renovate
  motivate
  salivate
  titivate
wait
  await
weight
  heavyweight
  overweight
  underweight, etc.
  accentuate
  actuate
  attenuate
  evacuate
  evaluate
  extenuate
  fluctuate
  graduate
  habituate
  infatuate
  insinuate
  perpetuate
  punctuate
  situate
(yate)
  affiliate (v)
  appreciate
  appropriate (v)
    misappropriate
  associate (v)
    disassociate
  conciliate
  depreciate
  differentiate
  enunciate
  humiliate

inebriate
mediate
negotiate
novitiate
officiate
permeate
propriate
  expropriate
radiate
  irradiate
repudiate
retaliate

AT
at
  hereat
  thereat
bat
  acrobat
brat
cat
  pussycat
  tabby cat
  tigercat
  wildcat (i), etc.
chat
(crat)
  aristocrat
  autocrat
  bureaucrat
  democrat
  plutocrat, etc.
drat
fat
flat
frat
gat
ghat
gnat
hat
  high-hat
mat
  automat
  diplomat
matte
pat

pit-a-pat
rat
sat
scat
slat
spat
sprat
stat
  photostat (i)
  rheostat (i)
  thermostat (i)
tat
  rat-a-tat-tat
vat
  cravat
(yat)
  proletariat
  secretariat

AT (OT)
squat
what
(*see* **OT**, *page 122*)

ATH (ATHE)
bathe
lathe
scathe
swathe

ATH (AITH)
faith
wraith

ATH
bath
Gath
lath
math
  aftermath
path
  bridal path
  towpath, etc.
  homeopath
  psychopath
  sociopath, etc.

wrath

AV (AIV)
brave
cave
  concave (i)
crave
gave
  forgave
grave
  engrave
(haiv)
  behave
    misbehave
lave
nave
knave
pave
(prave)
  deprave
rave
save
shave
slave
  enslave
stave
waive
wave

AV
calve
halve
have
salve

AV (OV)
Slav
suave
Zouave

AZ (AIZ)
blaze
  ablaze
braise
braze
chaise

craze
daze
  adaze
  nowadays
faze
gaze
glaze
graze
haze
laze
  malaise
maize
maze
  amaze
nays
  mayonnaise
  polonaise
praise
  appraise
  bepraise
vase (*British*)
(affrays, etc.)

AZ
as
  whereas
has
jazz
razz
(tazz)
  razzmatazz

AZ (OZ)
vase
(*see* **OZ,** *page 125*)

AZH (OZH)
(flage)
  camouflage
  persiflage
(nage)
  badinage
  menage

(rage)
  barrage
  entourage
  garage
  mirage

AZM
chasm
  sarcasm
(clasm)
  iconoclasm
plasm
  bioplasm
  ectoplasm
  metaplasm
  protoplasm
spasm
(tasm)
  phantasm
(yasm)
  enthusiasm

E

E (EE)
be
bee
  bumblebee
  honeybee, etc.
bree
Brie
  debris
Cree
  decree
  mimicry
Dee
  chickadee
  Dundee
  fiddle-de-dee
  grandee
  Ph. D.

bastardy (*i*)
comedy (*i*)
comédie (*French*)
custody (*i*)
jeopardy (*i*)
Lombardy (*i*)
malady
melody (*i*)
monody (*i*)
parody (*i*)
perfidy (*i*)
Picardy (*i*)
psalmody (*i*)
remedy (*i*)
rhapsody (*i*)
subsidy (*i*)

(dree)
  heraldry (*i*)
  husbandry (*i*)
  ribaldry (*i*)
fee
  apostrophe (*i*)
  atrophy (*i*)
  philosophy (*i*)
  theosophy (*i*)
  (graphy)
    geógraphy
    biography
    photography
    pornography
    thermography
    topography, etc.

flea
flee
free
  unfree
glee
(gree)
  gris-gris (*French*)
  agree
    disagree
degree
  first-degree
  second-degree, etc
  filigree
  pedigree
he
  hee-hee
gee
  gee-gee (*i*)
  apogee (*i*)
  mortgagee
  ogee
  refugee

  effigy (*i*)
  elegy (*i*)
  energy (*i*)
  eulogy (*i*)
  genealogy (*i*)
  lethargy (*i*)
  liturgy (*i*)
  prodigy (*i*)
  strategy (*i*)
  trilogy (*i*)

  (ology)
    astrology (*i*)
    biology (*i*)
    chronology (*i*)
    geology (*i*)
    mythology (*i*)
    theology (*i*)
    zoology (*i*), etc.
key
  Kankaki
  Waikiki
  (archy)

anarchy (*i*)
hierarchy (*i*)
oligarchy (*i*), etc.
quay
lea
  alea
lee
  anomaly (*i*)
  family (*i*)
  fleur-de-lis
  Galilee (*i*)
  homily (*i*)
  Italy (*i*)
  jubilee
  simile (*i*)
    facsimile (*i*)
  monopoly
(plus ly *adverbial*
  endings, awkward in
  rhyming)
me
  bonhomie
  sesame

alchemy (*i*)
anatomy (*i*)
astronomy (*i*)
autonomy (*i*)
bigamy (*i*)
blasphemy (*i*)
economy (*i*)
enemy (*i*)
epitome (*i*)
infamy (*i*)
monogamy
physiognomy (*i*)
polygamy (*i*)
(nee)
knee
  anemone (*i*)
  dominie
  examinee
  Gethsemane
  nominee

  accompany (*i*)

agony (*i*)
antiphony (*i*)
balcony (*i*)
barony (*i*)
botany (*i*)
calumny (*i*)
colony (*i*)
company (*i*)
destiny (*i*)
ebony (*i*)
Epiphany (*i*)
euphony (*i*)
felony (*i*)
Germany (*i*)
gluttony (*i*)
harmony (*i*)
irony (*i*)
litany (*i*)
mahogany (*i*)
monotony (*i*)
mutiny (*i*)
progeny (*i*)
Romany (*i*)
scrutiny (*i*)
simony (*i*)
symphony (*i*)
tympani (*i*)
tyranny (*i*)
villainy (*i*)
pea
  calliope (*i*)
  canopy (*i*)
  cap-a-pie
  recipe

  lycanthropy
  misanthropy
  philanthropy, etc.
plea
  panoply
(ree)
  diablerie
  jamboree
  Marie
    Sault Ste. Marie
  potpourri

referee

anniversary (*i*)
archery (*i*)
armory (*i*)
artillery (*i*)
augury (*i*)
bakery (*i*)
battery (*i*)
beggary (*i*)
bravery (*i*)
bribery (*i*)
burglary (*i*)
Calvary (*i*)
cavalry (*i*)
century (*i*)
chancery (*i*)
chivalry (*i*)
complimentary (*i*)
compulsory (*i*)
contradictory (*i*)
debauchery (*i*)
delivery (*i*)
diary (*i*)
directory (*i*)
discovery (*i*)
drapery (*i*)
drudgery (*i*)
effrontery (*i*)
elementary (*i*)
elusory (*i*)
factory (*i*)
feathery (*i*)
fiery (*i*)
finery (*i*)
flattery (*i*)
flummery (*i*)
forgery (*i*)
gallery (*i*)
greenery (*i*)
heathery (*i*)
history (*i*)
hostelry (*i*)
illusory (*i*)
imagery (*i*)
infirmary (*i*)

injury (*i*)
ivory (*i*)
jewelry (*i*)
jugglery (*i*)
knavery (*i*)
livery (*i*)
lottery (*i*)
luxury (*i*)
machinery (*i*)
masonry (*i*)
mastery (*i*)
memory (*i*)
mercury (*i*)
misery (*i*)
mockery (*i*)
mummery (*i*)
mystery (*i*)
notary (*i*)
nursery (*i*)
parliamentary (*i*)
penury (*i*)
peppery (*i*)
perfumery (*i*)
perfunctory (*i*)
perjury (*i*)
pillory (*i*)
popery (*i*)
precursory (*i*)
priory (*i*)
professory (*i*)
prudery (*i*)
quackery (*i*)
quandary (*i*)
raillery (*i*)
recovery (*i*)
rectory (*i*)
refractory (*i*)
revelry (*i*)
rivalry (*i*)
robbery (*i*)
rockery (*i*)
roguery (*i*)
rosemary (*i*)
rudimentary (*i*)
salary (*i*)
satisfactory (*i*)

unsatisfactory (*i*)
savagery (*i*)
savory (*i*)
unsavory (*i*)
scenery (*i*)
shivery (*i*)
silvery (*i*)
slavery (*i*)
slippery (*i*)
snuggery (*i*)
sorcery (*i*)
sugary (*i*)
summary (*i*)
theory (*i*)
thievery (*i*)
tracery (*i*)
treachery (*i*)
treasury (*i*)
trickery (*i*)
trumpery (*i*)
usury (*i*)
valedictory (*i*)
victory (*i*)
votary (*i*)
waggery (*i*)
watery (*i*)
wintery (*i*)
witchery (*i*)
yeomanry (*i*)

sea
see

addressee (*i*)
foresee
fricassee (*i*)
lessee
licensee
oversee
Pharisee
Tennessee

si (*Spanish*)

agency (*i*)
apostasy (*i*)
argosy (*i*)
aristocracy (*i*)
ascendancy (*i*)
brilliancy (*i*)

clemency (i)
  inclemency (i)
cogency
complacency (i)
consistency (i)
  inconsistency (i)
conspiracy (i)
constancy (i)
  inconstancy (i)
contingency
courtesy (i)
  discourtesy (i)
decency
  indecency
dependency
diplomacy (i)
discordancy (i)
discourtesy (i)
discrepancy (i)
ecstasy (i)
efficiency (i)
embassy (i)
emergency (i)
expectancy (i)
expediency (i)
fallacy (i)
fantasy (i)
fervency (i)
flagrancy (i)
flippancy (i)
fluency (i)
frequency (i)
galaxy (i)
heresy (i)
hypocrisy (i)
idiocy (i)
idiosyncrasy (i)
illiteracy (i)
inadvertency (i)
infancy (i)
insufficiency (i)
insurgency (i)
jealousy (i)
legacy (i)
leniency (i)
lunacy (i)

luxuriancy (i)
malignancy (i)
normalcy (i)
Odyssey (i)
papacy (i)
piracy (i)
pliancy (i)
poesy (i)
poignancy (i)
policy (i)
potency (i)
privacy (i)
proficiency (i)
prophecy (i)
pungency (i)
quiescency (i)
regency (i)
secrecy (i)
solvency (i)
stagnancy (i)
sufficiency (i)
  insufficiency (i)
supremacy (i)
tendency (i)
theocracy (i)
truancy (i)
urgency (i)
vacancy (i)
vagrancy (i)
valiancy (i)
verdancy (i)

she
  debauchee
  garnishee
(snee)
  snickersnee
spree
  esprit
tea
tee
  absentee
  appointee
  devotee
  goatee
  manatee (i)
  permittee

Q.T.
repartee
settee
suttee
trustee

ability (i)
  inability (i)
absurdity (i)
accessibility (i)
  inaccessibility (i)
acidity (i)
activity (i)
actuality (i)
adaptability (i)
adversity (i)
advisability (i)
affability (i)
affinity (i)
agility (i)
alacrity (i)
ambiguity (i)
amenability (i)
amenity (i)
amicability (i)
amity (i)
amnesty (i)
animosity (i)
annuity (i)
anonymity (i)
antiquity (i)
anxiety (i)
applicability (i)
aridity (i)
asperity (i)
atrocity (i)
audacity (i)
austerity (i)
authenticity (i)
authority (i)
avidity (i)
barbarity (i)
benignity (i)
brevity (i)
brutality (i)
calamity (i)

84

capability (*i*)
capacity (*i*)
  incapacity (*i*)
captivity (*i*)
casualty (*i*)
catholicity (*i*)
causticity (*i*)
cavity (*i*)
celebrity (*i*)
celerity (*i*)
certainty (*i*)
  uncertainty (*i*)
changeability (*i*)
charity (*i*)
chastity (*i*)
Christianity (*i*)
civility (*i*)
combustibility (*i*)
comity (*i*)
commodity (*i*)
community (*i*)
compatibility (*i*)
  incompatibility (*i*)
complexity (*i*)
complicity (*i*)
comprehensibility (*i*)
  incomprehensibil-
    ity (*i*)
conformity (*i*)
  nonconformity (*i*)
connubiality (*i*)
consanguinity (*i*)
contiguity (*i*)
contrariety (*i*)
conventionality (*i*)
convexity (*i*)
credulity (*i*)
  incredulity
criminality (*i*)
crotchety (*i*)
crudity (*i*)
cruelty (*i*)
cupidity (*i*)
curiosity (*i*)
debility (*i*)
declivity (*i*)

deformity (*i*)
deity (*i*)
density (*i*)
depravity (*i*)
deputy (*i*)
dexterity (*i*)
dignity (*i*)
  indignity (*i*)
diversity (*i*)
divinity (*i*)
docility (*i*)
domesticity (*i*)
dubiety (*i*)
duplicity (*i*)
dynasty (*i*)
eccentricity (*i*)
elasticity (*i*)
electricity (*i*)
enmity (*i*)
enormity (*i*)
entity (*i*)
equality (*i*)
  inequality (*i*)
equanimity (*i*)
equity (*i*)
eternity (*i*)
extremity (*i*)
facility (*i*)
faculty (*i*)
fallibility (*i*)
  infallibility (*i*)
falsity (*i*)
familiarity (*i*)
fatality (*i*)
fatuity (*i*)
fecundity (*i*)
felicity (*i*)
  infelicity (*i*)
ferocity (*i*)
fertility (*i*)
  infertility (*i*)
festivity (*i*)
fidelity (*i*)
  infidelity (*i*)
fidgety (*i*)
fixity (*i*)

formality (*i*)
  informality (*i*)
fortuity (*i*)
fragility (*i*)
fraternity (*i*)
frigidity (*i*)
frivolity (*i*)
frugality (*i*)
futility (*i*)
futurity (*i*)
gaiety (*i*)
garrulity (*i*)
generosity (*i*)
geniality (*i*)
gentility (*i*)
gratuity (*i*)
gravity (*i*)
guarantee (*i*)
heredity (*i*)
hilarity (*i*)
honesty (*i*)
hospitality (*i*)
hostility (*i*)
humanity (*i*)
  inhumanity (*i*)
humility (*i*)
identity (*i*)
imbecility (*i*)
immensity (*i*)
immunity (*i*)
impecuniosity (*i*)
impetuosity (*i*)
importunity (*i*)
impunity (*i*)
individuality (*i*)
inebriety (*i*)
inferiority (*i*)
infinity (*i*)
infirmity (*i*)
ingenuity (*i*)
iniquity (*i*)
insipidity (*i*)
instrumentality (*i*)
insularity (*i*)
integrity (*i*)
intensity (*i*)

intrepidity (*i*)
jollity (*i*)
joviality (*i*)
juvenility (*i*)
laity (*i*)
legality (*i*)
lenity (*i*)
levity (*i*)
liberality (*i*)
liberty (*i*)
limpidity (*i*)
longevity (*i*)
loquacity (*i*)
loyalty (*i*)
  disloyalty (*i*)
lubricity (*i*)
lucidity (*i*)
magnanimity (*i*)
majesty (*i*)
majority (*i*)
malignity (*i*)
maternity (*i*)
maturity (*i*)
  immaturity (*i*)
mediocrity (*i*)
mendacity (*i*)
minority (*i*)
mobility (*i*)
modesty (*i*)
  immodesty (*i*)
monstrosity (*i*)
morality (*i*)
  immorality (*i*)
mortality (*i*)
  immortality (*i*)
multiplicity (*i*)
municipality (*i*)
mutability (*i*)
nationality (*i*)
nativity (*i*)
necessity (*i*)
neutrality (*i*)
nobility (*i*)
notoriety (*i*)
novelty (*i*)
nudity (*i*)

nullity (*i*)
obesity (*i*)
obscurity (*i*)
oddity (*i*)
opportunity (*i*)
originality (*i*)
parity (*i*)
partiality (*i*)
particularity (*i*)
passivity (*i*)
  impassivity (*i*)
paternity (*i*)
peculiarity (*i*)
penalty (*i*)
perpetuity (*i*)
perplexity (*i*)
personality (*i*)
perspicuity (*i*)
pertinacity (*i*)
perversity (*i*)
piety (*i*)
  impiety (*i*)
polity (*i*)
pomposity (*i*)
popularity (*i*)
posterity (*i*)
poverty (*i*)
precocity (*i*)
priority (*i*)
probity (*i*)
proclivity (*i*)
prodigality (*i*)
profanity (*i*)
profundity (*i*)
prolixity (*i*)
promiscuity (*i*)
propensity (*i*)
property (*i*)
propinquity (*i*)
propriety (*i*)
  impropriety (*i*)
prosperity (*i*)
provinciality (*i*)
proximity (*i*)
publicity (*i*)
puerility (*i*)

purity (*i*)
  impurity (*i*)
pusillanimity (*i*)
putridity (*i*)
quality (*i*)
quantity (*i*)
rapacity (*i*)
rapidity (*i*)
rarity (*i*)
rascality (*i*)
reality (*i*)
reciprocity (*i*)
rickety (*i*)
rigidity (*i*)
rotundity (*i*)
royalty (*i*)
rusticity (*i*)
sagacity (*i*)
salubrity (*i*)
sanctity (*i*)
sanity (*i*)
satiety (*i*)
scarcity (*i*)
security (*i*)
senility (*i*)
sensibility (*i*)
sensuality (*i*)
sentimentality (*i*)
serenity (*i*)
servility (*i*)
severity (*i*)
sexuality (*i*)
similarity (*i*)
simplicity (*i*)
sincerity (*i*)
  insincerity (*i*)
singularity (*i*)
sobriety (*i*)
society (*i*)
solemnity (*i*)
solidity (*i*)
spontaneity (*i*)
stability (*i*)
sterility (*i*)
stolidity (*i*)
stupidity (*i*)

suavity (*i*)
subjectivity (*i*)
sublimity (*i*)
sublety (*i*)
superficiality (*i*)
superfluity (*i*)
superiority (*i*)
taciturnity (*i*)
technicality (*i*)
temerity (*i*)
tenacity (*i*)
timidity (*i*)
torpidity (*i*)
totality (*i*)
tranquility (*i*)
travesty (*i*)
trinity (*i*)
triviality (*i*)
ubiquity (*i*)
unanimity (*i*)
uniformity (*i*)
unity (*i*)
university (*i*)
urbanity (*i*)
utility (*i*)
validity (*i*)
vanity (*i*)
vapidity (*i*)
variety (*i*)
velocity (*i*)
velvety (*i*)
venality (*i*)
verbosity (*i*)
verity (*i*)
versatility (*i*)
vicinity (*i*)
virginity (*i*)
virility (*i*)
virtuosity (*i*)
viscosity (*i*)
vivacity (*i*)
volatility (*i*)
voracity (*i*)
vulgarity (*i*)
whimiscality (*i*)
thee

(thee)
antipathy (*i*)
apathy (*i*)
sympathy (*i*)
tree
axletree
Christmas tree
gallows tree
willow tree, etc.

ancestry (*i*)
artistry (*i*)
barratry (*i*)
bigotry (*i*)
coquetry (*i*)
Coventry (*i*)
deviltry (*i*)
errantry (*i*)
forestry (*i*)
gallantry (*i*)
geometry (*i*)
   telemetry (*i*)
   trigonometry (*i*),
   etc.
idolatry (*i*)
industry (*i*)
infantry (*i*)
knight-errantry (*i*)
ministry (*i*)
pageantry (*i*)
pedantry (*i*)
pleasantry (*i*)
poetry (*i*)
psychiatry (*i*)
sophistry (*i*)
symmetry (*i*)
tapestry (*i*)
tenantry (*i*)
(vee)
vis-a-vis
we
wee
whee
ennui *(French)*
billowy (*i*)
shadowy (*i*)

sinewy (*i*)
willowy (*i*)
ye
employee
hear ye
(zee)
bourgeoisie
chimpanzee
Zuyder Zee

EB (EEB)
grebe
plebe

EB
ebb
deb
web

ECH (EECH)
each
beach
beech
breach
breech
leach
leech
peach
impeach
preach
reach
(seech)
beseech
screech
speech
teach

ECH
etch
fetch
ketch
(catch)
kvetch *(Yiddish)*
letch
retch
sketch

stretch
vetch
wretch

ED (EED)
bead
bleed
breed
  inbreed
  interbreed
creed
deed
  indeed
  misdeed
feed
  overfeed
greed
heed
lead
  mislead
mead
Mede
  Ganymede
  Runnymede
meed
need
knead
  knock-kneed (i)
(pede)
  centipede
  impede
  stampede
  velocipede
read
  misread
reed
screed
seed
cede
  accede
  concede
  exceed
  intercede
  precede
  proceed
  recede

secede
succeed
supersede
speed
steed
Swede
teed
treed
tweed
weed
(agreed, etc.)

ED
bed
  abed
  flowerbed (i)
  riverbed (i), etc.
  truckle bed
  trundle bed, etc.
bread
  gingerbread, etc.
bred
  highbred
  inbred
  thoroughbred, etc.
dead
dread
fed
  overfed
  underfed
fled
head
  ahead
  behead
  chucklehead
  copperhead
  dunderhead
  featherhead
  figurehead
  fountainhead
  go-ahead
  maidenhead
  overhead
  thunderhead
led

misled
lead
(ped)
  biped
  quadriped
read
  misread
  unread
red
said
  aforesaid
    foresaid
  unsaid
shed
shred
sled
sped
spread
  bedspread
  bespread
  outspread
  overspread
stead
  bedstead (i)
  roadstead (i)
thread
  rethread
  unthread
tread
wed
  coed
zed *(British)*
(plus past-tense words
  ending in ed, all of
  which are imperfect
  and awkward as
  rhymes)

EF (EEF)
beef
brief
chief
fief
grief
leaf
lief

belief
　disbelief
　relief
reef
sheaf
thief

EF
chef
clef
deaf

EFT
eft
deft
heft
left
reft
　bereft
theft
weft

E (EEG)
league
(tigue)
　fatigue
(trigue)
　intrigue

EG
egg
beg
keg
leg
peg
yegg

EGZ
dregs
(eggs, etc.)

EJ (EEJ)
liege
siege
　besiege

EJ
edge
dredge
fledge
hedge
ledge
　allege
　privilege (*i*)
　sacrilege (*i*)
sledge
wedge

EK (EEK)
eke
beak
　Mozambique
bleak
　oblique
clique
creak
creek
geek
Greek
leak
leek
meek
　comique
(neek)
　Martinique
　unique
peak
peek
pique
reek
wreak
seek
　hide-and-seek
Sikh
　cacique
sheik
chic
shriek
sleek
sneak
speak
　bespeak

squeak
streak
teak
　antique
　critique
tweak
weak
week
Zeke
　physique

EK
beck
　Quebec
check
cheque
Czech
deck
　bedeck
fleck
heck
neck
　leatherneck (*i*)
peck
reck
wreck
spec
speck
trek

EKS
ex
flex
　circumflex
　reflex (*i*)
　Rolleiflex, etc.
nex
　annex
(plex)
　complex (*a*)
　duplex (*i*)
　multiplex
　perplex
rex
sex
　Essex (*i*)

Middlesex (*i*)
unisex (*i*)
Wessex (*i*)
Tex
vex
   convex
(decks, etc.)

EKST
next
text
   context (*i*)
   pretext (*i*)
(flexed, etc.)

EKT
(fect)
   affect
   defect
   effect
   infect
      disinfect
   perfect (*v*)
(flect)
   deflect
   genuflect
   inflect
   reflect
(glect)
   neglect
(ject)
   abject
   deject
   eject
   inject
   interject
   object
   project (*v*)
   reject
   subject
(lect)
   collect
      recollect
   dialect (*i*)
   elect
   intellect

select
(nect)
   connect
      disconnect
(rect)
   correct
      incorrect
   direct
      indirect
      misdirect
   erect
   resurrect
sect
   bisect
   dissect
   intersect
   trisect
(spect)
   circumspect
   expect
   inspect
   prospect (*v*)
   respect
      disrespect
      self-respect
   suspect
(tect)
   architect
   detect
   protect
(checked, etc.)

EL (EEL)
eel
(beal)
   mobile (*i*)
      automobile (*i*)
creel
deal
   misdeal
feel
heal
heel
he'll
(jeal)
   congeal

keel
Kiel
meal
   Camille
kneel
   anneal
   chenille
   O'Neill, Eugene
peal
   appeal
   repeal
   thunderpeal
peel
reel
seal
   conceal
   privy seal
she'll
speel
spiel
squeal
steal
steel
   bastille
   Castille
teal
   genteel
veal
   reveal
we'll
wheel
zeal

EL
el
bell
   Jezebel (*i*)
   rebel (*v*)
   dinnerbell
   passing bell
   vesper bell, etc.
belle
   southern belle
dell
   citadel (*i*)
   infidel (*i*)

dwell
fell
  befell
hell
(mell)
  béchamel
  Carmel
  pell-mell
knell
  personnel
  pimpernel (*i*)
  sentinel (*i*)
(rell)
  cockerel (*i*)
  doggerel (*i*)
sell
  carrousel
  undersell
cell
  excel
shell
  cockle-shell
smell
spell
tell
  bagatelle
  clientele
  foretell
  hotel
(vel)
  caravel
  Ravel, Maurice
well
  farewell
  unwell
yell
(zel)
  demoiselle
  gazelle
  mademoiselle

ELCH
belch
squelch
welch

ELD (EELD)
field
  afield
  battlefield (*i*)
  Chesterfield (*i*)
shield
wield
yield
(annealed, etc.)

ELD
geld
held
  beheld
  upheld
  withheld
meld
weld
(compelled, etc.)

ELF
elf
Guelph
self
  herself
  himself
  itself
  myself
  oneself
  yourself
shelf
  mantel shelf

ELM
elm
helm
realm
whelm
  overwhelm

ELP
help
kelp
whelp
yelp

ELT
belt
Celt
dealt
felt
  heartfelt (*i*)
  unfelt
gelt
knelt
melt
pelt
smelt
spelt
svelte
veldt
welt

ELTH
health
stealth
wealth
  commonwealth

ELV
delve
shelve
twelve

EM (EEM)
beam
  abeam
cream
  ice cream
deem
dream
(feem)
  blaspheme
gleam
(preme)
  supreme
ream
scheme
scream
seam
seem
  beseem

steam
　esteem
　　self-esteem
stream
　extreme
team
teem
　centime (*French*)
(zheem)
　regime

EM
em
(dem)
　condemn
　diadem
gem
　apothegm
　begem
　stratagem
hem
　ahem
　Bethlehem
phlegm
(rem)
　theorem (*i*)
stem
(tem)
　contemn
them
(yem)
　requiem (*i*)

EMT
dreamt
　undreamt
(kempt)
　unkempt
tempt
　attempt
　contempt
(yempt)
　preempt
(zempt)
　exempt

EMZ
Thames
(condemns, etc.)

EN (EEN)
bean
been
clean
　unclean
dean
　codeine
　gabardine
　incarnadine
　sardine
(feen)
Gene
　caffeine
glean
green
　bowling green
　evergreen
　peregrine
　wintergreen
(guine)
　beguine
keen
lean
lien
　colleen
　gasoline
　Magdalene
　opaline
　vaseline
mean
　demean
mien
(neen)
　mezzanine
peen
　atropine
preen
queen
　Dairy Queen (*i*)
　fairy queen (*i*)
(reen)
　careen

chorine
marine
　aquamarine
　submarine
Nazarene
nectarine
serene
tambourine
tureen
tangerine
wolverine
scene
　damascene
　epicene
　kerosene
　obscene
　plasticine
　Pleistocene
　Pliocene
seen
　foreseen
　　unforeseen
　unseen
sheen
　machine
spleen
teen
　Argentine
　Augustine
　barkentine
　brigantine
　canteen
　Constantine
　eighteen
　fifteen
　Florentine
　fourteen
　guillotine
　libertine
　nicotine
　nineteen
　quarantine
　routine
　sateen
　serpentine
　seventeen

sixteen
thirteen
velveteen
(tween)
  between
    go-between
    in-between
(veen)
  contravene
  convene
  intervene
  ravine
wean
  Halloween
  overween
(zeen)
  benzine
  cuisine
  magazine
  (plus proper names,
    such as Ernestine)

EN
en
den
fen
glen
hen
(jen)
  comedienne
  halogen (*i*)
  hydrogen (*i*)
  oxygen (*i*)
ken
Len
  Magdalen
men
  amen
  regimen (*i*)
  specimen (*i*)
pen
  fountain pen
  unpen
wren
Seine (River)
ten

then
wen
yen
zen
  citizen
  denizen
(zhen)
  Parisienne

ENCH
bench
clench
drench
French
quench
wrench
  monkey wrench
stench
trench
  entrench
  retrench
wench

END (EEND)
fiend
(cleaned, etc.)

END
end
bend
  unbend
blend
(dend)
  dividend
fend
  defend
  offend
friend
  befriend
hend
  apprehend
  comprehend
  reprehend
lend
mend
  amend

commend
  recommend
emend
pend
  append
  depend
  expend
  impend
penned
  unpenned
send
  ascend
  condescend
  descend
  transcend
spend
  misspend
  suspend
tend
  attend
  contend
  distend
  extend
  intend
    superintend
  portend
  pretend
  subtend
trend
vend
wend

ENGTH
length
strength

ENJ
(henge)
  Stonehenge (*i*)
venge
  avenge
  revenge

ENS (ENSE)
dense
  coincidence (*i*)

condense
confidence (*i*)
  self-confidence (*i*)
diffidence (*i*)
dissidence (*i*)
evidence (*i*)
impudence (*i*)
incidence (*i*)
  coincidence (*i*)
fence
  defense
    self-defense
  offense
(jence)
  indigence (*i*)
  negligence (*i*)
(lence)
  benevolence (*i*)
  corpulence (*i*)
  excellence
  flatulence (*i*)
  indolence
  insolence (*i*)
  malevolence (*i*)
  opulence
  pestilence (*i*)
  prevalence (*i*)
  redolence (*i*)
  somnolence (*i*)
  succulence (*i*)
  truculence (*i*)
  turbulence (*i*)
  violence (*i*)
  virulence (*i*)
(mence)
  commence
    recommence
  immense
  vehemence (*i*)
(nence)
  abstinence (*i*)
  continence (*i*)
    incontinence (*i*)
  eminence (*i*)
    preeminence (*i*)
  permanence (*i*)

impermanence (*i*)
pertinence (*i*)
  impertinence (*i*)
pence
  dispense
  expense
  recompense (*v*)
  suspense
(quence)
  consequence (*i*)
    inconsequence (*i*)
  eloquence (*i*)
    ineloquence (*i*)
  grandiloquence (*i*)
  magniloquence (*i*)
(rence)
  circumference (*i*)
  conference (*i*)
  deference (*i*)
  difference (*i*)
    indifference (*i*)
  inference (*i*)
  preference (*i*)
  reference (*i*)
  reverence (*i*)
    irreverence (*i*)
sense
  common sense
  sixth sense, etc.

beneficence (*i*)
incense (*v*)
  frankincense (*i*)
innocence (*i*)
magnificence (*i*)
maleficence (*i*)
munificence (*i*)
tense
  competence (*i*)
    incompetence (*i*)
  impotence (*i*)
    omnipotence (*i*)
  intense
  penitence (*i*)
    impenitence (*i*)
  pretense

thence
whence
  affluence (*i*)
  congruence (*i*)
    incongruence (*i*)
  influence (*i*)
(yence)
  convenience (*i*)
    inconvenience (*i*)
  expedience (*i*)
  experience (*i*)
    inexperience (*i*)
  incipience (*i*)
  obedience (*i*)
  omniscience (*i*)
  prescience (*i*)
  prurience (*i*)
  resilience (*i*)
  salience (*i*)
  sapience (*i*)
  subservience (*i*)

ENST
'gainst
  against
(fenced, etc.)

ENT
bent
  unbent
blent
dent
  accident (*i*)
  confident (*i*)
    self-confident (*i*)
  impudent (*i*)
  incident (*i*)
    coincident (*i*)
  indent
  occident (*i*)
  precedent (*i*)
  president (*i*)
  provident (*i*)
    improvident (*i*)
  resident (*i*)
gent

diligent (*i*)
intelligent (*i*)
Lent
lent
  benevolent (*i*)
  corpulent (*i*)
  malevolent (*i*)
  relent
  somnolent (*i*)
  succulent (*i*)
  truculent (*i*)
  turbulent (*i*)
  violent (*i*)
  virulent (*i*)
meant
  abandonment (*i*)
  acknowledgement (*i*)
  admonishment (*i*)
  advertisement (*i*)
  aggrandizement (*i*)
  ailment (*i*)
  apportionment (*i*)
    reapportionment (*i*)
  argument (*i*)
  armament (*i*)
    disarmament (*i*)
  banishment (*i*)
  battlement (*i*)
  betterment (*i*)
  bewilderment
  blandishment (*i*)
  blazonment (*i*)
  cement
  chastisement (*i*)
  cherishment (*i*)
  comment (*i*)
  complement (*i*)
  compliment (*i*)
  condiment (*i*)
  dazzlement (*i*)
  dement (*i*)
  detriment (*i*)
  development (*i*)
    redevelopment (*i*)
  devilment (*i*)
    bedevilment (*i*)

divertissement (*i*)
document (*i*)
element (*i*)
embarrassment (*i*)
embellishment (*i*)
embezzlement (*i*)
embitterment (*i*)
embodiment (*i*)
  disembodiment (*i*)
encouragement (*i*)
  discouragement (*i*)
enlightenment (*i*)
envelopment (*i*)
environment (*i*)
establishment (*i*)
experiment (*i*)
ferment (*i*)
filament (*i*)
firmament (*i*)
foment (*i*)
government (*i*)
impediment (*i*)
implement (*i*)
imprisonment (*i*)
lament (*i*)
ligament (*i*)
liniment (*i*)
management (*i*)
measurement (*i*)
merriment (*i*)
monument (*i*)
nourishment (*i*)
ornament (*i*)
parliament (*i*)
predicament (*i*)
presentiment (*i*)
punishment (*i*)
regiment (*i*)
replenishment (*i*)
rudiment (*i*)
sacrament (*i*)
sediment (*i*)
sentiment (*i*)
settlement (*i*)
supplement (*i*)
temperament (*i*)

tenement (*i*)
testament (*i*)
torment (*v*)
tournament (*i*)
well-meant (*i*)
wonderment (*i*)
worriment (*i*)
(nent)
  anent
  continent
    incontinent
  eminent (*i*)
    preeminent (*i*)
  permanent
    impermanent
  prominent
pent
  repent
(quent)
  consequent (*i*)
  frequent (*v*)
  grandiloquent (*i*)
  subsequent (*i*)
rent
  belligerent (*i*)
  reverent (*i*)
    irreverent (*i*)
scent
  ascent
  descent
sent
  assent
  consent
  unsent
cent
  accent
  beneficent
    maleficent
    munificent
  percent
  reticent (*i*)
spent
  overspent
  unspent
tent
  competent (*i*)

incompetent (*i*)
content (*a*) and (*v*)
  discontent
intent
omnipotent (*i*)
penitent (*i*)
portent (*i*)
vent
  circumvent
  event
  invent
  prevent
went
  fluent (*i*)
    affluent (*i*)
    confluent (*i*)
(yent)
  convenient (*i*)
    inconvenient (*i*)
  ingredient (*i*)
  orient (*i*)
    disorient (*i*)
(zent)
  present
    represent
      misrepresent
  resent

ENZ
cleanse
lens
(dens, etc.)

EP (EEP)
cheap
cheep
creep
deep
heap
keep
leap
  overleap
neap
peep
reap
seep

sheep
sleep
  asleep
  beauty sleep
  oversleep
steep
sweep
weep

EP
hep
pep
rep
step
  footstep (*i*)
  overstep
steppe

EPT
crept
(dept)
  adept
  kept
    unkept
sept
  accept
  except
  intercept
slept
  overslept
swept
  unswept
wept
  unwept
(stepped, etc.)

ER (EER)
ear
beer
  ginger beer, etc.
cheer
clear
  chanticleer
dear
  endear
deer

bombardier
brigadier
commandeer
grenadier
drear
fear
  interfere
gear
hear
  overhear
here
  adhere
  cohere
  inhere
jeer
kier
  fakir
leer
  cavalier
  chandelier
  fusileer
  gondolier
  pistoleer
mere
  emir
near
  auctioneer
  buccaneer
  cannoneer
  chiffonier
  domineer
  electioneer
  engineer
  mountaineer
  pioneer
  scrutineer
  veneer
peer
  appear
    disappear
    reappear
pier
queer
rear
  arrear
  career

seer
　overseer
sere
　cuirassier
　financier
　sincere
　　insincere
shear
sheer
　cashier
smear
　besmear
sneer
spear
sphere
　atmosphere
　hemisphere
　stratosphere
steer
　austere
tear
tier
　charioteer
　frontier
　gazetteer
　muleteer
　pamphleteer
　privateer
　racketeer
　volunteer
veer
　revere
　severe
　　persevere
weir
year

ERD (EERD)
beard
weird
(feared, etc.)

ERS (EERSE)
fierce
pierce

ES (EESE)
cease
　decease
　　predecease
　surcease
crease
　decrease
　increase
fleece
geese
grease
Greece
lease
　police
　release
　valise
Nice
niece
peace
piece
　apiece
　fowling piece
　frontispiece
　mantelpiece
　masterpiece (i)
(prese)
　caprice
(rese)
　cerise

ES
bless
chess
cress
(dess)
　stewardess (i)
dress
　address
　redress
　undress
(fess)
　confess
　profess
(gress)
　digress
　progress (v)

regress
transgress
guess
less
　coalesce
　convalesce
　fatherless (i)
　flavorless (i)
　limitless (i)
　more or less
　noblesse
　penniless (i)
　unless
　(plus all -less
　　endings)
mess
ness
　　Loch Ness

　baroness (i)
　finesse
　governess (i)

aggressiveness (i)
anxiousness (i)
artfulness (i)
bashfulness (i)
beastliness (i)
besottedness (i)
bitterness (i)
blissfulness (i)
breathlessness (i)
capriciousness (i)
childlessness (i)
churlishness (i)
cleanliness (i)
cleverness (i)
cliquishness (i)
cloudiness (i)
clumsiness (i)
coldheartedness (i)
comeliness (i)
conscientiousness (i)
consciousness (i)
　unconsciousness(i)
conspicuousness (i)

contentedness (*i*)
contrariness (*i*)
costliness (*i*)
courtliness (*i*)
craftiness (*i*)
craziness (*i*)
crustiness (*i*)
daintiness (*i*)
dauntlessness (*i*)
deadliness (*i*)
deceitfulness (*i*)
defenselessness (*i*)
delightfulness (*i*)
destructiveness (*i*)
distinctiveness (*i*)
dizziness (*i*)
dreaminess (*i*)
dreariness (*i*)
duskiness (*i*)
eagerness (*i*)
earliness (*i*)
earnestness (*i*)
earthiness (*i*)
earthliness (*i*)
easiness (*i*)
   uneasiness (*i*)
eeriness (*i*)
emptiness (*i*)
endlessness (*i*)
evasiveness (*i*)
exclusiveness (*i*)
expansiveness (*i*)
expressiveness (*i*)
farsightedness (*i*)
feeblemindedness (*i*)
fitfulness (*i*)
flabbiness (*i*)
flashiness (*i*)
fogginess (*i*)
foolishness
forgetfulness (*i*)
fragileness (*i*)
fretfulness (*i*)
friendlessness (*i*)
friendliness (*i*)
   unfriendliness (*i*)

fulsomeness (*i*)
gaudiness (*i*)
gentleness (*i*)
ghastliness (*i*)
ghostliness (*i*)
giddiness (*i*)
girlishness (*i*)
greasiness (*i*)
greediness (*i*)
griminess (*i*)
grittiness (*i*)
grogginess (*i*)
happiness (*i*)
   unhappiness (*i*)
hastiness (*i*)
haughtiness (*i*)
haziness (*i*)
holiness (*i*)
hollowness (*i*)
homelessness (*i*)
homeliness (*i*)
hopefulness (*i*)
hopelessness (*i*)
huskiness (*i*)
iciness (*i*)
idleness (*i*)
impulsiveness (*i*)
indebtedness (*i*)
joyfulness (*i*)
joylessness (*i*)
juiciness
kindliness (*i*)
   unkindliness (*i*)
lawlessness (*i*)
laziness (*i*)
likeliness (*i*)
   unlikeliness
listlessness
liveliness (*i*)
loftiness (*i*)
loneliness (*i*)
loveliness (*i*)
lovingness (*i*)
lustfulness (*i*)
massiveness (*i*)
mawkishness (*i*)

merriness (*i*)
mightiness (*i*)
mistiness (*i*)
modishness (*i*)
nakedness (*i*)
namelessness (*i*)
needlessness (*i*)
neighborliness (*i*)
nervousness (*i*)
nobleness (*i*)
noisiness (*i*)
nothingness (*i*)
obsequiousness (*i*)
obtrusiveness (*i*)
officiousness (*i*)
oiliness (*i*)
openness (*i*)
outlandishness (*i*)
outrageousness
paltriness (*i*)
plaintiveness (*i*)
playfulness (*i*)
portliness (*i*)
puffiness (*i*)
pugnaciousness (*i*)
queasiness (*i*)
quietness (*i*)
remorsefulness (*i*)
restiveness (*i*)
restlessness (*i*)
rockiness (*i*)
seediness (*i*)
seemliness (*i*)
   unseemliness (*i*)
selfishness (*i*)
   unselfishness (*i*)
senselessness (*i*)
seriousness
shabbiness (*i*)
shagginess (*i*)
shakiness (*i*)
shallowness (*i*)
shapelessness (*i*)
shiftiness (*i*)
shiftlessness
sickliness

sightliness
  unsightliness
silkiness (*i*)
slavishness (*i*)
sleaziness (*i*)
sleepiness (*i*)
sleeplessness (*i*)
slenderness (*i*)
smokiness (*i*)
sneakiness (*i*)
spaciousness (*i*)
speediness (*i*)
spiciness (*i*)
spitefulness (*i*)
stateliness (*i*)
steadiness (*i*)
stealthiness (*i*)
stickiness (*i*)
stinginess (*i*)
storminess (*i*)
stylishness (*i*)
suddenness (*i*)
sulkiness (*i*)
sullenness
sumptuousness (*i*)
sunniness (*i*)
superciliousness (*i*)
suppleness (*i*)
surliness (*i*)
swarthiness (*i*)
tastlessness (*i*)
thoughtfulness (*i*)
thoughtlessness (*i*)
thriftiness (*i*)
tidiness (*i*)
timeliness (*i*)
touchiness (*i*)
tracklessness (*i*)
tremendousness (*i*)
trustiness (*i*)
truthfulness (*i*)
tunefulness (*i*)
ugliness (*i*)
usefulness (*i*)
uselessness (*i*)
viciousness (*i*)

vindictiveness (*i*)
waxiness (*i*)
waywardness (*i*)
weariness (*i*)
wholesomeness (*i*)
wickedness (*i*)
willingness (*i*)
  unwillingness *i*)
wishfulness (*i*)
witlessness (*i*)
womanliness (*i*)
worldliness (*i*)
  unworldliness (*i*)
worthiness (*i*)
  unworthiness (*i*)
worthlessness (*i*)
wretchedness (*i*)
youthfulness (*i*)
press
  compress
  depress
  express
  impress
  oppress
  repress
  suppress
(ress)
  caress
  duress
  stress
(sess)
  assess
  excess
  obsess
  recess
  success
SOS
Tess
  politesse
tress
  distress
(vess)
  effervesce
yes
(zess)
  possess

dispossess
repossess

ESH (EESH)
(fiche)
  affiche
leash
  unleash
niche
quiche
(tische)
  schottische

ESH
crèche
flesh
fresh
  afresh
  refresh
mesh
  enmesh
(sesh)
  secesh
thresh

ESK
desk
(lesk)
  burlesque
(resk)
  picaresque
  picturesque
(tesk)
  grotesque
(wesk)
  statuesque, etc.

EST (EEST)
east
beast
feast
least
priest
(tiste)
  artiste
yeast
(pieced, etc.)

EST

best
  second-best
blest
breast
  abreast
chest
crest
dressed
  overdressed
  underdressed
(fest)
  infest
  manifest (*i*)
guessed
  unguessed
guest
(hest)
  behest
jest
  congest
  digest (*v*)
  ingest
  suggest
lest
  celeste
  molest
nest
pest
  Budapest (*i*)
pressed
  depressed
  expressed
    unexpressed
  impressed
quest
  bequest
  conquest (*i*)
  request
rest
  arrest
    Bucharest (*i*)
  interest (*i*)
  unrest
wrest
(sest)

obsessed
recessed
stressed
  distressed
test
  attest
  contest (*v*)
  detest
  protest
vest
  divest
  invest
west
yessed
  Trieste
zest
  possessed
(blessed, etc.)
(*plus superlatives
  ending in* est, *which
  are awkward as
  masculine rhymes
  since the stress would
  not normally fall on
  the final syllable.*)

ET (EET)

eat
  overeat
beat
beet
bleat
cheat
cleat
Crete
  accrete
  concrete
  discrete
  secrete
feat
  defeat
feet
fleet
greet
heat
(keet)

parakeet (*i*)
(leet)
  athlete (*i*)
  delete
  elite
  obsolete (*i*)
meat
meet
mete
neat
peat
  compete
  repeat
pleat
  complete
    incomplete
  deplete
  replete
(screet)
  discreet
    indiscreet
seat
  conceit
  deceit
    self-deceit
  receipt
sheet
skeet
sleet
street
suite
sweet
  bittersweet (*i*)
teat
treat
  entreat
  mistreat
  retreat
wheat

ET

et
bet
  alphabet
  Tibet
(bret)

soubrette
debt
  cadet
  vedette
fret
get
  beget
  forget
(gret)
  regret
  vinaigrette
jet
  suffragette
(ket)
  coquette
  croquette
  etiquette
let
  amulet
  coverlet
  novelette
  omelet (i)
  rivulet
  roulette
  toilette
  violet
met
  calumet
  well-met
net
  Antoinette, Marie
  bassinet
  bayonet
  brunette
  cabinet (i)
  castanet
  chansonette
  clarinet
  cornet
  coronet
  luncheonette
  marionette
  martinet
  mignonette
pet
  parapet

pipette
ret
  cigarette
  farmerette
  minaret
set
  anisette
  beset
  crystal set
  marmoset
  offset
  somerset
  Somerset
  sunset (i)
  upset (i)
(shet)
  brochette
  planchette
stet
sweat
Tet (*Vietnamese*)
  motet
  octet
  quartet
  quintet
  septet
  sestet
  sextet
(thet)
  epithet
threat
vet
  corvette
wet
  duet
  minuet
  pirouette
  silhouette
  statuette
yet
  Joliet
  Juliet
  oubliette (*French*)
  serviette
(zet)
  gazette

musette
rosette
(*plus other diminu-
tives and proper
names ending in -ette*)

ETH (EETH)
heath
'neath
  beneath
  underneath
sheath
teeth
wreath

ETH
Beth
  Elizabeth (i)
  Macbeth
breath
death
(leth)
  shibboleth (i)
(*plus antique verbs,
such as answereth*)

EVE
eave
eve
Eve
  Christmas Eve
  New Year's Eve
(chieve)
  achieve
grieve
  aggrieve
heave
leave
  believe
    disbelieve
  relieve
(preve)
  reprieve
reave
  bereave
reeve

(seve)
  conceive
    misconceive
    preconceive
  perceive
  receive
sheave
sleave
sleeve
(teve)
  recitative
thieve
(treve)
  retrieve
weave
  interweave

EX
(*see* **EKS** *and* **EK** *in the plural, page 82*)

EZE
ease
breeze
cheese
(clees)
  Androcles

Pericles
Sophocles
(dees)
  antipodes
  B.V.D.s
  Hesperides
  Pleiades
freeze
  unfreeze
frieze
(gueez)
  Portuguese
lees
  Hercules (*i*)
  isosceles
  journalese
  Praxiteles
(meez)
  Annamese
  Burmese
  chemise
  Siamese
  Vietnamese
(neez)
  aborigines
  Ceylonese

Chinese
Diogenes
Japanese
Javanese
Milanese
Pyrenees
Viennese
peas
  appease
  trapeze
please
  displease
seize
  analyses
  antitheses
  parentheses
  syntheses
  vortices
squeeze
tease
  D.T.s
these
wheeze
(zees)
  disease
(absentees, sees, etc.)

I

I
aye
  aye aye
eye
I
buy
by
  alibi
  by-and-by
  by the by
  go-by (*i*)
  hushaby

lullaby
passerby
thereby
whereby
bye
  bye-bye
  good-bye
cry
  decry
  descry
die

dye
dry
  bone-dry
  high-and-dry
fie
  amplify (*i*)
  beautify (*i*)
  certify (*i*)
  clarify (*i*)
  classify (*i*)
  codify (*i*)

crucify (*i*)
defy (*i*)
deify (*i*)
dignify (*i*)
edify (*i*)
electrify (*i*)
exemplify (*i*)
falsify (*i*)
glorify (*i*)
gratify (*i*)
horrify (*i*)
identify (*i*)
indemnify (*i*)
intensify (*i*)
justify (*i*)
magnify (*i*)
modify (*i*)
mollify (*i*)
mortify (*i*)
mystify (*i*)
notify (*i*)
ossify (*i*)
pacify (*i*)
personify (*i*)
petrify (*i*)
purify (*i*)
qualify (*i*)
  disqualify (*i*)
ratify (*i*)
rectify (*i*)
revivify (*i*)
sanctify (*i*)
satisfy (*i*)
  dissatisfy (*i*)
signify (*i*)
simplify (*i*)
solidify (*i*)
specify (*i*)
terrify (*i*)
testify (*i*)
transmogrify (*i*)
typify (*i*)
unify (*i*)
verify (*i*)
versify (*i*)
  diversify (*i*)

vilify (*i*)
vitrify (*i*)
fly
  butterfly
  dragonfly
  firefly (*i*)
fry
guy
hi
hie
high
lie
lye
  alkali
  ally (*v*)
  belie
  July
  rely
  underlie
my
nigh
  deny
pi
pie
  apple pie
  humble pie, etc.
  occupy
    preoccupy
ply
  imply
pry
rye
wry
  awry
shy
sigh
sky
Skye, Isle of
sly
spry
spy
  espy
sty
Thai
  Mai-tai
thigh

tie
try
why

IB (IBE)
(bibe)
  imbibe
bribe
jibe
scribe
  ascribe
  circumscribe (*i*)
  describe
  inscribe
  prescribe
  proscribe
  subscribe
  transcribe
tribe
  diatribe

IB
crib
drib
fib
glib
jib
(lib)
  ad lib
nib
rib
squib

ICH
itch
bitch
ditch
flitch
hitch
niche
pitch
rich
  enrich
stitch
switch
twitch

which
witch
  bewitch

ID (IDE)
eyed
  cockeyed
  eagle-eyed
  goggle-eyed
  open-eyed
  pie-eyed, etc.
bride
chide
died
  iodide
(fied)
  bonafide
  confide
  countrified
  dignified (i), etc.
guide
  misguide
hide
lied
  collide
  elide
(mide)
  bromide
pied
pride
ride
  deride
  override
side
  aside
  beside
  coincide
  countryside
  decide
  fireside (i)
  fratricide
  hillside (i)
  homicide
  infanticide
  insecticide
  inside

matricide
outside
parenticide
parricide
patricide
preside
regicide
reside
riverside
seaside (i)
sororicide
subside
suicide
tyrannicide
underside
waterside
slide
snide
stride
  astride
  bestride
  outstride
tide
  betide
  ebb tide (i)
  eventide (i)
  high tide (i)
  low tide (i)
  neap tide (i)
  springtide (i)
  Whitsuntide (i)
  yuletide (i)
tried
  untried
vied
  divide
    subdivide
  provide
wide
  nationwide, etc.
(applied, etc.)

ID
id
bid
  forbid

outbid
overbid
did
  katydid
  outdid
  overdid
  undid
(drid)
  Madrid
grid
hid
lid
  invalid (i)
mid
  amid
  pyramid
quid
rid
Sid
  El Cid
skid
slid
squid

IF (IFE)
fife
knife
life
  afterlife
  halflife (i)
rife
strife
wife
  housewife

IF
if
biff
(chif)
  kerchief (i)
    handkerchief (i)
    neckerchief (i)
cliff
glyph
  hieroglyph
jiff

miff
skiff
sniff
  Pecksniff (*i*)
stiff
tiff
whiff

IFT
drift
  adrift
  snowdrift (*i*)
  spindrift (*i*)
gift
lift
  uplift
rift
shift
shrift
sift
swift
thrift
  spendthrift (*i*)
tift
(biffed, etc.)

IG
big
brig
dig
fig
gig
  whirligig
jig
  thingumajig (*i*)
pig
  guinea pig (*i*)
prig
rig
sprig
swig
trig
twig
Whig
wig

IJ
bridge
  abridge
'fridge
ridge

IK (IKE)
bike
hike
like
  alike
  dislike
  unlike
mike
pike
shrike
spike
strike
tyke

IK
brick
chick
click
crick
flick
hick
kick
lick
  Catholic (*i*)
nick
  arsenic (*i*)
pick
prick
quick
  double-quick
rick
  hayrick (*i*)
  limerick (*i*)
  maverick (*i*)
sic
sick
  heartsick
  love-sick
slick
snick

stick
  candlestick (*i*)
  pogo stick
  walking stick
thick
tic
  arithmetic (*i*)
  heretic (*i*)
  lunatic (*i*)
  politic (*i*)
    impolitic (*i*)
tick
wick
  bailiwick
  candlewick (*i*)

IKS
Dix, Dorothea & Fort
fix
  affix
  crucifix
  prefix
  transfix
licks
  prolix
mix
  intermix
nix
six
sticks
  fiddlesticks
Styx
ticks
  acrobatics
  mathematics (*i*)
  politics (*i*)
tricks
  aviatrix
  cicatrix (*i*)
  executrix
(bricks, etc.)

IKST
'twixt
  betwixt
(fixed, etc.)

IKT
(dict)
  addict
  contradict
  predict
flicked
  afflict
  conflict (*v*)
  inflict
licked
  derelict
Pict
  depict
strict
  constrict
  restrict
(vict)
  convict
  evict
(bricked, etc.)

IL (ILE)
aisle
isle
bile
(dile)
  crocodile
file
  Anglophile, etc.
  bibliophile
  defile
guile
  beguile
mile
  camomile
Nile
  juvenile
pile
  compile
rile
  puerile (*i*)
(sile)
  ensile
  reconcile
smile
stile

style
tile
  infantile
  mercantile
  versatile (*i*)
  volatile (*i*)
vile
  revile
while
  awhile
  erstwhile (*i*)
  meanwhile (*i*)
  worthwhile
wile

IL
ill
bill
chill
dill
  daffodil
drill
  escadrille
  quadrille
fill
  fulfill
frill
  befrill
gill
grill
grille
hill
  downhill
  uphill
kill
mill
nil
quill
rill
shrill
sill
  codicil
  imbecile
  windowsill
skill
spill

still
  distill
  instill
swill
thrill
till
  until
  mercantile (*i*)
  volatile (*i*)
trill
twill
(vill)
  Seville
  Evansville, etc.
will
  goodwill
  ill will
  whippoorwill

ILCH
filch
zilch

ILD (ILED)
child
mild
wild
(smiled, etc.)

ILD
build
  rebuild
gild
guild
(chilled, etc.)

ILK
ilk
bilk
milk
silk

ILT
built
  rebuilt
  Vanderbilt

gilt
guilt
hilt
jilt
kilt
lilt
milt
quilt
silt
spilt
stilt
tilt
  atilt
wilt

ILZ (ILEZ)
wiles
(beguiles, etc.)

IM (IME)
I'm
(blime)
  sublime
climb
clime
crime
dime
grime
lime
mime
  pantomime
prime
rhyme
rime
slime
thyme
time
  daytime (*i*)
  lifetime (*i*)
  maritime (*i*)
  overtime (*i*)
  summertime (*i*)

IM
(bim)
  cherubim (*i*)

brim
dim
  bedim
(fim)
  seraphim
grim
gym
him
hymn
limb
(nym)
  antonym (*i*)
  pseudonym (*i*)
  synonym (*i*)
prim
rim
shim
skim
slim
swim
trim
vim
whim

IMF
lymph
nymph

IMP
imp
blimp
crimp
gimp
limp
pimp
primp
scrimp
shrimp
simp
skimp
tymp
wimp

IN (INE)
(bine)
  columbine

combine
concubine
brine
(cline)
  decline
  incline
    disincline
  recline
dine
  anodyne
  incarnadine
fine
  confine
  define
  refine
line
  align
  alkaline
  aniline
  aquiline
  malign
  opaline
  underline
mine
  undermine
nine
  asinine
  benign
  leonine
  saturnine
pine
  porcupine
  rapine (*i*)
  repine
  supine (*i*)
Rhine
shine
  ashine
  outshine
shrine
  enshrine
sign
  assign
  consign
  countersign
spine

spline
stein
　Beckstein
　Celestine
　Philistine
swine
thine
tine
　Byzantine
　Florentine
　serpentine
　turpentine
　valentine
trine
twine
　entwine
　intertwine
vine
　divine
whine
wine
　apple wine
　May wine (*i*) etc.
(zine)
　"Auld Lang Syne"
　design
　resign

IN
in
　herein
　therein
　wherein
　within
inn
been
bin
chin
din
　incarnadine (*i*)
　paladin
fin
Finn, Huckleberry
'gin
　begin
gin

origin
grin
　agrin
　chagrin
kin
　mannequin
Lynn
　Berlin
　Boleyn, Ann
　crinoline (*i*)
　mandolin
　masculine (*i*)
　violin
(nin)
　feminine (*i*)
pin
(plin)
　discipline
Quinn
　harlequin
(rin)
　aspirin (*i*)
　mandarin
　saccharine (*i*)
shin
sin
　clavecin (*i*)
　moccasin (*i*)
skin
spin
thin
　thick-and-thin
tin
　gelatin (*i*)
　Rin Tin Tin
twin
win
　genuine
　heroine

INCH
inch
cinch
chinch
clinch
finch

flinch
lynch
pinch
winch

IND (INED)
bind
blind
find
　confined
　　unconfined
　refined
　　unrefined
grind
hind
　behind
kind
　humankind
　mankind
　unkind
　womankind
mind
　mastermind
　remind
rind
signed
　undersigned
　unsigned
twined
　intertwined
wind
　unwind
(combined, etc.)

IND
(plined)
　disciplined (*i*)
(rind)
　tamarind (*i*)
sinned
　rescind
wind
　sea-wind
(grinned, etc.)

ING
bing
bring
cling
ding
fling
king
  fairy-king
Ming
(ning)
  evening (*i*)
ping
ring
  signet ring, etc.
sing
sling
spring
sting
string
swing
thing
  anything
  everything (*i*)
ting
wing
wring
(*plus present*
  participles)

INGKT
succinct
(blinked, etc.)

INJ
binge
cringe
fringe
  infringe
hinge
  unhinge
(pinge)
  impinge
singe
tinge
twinge

INK
ink
blink
brink
chink
clink
dink
drink
fink
kink
mink
pink
rink
shrink
sink
skink
slink
stink
think
wink
zinc

INKS
jinx
lynx
minx
sphinx
thinks
  methinks
(blinks, etc.)

INS (INSE)
mince
prince
quince
rinse
since
Vince
  convince
  evince
wince
(dints, etc.)

INT
dint
flint

glint
hint
lint
mint
  spearmint (*i*)
print
  imprint (*v*)
  misprint (*v*)
  reprint (*v*)
splint
sprint
squint
stint
tint
  aquatint
  mezzotint

INTH
plinth
(rinth)
  labyrinth
(sinth)
  hyacinth (*i*)

INTS
chintz
dints, etc.
(convinced, etc.)

IP (IPE)
gripe
hype
ripe
  overripe
  unripe
snipe
  guttersnipe
stripe
swipe
tripe
type
  archetype (*i*)
  daguerreotype
  electrotype
  linotype
  logotype

prototype
stereotype
teletype
tintype (*i*) etc.
wipe

IP
chip
clip
dip
drip
flip
grip
grippe
gyp
hip
kip
lip
nip
pip
quip
  equip
rip
scrip
ship
  battleship (*i*)
slip
snip
strip
  outstrip
  weather strip
tip
trip
  pleasure trip
whip
  buggy whip
  horsewhip (*i*)
zip

IPS
clips
  eclipse
lips
  ellipse
  apocalypse
(chips, etc.)

IPT
crypt
script
  manuscript (*i*)
  nondescript
  transcript
(chipped, etc.)

IRE (IRE)
ire
dire
drier
dryer
fire
  afire
  signal fire
hire
mire
  admire
pyre
quire
  acquire
  enquire
  esquire
  inquire
  require
choir
shire
sire
spire
  aspire
  conspire
  expire
  inspire
  perspire
  respire
  suspire
  transpire
squire
tire
  attire
  entire
  retire
Tyre
wire
(zire)

desire
(see **I-ur,** *page 252)*

IS (ISE)
ice
dice
  paradise
(fice)
  sacrifice
    self-sacrifice
  suffice
lice
mice
nice
price
rice
(sise)
  concise
  precise
spice
splice
thrice
(tice)
  entice
trice
twice
vice
  advice
  device

IS (ISS)
(biss)
  abyss
  cannabis
bliss
(diss)
  cowardice (*i*)
  prejudice (*i*)
(fiss)
  artifice (*i*)
  edifice (*i*)
  orifice (*i*)
(friss)
  dentifrice (*i*)
(griss)
  ambergris (*i*)

verdigris
hiss
kiss
(liss)
  acropolis (*i*)
  metropolis (*i*)
  necropolis (*i*)
miss
  amiss
  dismiss
  remiss
piss
  precipice (*i*)
(riss)
  avarice (*i*)
  liquorice (*i*)
  sui generis (*i*)
sis
  analysis (*i*)
  antithesis (*i*)
  biogenesis (*i*)
  dialysis (*i*)
  emphasis (*i*)
  genesis (*i*)
  hypothesis (*i*)
  metamorphosis (*i*)
  metastasis (*i*)
  nemesis (*i*)
  paralysis (*i*)
  parenthesis (*i*)
  synthesis (*i*)
Swiss
this
(tiss)
  armistice (*i*)
(triss)
  cicatrice (*i*)

ISH
dish
fish
(rish)
  gibberish
  impoverish
squish
swish

wish
(devilish, etc.)

ISK
bisque
brisk
disc
frisk
(lisk)
  basilisk (*i*)
  obelisk (*i*)
  odalisque (*i*)
risk
  asterisk
whisk

ISP
crisp
lisp
wisp

IST
cist (*i*)
  classicist (*i*)
  exorcist (*i*)
  pharmacist (*i*)
  physicist (*i*)
  romanticist (*i*), etc.
cyst
(sist)
  assist
  consist
  desist
  subsist
(dist)
  chiropodist (*i*)
  melodist (*i*)
  Methodist (*i*)
  rhapsodist (*i*)
fist
gist
  anthropologist (*i*)
  apologist (*i*)
  archaeologist (*i*)
  biologist (*i*)
  demonologist (*i*)

ecologist (*i*)
entomologist (*i*)
etymologist (*i*)
meteorologist (*i*)
mineralogist (*i*)
mythologist (*i*)
necrologist (*i*)
ontologist (*i*)
pathologist (*i*)
penologist (*i*)
philologist (*i*)
phrenologist (*i*)
physiologist (*i*)
psychologist
seismologist (*i*)
sociologist (*i*)
strategist (*i*)
technologist (*i*)
teleologist (*i*)
theologist (*i*)
toxicologist (*i*)
zoologist (*i*)
grist
hissed
kissed
  unkissed
  anarchist
  monarchist
list
  agriculturalist (*i*)
  analyst (*i*)
  capitalist (*i*)
  Congregationalist (*i*)
  evangelist (*i*)
  fatalist (*i*)
  herbalist (*i*)
  idealist (*i*)
  imperialist (*i*)
  instrumentalist (*i*)
  internationalist (*i*)
  journalist (*i*)
  loyalist (*i*)
  materialist (*i*)
  monopolist (*i*)
  moralist (*i*)
  nationalist (*i*)

naturalist (*i*)
nihilist (*i*)
novelist (*i*)
oculist (*i*)
Orientalist (*i*)
philatelist (*i*)
pluralist (*i*)
pugilist (*i*)
revivalist (*i*)
royalist (*i*)
sensualist (*i*)
sentimentalist (*i*)
socialist (*i*)
specialist (*i*)
symbolist (*i*)
traditionalist (*i*)
transcendentalist (*i*)
universalist (*i*)
vocalist (*i*)
missed
  dismissed
  unmissed
mist
  academist (*i*)
  anatomist (*i*)
  bigamist (*i*)
  monogamist (*i*)
  pessimist (*i*)
  polygamist (*i*)
(nist)
  abolitionist (*i*)
  accompanist (*i*)
  antagonist (*i*)
  botanist (*i*)
  Calvinist (*i*)
  colonist (*i*)
  communist (*i*)
  contortionist (*i*)
  evolutionist (*i*)
  excursionist (*i*)
  hedonist (*i*)
  humanist (*i*)
  illusionist (*i*)
  imperialist (*i*)
  insurrectionist (*i*)
  mechanist (*i*)

obstructionist (*i*)
organist (*i*)
perfectionist (*i*)
pianist (*i*)
Platonist (*i*)
  Neoplatonist (*i*)
prohibitionist (*i*)
projectionist (*i*)
protagonist (*i*)
Satanist (*i*)
saxophonist (*i*)
secessionist (*i*)
telephonist (*i*)
tobacconist (*i*)
trombonist (*i*)
unionist (*i*)
(pist)
  misanthropist
  philanthropist
(quist)
  ventriloquist
(rist)
wrist
  allegorist (*i*)
  amorist (*i*)
  aphorist (*i*)
  colorist (*i*)
  horticulturist (*i*)
  humorist (*i*)
  mesmerist (*i*)
  motorist (*i*)
  plagiarist (*i*)
  satirist (*i*)
  terrorist (*i*)
  theorist (*i*)
(tist)
  absolutist (*i*)
  diplomatist (*i*)
  dramatist (*i*)
  egotist (*i*)
  pragmatist (*i*)
  scientist (*i*)
tryst
twist
  untwist
(vist)

Bolshevist (*i*)
whist
  egoist (*i*)
  soloist (*i*)
(yist)
  essayist (*i*)
  lobbyist (*i*)
(zist)
  exist
    coexist

IT (ITE)
bite
  Jacobite
  Moabite
blight
bright
(dite)
  erudite
  expedite
  indite
  recondite
fight
  neophyte
flight
fright
  affright
height
  Fahrenheit
kite
light
  acolyte
  aerolite
  alight
  cosmopolite
  daylight (*i*)
  delight
  electrolyte
  headlight (*i*)
  Israelite
  moonlight (*i*)
  polite
    impolite
  proselyte
  satellite
  starlight (*i*)

sunlight (*i*)
theodolite
twilight (*i*)
zoolite
might
mite
  dolomite
  dynamite
  Islamite
night
  benight
  good-night
  midnight (*i*)
  overnight
(nite)
  ebonite
  ignite
  mammonite
  unite
    reunite
knight
plight
quite
  requite
right
  aright
  copyright
  forthright (*i*)
  outright (*i*)
rite
  anchorite
  meteorite
  sybarite
write
  underwrite
site
  parasite
sight
  oversight
  second-sight
cite
  anthracite
  excite
  incite
  plebiscite
  recite

sleight
slight
smite
spite
  despite
sprite
  water sprite
tight
  appetite
  water tight
trite
  contrite
(vite)
  invite
white
  snow-white (*i*)

IT
it
bit
bitt
chit
(crit)
  hypocrite (*i*)
fit
  befit
  benefit
  counterfeit (*i*)
  misfit (*i*)
  outfit (*i*)
  refit
  unfit (*i*)
flit
grit
hit
kit
lit
mitt
  admit
  commit
  emit
  omit
  permit (*v*)
  remit
  submit
  transmit

nit
  definite (*i*)
    indefinite (*i*)
  infinite (*i*)
knit
pit
quit
  acquit
rit
  favorite (*i*)
  preterite (*i*)
sit
slit
spit
split
sprit
tit
  tomtit
twit
whit
wit
  Jesuit (*i*)
  motherwit (*i*)
  nitwit (*i*)
  outwit
writ
zit
  exquisite
  opposite
  perquisite
  requisite
    prerequisite

ITH (ITHE)
blithe
lithe
scythe
withe
writhe

ITH
kith
lith
  monolith (*i*)
myth
pith

smith
with
  forthwith (*i*)
  herewith (*i*)
  therewith (*i*)
  wherewith (*i*)

IV (IVE)
chive
Clive
dive
drive
five
hive
jive
live
  alive
(nive)
  connive
(prive)
  deprive
rive
  arrive
  derive
shrive
strive
thrive
(trive)
  contrive
(vive)
  revive
  survive
wive (*v*)

IV
give
  forgive
live
  outlive
sieve
(tive)
  acquisitive (*i*)
  affirmative (*i*)
  alternative (*i*)
  argumentative (*i*)
  causative (*i*)
  combative (*i*)

comparative (*i*)
compensative (*i*)
competitive (*i*)
confirmative (*i*)
consecutive
conservative (*i*)
contemplative (*i*)
contributive (*i*)
correlative (*i*)
curative (*i*)
declarative (*i*)
definitive (*i*)
demonstrative (*i*)
derivative (*i*)
derogative (*i*)
diminutive (*i*)
distributive (*i*)
evocative (*i*)
exclamative (*i*)
executive (*i*)
expletive (*i*)
figurative (*i*)
formative
fugitive
genitive (*i*)
illustrative (*i*)
imperative (*i*)
indicative (*i*)
infinitive (*i*)
informative (*i*)
inquisitive (*i*)
interrogative (*i*)
intuitive (*i*)
laudative (*i*)
lucrative (*i*)
narrative (*i*)
negative (*i*)
nominative (*i*)
nutritive (*i*)
positive (*i*)
preparative (*i*)
prerogative (*i*)
preservative (*i*)
primitive (*i*)
prohibitive (*i*)
provocative (*i*)

punitive (*i*)
putative (*i*)
quantitative (*i*)
reformative (*i*)
relative (*i*)
representative (*i*)
restorative (*i*)
sedative (*i*)
sensitive (*i*)
  insensitive (*i*)
substantive (*i*)
superlative (*i*)
talkative (*i*)
tentative (*i*)
transitive (*i*)

IZ (IZE)
eyes
dies
  gormandize (*i*)
  jeopardize (*i*)
  merchandise (*i*)
  oxidize (*i*)
  rhapsodize (*i*)
  subsidize (*i*)
(fize)
  philosophize (*i*)
guise
  disguise
(jize)
  apologize (*i*)
  energize (*i*)
  eulogize (*i*)
lies
  analyze (*i*)
  brutalize (*i*)
  capitalize (*i*)
  centralize (*i*)
  civilize (*i*)
  devitalize (*i*)
  equalize (*i*)
  evangelize (*i*)
  fertilize (*i*)
  formalize (*i*)
  generalize
  idealize (*i*)

idolize (*i*)
immortalize (*i*)
individualize (*i*)
journalize (*i*)
legalize (*i*)
liberalize (*i*)
localize (*i*)
materialize (*i*)
memorialize (*i*)
mobilize (*i*)
monopolize (*i*)
moralize (*i*)
nationalize (*i*)
naturalize (*i*)
neutralize (*i*)
novelize (*i*)
paralyze (*i*)
penalize (*i*)
personalize (*i*)
pluralize (*i*)
provincialize (*i*)
rationalize (*i*)
realize (*i*)
ruralize (*i*)
scandalize (*i*)
sentimentalize (*i*)
socialize (*i*)
specialize (*i*)
sterilize (*i*)
symbolize (*i*)
tantalize (*i*)
tranquilize (*i*)
utilize (*i*)
verbalize (*i*)
visualize (*i*)
vocalize (*i*)
(mize)
anatomize (*i*)
atomize (*i*)
compromise (*i*)
demise (*i*)
economize (*i*)
emblemize (*i*)
epitomize (*i*)
minimize (*i*)
remise (*i*)

surmise (*i*)
systemize (*i*)
victimize (*i*)
(nize)
agonize (*i*)
antagonize (*i*)
canonize (*i*)
Christianize (*i*)
colonize (*i*)
fraternize (*i*)
galvanize (*i*)
harmonize (*i*)
Hellenize (*i*)
humanize (*i*)
modernize (*i*)
organize (*i*)
   disorganize (*i*)
patronize (*i*)
recognize (*i*)
revolutionize (*i*)
scrutinize (*i*)
sermonize (*i*)
solemnize (*i*)
synchronize (*i*)
tyrannize (*i*)
vulcanize (*i*)
prize
apprise (*i*)
comprise (*i*)
enterprise (*i*)
reprise (*i*)
surprise (*i*)
(quize)
soliloquize (*i*)
rise
arise
moonrise (*i*)
sunrise (*i*)

authorize (*i*)
bowdlerize (*i*)
cauterize (*i*)
characterize (*i*)
deodorize (*i*)
extemporize (*i*)
familiarize (*i*)

memorize (*i*)
mesmerize (*i*)
plagiarize (*i*)
polarize (*i*)
popularize (*i*)
pulverize (*i*)
rapturize (*i*)
satirize (*i*)
summarize (*i*)
temporize (*i*)
terrorize (*i*)
theorize (*i*)
vaporize (*i*)
vulgarize (*i*)
size
Anglicize (*i*)
assize (*i*)
capsize (*i*)
criticize (*i*)
emphasize (*i*)
excise (*i*)
exercise (*i*)
exorcise (i)
incise (*i*)
italicize (*i*)
ostracize (*i*)
synthesize (*i*)
spies
despise
thighs
sympathize (*i*)
ties
acclimatize (*i*)
advertise (*i*)
anathematize (*i*)
baptize (*i*)
chastise (*i*)
democratize (*i*)
deputize (*i*)
dramatize (*i*)
hypnotize (*i*)
hypothesize (*i*)
magnetize (*i*)
proselytize (*i*)
stigmatize (*i*)
vise

advise
devise
improvise (*i*)
revise
supervise (*i*)
wise
  anywise (*i*)
  contrariwise (*i*)
  otherwise (*i*)
  overwise (*i*)
  unwise (*i*)

(buys, etc.)

IZ
is
biz
  show biz
(diz)
  Cadiz
fizz
  gin fizz

friz
his
phiz
quiz
'tis
whiz

IZM
(abolitionism, etc.)
(see **IST,** *page 104)*

O

O (OH)
O
oh
  oh-oh
owe
beau
blow
  Fontainebleau
  tableau
bo
  gazebo
  hobo (*i*)
  oboe (*i*)
bow
  crossbow (*i*)
  longbow (*i*)
  rainbow (*i*)
(co)
  calico
  magnifico (*Spanish*)
  Mexico
  Quantico (*i*)
crow
doe
dough
  Bordeaux

floe
  ice floe (*i*)
flow
  overflow
foe
  comme-il-faut
  (*French*)
fro
  to-and-fro
glow
  aglow
go
  ago
    archipelago (*i*)
    long-ago
  forgo
  indigo
  undergo
  vertigo
grow
  outgrow
  overgrow
ho
  Coho
  heigh ho
  ho-ho

  Soho
  tally-ho
  Westward ho, etc.
hoe
Joe
  banjo (*i*)
lo
  buffalo
  gigolo
  tremolo
low
  below
  bungalow (*i*)
  furbelow (*i*)
mow
  bravissimo (*i*)
  Eskimo (*i*)
  fortissimo (*i*)
  generalissimo (*i*)
  pianissimo (*i*)
no
  domino (*i*)
know
  foreknow
Po (River)
Poe

chapeau
depot (*i*)
quo
  in statu quo (*Latin*)
  quid pro quo (*Latin*)
  status quo (*Latin*)
roe
row
sew
so
  so-and-so
  Rousseau
  trousseau
  Tussaud, Madame
(scrow)
  escrow
sloe
slow
snow
stow
  bestow
though
  although
throe
throw
  overthrow
toe
  incognito
  mistletoe
  tiptoe
tow
  undertow
  bateau
  château
  plateau
  portmanteau
woe
yo
  adagio (*i*)
  Boccaccio (*i*)
  braggadocio (*i*)
  embroglio (*i*)
  embryo (*i*)
  folio (*i*)
  impresario (*i*)
  Lothario (*i*)

mustachio (*i*)
oleo (*i*)
oratorio (*i*)
Pinocchio (*i*)
pistachio (*i*)
portfolio (*i*)
punctilio (*i*)
ratio (*i*)
seraglio (*i*)
studio (*i*)
Tokyo (*i*)
Yo-Yo (*i*)

O (AH)
ah
awe
  overawe
bah
caw
  macaw
chaw
craw
daw
draw
  overdraw
  withdraw
fa
  guffaw
flaw
jaw
la
  la-la
  tra-la
law
  brother-in-law
  son-in-law, etc.
maw
nah
gnaw
paw
raw
saw
  foresaw
  oversaw
  seesaw (*i*)
  Arkansas

shah
slaw
squaw
straw
thaw
yaw
(see **A (AH)**, *page 60)*

OB (OBE)
globe
Job
probe
robe
  disrobe
strobe

OB
blob
bob
cob
fob
gob
hob
job
lob
mob
nob
  hobnob (*i*)
knob
rob
slob
snob
sob
squab
swab
throb
  athrob

OCH (OACH)
broach
brooch
coach
(croach)
  encroach
poach
(proach)

approach
reproach
  self-reproach
roach
  cockroach (i)

OCH
blotch
botch
  debauch
crotch
nautch
notch
Scotch
  hopscotch (i)
splotch
swatch
watch
  wristwatch (i)

OD (OAD)
ode
bode
  abode
  forebode
code
goad
load
  overload
  unload
lode
  mother lode
mode
  à la mode
  commode
    discommode
node
(plode)
  explode
  implode
(pode)
  antipode
road
rode
  corrode
  erode
(sode)

episode
Spode
strode
  bestrode
toad
  pigeon-toed
(crowed, etc.)

OD
odd
bawd
broad
  abroad
clod
cod
fraud
  defraud
God
hod
laud
nod
plod
  applaud
pod
prod
quad
quod
rod
  divining rod
  goldenrod
  maraud
  piston rod
shod
  roughshod (i)
  slipshod (i)
  unshod
sod
  Sade, Marquis de
squad
trod
  untrod
wad
(awed, etc.)

OF (OAF)
oaf

loaf

OFF
off
cough
doff
prof
scoff
soph
  philosophe (*French*)
toff
trough

OFT
oft
croft
loft
  aloft
soft
toft
(doffed, etc.)

OG (OAG)
brogue
rogue
  pirogue
  prorogue
vogue

OG
bog
clog
  unclog
cog
dog
  hot dog (i)
  prairie dog
flog
fog
  befog
  pettifog
frog
Gog
  agog
demagogue
Magog (i)
pedagogue

synagogue
grog
hog
  hedgehog
jog
log
  analogue (*i*)
  catalog (*i*)
  dialogue
  epilogue
  monologue
  theologue
  travelog
Prague
wog *(British)*
  polliwog (*i*)

OI
boy
buoy
cloy
coy
  decoy (*v*)
(hoy)
  ahoy
  hobbledehoy
joy
  enjoy
  overjoy
(loy)
  alloy
(noy)
  annoy
  Illinois
ploy
  employ
poi
  sepoy (*i*)
Roy
  corduroy
  viceroy
soy
(stroy)
  destroy
toy
troy
(voy)

convoy (*i*)
Savoy

OID
Freud, Sigmund
Lloyd
  alkaloid (*i*)
  mongoloid
  paraboloid
  tabloid (*i*)
(poid)
  anthropoid (*i*)
(roid)
  asteroid
void
  avoid
(cloyed, etc.)
(plus N.Y.C. pronunciation of bird, word, etc.)

OIL
oil
boil
  aboil
broil
  embroil
coil
  recoil
  uncoil
foil
  counterfoil (*i*)
  fencing foil
moil
  turmoil (*i*)
roil
soil
spoil
  despoil
toil
(plus N.Y.C. pronunciation of girl, etc.)

OIN
coin
groin

join
  adjoin
  conjoin
  enjoin
  rejoin
loin
  purloin
  sirloin (*i*)
  tenderloin
(moin)
  Des Moines
(plus N.Y.C. pronunciation of burn, etc.)

OINT
joint
  conjoint
  disjoint
(noint)
  anoint
point
  appoint
    disappoint
    reappoint
  counterpoint
(plus N.Y.C. pronunciation of burnt, etc.)

OIS
choice
Joyce, James
  rejoice
voice
  invoice (*i*)

OIST
foist
hoist
joist
moist
(voiced, etc.)

OIT
(droit)
  adroit
    maladroit

(ploit)
  exploit
(troit)
  Detroit

OIZ
noise
poise
  counterpoise (*i*)
  equipoise (*i*)

OJ (OZH)
doge
loge
  horologe

OJ
dodge
lodge
  dislodge
(podge)
  hodgepodge (*i*)
raj

OK (OAK)
oak
bloke
broke
choke
  artichoke (*i*)
cloak
coak
coke
croak
folk
  gentlefolk (*i*)
  townsfolk (*i*), etc.
joke
poke
(roke)
  baroque
smoke
soak
spoke
  bespoke
stoke

stroke
  counterstroke
  masterstroke
  thunderstroke
toke
toque
(voke)
  convoke
  evoke
  invoke
  provoke
  revoke
woke
  awoke
yoke
  unyoke
yolk

OK
auk
Bach, Johann Sebastian
clock
cock
  Bangkok (*i*)
  peacock (*i*)
  poppycock
  weathercock
crock
dock
  Médoc
flock
frock
  defrock
  unfrock
gawk
hawk
  Mohawk (*i*)
  tomahawk (*i*)
hock
  hollyhock (*i*)
jock
knock
loch
lock
  deadlock (*i*)
  fetlock (*i*)

flintlock (*i*)
padlock (*i*)
unlock
mock
amok
pock
roc
rock
  Little Rock
  Ragnarok
shock
smock
sock
squawk
stalk
  beanstalk, etc.
stock
  livestock, etc.
talk
  small talk (*i*)
  table talk (*i*)
walk
  sidewalk
wok
(yock)
  Antioch

OKS (OAKS)
coax
hoax
(oaks, etc.)

OKS
ox
box
  mailbox (*i*)
  powder box
  signal box
(dox)
  orthodox (*i*)
  paradox (*i*)
fox
(nox)
  equinox (*i*)
pox
  chickenpox (*i*)

smallpox (*i*)
vox
(auks, etc.)

OKT
cocked
  concoct
  decoct
(blocked, etc.)

OL (OAL)
bole
bowl
  Cotton Bowl
  Orange Bowl
  Rose Bowl etc.
  wassail bowl
coal
cole
  Ole King Cole
dole
  condole
doll
droll
foal
goal
hole
  buttonhole
  gloryhole
  Jackson Hole
  loophole (*i*)
  pigeonhole
  porthole (*i*)
  Wood's Hole
whole
(jole)
  cajole
mole
(nole)
  Seminole
knoll
pole
  Maypole (*i*)
  tadpole (*i*)
Pole
poll

role
  barcarolle
  casserole
  escarole
  parole
  rigmarole
roll
  enroll
  unroll
scroll
toll
  extoll
troll
  comptrol
  control
    self-control
  patrol
vole
(yole)
  aureole
  oriole
  variole

OL (ALL)
all
  all-in-all
  withal
    therewithal
    wherewithal
awl
ball
  baseball (*i*)
  football (*i*), etc.
bawl
brawl
call
  recall
  mail call
  trumpet call, etc.
caul
  protocol
crawl
doll
drawl
fall
  befall

footfall (*i*)
nightfall (*i*)
pitfall (*i*)
rainfall (*i*)
snowfall (*i*)
waterfall (*i*)
windfall (*i*), etc.
gall
  Bengal
Gaul
  De Gaulle, Charles
haul
  overhaul
loll
mall
maul
moll
  gun moll (*i*)
pall
  Paul, Saint
scrawl
shawl
small
sol
  parasol
sprawl
squawl
stall
  forestall
  install
tall
thrall
  enthrall
wall
  sea wall (*i*)
waul
  caterwaul
y'all
  vitriol
yawl
  Montreal

OLD
old
bold
cold

fold
  blindfold (*i*)
  centerfold (*i*)
  enfold
  manifold (*i*)
  multifold
  refold
  unfold
  twofold, etc.
gold
  marigold
hold
  ahold
  behold
  foothold (*i*)
  household (*i*)
  uphold
  withhold
mold
mould
scold
sold
  unsold
soled
  half-soled
told
  foretold
  retold
  untold
(cajoled, etc.)

OLD (AULD)
auld
bald
scald
(appalled, etc.)

OLT
bolt
  thunderbolt
  unbolt
colt
dolt
holt
jolt
molt

volt
  revolt

OLT (ALT)
(balt)
  cobalt
fault
gault
halt
malt
salt
  assault
  basalt
  somersault
vault
(zalt)
  exalt

OLTZ
waltz
(exalts, etc.)

OLV
solve
  absolve
  dissolve
(volve)
  convolve
  devolve
  evolve
  involve
  revolve

OM (OAM)
chrome
  monochrome
  polychrome
comb
  catacomb
  currycomb
  honeycomb
dome
(drome)
  hippodrome
  palindrome
foam

afoam
home
  harvest home
loam
Nome
  metronome
gnome
pome
roam
Rome
(soam)
  chromosome
tome

OM
om
balm
  embalm
  tannenbaum
    (*German*)
bomb
calm
from
  therefrom
(grom)
  pogrom
Guam
(lom)
  salaam
Mom
  imam
palm
  pom pom
(plom)
  aplomb
psalm
qualm

OMP
comp
pomp
romp
stomp
swamp
tromp

OMPT
prompt
(romped, etc.)

ON (OAN)
own
　disown
blown
　full-blown
　outblown
　unblown
　weather-blown
bone
　backbone (*i*)
　knucklebone
　marrowbone
　trombone
clone
　cyclone (*i*)
cone
crone
(done)
　condone
drone
flown
　high-flown
groan
grown
　full-grown
　moss-grown (*i*)
　mossy-grown
　overgrown
　ungrown
Joan, Saint
known
　foreknown
　unknown
loan
lone
　alone
　Cologne
　　eau-de-cologne
moan
　bemoan
mown
phone

dictaphone
gramaphone
megaphone
microphone
saxophone
telephone
xylophone
pone
　corn pone (*i*)
　postpone
prone
roan
　chaperone
Rhone (River)
sewn
shown
sown
　unsown
stone
　brimstone (*i*)
　cornerstone (*i*)
　flagstone (*i*)
　foundation stone (*i*)
　grindstone (*i*)
　hailstone (*i*)
　headstone (*i*)
　milestone (*i*)
　millstone (*i*)
throne
　dethrone
　enthrone
thrown
　overthrown
tone
　atone
　baritone (*i*)
　intone
　monotone
　semitone
　undertone
zone

ON
on
　hangers-on
　hereon

thereon
whereon
Bonn
　autobahn (*German*)
　bonbon
brawn
con
　lexicon
　Rubicon
　silicon
　stereopticon
dawn
don
　Glyptodon
　iguanodon
　mastodon
drawn
　withdrawn
fawn
　chiffon
gone
　begone
　hexagon
　octagon
　Oregon
　paragon
　pentagon
　polygon
　tarragon
　undergone
　woebegone
John
　demijohn
lawn
　Babylon
　Ceylon
　echelon
non
　anon
　sine qua non
pawn
　impawn
　upon
　　hereupon
　　put-upon
　　thereupon

whereupon
prawn
(ton)
 wonton
wan
 Saskatchewan
yawn
(zon)
 Amazon
 Luzon
 Lausanne

ONCH
conch
launch
paunch
raunch

OND
blond
bond
 vagabond
fond
 overfond
frond
monde
 demimonde
pond
(scond)
 abscond
spawned
 respond
  correspond
wand
yawned
 beyond
(dawned, etc.)

ONG
bong
dong
 ding-dong (*i*)
gong
(kong)
 Hong Kong
 King Kong

(jong)
 mah-jong
long
 along
  all along (*i*)
 belong
 headlong (*i*)
 lifelong (*i*)
 overlong
pong
 Ping-Pong
prong
wrong
song
 battlesong
 drinking song
 evensong
 singsong
strong
 headstrong (*i*)
thong
throng
tong

ONGK
conch
conk
honk
tonk
 honky-tonk

ONS
nonce
sconce
 ensconce
(sponse)
 response
(daunts, etc.)

ONT (OANT)
don't
won't
wont

ONT
daunt

flaunt
gaunt
haunt
jaunt
taunt
 debutante
want

ONZ
bonze
bronze
johns
 longjohns (*i*)
pons
dawns, etc.
(bonds, etc.)

OOD (UD)
could
good
hood
 babyhood
 brotherhood
 fatherhood
 likelihood
 livelihood
 motherhood
 neighborhood
 priesthood (*i*)
 sisterhood
 womanhood, etc.
should
stood
 understood
  misunderstood
 withstood
wood
 Hollywood
 firewood (*i*)
 sandalwood, etc.
 Underwood
would

OOD (YOOD)
(feud, etc.)
(*see* **UD (YOOD)**, *page 127*)

OOD
(food, etc.)
(see **UD (OOD),**
page 128)

OOK (UK)
book
  bankbook (*i*)
  black book (*i*)
  holy book
  picture book
  pocketbook (*i*), etc.
brook
cook
  pastry cook
crook
hook
  unhook
look
  outlook (*i*)
  overlook
nook
rook
shook
(sook)
  forsook
took
  betook
  mistook
  overtook
  partook
  undertook

OOK (YOOK)
uke
duke
juke
puke
(ruke)
  peruke
(tuke)
  Hexateuch
  Pentateuch

OOK
fluke
kook

spook

OOL
bull
  cock-and-bull
full
pull
wool
beautiful (*plus* ful
  endings. This rhyme
  is awkward.)

OOL
pool, etc.
(see **UL (OOL),**
page 129)

OOT
foot
  afoot
  fiddle-foot
  pussyfoot
  tenderfoot
  underfoot, etc.
put

OP (OAP)
ope
cope
dope
grope
hope
lope
  antelope (*i*)
  cantaloupe (*i*)
  elope
  envelope (*n*)
  interlope
mope
pope
rope
scope
  astroscope (*i*)
  electroscope (*i*)
  galvanoscope (*i*)
  gyroscope (*i*)
  horoscope (*i*)

kaleidoscope (*i*)
microscope (*i*)
spectroscope (*i*)
stethoscope (*i*)
telescope (*i*), etc.
slope
soap
taupe
(thrope)
  misanthrope (*i*)
tope
trope
  heliotrope

OP
chop
cop
crop
drop
  eavesdrop (*i*)
  raindrop (*i*)
  snowdrop (*i*)
flop
fop
hop
lop
mop
plop
pop
  lollipop
  soda pop
prop
shop
slop
sop
  milksop
strop
swap
  atop
  tip-top (*i*)
whop

OPT
opt
Copt
(dopt)

adopt
(dropped, etc.)

OR
or
oar
ore
boar
Boer
bore
  forbore
chore
core
  albacore
  encore
corps
door
  adore
  ambassador
  battledore
  commodore
  corridor
  Ecuador
  Labrador
  matador
  mirador
  picador
  stevedore
  troubadour
drawer
floor
for
fore
  afore
  before
  heretofore
  metaphor
  pinafore
  semaphore
  therefore (*i*)
four
hoar
  abhor
whore
lore
  bachelor (*i*)

chancellor (*i*)
folklore (*i*)
galore (*i*)
more
  amor
  Baltimore
  evermore
  furthermore
  nevermore
  paramour
  sophomore
  sycamore
nor
  governor (*i*)
  ignore
(plore)
  deplore
  explore
  implore
pore
  Singapore
pour
  downpour (*i*)
rapport
roar
  emperor (*i*)
  uproar (*i*)
score
  underscore (*i*)
shore
  ashore
    offshore
  onshore
  seashore (*i*)
soar
sore
  footsore (*i*)
  heartsore (*i*)
  dinosaur
  ichthyosaur
  plesiosaur, etc.
snore
spore
store
  restore
swore

forswore
Thor
tor
  auditor (*i*)
  competitor (*i*)
  conspirator (*i*)
  contributor (*i*)
  editor (*i*)
  executor (*i*)
  guarantor (*i*)
  inquisitor (*i*)
  minotaur (*i*)
  orator (*i*)
  progenitor (*i*)
  senator (*i*)
  solicitor (*i*)
  visitor (*i*)
tore
war
  man-o'-war
yore
  anterior (*i*)
  excelsior (*i*)
  exterior (*i*)
  inferior (*i*)
  señor
  ulterior (*i*)
your

ORB
orb
(zorb)
  absorb

ORCH
porch
scorch
torch

ORD
Orde, Fort
board
  aboard
  overboard
  shuffleboard
chord

harpsichord (*i*)
cord
  accord
  misericord
ford
  afford
hoard
lord
  milord
  overlord
soared
sword
ward
  award
  reward
(yord)
  fjord
(bored, etc.)

ORF
Orff, Carl
dwarf
wharf

ORJ
forge
George
  by George
gorge
  disgorge
  engorge

ORK
cork
  uncork
fork
pork
stork
torque
York

ORM
form
  chloroform
  conform
  cruciform

cuneiform
deform
inform
  misinform
multiform
perform
reform
transform
uniform
vermiform
norm
storm
  snowstorm (*i*), etc.
swarm
warm

ORN
Orne (River)
born
  firstborn (*i*)
  highborn (*i*)
  inborn (*i*)
  stillborn (*i*)
  suborn
  unborn, etc.
borne
  airborne (*i*)
  seaborne (*i*)
bourn
corn
  barleycorn
  Capricorn
  popcorn (*i*)
  unicorn
(dorn)
  adorn
horn
  alpenhorn
  Cape Horn
  drinking horn
  English horn
  foghorn (*i*)
  French horn (*i*)
  greenhorn (*i*)
  hunting horn

Matterhorn
powder horn
priming horn
lorn
  forlorn
  lovelorn
morn
mourn
Norn
scorn
  self-scorn
shorn
  unshorn
sworn
  forsworn
  unsworn
warn
  forewarn
worn
  footworn (*i*)
  outworn
  waterworn
  wayworn (*i*)

ORPS
corpse
warps

ORS
coarse
course
  discourse
  intercourse
  recourse
  watercourse
(dorse)
  endorse
force
  enforce
  perforce
  reinforce
gorse
hoarse
horse
  hobbyhorse
  stalking-horse

unhorse
Morse
  remorse
Norse
source
  resource
(vorse)
  divorce

ORT
bort
  abort
court
  county court
  escort
fort
  comfort (i)
mort
port
  comport
  davenport
  deport
  export
  import
  passport (i)
  report
  support
quart
short
snort
sort
  assort
  consort
sport
  disport
  transport
thwart
  athwart
tort
  contort
  distort
  extort
  retort
(vort)
  cavort
wart

(zort)
  exhort
  resort

ORTH
forth
  Firth of Forth
  henceforth
  thenceforth
fourth
north

ORTS
quartz
shorts
(aborts, etc.)

ORZ
doors
  indoors
  outdoors
(torz)
  quatorze (*French*)
(zores)
  Azores
(bores, etc.)

OS (OSE)
(bose)
  verbose
close
(cose)
  bellicose
  glucose
  varicose
dose
  overdose
gross
  engross
(lose)
  cellulose
(nose)
  diagnose
(pose)
  adipose (i)
(rose)

morose
(tose)
  comatose
(yose)
  grandiose
  otiose

OS
boss
  emboss
cross
  across
  double-cross
  lacrosse
  recross
dross
floss
gloss
hoss
joss
loss
moss
Ross
  rhinoceros (i)
sauce
  applesauce, etc.
toss
(tross)
  albatross

OSH
bosh
  kibosh (i)
frosh
gosh
josh
(losh)
  galosh
posh
quash
slosh
squash
swash
(tosh)
  mackintosh
wash

awash
hogwash (*i*)
Siwash (*i*)
(yosh)
brioche

OSHE
boche
Foch, Marshal
gauche

OSK
mosque
(yosk)
kiosk (*i*)

OST (OAST)
boast
coast
ghost
host
most
foremost (*i*)
furthermost
hindermost
innermost
northernmost
outermost
southernmost
uppermost
uttermost
post
riposte
trading post
whipping post, etc.
roast
toast
(dosed, etc.)

OST
cost
accost
holocaust
Pentecost
frost
lost

tossed
tempest-tossed
(zaust)
exhaust
(crossed, etc.)

OT (OAT)
oat
bloat
boat
pilotboat
riverboat
coat
overcoat
petticoat
dote
antidote
float
afloat
gloat
goat
redingote
groat
moat
mote
promote
remote
note
connote
denote
footnote (*i*)
quote
misquote
rote
wrote
underwrote
shote
smote
stoat
throat
tote
vote
devote
outvote

OT
aught
ought
blot
bought
unbought
brought
caught
uncaught
clot
cot
apricot
cocotte
dot
fought
hardfought
unfought
fraught
got
begot
misbegot
forgot
unforgot
hot
jot
lot
Camelot
shallot
Lot
naught
aeronaut (*i*)
argonaut (*i*)
astronaut (*i*)
cosmonaut (*i*)
juggernaut (*i*)
not
forget-me-not
Huguenot
knot
love knot, etc.
plot
counterplot
pot
(quot)
aliquot
kumquat (*i*)

rot
  dry rot
  tommyrot
wrought
  overwrought
Scot
shot
  overshot
  undershot
slot
sot
  besot
sought
  besought
spot
  beauty-spot
squat
swat
taught
  self-taught
  untaught
taut
thought
  afterthought
  bethought
  forethought
tot
  Hottentot
trot
  distraught
(vot)
  gavotte
watt
what
  somewhat
yacht
  compatriot

OTHE
clothe
loathe

OTH (OATH)
oath
both
growth

overgrowth
undergrowth
loath
sloth
Thoth
troth
  betroth

OTH
broth
cloth
  broadcloth (*i*)
  saddlecloth (*i*)
froth
Goth
  Ostrogoth (*i*)
  Visigoth (*i*)
moth
  behemoth (*i*)
swath
troth
  betroth
wrath
wroth

OU
ow
bough
bow
brow
chow
  Foochow
  Soochow
ciao (*Italian*)
cow
  Hankow
dhow
dow
  endow
  landau (*i*)
frau
frow
(gow)
  hoosegow (*i*)
how
  anyhow

somehow
(lau)
  allow
    disallow
now
plough
plow
prow
row
scow
slough
sow
(tau)
  kowtow (*i*)
thou
vow
  avow
  disavow
wow
  bow-wow (*i*)
  pow-wow (*i*)
  Luau (*i*)

OUCH
ouch
couch
crouch
grouch
pouch
slouch
vouch

OUD
cloud
  becloud
  encloud
  overcloud
  thundercloud, etc.
crowd
  overcrowd
loud
  aloud
proud
shroud
  beshroud
  enshroud
(allowed, etc.)

OUL
owl
cowl
dowel
foul
  afoul
  befoul
fowl
  guinea fowl
  waterfowl
growl
howl
jowl
prowl
scowl

OUN
brown
clown
crown
  uncrown
down
  eiderdown
  hand-me-down
  tumble-down
  upside down
drown
frown
gown
noun
  renown
town
  downtown (*i*)
  uptown

OUND
bound
  abound
  hill-bound (*i*)
  icebound (*i*)
  ironbound (*i*)
  outward-bound
  spellbound (*i*)

unbound
downed
  redound
found
  confound
  dumbfound (*i*)
  profound
ground
  aground
  background (*i*)
  battleground (*i*)
  underground
hound
  bloodhound (*i*)
mound
(nound)
  renowned
pound
  compound
  expound
  impound
  propound
round
  around
  merry-go-round
  surround
sound
  resound
(stound)
  astound
wound
(browned, etc.)

OUNJ
lounge
scrounge

OUNSE
ounce
bounce
flounce
(nounce)
  announce
  denounce
  pronounce
  renounce

pounce
trounce
(counts, etc.)

OUNT
count
  account
  discount
  miscount
  recount
fount
mount
  amount
  dismount
  paramount (*i*)
  remount
  surmount
  tantamount (*i*)

OUR
our
hour
flour
scour
sour
(vour)
  devour)
(see **OUR-ur,** *page 281)*

OUS
blouse
douse
grouse
house (*n*)
  chapterhouse (*i*)
  charnel house (*i*)
  custom house (*i*)
  madhouse (*i*).
  outhouse (*i*)
  penthouse (*i*)
  pleasure house (*i*)
  prison house (*i*)
  public house (*i*)
  slaughterhouse (*i*)
louse
mouse

fliedermaus
  (*German*)
Mickey Mouse
souse
spouse
(Strauss, Johann, etc.)

OUST
oust
roust
(doused, etc.)

OUT
out
  knockout (*i*)
  lookout (*i*)
  out-and-out
  throughout
  without
pout
rout
scout
shout
snout
spout
  waterspout (*i*)
sprout
stout
tout
trout
(vout)
  devout

OUTH
mouth
south

OUZ
blouse

browse
drowse
house (*v*)
rouse
  arouse
  carouse
(spouze)
  espouse

OV (OVE)
clove
cove
dove (*v*)
drove
grove
hove
Jove
  by Jove
mauve
rove

OZ (OZE)
chose
close
  disclose
  enclose
  foreclose
  inclose
  unclose
doze
froze
  refroze
  unfroze
hose
nose
pose
  compose
    decompose

    recompose
  depose
  impose
  interpose
  superpose
  suppose
    presuppose
prose
rose
  arose
    rearose
  moss rose (*i*)
  tea rose (*i*) etc.
(sclose)
  disclose
(spose)
  dispose
    indispose
    predispose
  expose
  transpose
those
(owes, etc.)

OZ
Oz, Wizard of
cause
  because
clause
  Santa Claus
gauze
pause
  menopause
(plause)
  applause
vase
was
yaws
(laws, etc.)

U

U (YOO)

*This group of words
rhymes correctly with
the one immediately
following it.*

ewe
yew
you
  bayou
  I.O.U.
(bue)
  debut
  imbue
chew
  achoo
  choo-choo (*i*)
  kerchoo
cue
  barbecue
dew
  honeydew
  mountain dew, etc.
due
  adieu
  endue
  overdue
  residue
  subdue
  undue
few
  curfew
phew
hew
hue
Jew
lieu
  curlew
mew
new
  anew
  renew
knew

avenue
foreknew
ingénue
retinue
revenue
pew
spew
sue
  ensue
  pursue
thew
view
  interview
  preview (*i*)
  review

U (OO)

blew
blue
  baby blue
  sky blue (*i*) etc.
boo
  bamboo
  caribou
  peekaboo
  taboo
brew
clue
coo
  cuckoo
coup
crew
  accrue
do
  ado
  derring-do
  outdo
  overdo
  to-do
  undo
  well-to-do
  billet-doux

Hindu (*i*)
hoodoo (*i*)
skiddoo
voodoo (*i*)
drew
  withdrew
flew
flue
glue
  igloo (*i*)
  unglue
goo
  goo-goo
  ragout
grew
hoo
  ballyhoo
  boohoo
  wahoo (*i*)
  Yahoo (*i*)
who
loo (*British*)
  halloo
    view halloo
  hullabaloo
  Zulu (*i*)
moo
  emu
gnu
poo
  shampoo
roux
  kangaroo
  Peru
rue
screw
  unscrew
shoe
shoo
  cashew
  eschew
  issue (*i*)

133

tissue (*i*)
shrew
slew
slue
stew
strew
  bestrew
  construe
    misconstrue
sou (*French*)
Sioux
threw
  overthrew
through
to
  hereto
  hitherto
  into
    hereinto
    thereinto
  thereto
  thitherto
  whitherto
  unto
    thereunto
    whereunto
too
  impromptu (*French*)
  in transitu (*Latin*)
  manitou (*Indian*)
  passe-partout
    (*French*)
  tattoo
two
true
  too true
  untrue
vous (*French*)
  rendezvous
woo
zoo
  Kalamazoo
  kazoo

UB (OOB)
boob
cube
rube
tube

UB
bub
  Beelzebub
  hubbub
chub
club
  men's club (*i*)
  golf club (*i*) etc.
cub
drub
dub
  rub-a-dub-dub
grub
hub
nub
pub
rub
scrub
shrub
snub
stub
sub
tub

UCH (OOCH)
cooch
hooch
mooch
pooch

UCH
clutch
crutch
Dutch
hutch
much
  inasmuch
such
touch
  retouch

UD (YOOD)
This group of words rhymes correctly with the one immediately following it.
you'd
dude
  subdued
    unsubdued
feud
lewd
  allude
  delude
  interlude
  prelude (*i*)
nude
  denude
  renewed
sued
  pursued
    unpursued
(tude)
  altitude (*i*)
  amplitude (*i*)
  aptitude (*i*)
    ineptitude (*i*)
  attitude (*i*)
  beatitude (*i*)
  certitude (*i*)
    incertitude (*i*)
  decrepitude (*i*)
  definitude (*i*)
  desuetude (*i*)
  exactitude (*i*)
    inexactitude (*i*)
  finitude (*i*)
    infinitude (*i*)
  fortitude (*i*)
  gratitude (*i*)
    ingratitude (*i*)
  habitude (*i*)
  lassitude (*i*)
  latitude (*i*)
  longitude (*i*)
  magnitude (*i*)
  multitude (*i*)

necessitude (*i*)
platitude (*i*)
plenitude (*i*)
promptitude (*i*)
pulchritude (*i*)
quietude (*i*)
  disquietude (*i*)
rectitude (*i*)
servitude
similitude
solicitude
solitude
turpitude
(zude)
  exude

UD (OOD)
brood
  abrood
clued
  conclude
  exclude
  include
  occlude
  preclude
  seclude
crude
dude
food
glued
  unglued
hued
  amber-hued
  rainbow-hued, etc.
mood
prude
rood
rude
shrewd
snood
strewed
  extrude
(trude)
  intrude
  obtrude
  protrude

(chewed, etc.)

UD
*(see **OOD,** page 118)*

UD
blood
bud
cud
dud
flood
mud
scud
spud
stud
thud

UDZ
suds
(bloods, etc.)

UF (OOF)
goof
hoof
(loof)
  aloof
proof
  bulletproof
  disproof
  reproof
  waterproof
  weatherproof, etc.
roof
spoof
(toof)
  Tartuffe
woof

UF
bluff
buff
  blindman's buff
  rebuff
chuff
cuff
duff

fluff
gruff
huff
muff
(nuff)
  enough
puff
  powder puff
rough
ruff
scruff
scuff
slough
snuff
stuff
tough

UFT
tuft
(bluffed, etc.)

UG
bug
  doodlebug (*l*), etc.
drug
dug
hug
  bunny hug (*i*)
jug
lug
mug
plug
pug
rug
shrug
slug
smug
snug
thug
tug

UJ (OOJ)
(fuge)
  centrifuge
  subterfuge
huge

Scrooge
stooge

UJ
budge
drudge
fudge
grudge
　begrudge
judge
　forejudge
　misjudge
　prejudge
nudge
sludge
smudge
trudge

UK (YOOK)
This group of words rhymes correctly with the one immediately following it.
uke
duke
juke
puke
(ruke)
　peruke
(tuke)
　Hexateuch
　Pentateuch

UK (OOK)
fluke
kook
spook

UK (OOK)
book, etc.
(see OOK, page 118)

UK
buck
chuck
cluck

duck
　Donald Duck
luck
　potluck
muck
　amuck
(nuck)
　Canuck
pluck
puck
ruck
shuck
struck
　horror-struck, etc.
stuck
suck
truck
tuck

UKS
crux
flux
lux
shucks
(bucks, etc.)

UKT
duct
　abduct
　aqueduct (*i*)
　conduct
　deduct
　induct
　viaduct (*i*)
(struct)
　construct
　instruct
　obstruct
(ducked, etc.)

UL (YULE)
This group of words rhymes correctly with the one immediately following it.
yule

(bule)
　vestibule
(cule)
　molecule (*i*)
　ridicule (*i*)
mule

UL (OOL)
cool
drool
fool
　April fool
ghoul
pool
　Liverpool
　whirlpool (*i*)
rule
　misrule
　overrule
school
spool
stool
tool
tulle

UL (OOL)
wool
(see OOL, page 118)

UL
cull
dull
gull
hull
lull
mull
null
　annul
scull
skull

ULCH
gulch
mulch

ULJ
bulge
(dulge)
  indulge
(vulge)
  divulge

ULK
bulk
hulk
skulk
sulk

ULKT
mulct
(hulked, etc.)

ULP
gulp
pulp

ULS
pulse
  impulse (i)
  repulse
(vulse)
  convulse

ULT
cult
  difficult (i)
  occult
(dult)
  adult
(pult)
  catapult (i)
(sult)
  consult
  insult (v)
(zult)
  exult
  result

UM (YUME)
*This group of words
rhymes correctly with*
*the one immediately
following it.*
fume
  perfume
(gume)
  legume
(lume)
  illume
spume
(sume)
  assume
  consume
  subsume
(tume)
  costume (i)
(zume)
  exhume
  presume
  resume

UM (OOM)
bloom
  abloom
boom
broom
brume
doom
flume
gloom
groom
  bridegroom (i)
whom
loom
rheum
room
  anteroom
  dining room
  elbow room
  reading room, etc.
tomb
  entomb
    disentomb
  Khartoum
womb
zoom

UM
bum
chum
come
  become
  modicum (i)
  overcome
  succumb
crumb
drum
  kettledrum (i)
dumb
  Christendom (i)
  kingdom (i)
  martyrdom (i) etc.
  Tweedledum
(fum)
  fee-fi-fo-fum
glum
gum
hum
(lum)
  curriculum
  pendulum
mum
  chrysanthemum
  maximum (i)
  minimum (i)
numb
  benumb
  laudanum (i)
  platinum (i)
  tympanum (i)
plum
  sugar-plum
rum
scum
slum
some
  burdensome (i)
  cumbersome (i)
  frolicsome (i)
  meddlesome (i)
  quarrelsome (i)
  troublesome (i)
  venturesome (i)

wearisome (*i*)
worrisome (*i*)
sum
strum
swum
thumb
(tum)
  ad libitum
yum
  aquarium (*i*)
  auditorium
  compendium (*i*)
  cranium (*i*)
  crematorium (*i*)
  emporium (*i*)
  encomium (*i*)
  geranium
  gymnasium (*i*)
  medium (*i*)
  millennium (*i*)
  moratorium (*i*)
  museum (*i*)
  odium (*i*)
  opium (*i*)
  palladium (*i*)
  pandemonium (*i*)
  petroleum (*i*)
  premium (*i*)
  radium (*i*)
  sanatorium (*i*)
  symposium (*i*)
  tedium (*i*)
  uranium (*i*)
  yum-yum (*i*)

UMP
bump
chump
clump
crump
dump
frump
hump
jump
lump
plump

rump
slump
stump
sump
thump
trump

UMPS
mumps
(bumps, etc.)

UN (YUNE)
This group of words
rhymes correctly with
the one immediately
following it.
(yune)
  picayune
dune
hewn
June
(mune)
  commune
  immune
(pune)
  impugn
tune
  attune
  importune
  opportune
    inopportune

UN (OON)
(bloon)
  doubloon
boon
  baboon
coon
  cocoon
  raccoon
  tycoon
croon
(foon)
  buffoon
  typhoon
(droon)

gadroon
quadroon
goon
  dragoon
  lagoon
  Rangoon
loon
  balloon
  galloon
  pantaloon
  saloon
  Walloon
moon
  harvest moon
  honeymoon, etc.
noon
  afternoon
  forenoon (*i*)
poon
  harpoon
  lampoon
prune
rune
  macaroon
  maroon
  octoroon
soon
  bassoon
  monsoon
swoon
(troon)
  patroon
  poltroon
(toon)
  cartoon
  platoon
  pontoon
  Saskatoon
  spittoon

UN
bun
done
  outdone
  overdone
  undone

dun
fun
gun
  begun
    unbegun
hon
Hun
none
  phenomenon
nun
pun
run
  outrun
  overrun
shun
son
  benison (*i*)
  caparison (*i*)
  comparison (*i*)
  foster son
  garrison
  jettison
  orison
  unison
  venison
stun
  Galveston
sun
ton
  simpleton (*i*)
  skeleton (*i*)
tun
won
  hard-won
one
  anyone
  everyone
  number one
(yun)
  oblivion

UNCH
brunch
bunch
crunch
hunch

lunch
munch
punch
scrunch

UND
bund
  cumberbund (*i*)
  moribund (*i*)
(cund)
  rubicund
fund
  refund (*v*)
(tund)
  orotund
  rotund
(shunned, etc.)

UNG
bung
clung
dung
flung
hung
  overhung
  unhung
lung
(mung)
  among
rung
wrung
slung
sprung
strung
  high-strung
  unstrung
stung
sung
  unsung
swung
tongue
  mother tongue
young

UNGK
bunk

chunk
clunk
dunk
drunk
flunk
funk
hunk
junk
monk
plunk
punk
shrunk
skunk
slunk
spunk
stunk
sunk
trunk

UNGKT
funked
  defunct
junked
  conjunct
  disjunct
(bunked, etc.)

UNJ
lunge
plunge
sponge
  expunge

UNS
dunce
once
(blunts, etc.)

UNT
blunt
brunt
bunt
front
  affront
  confront
  forefront

grunt
hunt
punt
runt
shunt
stunt
(yunt)
  exeunt

UP (OOP)
coop
  recoup
croup
droop
dupe
group
hoop
loop
  Guadeloupe (*i*)
poop
  nincompoop
scoop
sloop
soup
stoop
stoup
swoop
troop
troupe
whoop

UP
up
  fed up
  hard-up
  keyed-up
  up-and-up, etc.
cup
  buttercup
  loving cup
  stirrup cup
  wassail cup, etc.
pup
sup

UPT
(brupt)
  abrupt
cupped
(rupt)
  corrupt
  disrupt
  erupt
  interrupt
supped

UR (YUR)
This group of words rhymes imprecisely with the one immediately following it.
your
cure
  epicure
  insecure
  liqueur
  manicure
  pedicure
  procure
  secure
  sinecure
(dure)
  endure
(jure)
  abjure
  adjure
lure
  allure
(mure)
  demure
  immure
(nure)
  inure
  manure
pure
  impure
(scure)
  obscure
sure
  assure
    reassure

brochure
cocksure
cynosure
ensure
insure
  reinsure
unsure
(ture) (chure)
  aperture (*i*)
  armature (*i*)
  candidature (*i*)
  caricature (*i*)
  discomfiture (*i*)
  divestiture (*i*)
  entablature (*i*)
  expenditure (*i*)
  forfeiture (*i*)
  furniture
  investiture (*i*)
  ligature (*i*)
  literature (*i*)
  mature
    immature (*i*)
    premature
  miniature (*i*)
  overture (*i*)
  portraiture (*i*)
  primogeniture (*i*)
  signature (*i*)
  tablature (*i*)
  temperature
  vestiture (*i*)
    investiture (*i*)

UR
blur
cur
  concur
  incur
  occur
  recur
fir
fur
  chauffeur
  confer
  defer

infer
prefer
transfer (*v*)
her
myrrh
  demur
per
purr
shirr
sir
  Big Sur
  connoisseur
slur
spur
stir
  astir
  bestir
(tur)
  amateur
  deter
  hauteur
  inter
    disinter
  restaurateur
(ver)
  aver
were
whir
(zhur)
  voyageur*

UR (OOR)
boor
moor
  amour
  blackamoor
  paramour
poor
spoor
tour
  contour (*i*)
  detour

URB
blurb
(burb)

suburb (*i*)
curb
herb
(perb)
  superb
Serb
(sturb)
  disturb
(turb)
  perturb
verb

URCH
birch
church
lurch
perch
search
  research
smirch
  besmirch

URD
bird
  frigate bird
  gallows bird
  hummingbird
  ladybird
  mockingbird
  pilot bird, etc.
curd
gird
  engird
heard
  overheard
herd
shirred
surd
  absurd
third
word
(zurd)
  absurd
(abjured, etc.)

URF
serf
surf
turf

URJ
urge
dirge
merge
  emerge
  immerge
  submerge
purge
scourge
serge
splurge
surge
verge
  converge
  diverge

URK
irk
clerk
dirk
jerk
kirk
lurk
murk
perk
quirk
shirk
smirk
Turk
work
  fancywork (*i*)
  handiwork (*i*)
  overwork
  wonderwork (*i*)

URL
earl
burl
churl
curl
  uncurl

furl
　unfurl
girl
hurl
knurl
pearl
　mother-of-pearl
purl
skirl
swirl
twirl
whirl

URLD
world
　underworld
(curled, etc.)

URM
firm
　affirm
　　reaffirm
　confirm
　infirm
germ
sperm
squirm
term
worm

URN
earn
urn
burn
churn
durn
fern
(journ)
　adjourn
　sojourn (i)
kern
learn
　unlearn
spurn
stern
　astern

(surn)
　concern
　　unconcern
　discern
　Lucerne
tern
　intern (v)
　subaltern (i)
turn
　overturn
　return
　taciturn (i)
Verne, Jules
yearn

URNT
earnt
burnt
　unburnt
learnt
　unlearnt
weren't

URP
Earp, Wyatt
blurp
chirp
(surp)
　usurp
twirp

URPT
(zerpt)
　excerpt
(chirped, etc.)

URS
burse
　disburse
　imburse
　　reimburse
curse
　accurse
　precurse
hearse
　rehearse

(merse)
　immerse
　submerse
nurse
purse
　cutpurse (i)
(spurse)
　disperse
　intersperse
terse
verse
　adverse
　averse
　converse
　diverse
　inverse
　reverse
　subverse
　transverse
　traverse
　universe
worse

URST
burst
　outburst (i)
curst
　accurst
durst
first
thirst
　athirst
versed
　unversed
verst
worst
(cursed, etc.)

URT
blurt
curt
dirt
flirt
girt
　begirt
　yogurt

hurt
  unhurt
(lert)
  alert
(nert)
  inert
pert
shirt
skirt
spurt
  expert (i)
squirt
(surt)
  concert (v)
    disconcert
  insert
(vurt)
  avert
  controvert (i)
  convert
  divert
  evert
  extrovert (i)
  introvert (i)
  invert
  obvert
  pervert (v)
  revert
  subvert
yurt
(zurt)
  desert (i)
  dessert
  exert

URTH
earth
  unearth
berth
birth
dearth
firth
girth
mirth
worth

URV
curve
nerve
  unnerve
serve
  conserve
  deserve
  observe
  preserve
  reserve
  subserve
swerve
verve

US (UCE)
*This group of words
rhymes correctly with
the one immediately
following it.*
use (n)
  abuse (n)
  disuse (n)
  misuse (n)
(cuse)
  Syracuse (i)
deuce
  adduce
  deduce
  educe
  induce
  introduce
  produce
    reproduce
  reduce
  seduce
  traduce
(fuse)
  diffuse (a)
  profuse (a)
juice
(nuse)
  hypotenuse
puce
(scuse)
  excuse
(tuse)

obtuse

US (OOS)
(boose)
  caboose
  calaboose
(cloose)
  recluse
goose
loose
moose
  vamoose
noose
  burnoose
(poose)
  papoose
Russe
  charlotte russe
sluice
spruce
(stroose)
  abstruse
truce

US
us
bus
  incubus (i)
  omnibus (i)
  succubus (i)
  syllabus (i)
buss
  blunderbuss (i)
cuss
  abacus (i)
  discuss
  Leviticus
fuss
Gus
  esophagus (i)
  sarcophagus (i)
(lus)
  angelus (i)
  cumulus (i)
  nautilus (i)
  ranunculus (i)

stimulus (*i*)
Tantalus (*i*)
muss
　animus (*i*)
　hippopotamus (*i*)
(nus)
　terminus (*i*)
plus
pus
　octopus (*i*)
　platypus (*i*)
Russ
　humerus (*i*)
　phosphorous (*i*)
(sus)
　Pegasus (*i*)
thus
truss

(brus)
　tenebrous
(crus)
　ludicrous
(dus)
　hazardous
(lus)
　acidulous (*i*)
　anomalous (*i*)
　bibulous (*i*)
　crapulous (*i*)
　credulous (*i*)
　　incredulous (*i*)
　fabulous (*i*)
　frivolous (*i*)
　garrulous (*i*)
　libelous (*i*)
　marvelous (*i*)
　meticulous (*i*)
　miraculous (*i*)
　nebulous (*i*)
　pendulous (*i*)
　perilous (*i*)
　populous (*i*)
　querulous (*i*)
　scandalous (*i*)
　scrofulous (*i*)

scrupulous (*i*)
　unscrupulous (*i*)
scurrilous (*i*)
sedulous (*i*)
tintinnabulous (*i*)
tremulous (*i*)
tuberculous (*i*)
undulous (*i*)
(mus)
　anonymous (*i*)
　bigamous (*i*)
　blasphemous
　diatomous (*i*)
　famous (*i*)
　　infamous (*i*)
　magnanimous (*i*)
　monogamous (*i*)
　polygamous (*i*)
　posthumous (*i*)
　pseudonymous (*i*)
　synonymous (*i*)
　unanimous (*i*)
　venomous (*i*)
(nus)
　androgenous (*i*)
　bituminous (*i*)
　cavernous (*i*)
　diaphanous (*i*)
　fortitudinous (*i*)
　gelatinous (*i*)
　glutinous (*i*)
　gluttonous (*i*)
　indigenous (*i*)
　libidinous (*i*)
　luminous (*i*)
　monotonous (*i*)
　mountainous (*i*)
　multitudinous (*i*)
　mutinous (*i*)
　ominous (*i*)
　platitudinous (*i*)
　poisonous (*i*)
　ravenous (*i*)
　ruinous (*i*)
　synchronous (*i*)
　treasonous (*i*)

tyrannous (*i*)
verminous (*i*)
villainous (*i*)
voluminous (*i*)
(rus)
adulterous (*i*)
adventurous (*i*)
amorous (*i*)
arborous (*i*)
barbarous (*i*)
blusterous (*i*)
boisterous (*i*)
cancerous (*i*)
cankerous (*i*)
cantankerous (*i*)
carboniferous (*i*)
carnivorous (*i*)
chivalrous (*i*)
　unchivalrous (*i*)
clamorous (*i*)
dangerous (*i*)
decorous
　indecorous
dexterous (*i*)
doloriferous (*i*)
dolorous (*i*)
generous
　ungenerous (*i*)
languorous (*i*)
lecherous (*i*)
murderous (*i*)
numerous (*i*)
obstreperous (*i*)
odoriferous (*i*)
odorous (*i*)
　malodorous (*i*)
omnivorous (*i*)
onerous (*i*)
oviparous (*i*)
perjurous (*i*)
pestiferous (*i*)
ponderous (*i*)
preposterous (*i*)
prosperous (*i*)
rancorous (*i*)
rapturous (*i*)

rigorous (*i*)
roisterous (*i*)
savorous (*i*)
slanderous (*i*)
slumberous (*i*)
somniferous (*i*)
sulphurous (*i*)
thunderous (*i*)
timorous (*i*)
torturous (*i*)
traitorous (*i*)
treacherous (*i*)
valorous (*i*)
vaporous (*i*)
venturous (*i*)
vigorous (*i*)
viperous (*i*)
viviparous (*i*)
vociferous (*i*)
vulturous (*i*)
truss
  idolatrous (*i*)
(tuss)
  calamitous (*i*)
  circuitous (*i*)
  covetous (*i*)
  fortuitous (*i*)
  felicitous
    infelicitous (*i*)
  gratuitous
  iniquitous (*i*)
  necessitous (*i*)
  precipitous (*i*)
  riotous (*i*)
  solicitous (*i*)
  ubiquitous (*i*)
(wus)
  ambiguous (*i*)
  arduous (*i*)
  assiduous (*i*)
  congruous (*i*)
    incongruous (*i*)
  conspicuous (*i*)
    inconspicuous (*i*)
  contemptuous (*i*)
  contiguous (*i*)

continuous (*i*)
deciduous
fatuous (*i*)
impetuous (*i*)
incestuous (*i*)
ingenuous (*i*)
  disingenuous (*i*)
innocuous (*i*)
mellifluous (*i*)
presumptuous (*i*)
promiscuous (*i*)
sensuous (*i*)
  insensuous
sinuous (*i*)
strenuous (*i*)
sumptuous (*i*)
superfluous (*i*)
tempestuous (*i*)
tenuous (*i*)
tortuous (*i*)
tumultuous (*i*)
vacuous (*i*)
virtuous (*i*)
voluptuous (*i*)
(yus)
abstemious (*i*)
amphibious (*i*)
aqueous (*i*)
beauteous (*i*)
bounteous (*i*)
calumnious (*i*)
censorious (*i*)
ceremonious (*i*)
commodious (*i*)
compendious (*i*)
contemporaneous (*i*)
copious (*i*)
courteous (*i*)
  discourteous (*i*)
curious (*i*)
deleterious (*i*)
delirious (*i*)
devious (*i*)
dubious (*i*)
duteous (*i*)
envious (*i*)

erroneous (*i*)
extemporaneous (*i*)
extraneous (*i*)
fastidious (*i*)
felonious (*i*)
furious (*i*)
glorious (*i*)
  inglorious (*i*)
  vainglorious (*i*)
gregarious (*i*)
harmonious (*i*)
  inharmonious (*i*)
heterogeneous
hideous
hilarious
homogeneous
igneous (*i*)
ignominious (*i*)
illustrious (*i*)
impecunious (*i*)
imperious (*i*)
impervious (*i*)
impious (*i*)
industrious (*i*)
ingenious (*i*)
injurious (*i*)
inquisitorious (*i*)
insidious (*i*)
instantaneous (*i*)
invidious (*i*)
laborious (*i*)
lascivious (*i*)
ligneous (*i*)
lugubrious (*i*)
luxurious (*i*)
melodious (*i*)
meritorious (*i*)
miscellaneous (*i*)
multifarious (*i*)
mysterious (*i*)
nauseous (*i*)
nefarious (*i*)
notorious (*i*)
oblivious (*i*)
obsequious (*i*)
odious (*i*)

opprobrious (*i*)
parsimonious (*i*)
penurious (*i*)
perfidious (*i*)
piteous (*i*)
plenteous (*i*)
precarious (*i*)
punctilious (*i*)
rebellious (*i*)
sanctimonious (*i*)
serious (*i*)
simultaneous (*i*)
spontaneous (*i*)
spurious (*i*)
stentorious (*i*)
studious (*i*)
subterraneous (*i*)
supercilious (*i*)
tedious
uproarious (*i*)
usurious (*i*)
various (*i*)
vicarious (*i*)
victorious (*i*)
vitreous (*i*)

USH (OOSH)
bouche (*French*)
   debouch
douche
(koosh)
   Hindu Kush
mouche
(toosh)
   cartouche

USH (OOSH)
bush
   bramblebush, etc.
push

USH
blush
brush
   underbrush (*i*)
crush

flush
gush
hush
lush
mush
plush
rush
slush
thrush

USK
brusque
busk
dusk
husk
musk
rusk
tusk

UST (OOST)
boost
joust
roost
(loosed, etc.)

UST
bust
   robust
crust
   encrust
gust
   august (*a*)
   disgust
just
   adjust
   unjust
lust
must
rust
thrust
trust
   distrust
   entrust
   mistrust
(bussed, etc.)

UT (YUTE)
*This group of words
rhymes correctly with
the one immediately
following it.*
Ute
beaut
butte
   attribute (*n*)
cute
   acute
   electrocute
   execute
   persecute
   prosecute
(fute)
   confute
   refute
lute
   absolute
   dilute
   dissolute
   pollute
   resolute
mute
   commute
   permute
   transmute
newt
   minute (*a*)
(pute)
   compute
   depute
   dispute
   repute
      disrepute
suit
   hirsute
   pursuit
(tute)
   astute
   constitute (*i*)
   destitute (*i*)
   prostitute (*i*)
   substitute (*i*)

UT (OOT)
boot
brute
coot
(croot)
  recruit
flute
fruit
hoot
loot
  galoot
moot
root
  arrowroot
  cheroot
  uproot
route
  en route
  reroute
scoot
shoot
  overshoot
chute
  parachute (i)
snoot
toot

UT
but
  abut
  halibut
butt
  scuttlebutt
cut
  uncut
glut
gut
hut
jut
mutt
nut
  coconut (i), etc.
putt
  Lilliput
rut
scut

shut
slut
smut
  besmut
strut
tut
  King Tut

UTH (OOTHE)
smooth
soothe

UTH (OOTH)
booth
couth
  uncouth
(looth)
  Duluth
ruth
sleuth
sooth
  forsooth
tooth
truth
  untruth
youth

UTS (OOTS)
hoots
  cahoots
(boots, etc.)

UV (OOV)
groove
(hoove)
  behoove
move
  remove
prove
  approve
    disapprove
  disprove
  improve
  reprove

UV
Basically, there are five rhymes in this group. Of will work, but it is not quite correct.
(buv)
  above
dove
  mourning dove
  ring dove (i)
  rock dove (i)
  stock dove (i)
  turtle dove (i)
  wood dove (i)
glove
  boxing glove
  kid glove (i), etc.
love
  lady love
  true love, etc.
shove
(*also: of*)

UZ (YOOZ)
This group of words rhymes correctly with the one immediately following it.
use (v)
  abuse (v)
    disabuse (v)
  misuse (v)
  peruse
cues
  accuse
  excuse
fuse
  confuse
  diffuse (v)
  effuse (v)
  infuse
  perfuse
  refuse (v)

UZ (OOZ)
ooze
blues
booze
bruise
choose
cruise
   Santa Cruz
   Vera Cruz
lose
ruse
snooze
whose
(chews, etc.)

UZ
buzz
   abuzz
coz
does
fuzz
was

*The -er endings, which function in English to designate professions and practices and to express the comparative— *worker* and *skier; bigger* and *fuller*—can be attached to countless verbs, adjectives and adverbs. But since the stress is never on the final syllable, none of these words works as a masculine rhyme.

Feminine
Rhymes

A

A-ans
(beyance)
  abeyance
(veyance)
  conveyance
  purveyance

A-ber
(see **A-bur,** *page 145)*

A-bi
baby
maybe

AB-i
abbey
cabby
crabby
flabby
grabby
scabby
shabby
tabby

AB-id
rabid
tabid

AB-ing
blabbing
cabbing
  taxicabbing
crabbing
dabbing
gabbing
grabbing
jabbing
nabbing
stabbing
tabbing

AB-it
habit
  cohabit
  inhabit
  riding habit
rabbit
(grab it, etc.)

A-bl
Abel
able
  disable
  enable
  unable
cable
fable
gable
label
sable
stable
  unstable
table

AB-l
babble
dabble
gabble
rabble
scrabble

AB-ling
babbling
dabbling
gabbling

AB-lur
babbler
dabbler
gabbler

AB-ot
abbot

Cabot
(habit, etc.)

A-bur
caber
labor
  belabor
neighbor
saber

AB-ur
blabber
grabber
jabber
(grab 'er, etc.)

AB-urd
blabbered
jabbered
scabbard
tabard

ACH-et
hatchet
latchet
ratchet
(catch it, etc.)

ACH-ez
batches
catches
hatches
latches
  unlatches
matches
Natchez
patches
  dispatches
scratches
snatches
(tatches)
  attaches

detaches
thatches

ACH-i
catchy
patchy
Apache
scratchy

ACH-ing
batching
catching
hatching
latching
unlatching
matching
patching
dispatching
scratching
snatching
(taching)
attaching
detaching

ACH-less
matchless
patchless
scratchless
thatchless

ACH-ment
catchment
(tachment)
attachment
detachment

ACH-ur
catcher
hatcher
matcher
patcher
dispatcher
scratcher
back scratcher (i)
body snatcher (i)
(tacher)

attacher
detacher
thatcher

ACH-wurk
catchwork
patchwork

A-dai
gay day
gray day
heyday
Mayday
payday
play day

AD-a (OD-a)
dada
da-da
(mada)
armada
nada (*Spanish*)
Granada
(vada)
Nevada
Sierra Nevada

AD-am
Adam
MacAdam
madam
(had 'em, etc.)

A-ded
aided
unaided
braided
abraded
upbraded
(caded)
barricaded
blockaded
brocaded
faded
unfaded
graded

degraded
jaded
(naded)
cannonaded
serenaded
raided
masqueraded
paraded
(saded)
crusaded
(scaded)
ambuscaded
cascaded
shaded
unshaded
(suaded)
dissuaded
persuaded
waded
(vaded)
evaded
invaded
pervaded

AD-ed
added
gadded
padded
plaided

A-den
Aden
laden
heavy-laden
overladen
unladen
maiden

Ad-en
gladden
madden
sadden

AD-est
"baddest"
gladdest

maddest
saddest

A-di
glady
lady
shady

AD-i
baddy
caddy
daddy
  sugar daddy
(haddy)
  finnan haddie
laddie
paddy

AD-ik
(gadic)
  haggadic
(madic)
  nomadic
(nadic)
  monadic
(radic)
  sporadic
(yadic)
  triadic

A-din
fade-in
(wade in, etc.)

A-ding
aiding
braiding
  abrading
  upbraiding
(cading)
  ambuscading
  barricading
  blockading
  cascading
fading
  unfading

grading
  degrading
lading
(nading)
  cannonading
  serenading
raiding
  masquerading
  parading
(sading)
  crusading
shading
spading
(suading)
  dissuading
  persuading
trading
(vading)
  evading
  invading
  pervading
wading

AD-ing
adding
gadding
madding
padding

AD-ish
baddish
caddish
faddish
gladdish
radish
saddish

A-dl
cradle
ladle
(maid'll etc.)

AD-l
addle
(daddle)
  skedaddle

faddle
  fiddle-faddle
paddle
saddle
  unsaddle
straddle
  astraddle
  bestraddle
(dad'll etc.)

A-dless
bladeless
braidless
fadeless
gradeless
maidless
shadeless
tradeless

A-dli
gradely
  retrogradely
staidly

AD-li
badly
gladly
madly
sadly

A-dling
cradling
ladling

AD-ling
addling
(daddling)
  skedaddling
paddling
saddling
  unsaddling
spraddling
straddling

AD-lur
addler

AD-lur

(daddler)
  skedaddler
paddler
saddler
straddler

AD-ness
badness
gladness
madness
sadness

A-do
dado
(nado)
  bastinado
  tornado
(pado)
  strappado
  play dough
(rado)
  desperado
  Laredo

AD-o
shadow
  foreshadow
  overshadow

AD-o (OD-o)
(cado)
  avocado
  Mikado
(pado)
  strappado
(rado)
  Colorado
  desperado
  El Dorado
(vado)
  bravado
(yado)
  amontillado

AD-ok
haddock

paddock

AD-pol
tadpole
(sad Pole, etc.)

AD-sum
gladsome
madsome
(had some)

A-dur
aider
braider
  abrader
  upbraider
nadir
  serenader
raider
  parader
Seder (*Hebrew*)
  crusader
(suader)
  persuader
trader
(vader)
  evader
  invader
wader

AD-ur
adder
bladder
gladder
ladder
madder
padder
sadder

A-est
gayest
grayest

A-fair
Mayfair
Playfair

wayfare

AF-i
daffy
taffy

AF-ik
graphic
graphic *and its compounds have three rhymes,* Sapphic, seraphic, *and* traffic. *The rest are identities.*

  autobiographic
  biographic
  cartographic
  choreographic
  cinematographic
  lexicographic
  monographic
  photographic
  pornographic
  telegraphic
  topographic, etc.
(raffic)
  seraphic
Sapphic
traffic

AF-ing
chaffing
graphing
  lithographing, etc.
laughing
strafing

AF-1
baffle
raffle
snaffle

AF-ling
baffling
raffling
snaffling

AF-old
scaffold
(baffled, etc.)

AF-ted
drafted
grafted
rafted
shafted
wafted

AF-ti
crafty
drafty

AF-ting
drafting
grafting
rafting
shafting

AFT-less
craftless
draftless
raftless
shaftless

AFTS-man
craftsman
    handicraftsman
draftsman
raftsman

AF-tur
after
grafter
laughter
rafter
    hereafter
    thereafter

A-ful
playful
trayful

A-fur
safer
wafer

AF-ur
chaffer
gaffer
laugher

AG-a
(baga)
    rutabaga
saga

A-gan
Fagin
pagan
ray gun
Ronald Reagan

AG-ard
haggard
laggard
staggard
staggered
swaggered

AG-at (AG-ut)
agate
faggot
maggot
(flag it, etc.)

AG-ed
jagged
ragged

AG-i
aggie
baggy
craggy
draggy
faggy
gaggy
laggy
raggy

saggy
scraggy
shaggy
slaggy
snaggy
swaggy
waggy

AG-ing
bagging
bragging
dragging
fagging
flagging
    unflagging
gagging
lagging
nagging
ragging
sagging
scragging
shagging
tagging
wagging

AG-l
draggle
    bedraggle
gaggle
haggle
straggle
waggle

AG-ling
draggling
    bedraggling
gaggling
haggling
straggling
waggling

AG-lur
draggler
    bedraggler
haggler
straggler

waggler

AG-man
bagman
dragman
flagman
gagman
ragman

AG-nat (AG-nait)
magnate
stagnate

A-go
(bago)
  lumbago
(rago)
  farrago
(yago)
  Diego
  San Diego
(day go, etc.)

AG-o (OG-o)
(cago)
  Chicago
Iago
  Santiago

AG-on
dragon
flagon
wagon
(braggin', etc.)

AG-ot
agate
faggot
maggot

AG-rans
flagrance
fragrance
vagrants

AG-rant
flagrant
fragrant
vagrant

AG-ur
bagger
  carpetbagger (i)
  three-bagger
  two-bagger
bragger
dagger
dragger
flagger
stagger
swagger
wagger

AH-hoo
wahoo
Yahoo
(saw who)

A-ik
(braic)
  algebraic
  Hebraic
(caic)
  archaic
  trochaic
(daic)
  Judaic
(maic)
  Aramaic
  Ptolemaic
(saic)
  Passaic
  Pharisaic

A-ing
baying
  obeying
    disobeying
braying
(caying)
  decaying

flaying
fraying
  defraying
graying
haying
laying
  allaying
  belaying
  delaying
  inlaying
  mislaying
  relaying
  waylaying
(maying)
  dismaying
naying
neighing
paying
  overpaying
  prepaying
  repaying
  unpaying
playing
  displaying
  overplaying
  underplaying
praying
preying
raying
  arraying
  hurraying
saying
  assaying
  essaying
  gainsaying (i)
  soothsaying (i)
slaying
spraying
staying
  outstaying
  overstaying
straying
swaying
(traying)
  betraying
  portraying

(veying)
  conveying
  inveighing
  purveying
  surveying
weighing
  outweighing

A-ing (AH-ing)
awing
(see **O-ing,** *page 259)*

A-ish
clayish
gayish
grayish

A-jez
ages
cages
gages
  engages
    disengages
gauges
pages
rages
  enrages
  outrages
sages
  presages (*i*)
stages
wages
  assuages

A-ji
cagey
stagey

AJ-ik
(lagic)
  pelagic
magic
tragic

AJ-il
agile

fragile

A-jing
aging
caging
gaging
  engaging
gauging
paging
raging
  enraging
staging
waging
  assuaging

AJ-ing
badging
cadging

AJ-less (AIJ-less)
cageless
pageless
rageless
sageless
stageless
wageless

A-jment (AIJ-ment)
(cagement)
  encagement
(gagement)
  engagement

A-jur
cager
major
  sergeant major
pager
sager
stager
wager
  assuager

AJ-ur
badger
cadger

A-jus
(pageous)
  rampageous
(rageous)
  courageous
  outrageous
(tageous)
  advantageous
    disadvantageous
  contagious

AK-a
(laca)
  Malacca
(paca)
  alpaca

A-kdown (AIK-down)
breakdown
shakedown

A-ken
bacon
kraken
makin'
  Jamaican
(saken)
  forsaken
shaken
  unshaken
taken
  mistaken
  overtaken
  partaken
  undertaken
waken
  awaken
(achin' etc.)

AK-en
blacken
bracken
slacken
(crackin' etc.)

AK-est
blackest
slackest

AK-et
bracket
jacket
packet
racket
(crack it, etc.)

A-ki
achey
caky
fakey
flaky
quaky
shaky
snaky

AK-i
(cracky)
  by cracky
lackey
tacky

AK-ij
package
trackage

A-king
aching
baking
braking
breaking
  heartbreaking (i)
caking
faking
flaking
making
  remaking (i)
  unmaking
quaking
raking
(saking)
  forsaking

shaking
slaking
staking
  mistaking
taking
  overtaking
  partaking
  undertaking
waking
  awaking

AK-ing
backing
blacking
clacking
cracking
hacking
lacking
packing
  repacking
  unpacking
quacking
racking
sacking
  ransacking
shacking
slacking
smacking
tacking
  attacking
tracking
whacking
  bivouacking (i)

AK-ish
blackish
brackish

AK-l
cackle
crackle
grackle
hackle
shackle
  ramshackle
tackle

AK-ling
cackling
crackling
shackling
tackling

AK-log
backlog

AK-lur
cackler
crackler
shackler
tackler

AK-man
black man
jackman
packman

AK-ness
blackness
slackness

AK-ni
acne
hackney

A-koff
break off
make off
rake-off
takeoff

A-kon
bacon
Macon
(takin', etc.)
(see A-ken, page 151)

AK-out
blackout
(back out, etc.)

AK-pot
crackpot
jackpot

AK-ron
Akron
Dacron

AK-rum
(lacrum)
  simulacrum
sacrum

AK-sez
axes
  battle-axes (*i*)
(laxes)
  relaxes
taxes
waxes

AK-shun
action
  counteraction
  inaction
  interaction
  reaction
  retroaction
  transaction
(daction)
  redaction
faction
  benefaction
  dissatisfaction
  lubrifaction
  malefaction
  putrefaction
  rarefaction
  satisfaction
  stupefaction
fraction
  infraction
  refraction
(straction)
  abstraction
  distraction
  extraction
(straction)

traction
  attraction
  contraction
  detraction
  protraction
  retraction
  subtraction

AK-shus
factious
fractious

AKS-ing
axing
(laxing)
  relaxing
taxing
waxing

AKS-man
cracksman
sax man
tax man
(relax, man)

AK-son
flaxen
Jackson, Andrew
klaxon
Saxon
  Anglo-Saxon
(taxin', etc.)

AK-ted
acted
  counteracted
  enacted
  exacted
  overacted
  reacted
  transacted
  underacted
(fracted)
  refracted
(pacted)
  compacted

impacted
(stracted)
  distracted
  extracted
(tracted)
  attracted
  contracted
  detracted
  protracted
  subtracted

AK-tik
(dactic)
  didactic
lactic
  galactic
  parallactic
  prophylactic
tactic

AK-til
dactyl
  pterodactyl
tactile
tractile
  retractile

AK-ting
acting
  counteracting
  enacting
  overacting
  reacting
  underacting
(fracting)
  refracting
(stracting)
  abstracting
  distracting
(tracting)
  attracting
  contracting
  detracting
  protracting
  retracting
  subtracting

(zacting)
  exacting
  transacting

AK-tiv
active
  counteractive
  enactive
  inactive
  overactive
  radioactive
  reactive
  retroactive
  underactive
(fractive)
  refractive
(stractive)
  distractive
  extractive
tractive
  attractive
  contractive
  detractive
  protractive
  subtractive

AKT-less
actless
factless
tactless
tractless

AKT-li
(factly)
  matter-of-factly
(pactly)
  compactly
(zactly)
  exactly

AKT-ness
(pactness)
  compactness
(tactness)
  intactness
(zactness)

  exactness

AK-tress
actress
(factress)
  benefactress

AK-tur (AK-chur)
(facture)
  manufacture
fracture

AK-tur
actor
factor
  benefactor
  malefactor
(fractor)
  refractor
(stracter)
  distracter
  extractor
tractor
  contractor
  detractor
  subtracter
(yacter)
  reactor
(zacter)
  exacter
  transactor

A-kup
breakup
make-up
rake up
shake-up
take up
wake up

AK-up
backup
crack-up
jack up
pack up
rack up

shack up
smack-up
stack up
tack up

A-kur
acre
baker
breaker
  heartbreaker
  strikebreaker, etc.
faker
maker
  dressmaker (i)
  matchmaker (i)
  mischief-maker (i)
  pacemaker (i)
  peacemaker (i)
  troublemaker
  watchmaker (i), etc.
nacre
Quaker
shaker
taker
  partaker
  undertaker

AK-ur
backer
blacker
cracker
  nutcracker
(jacker)
  hijacker (i)
knacker
packer
sacker
  ransacker
slacker
smacker
tacker
  attacker
tracker

A-kurz
breakers
(bakers, etc.)

AL-ad (AL-ud)
ballad
pallid
salad
valid
  invalid (a)

AL-ans
balance
valance

A-lant
(halant)
  inhalant
(sailant)
  assailant

AL-as
Alice
chalice
Dallas
malice
palace
phallus

A-lburd (AIL-burd)
jailbird
railbird

A-lee
(see **A-li**, page 155)

AL-ent
gallant
  topgallant
  ungallant
talent

AL-et
mallet
palate
palette
valet

A-lful (AIL-ful)
baleful

pailful

A-li
Bailey
  Old Bailey
daily
gaily
grayly
(laily)
  shillelagh
  ukulele
(zraily)
  Israeli
  Benjamin Disraeli

Al-i
alley
bally (*English*)
dally
Cali
Kali
pally
rally
sally
shally
  shilly-shally
tally
valley

AL-i (OL-lee)
brolly (*English*)
collie
  melancholy
crawly
dolly
folly
golly
holly
jolly
Kali
lolly
  loblolly (i)
Molly
  tamale
(nolly)
  finale

Polly
scrawly
sprawly
squally
trolley
volley

A-lif
bailiff
Caliph
(sail if, etc.)

AL-ik
Gallic
phallic
  cephalic
    brachycephalic
    encephalic
    macrocephalic
salic
  oxalic
(talic)
  italic
  metallic
    bimetallic
    nonmetallic

A-ling
ailing
bailing
baling
galing
  regaling
grayling
hailing
haling
  exhaling
  inhaling
jailing
mailing
  blackmailing
nailing
paling
  empaling
  impaling
quailing

railing
  derailing
sailing
  assailing
  outsailing
  wholesaling
scaling
tailing
  curtailing
  detailing
  entailing
  retailing
trailing
veiling
  availing
    unavailing
  countervailing
  prevailing
  unveiling
wailing
  bewailing
whaling

AL-is
chalice
(see **AL-as,** *page 155)*

AL-jik
(ralgic)
  neuralgic
(stalgic)
  nostalgic

A-lkar (AIL-kar)
mail car
railcar

A-lment (AIL-ment)
ailment
(galement)
  regalement
(palement)
  empalement
  impalement
(tailment)
  curtailment

detailment
entailment

A-lness (AIL-ness)
frailness
haleness
paleness
staleness

A-lo
halo
(stay low, etc.)

AL-o
aloe
callow
fallow
hallow
mallow
  marshmallow
shallow
tallow

AL-o (AH-lo)
follow
hollow
(pollo)
  Apollo
  São Paulo
swallow
wallow

AL-on
gallon
talon

AL-op
gallop
scallop

AL-ot
ballot
shallot *(i)*

AL-oz
gallows

(hallows, etc.)

AL-to
alto
  contralto
  Palo Alto
(yalto)
  rialto

A-lur
frailer
haler
  inhaler
jailer
mailer
nailer
paler
  impaler
sailor
staler
tailor
  retailer *(i)*
trailer
wailer
whaler

AL-ur
pallor
valor

A-lya (AIL-yuh)
dahlia
(galia)
  regalia
(nalia)
  Bacchanalia
  paraphernalia
  Saturnalia
Thalia
(zalia)
  azalea

A-lyan (AIL-yun)
alien
(malian)
  mammalian

(nalian)
  Bacchanalian
  Saturnalian
(palian)
  Episcopalian
(stralian)
  Australian

AL-yun
(dallion)
  medallion
scallion
  rapscallion
stallion
(talion)
  battalion
  Italian

AM-a
'Bama
  Alabama
drama

AM-a (OM-a)
Brahma
comma
drama
  melodrama
(hama)
  Bahama
  Yokahama
(jama)
  pajama
lama
  Dalai Lama
llama
mamma
Rama
  cyclorama
  diorama
  panorama
(yama)
  Fujiyama

A-man
cayman

dayman
layman
stamen

AM-bit
ambit
damn bit
gambit

AM-bl
amble
bramble
gamble
gambol
ramble
scramble
shamble
(yamble)
  preamble

AM-bling
ambling
gambling
rambling
scrambling
shambling

AM-blur
ambler
gambler
rambler
scrambler
shambler

AM-bur
amber
clamber
timbre

AM-el
camel
mammal
(namel)
  enamel
trammel

AM-eld
(nameld)
  enameled
trammelled
  untrammelled

A-men (AI-men)
amen
Bremen
daymen
draymen
laymen
stamen

A-ment (AI-ment)
claimant
(layment)
  allayment
payment
raiment
(they meant, etc.)

A-mful (AIM-ful)
blameful
shameful

A-mi
gamy
(pay me, etc.)

AM-i (AM-ee)
ami (i) *French*
  bon ami (i) *French*
  mon ami (i) *French*
chamois
clammy
hammy
mammy
shammy
tammy
whammy
(yammy)
  Miami

AM-i (OM-i)
ah me

balmy
(lami)
　salami
(strommy)
　pastrami
swami
Tommy

AM-ik
(namic)
　dynamic
　　electrodynamic
　　hydrodynamic,
　　　etc.
(ramic)
　ceramic
　cycloramic
　panoramic
(zlamic)
　Islamic

AM-in
famine
gamin
(zamine)
　examine
(*see* **AM-on,**
　page 158)

A-ming
aiming
blaming
claiming
　acclaiming
　declaiming
　disclaiming
　exclaiming
　proclaiming
　reclaiming
(faming)
　defaming
flaming
　inflaming
framing
gaming
laming

maiming
naming
　misnaming
　nicknaming (*i*)
　renaming
shaming
taming

AM-ing
cramming
damming
damning
hamming
jamming
lamming
ramming
scramming
shamming
slamming

AM-ing (OM-ing)
balming
　embalming
bombing
calming
　becalming
(lomming)
　salaaming
palming

AM-ist
palmist
psalmist

A-mless (AIM-less)
aimless
blameless
claimless
fameless
flameless
frameless
gameless
nameless
shameless
tameless

A-mli (AIM-li)
gamely
lamely
namely
tamely

A-mness (AIM-ness)
lameness
sameness
tameness

AM-on
gammon
　backgammon
Mammon
salmon
shaman
(crammin', etc.)

AM-part
rampart
(am part, etc.)

AMP-ing
camping
　decamping
　encamping
clamping
cramping
damping
stamping
tramping
vamping

AMP-l
ample
sample
trample
(zample)
　example

AMP-ling
sampling
trampling

AMP-lur
ampler
sampler
trampler

AM-pur
camper
cramper
damper
hamper
pamper
scamper
stamper
tamper
tramper

AMP-us
campus
cramp us
grampus
stamp us

A-mur
blamer
claimer
  acclaimer
  declaimer
  disclaimer
  exclaimer
  proclaimer
  reclaimer
femur
  defamer
flamer
  inflamer
framer
lamer
maimer
namer
tamer

AM-ur
clamor
crammer
dammer
damner

glamor
grammar
hammer
  sledgehammer (*i*)
  yellowhammer (*i*),
  etc.
rammer
shammer
slammer
stammer
yammer

AM-ur (OM-ur)
(balmer)
  embalmer
bomber
calmer
palmer

A-mus
(damus)
  mandamus
famous
ramus
  ignoramus
squamous
(shame us, etc.)

AN-a
(bana)
  Urbana
(cana)
  Americana
  arcana
    Texarkana
(dana)
  bandanna
Hannah
  Susquehanna
manna
  vox humana
Nana
  banana
(vana)
  Havana
  Nirvana

savanna
Savannah
(yana)
  Diana
    Indiana
  Guiana
  liana
  Louisiana
  poinciana
  Pollyanna
(zana)
  hosanna
(*U.S. southern:
  scanner, etc.*)

AN-a (AH-nuh)
(cana)
  Americana
(vana)
  Nirvana
(yana)
  liana
(*U.S. southern: honor.
  corner, etc.*)

AN-al
annal
channel
flannel
panel
  empanel
  impanel

AN-alz
annals
(flannels, etc.)

AN-chez (ON-chez)
haunches
launches
paunches
staunches

AN-chez
blanches
branches

(lanches)
  avalanches
ranches

AN-chi (ON-chee)
paunchy
raunchy

AN-ching (ON-ching)
launching
staunching

AN-ching
blanching
branching
ranching

AN-da (AN-duh)
(ganda)
  propaganda
  Uganda
panda
(randa)
  jacaranda
  memoranda
  veranda
(*U.S. southern:*
  candor, etc.)

AND-bag
handbag
sandbag

AND-bal
grand ball
handball
sand ball

AND-boks
bandbox
sandbox

AND-ed
banded
  disbanded
handed

backhanded
cleanhanded
emptyhanded
evenhanded
high-handed
left-handed
one-handed
openhanded
red-handed
right-handed
shorthanded
single-handed
two-handed
underhanded
unhanded, etc.
landed
(manded)
  commanded
  countermanded
  demanded
  remanded
  reprimanded
sanded
(spanded)
  expanded
stranded

AN-dest
blandest
grandest

AN-di
Andy
  handy Andy
bandy
brandy
candy
  rock candy (*i*)
  sugar candy, etc.
dandy
  jack-a-dandy
  Jim Dandy
grandee
  Rio Grande
handy
randy

sandy
shandy

AN-did (AN-deed)
brandied
candied

AND-ing
banding
  disbanding
branding
handing
  unhanding
landing
(manding)
  commanding
  countermanding
  demanding
  remanding
  reprimanding
sanding
standing
  outstanding
  understanding
  withstanding
    notwithstanding

A-ndir (AIN-deer)
reindeer
(explain, dear, etc.)

AND-ish
blandish
brandish
grandish
(landish)
  outlandish
Standish, Miles

AND-ist
(bandist)
  contrabandist
(gandist)
  propagandist

AND-it
bandit
(command it,
fanned it, etc.)

AN-diz (AN-dees)
Andes
(brandies, etc.)

AND-l
candle
dandle
handle
sandal
scandal
vandal
(band'll, etc.)

AND-less
bandless
brandless
glandless
handless
landless
sandless

AND-li
blandly
grandly

AND-lord
landlord
(grand lord, command,
Lord, etc.)

AND-lur
chandler
dandler
handler

AND-maid
handmade
handmaid
(demand made, etc.)

AND-mark
brand mark
hand mark
landmark

AND-ment
(bandment)
  disbandment
(mandment)
  commandment

AND-ness
blandness
grandness

AND-o
(lando)
  Orlando
  parlando
(mando)
  commando
(nando)
  Fernando
    San Fernando

AND-ril
band drill
hand drill
mandril

AND-stand
bandstand
grandstand
handstand

AND-um
random
  memorandum
tandem
(land 'em, etc.)

AND-ur
blander
brander
candor
  Afrikander

dander
gander
  Goosey Gander
  Michigander
Gander
grander
hander
  left-hander
  right-hander
lander
  moon lander
  philander
(mander)
  commander
  gerrymander
  remander
  reprimander
  salamander
(nander)
  Menander
pander
slander
(spander)
  expander
stander
(yander)
  coriander
  Leander
  meander
  oleander

AND-ur (ON-dur)
launder
maunder
wander
  *(see **ON-dur**, page 26)*

AND-urd
standard
(pandered, etc.)

ANDZ-man
bandsman
landsman

168

A-ness
gayness
grayness
heinous

A-nest
(banest)
 urbanest
(manest)
 humanest
(nanest)
 inanest
plainest
sanest
 insanest
vainest

AN-et
gannet
granite
 pomegranate
Janet
planet
(fan it, etc.)

A-nful (AIN-ful)
baneful
(dainful)
 disdainful
gainful
painful

A-ngang (AIN-gang)
chain gang
train gang
(cocaine gang, etc.)

ANG-gl
angle
 triangle
bangle
dangle
(drangle)
 quadrangle
jangle
mangle

spangle
 bespangle
strangle
tangle
 entangle
  disentangle
 untangle
wrangle

ANG-gld
fangled
 newfangled
jangled
(dangled, etc.)

ANG-gling
angling
(dangling, etc.)

ANG-glur
angler
(dangler, etc.)

ANG-go
(dango)
 fandango
mango
tango

ANG-gur
anger
clangor
languor

ANG-gwish
anguish
languish

ANG-i
bangy
clangy
slangy
tangy

ANG-ing
banging

clanging
ganging
hanging
 overhanging
 paperhanging (i)
(ranging)
 haranguing
twanging

ANG-kest
blankest
dankest
frankest
rankest

ANG-ket
blanket
(bank it, etc.)

ANGK-ful
tankfull
thankful

ANG-ki
cranky
hanky
lanky
(panky)
 hanky-panky
Yankee

ANG-king
banking
clanking
flanking
 outflanking
franking
planking
ranking
 outranking
spanking
thanking
yanking

ANG-kl
ankle

169

rankle

ANG-kles
bankless
prankless
rankless
thankless

ANG-kli
blankly
dankly
frankly

ANGK-ness
blankness
dankness
frankness
lankness
rankness

ANG-kur
anchor
banker
canker
clanker
danker
flanker
franker
hanker
rancor
ranker
spanker
tanker
thanker

ANG-kurd
anchored
tankard

ANG-ur
banger
clangor
(ganger)
    doppelgänger
hangar
hanger

cliff-hanger
coat hanger
paperhanger
straphanger, etc.
(ranger)
    haranguer
(rang'er, etc.)

A-ni
brainy
(gainy)
    Allegheny
grainy
rainy
veiny
zany

AN-i (EN-i)
any
(see **EN-i,** *page 209)*

AN-i
Annie, Little Orphan
canny
    uncanny
cranny
fanny
granny
nanny
(panny)
    frangipani
(stanny)
    Hindustani

AN-ik
(canic)
    mechanic
    volcanic
(ganic)
    organic
(lanic)
    Magellanic
manic
    aldermanic
    Germanic
    monomanic

Romanic
panic
(spanic)
    Hispanic
tannic
    Britannic
    satanic
    sultanic
    titanic
(vanic)
    galvanic
(yanic)
    Messianic
    oceanic
        interoceanic

A-ning
braining
caning
chaining
    enchaning
    unchaning
craning
deigning
    disdaining
    ordaining
        foreordaining
        preordaining
feigning
    profaning
    unfeigning
(fraining)
    refraining
gaining
    regaining
(maining)
    remaining
paining
    campaigning
planing
    complaining
        uncomplaining
    explaining
    hyroplaning
raining
reigning

reining
spraining
staining
  abstaining
  bestaining
  restaining
  substaining
straining
  constraining
  restraining
(taining)
  appertaining
  ascertaining
  attaining
  containing
  detaining
  entertaining
  maintaining
  obtaining
  pertaining
  retaining
training
  entraining
veining
waning

AN-ing
banning
canning
fanning
flanning
manning
panning
  trepanning
planning
scanning
spanning
tanning

AN-ish
banish
clannish
mannish
Spanish
vanish

AN-jent
plangent
tangent

A-njez (AIN-jez)
changes
  exchanges
  interchanges
granges
ranges
  arranges
    disarranges
  deranges
(stranges)
  estranges

A-nji (AIN-jee)
mangy
rangy

A-njing (AIN-jing)
changing
  exchanging
  interchanging
  unchanging
ranging
  arranging
    disarranging
    rearranging
  deranging
(stranging)
  estranging

A-njless (AINJ-less)
changeless
rangeless

A-njment (AINJ-ment)
changement
  exchangement
  interchangement
(rangement)
  arrangement
    disarrangement
    rearrangement
  derangement

(strangement)
  estrangement

A-njur (AIN-jur)
changer
  exchanger
  money-changer
danger
  endanger
manger
ranger
  arrranger
  forest ranger
  Texas Ranger, etc.
stranger

A-nless (AIN-less)
brainless
caneless
chainless
gainless
rainless
stainless

AN-less
clanless
fanless
manless
planless
tanless

A-nli (AIN-li)
(fanely)
  profanely
gainly
  ungainly
mainly
  humanely
  inhumanely
(nanely)
  inanely
sanely
  insanely
vainly

AN-li (AN-lee)
manly
  unmanly
Stanley

A-nment (AIN-ment)
(rainment)
  arraignment
(tainment)
  attainment
  entertainment
  ordainment

A-ness (AIN-ness)
(maneness)
  humaneness
plainness

A-no
(cano)
  volcano
Draino
(say no, they know, etc.)

AN-o
anno
(prano)
  soprano
(yano)
  piano

AN-on
cannon
canon
Shannon (*River*)

AN-sel
cancel
chancel

AN-sez
chances
  mischances
dances
glances
(hances)

enhances
lances
manses
  romances
(nances)
  finances
prances
(spanses)
  expanses
trances
  entrances (*v*)
(vances)
  advances

AN-shal (AN-shul)
(nancial)
  financial
(stantial)
  circumstantial
  substantial

AN-she
banshee
can she

AN-shun
mansion
scansion
(spansion)
  expansion
stanchion

AN-si
antsy
chancy
fancy
(gancy)
  extravagancy (*i*)
(mancy)
  necromancy
Nancy
  consonancy (*i*)

AN-sing
chancing
dancing

glancing
(hancing)
  enhancing
lancing
Lansing
(mancing)
  necromancing
  romancing
(trancing)
  entrancing
(vancing)
  advancing

ANS-ment
(hancement)
  enhancement
(trancement)
  entrancement
(vancement)
  advancement

AN-sum
handsome
hansom
ransom
transom
(ban some etc.)

AN-sur
answer
cancer
chancer
(ganser)
  merganser
glancer
lancer
(manser)
  romancer
    chiromancer (*i*)
    geomancer (*i*)
    necromancer (*i*),
      etc.
prancer
(trancer)
  entrancer
(can, sir, etc.)

AN-ta (ANTA)
(danta)
  Vedanta
(fanta)
  infanta (*Spanish*)
(lanta)
  Atlanta
Santa

AN-tam (AN-tum)
bantam
phantom

A-nted (AIN-ted)
fainted
feinted
painted
  repainted
  unpainted
(quainted)
  acquainted
sainted
tainted

AN-ted
canted
chanted
  enchanted
    disenchanted
granted
panted
planted
  implanted
    reimplanted
  replanted
  transplanted
ranted
slanted

A-ntest (AINT-est)
faintest
quaintest

AN-ti
aunty
panty

scanty
shanty

AN-tik
antic
(dantic)
  pedantic
  Vedantic
(fantic)
  sycophantic
frantic
(gantic)
  gigantic
(lantic)
  Atlantic
    transatlantic
(mantic)
  romantic
    chiromantic
    necromantic

ANT-ine
(fantine)
  elephantine
(mantine)
  adamantine
(vantine)
  Levantine
(zantine)
  Byzantine

A-nting (AINT-ing)
fainting
feinting
painting
(quainting)
  acquainting
    reacquainting
tainting
  attainting

ANT-ing
canting
  decanting
  recanting
chanting

enchanting
  disenchanting
granting
panting
planting
  implanting
  replanting
  supplanting
  transplanting

AN-tis
(lantis)
  Atlantis
mantis

ANT-l
cantle
mantel
mantle
  dismantle

A-ntli (AINT-li)
faintly
quaintly
saintly

A-ntlike (AINT-like)
saintlike
(ain't like, etc.)

ANT-lur
antler
(mantler)
  dismantler

A-ntness (AINT-ness)
faintness
quaintness

ANT-or
cantor
grantor

ANT-ri (ANT-ree)
gantry
pantry

A-ntur (AINT-ur)
fainter
painter
quainter

ANT-ur
banter
canter
  decanter
  recanter
cantor
chanter
  enchanter
granter
planter
ranter
(stanter)
  instanter

ANT-urn
lantern
(can turn, etc.)

A-nur (AIN-ur)
chainer
  enchainer
(daner)
  ordainer
(faner)
  profaner
gainer
(paner)
  campaigner
plainer
  complainer
(raner)
  arraigner
saner
(splaner)
  explainer
stainer
  abstainer
    nonabstainer
  sustainer
strainer
  restrainer

(taner)
  container
  detainer
  entertainer
  maintainer
  obtainer
  retainer
trainer
vainer

AN-ur
banner
canner
fanner
manner
manor
planner
scanner
spanner
tanner

AN-urd
bannered
mannered
  ill-mannered
  unmannered
  well-mannered

A-nus (AIN-us)
anus
heinous
Janus
veinous
(explain us, etc.)

A-nwurk (AIN-wurk)
brainwork
canework
chain work
(gain work, etc.)

AN-yan (AN-yun)
banyan
canyon
(panion)
  companion

AN-yel
Daniel
spaniel
  cocker spaniel
  water spaniel

AN-za
(ganza)
  extravaganza
(nanza)
  bonanza
stanza

A-on
crayon
rayon
(play on, etc.)

A-os
chaos
Laos

AP-en
happen
(nappin' etc.)

AP-i
chappy
crappie
happy
  slaphappy
nappy
knappy
pappy
sappy
scrappy
yappy

AP-id
rapid
sapid
vapid

A-ping
aping
draping

A-ping
gaping
raping
saping
(scaping)
   escaping
   landscaping (*i*)
scraping

AP-ing
capping
   handicapping
clapping
dapping
flapping
gapping
lapping
   overlapping
mapping
napping
rapping
wrapping
   enwrapping
   unwrapping
sapping
scrapping
slapping
snapping
strapping
tapping
trapping
   entrapping
yapping

A-pist
papist
rapist
(scapist)
   escapist
landscapist (*i*)

A-pl
maple
papal
staple

AP-l
apple
chapel
dapple
grapple
scrapple

A-pless
capeless
scrapeless
shapeless
tapeless

AP-less
capless
hapless

AP-ling
dappling
grappling
sapling

A-plz
maples
Naples
staples

AP-nel
grapnel
shrapnel

AP-shun
caption
(traption)
   contraption

AP-tiv
captive
(daptive)
   adaptive

APT-li
aptly
   inaptly
raptly

APT-ness
aptness
   inaptness
raptness

AP-tur
apter
captor
chapter
(dapter)
   adapter
raptor

AP-ture
capture
   recapture
rapture
   enrapture

A-pur
aper
caper
draper
paper
raper
(scaper)
   escaper
scraper
   skyscraper (*i*)
shaper
taper
tapir

AP-ur
capper
   handicapper (*i*)
clapper
dapper
flapper
mapper
napper
rapper
wrapper
sapper
slapper
snapper

whippersnapper (*i*)
tapper
  wiretapper (*i*)
yapper

AR-a
Bara, Theda
Clara
  Santa Clara
(hara)
  Sahara
(yara)
  tiara

AR-ab
Arab
  street Arab
scarab

AR-ak
arrack
barrack

AR-ans (ER-ans)
(berrance)
  aberrance
  forbearance
(parence)
  apparence
  transparence

AR-ant (ER-ant)
(berrant)
  aberrant
  forbearant
parent
  apparent

AR-ant (OR-ant)
warrant
(see OR-ent, page 271)

AR-bl
garble
marble

AR-bord
larboard
starboard

AR-bur
arbor
barber
harbor

ARCH-ez
arches
  overarches
larches
marches
  countermarches
  outmarches
parches
starches

ARCH-ing
arching
  overarching
marching
  countermarching
  outmarching
parching
starching

ARCH-ur
archer
marcher

ARD-ed
(barded)
  bombarded
carded
guarded
  regarded
    disregarded
  unguarded
larded
(scarded)
  discarded
(tarded)
  retarded
    unretarded

ARD-en
garden
harden
pardon

ARD-end
gardened
hardened
  case-hardened
pardoned
  unpardoned

ARD-i
hardy
  foolhardy (*i*)
tardy

ARD-ing
(barding)
  bombarding
carding
  discarding
  placarding (*i*)
guarding
regarding
  disregarding
  unregarding
(tarding)
  retarding

ARD-less
cardless
guardless
  regardless

ARD-ning
gardening
hardening

ARD-nur
gardener
hardener
pardner

ARD-ur
ardor

harder
larder

AR-el
barrel
carol
  Christmas carol
  Lewis Carroll
(parel)
  apparel

AR-ens (ER-ens)
(berrance)
  aberrance
  forbearance
(parence)
  apparence
  transparence

AR-ent
parent
  apparent
  grandparent (*i*)
sparent)
  transparent

AR-est (AIR-est)
barest
fairest
rarest
squarest

AR-et
carat
caret
carrot
karat
claret
garret
garrote
parrot

AR-for (AIR-for)
therefore
wherefore
(care for, etc.)

AR-go
Argo
argot
(bargo)
  embargo
cargo
Fargo
  Wells Fargo
largo
  Key Largo

AR-gon
argon
Argonne
far gone
jargon
(car gone, etc.)

AR-i (AIR-ee)
airy
berry
bury
cherry
dairy
  dromedary
  legendary
  hebdomadary
Derry
fairy
ferry
glairy
hairy
Jerry
Kerry
  apothecary
(lairy)
  capillary
  constabulary
  corollary
  epistolary
  formulary
  maxillary
  titulary
  tutelary
  vocabulary
Mary

Queen Mary
St. Mary
customary
  accustomary
nary
canary
cautionary
centenary (*a*)
  bicentenary (*a*)
  confectionary
  culinary
dictionary
disciplinary
discretionary
elocutionary
evolutionary
functionary
imaginary
insurrectionary
legionary
luminary
mercenary
millinery
missionary
ordinary
  extraordinary
pensionary
processionary
pulmonary
reactionary
reversionary
revolutionary
sanguinary
seditionary
seminary
stationary
traditionary
veterinary
visionary
  provisionary
  revisionary
perry
prairie (*i*)
quary
  antiquary
  reliquary

(rary)
  honorary
  literary
  temporary
  Tipperary (i)
(sary)
  adversary
  commissary
  lamasery
  necessary
scary
skerry
sherry
Terry
  commentary
  contributary
  depositary
  dietary
  dignitary
  fragmentary
  hereditary
  military
  momentary
  monetary
  planetary
  presbytery
  proprietary
  salutary
  sanitary
  secretary
  sedentary (i)
  solitary
  tributary
  voluntary
(trary)
  arbitrary
very
  salivary
wary
  actuary
  cassowary
  estuary
  February
  January
  mortuary
  obituary

sanctuary
statuary
sumptuary
unwary
(yary)
  beneficiary
  fiduciary
  incendiary
  intermediary
  pecuniary
  subsidiary

AR-i
carry
  hari-kari
  miscarry
marry
  intermarry
parry
tarry
vary

AR-i (ARR-i)
scarry
starry
tarry

AR-id (AR-eed)
(carried, etc.)

AR-ij
carriage
  miscarriage
marriage
  intermarriage
(sparage)
  disparage

AR-ing (AIR-ing)
airing
baring
bearing
  forbearing
  overbearing
blaring
caring

uncaring
chairing
(claring)
  declaring
daring
  outdaring
faring
  seafaring
  wayfaring
glaring
pairing
  impairing
  repairing
paring
  comparing
  preparing
scaring
sharing
snaring
  ensnaring
sparing
  despairing
  unsparing
squaring
staring
  outstaring
swearing
  forswearing
tearing
wearing
  outwearing

AR-ing
barring
  debarring
  disbarring
jarring
marring
scarring
sparring
starring
tarring

AR-ingks
larynx
pharynx

AR-is
(laris)
  Polaris
Paris

AR-ish (AIR-ish)
bearish
fairish
squarish

AR-jent
argent
sergeant

AR-jez
barges
charges
  discharges
(larges)
  enlarges
marges

AR-jin
margin
(barge in, chargin', etc.)

AR-jing
barging
charging
  discharging
  overcharging
(larging)
  enlarging

ARJ-ur
charger
larger
  enlarger

ARK-en
darken
hearken
(barkin', etc.)

ARK-est
darkest

starkest

ARK-et
market
(park it, etc.)

ARK-i (ARK-ee)
barky
car key
(garchy)
  oligarchy
(larky)
  malarkey
marquee
marquis
(rarchy)
  hierarchy
snarky (*British*)
(yarky)
  patriarchy

ARK-ik
(garchic)
  oligarchic
(narchic)
  anarchic
  monarchic
(rarchic)
  hierarchic
(tarchic)
  heptarchic
(yarchic)
  patriarchic

ARK-ing
barking
  embarking
    disembarking
harking
larking
  skylarking (*i*)
marking
  remarking
parking

ARK-li (ARK-lee)
darkly
starkly

ARK-ling
darkling
sparkling

ARK-som
darksome
(spark some, etc.)

ARK-ur
barker
darker
marker
parker
sparker
starker

AR-land
garland
  engarland
(bizarre land, far
  land, etc.)

AR-less (AIR-less)
airless
heirless
careless
hairless
  Mexican hairless
prayerless
snareless
(care less, etc.)

AR-less
carless
scarless
starless
(far less, etc.)

AR-let
harlot
scarlet
starlet

varlet

AR-li (AIR-li)
barely
fairly
  unfairly
rarely

AR-li (AR-li)
barley
parley

AR-line (AIR-line)
airline
hairline
(their line, etc.)

AR-ling
darling
snarling
starling

AR-lite
car light
far light
starlight

AR-lot
car lot
  used-car lot
Charlotte
harlot
(scarlet, etc.)

AR-man (AIR-man)
airman
chairman
(fair man, their
  man, etc.)

AR-ment
(barment)
  debarment
  disbarment
garment

ARM-ful
armful
charmful
harmful
  unharmful

AR-mi
army
barmy (*British*)
smarmy
(bar me, etc.)

ARM-ing
arming
  disarming
  forearming
farming
harming
(larming)
  alarming

ARM-less
armless
charmless
farmless
harmless

ARM-let
armlet
charmlet

AR-mur
armor
  disarmer
charmer
farmer

AR-nal
carnal
charnel

AR-ness (AIR-ness)
bareness
  threadbareness (*i*)
fairness

unfairness
rareness
spareness
squareness
whereness
  awareness
    unawareness

AR-ness
farness
harness

AR-ni
blarney
carnie
  chile con carne
(larney)
  Killarney

AR-nish
garnish
tarnish
varnish

AR-nisht
garnished
  ungarnished
tarnished
  untarnished
varnished
  unvarnished

AR-o (AIR-o)
(brero)
  sombrero
faro
pharaoh
(kero)
  vaquero
(lero)
  bolero
(nero)
  Rio do Janeiro
(yero)
  caballero *(Spanish)*

AR-o
arrow
barrow
farrow
harrow
marrow
narrow
sparrow
tarot
yarrow

AR-old
Harold, King
(caroled, etc.)

AR-on
baron
barren

ARP-ing
carping
harping
sharping

ARP-ur
carper
harper
sharper

ARP-urz
scarpers (*British*)
(carpers, etc.)

ARSH-al
marshal
  field marshal (*i*)
partial
  impartial

ARS-ness (AIRS-ness)
scarceness
sparseness

AR-son
arson
Carson

parson

ART-ed
carted
charted
  uncharted
darted
(hearted)
  brokenhearted
  chickenhearted
  coldhearted
  downhearted
  fainthearted
  false-hearted
  flint-hearted
  full-hearted
  gentle-hearted
  greathearted
  halfhearted
  hardhearted
  kindhearted
  lionhearted, etc.
parted
  departed
  imparted
smarted
started
  restarted

ART-en
barton
carton
(garten)
  kindergarten
hearten
  dishearten
marten
martin
smarten
Spartan
tartan
(startin', etc.)

ART-ful
artful
cartful

heart full

ART-i
arty
hearty
party
smarty
(starty)
  Astarte
tarty

ART-ing
carting
darting
parting
  departing
  imparting
smarting
starting

ART-ist
artist
chartist

ART-less
artless
heartless

ART-li
partly
smartly
tartly

ART-ment
(partment)
  apartment
  compartment
  department
(heart meant, etc.)

ART-ness
smartness
tartness

ART-rij
cartridge

partridge

ART-ur
barter
carter
charter
darter
garter
martyr
smarter
starter
Tartar
tarter

AR-um
carrom
harem
marum (*Latin*)
(scarum)
  harum-scarum

AR-ur (AIR-ur)
barer
bearer
  arms-bearer (*i*)
  standard-bearer (*i*)
  sword-bearer (*i*)
  talebearer (*i*)
fairer
  seafarer (*i*)
  wayfarer (*i*)
parer
  impairer
  preparer
  repairer
sharer
snarer
sparer
squarer
starer
swearer
tearer
wearer

AR-val
carvel

larval
marvel

AR-ven
carven
(starvin', etc.)

AR-ving
carving
starving

AR-wel (AIR-well)
farewell
(bear well, etc.)

AR-worn (AIR-worn)
careworn
prayerworn

A-sens
(beisance)
  obeisance
(jacence)
  adjacence
nascence
  renascence
(placence)
  complacence

A-sent
(jacent)
  adjacent
nascent
  renascent
(bay scent, etc.)

AS-et
asset
basset
facet
(pass it, etc.)

A-sez
aces
bases
  debases

braces
  embraces
cases
  ukases
chases
  steeplechases (*i*)
faces
  defaces
  effaces
graces
  disgraces
laces
  enlaces
  unlaces
maces
paces
  outpaces
places
  commonplaces (*i*)
  displaces
  hiding places (*i*)
  misplaces
  replaces
races
  chariot races (*i*)
  footraces (*i*)
  horse-races (*i*)
spaces
  breathing spaces (*i*)
traces
  retraces

AS-ez
asses
brasses
classes
gases
glasses
grasses
lasses
  molasses
masses
  amasses
passes
  surpasses

A-sful (AIS-ful)
graceful
　disgraceful
　ungraceful

ASH-ai
cachet
sachet
sashay
taché (*French*)
　attaché

A-shal
facial
glacial
(latial)
　palatial
racial
spatial

ASH-bord
dashboard
splashboard

ASH-ez
ashes
bashes
　abashes
caches
cashes
clashes
crashes
dashes
flashes
gashes
hashes .
　rehashes
lashes
mashes
gnashes
rashes
sashes
slashes
smashes
splashes
stashes

mustaches

ASH-i
ashy
flashy
hashy
mashie
plashy
splashy
trashy

ASH-ing
bashing
　abashing
clashing
crashing
dashing
Fasching (*German*)
flashing
gashing
hashing
　rehashing
mashing
gnashing
plashing
slashing
smashing
splashing
thrashing
trashing

A-shun
(bation)
　approbation
　exacerbation
　incubation
　libation
　probation
(bration)
　adumbration
　celebration
　vibration
(cation)
　adjudication
　altercation
　amplification

Anglification
application
authentication
beatification
beautification
bifurcation
calcification
　decalcification
clarification
classification
codification
communication
　excommunication
　intercom-
　　munication
complication
damnification
debarkation
　embarkation
dedication
　rededication
defecation
deification
demarcation
deprecation
desiccation
domestication
duplication
edification
education
electrification
eradication
explication
extrication
fabrication
falsification
fortification
fructification
glorification
gratification
identification
implication
imprecation
inculcation
indemnification
indication

183

intensification
intoxication
justification
location
   allocation
   dislocation
   relocation
magnification
mastication
medication
modification
mollification
mortification
multiplication
mummification
mystification
notification
nullification
ossification
pacification
personification
predication
prevarication
prognostication
prolification
publication
purification
qualification
   disqualification
ramification
ratification
reciprocation
replication
revivification
sanctification
scarification
simplification
solidification
sophistication
specification
stratification
stultification
suffocation
supplication
testification
transmogrification

triplication
truncation
typification
unification
vacation
verification
versification
   diversification
vilification
vindication
vitrification
vocation
   advocation
   avocation
   convocation
   equivocation
   invocation
   provocation
   revocation
(cration)
   consecration
     deconsecration
     reconsecration
   desecration
   execration
(dation)
   accommodation
   commendation
     recommendation
   consolidation
   denudation
   depredation
   dilapidation
   elucidation
   emendation
   exudation
   foundation
   gradation
     degradation
   intimidation
   inundation
   laudation
   liquidation
   oxidation
   retardation
   sedation

trepidation
validation
   invalidation
(flation)
   deflation
   inflation
(gation)
   aggregation
   castigation
   congregation
   conjugation
   corrugation
   divagation
   divulgation
   fumigation
   instigation
   investigation
   irrigation
   legation
     allegation
     delegation
     relegation
   mitigation
   navigation
     circumnavigation
   negation
     abnegation
   obligation
   prolongation
   promulgation
   propagation
   purgation
     expurgation
   rogation
     arrogation
     derogation
     subrogation
   segregation
     desegregation
   subjugation
   variegation
(gration)
   conflagration
   integration
     disintegration
   migration

emigration
immigration
transmigration
(lation)
  accumulation
  adulation
  ambulation
    perambulation
    somnambulation
  Appalachian
  appelation
  articulation
  assimilation
  calculation
    miscalculation
  cancellation
  capitulation
    recapitulation
  circulation
  coagulation
  collation
  compilation
  confabulation
  congratulation
  consolation
  constellation
  copulation
  denticulation
  desolation
  dilation
  distillation
  ejaculation
  elation
  emasculation
  emulation
  flagellation
  granulation
  halation
    exhalation
    inhalation
  immolation
  inoculation
  installation
    reinstallation
  insulation
  interpolation

isolation
jubilation
manipulation
matriculation
modulation
mutilation
oscillation
osculation
peculation
percolation
population
  depopulation
postulation
regulation
  deregulation
relation
  correlation
  interrelation
reticulation
revelation
scintillation
simulation
  dissimulation
speculation
stimulation
stipulation
strangulation
tabulation
tessellation
tintinnabulation
triangulation
tribulation
ululation
undulation
ventilation
violation
(mation)
  acclamation
  acclimation
  affirmation
  amalgamation
  animation
    inanimation
    reanimation
  approximation
  confirmation

cremation
Dalmatian
decimation
declamation
defamation
estimation
exclamation
exhumation
formation
  conformation
  deformation
  information
  malformation
  reformation
  transformation
inflammation
inhumation
intimation
proclamation
reclamation
sublimation
summation
  consummation
ultimation
nation
  abomination
  alienation
  alternation
  assassination
  assignation
  carnation
    incarnation
      reincarnation
  cognation
  combination
  condemnation
  consternation
  contamination
    decontamination
  coronation
  crimination
    discrimination
      indiscrimination
    incrimination
    recrimination
  culmination

damnation
declination
destination
  predestination
divination
domination
donation
  condonation
elimination
emanation
examination
explanation
fascination
germination
hallucination
hibernation
imagination
impersonation
impregnation
incineration
inclination
  disinclination
indignation
indoctrination
  reindoctrination
intonation
machination
miscegenation
nomination
  denomination
  renomination
ordination
  coordination
  subordination
    insubordination
origination
pagination
peregrination
pollination
procrastination
profanation
ratiocination
rejuvenation
reparation
resignation
ruination

rumination
salination
semination
  dissemination
  insemination
stagnation
subornation
tarnation
termination
  determination
    indetermination
  extermination
vaccination
  revaccination
(pation)
  anticipation
  emancipation
  exculpation
  occupation
    preoccupation
    reoccupation
  participation
(plation)
  contemplation
(quation)
  equation
ration
aberration
abjuration
admiration
adoration
aeration
agglomeration
alliteration
alteration
asseveration
botheration
coloration
  discoloration
commiseration
conglomeration
consideration
  inconsideration
  reconsideration
corporation
  incorporation

corroboration
declaration
decoration
  redecoration
defloration
desperation
deterioration
duration
elaboration
enumeration
evaporation
exaggeration
exasperation
exhilaration
exoneration
expectoration
exploration
federation
  confederation
figuration
  configuration
  disfiguration
  transfiguration
generation
  degeneration
  regeneration
inauguration
incarceration
incineration
inspiration
invigoration
  reinvigoration
laceration
liberation
  deliberation
maceration
maturation
mensuration
moderation
  immoderation
narration
obliteration
obscuration
operation
  cooperation
oration

peroration
perforation
perspiration
preparation
protruberation
recuperation
refrigeration
reiteration
remuneration
reparation
respiration
restoration
reverberation
saturation
separation
suppuration
suspiration
toleration
  intoleration
transliteration
transpiration
ulceration
veneration
vituperation
vociferation
(sation)
  cessation
compensation
condensation
conversation
dispensation
fixation
laxation
  relaxation
pulsation
sensation
tergiversation
(scation)
  corruscation
  obfuscation
(slation)
  legislation
station
  bus station
  radio station
  railway station

television station
(way station, etc.)

crustacean
degustation
devastation
divestation
gestation
  ingestion
infestation
  manifestation
molestation
testation
  attestation
  detestation
  protestation
(stration)
  demonstration
frustration
lustration
  illustration
ministration
  administration
orchestration
prostration
registration
remonstration
(tation)
  accreditation
adaptation
affectation
agitation
amputation
cetacean
citation
  excitation
  recitation
cogitation
computation
confrontation
confutation
crepitation
  decrepitation
debilitation
decantation
decapitation

delectation
dentation
  indentation
deportation
deputation
dictation
digitation
  prestidigitation
dilatation
dotation
eructation
exaltation
exhortation
expectation
exploitation
exportation
exultation
felicitation
flirtation
flotation
habitation
  cohabitation
  inhabitation
hesitation
imitation
importation
imputation
incantation
incapacitation
interpretation
  misinterpretation
  reinterpretation
invitation
irritation
lactation
levitation
limitation
  delimitation
meditation
  premeditation
mentation
  alimentation
  augmentation
  documentation
  experimentation
  fermentation

instrumentation
integumentation
lamentation
ornamentation
sedimentation
segmentation
supplementation
mutation
  commutation
  permutation
necessitation
notation
  annotation
  connotation
  denotation
occultation
orientation
ostentation
palpitation
plantation
  implantation
  replantation
  supplantation
  transplantation
precipitation
presentation
  representation
quotation
recantation
refutation
rehabilitation
reputation
rotation
salutation
sanitation
solicitation
transportation
vegetation
visitation
(tration)
  arbitration
  concentration
  filtration
    infiltration
  penetration
  perpetration

(vation)
  activation
    deactivation
    reactivation
  aggravation
  captivation
  conservation
  cultivation
  depravation
  derivation
  elevation
  enervation
  excavation
  observation
  ovation
    innovation
    renovation
  preservation
    self-preservation
  privation
    deprivation
  reservation
  salvation
(wation)
  attenuation
  continuation
    discontinuation
  evacuation
  eventuation
  extenuation
  graduation
  habituation
    rehabituation
  infatuation
  insinuation
  perpetuation
  punctuation
  superannuation
(yation)
  abbreviation
  affiliation
  alleviation
  annunciation
  appreciation
  appropriation
  asphyxiation

association
  dissociation
calumniation
conciliation
  reconciliation
creation
  procreation
  recreation
delineation
denunciation
depreciation
differentiation
emaciation
enunciation
excruciation
expatiation
expatriation
expiation
expropriation
foliation
  defoliation
humiliation
ideation
inebriation
ingratiation
initiation
luxuriation
mediation
negotiation
  renegotiation
obviation
permeation
pronunciation
  mispronunciation
propitiation
radiation
  irradiation
renunciation
repatriation
repudiation
retaliation
satiation
spoliation
striation
substantiation
  transubstantiation

variation
vitiation
(zation)
 acclimitization
 accusation
 actualization
 aggrandization
 Americanization
 Anglicization
 annexation
 atomization
 authorization
 brutalization
 canalization
 canonization
 capitalization
 carbonization
 cathechization
 causation
 cauterization
 centralization
  decentralization
 characterization
 Christianization
 civilization
 colonization
 crystallization
 deodorization
 economization
 effeminization
 equalization
 evangelization
 familiarization
 fraternization
 generalization
 harmonization
 Hellenization
 humanization
 hybridization
 idealization
 improvisation
 individualization
 Latinization
 legalization
 localization
 materialization

mesmerization
mobilization
modernization
moralization
 demoralization
naturalization
neutralization
normalization
organization
 disorganization
 reorganization
patronization
polarization
pulverization
realization
secularization
solemnization
specialization
symbolization
synchronization
systemization
tantalization
temporization
 extemporization
tranquilization
utilization
verbalization
vitalization
 devitalization
 revitalization
vocalization
vulcanization

ASH-un
ashen
(cashun)
 Circassian
fashion
passion
 compassion
 impassion
(bashin', etc.)

ASH-und
fashioned
 old-fashioned

 refashioned
passioned
 impassioned
  unimpassioned

ASH-ur
brasher
crasher
 gate-crasher (*i*)
dasher
 haberdasher
flasher
masher
slasher
smasher
splasher
thrasher

A-shus
(baceous)
 herbaceous
 sebaceous
(cacious)
 efficacious
  inefficacious
 perspicacious
(dacious)
 audacious
 mendacious
(gacious)
 sagacious
gracious
 ungracious
(lacious)
 fallacious
 salacious
(maceous)
 contumaceous
(nacious)
 carbonaceous
 pertinacious
 pugnacious
 tenacious
(pacious)
 capacious
 rapacious

(quacious)
  loquacious
(racious)
  veracious
  voracious
(satious)
  vexatious
spacious
(tatious)
  cetaceous
  disputatious
  flirtatious
  ostentatious
  setaceous
(vacious)
  vivacious

AS-i
brassy
chassis
classy
gassy
  Malagasy
glassy
grassy
(hassee)
  Tallahassee
lassie
sassy

A-side
A side
bayside
braeside
wayside

AS-id
acid
placid

AS-ik
classic
(racic)
  boracic
  Jurassic
  thoracic

(yasic)
  Triassic

A-sin
basin
caisson
chasten
hasten
Jason
mason
(racin', etc.)

AS-in
(sassin)
  assassin
(passin', etc.)

A-sing
acing
basing
  abasing
    self-abasing
  debasing
bracing
  embracing
casing
  encasing
chasing
facing
  defacing
  effacing
gracing
  disgracing
lacing
  enlacing
  unlacing
pacing
placing
  displacing
  misplacing
  replacing
racing
  erasing
spacing
tracing
  retracing

AS-ing
classing
gassing
massing
  amassing
passing
  surpassing

A-sis
basis
(wasis)
  oasis
(face is, place is,
  traces, etc.)

AS-it
(see **AS-et,** *page 175)*

A-siv
suasive
  dissuasive
  persuasive
(vasive)
  evasive
  invasive
  pervasive

AS-ive
massive
passive
  impassive

AS-ket
basket
casket
gasket
(ask it)

AS-king
asking
basking
masking
  unmasking
tasking

AS-ko
(basco)
 Tabasco
(lasco)
 Belasco
(yasco)
 fiasco

AS-kur
asker
basker
masker

AS-kus
Damascus
(ask us, mask us, etc.)

AS-l
castle
tassel
vassal
"wrassle"

A-sless (AIS-less)
baseless
faceless
graceless
laceless
placeless
raceless
spaceless
traceless

AS-man
classman
 upperclassman
gas man
glass man

A-sment (AIS-ment)
basement
 abasement
  self-abasement
 debasement
casement
 encasement

(facement)
 defacement
 effacement
placement
 displacement
 replacement

AS-o
basso
(gasso)
 Sargasso
lasso

AS-ok
cassock
hassock
Masoch

AS-pen
aspen
(graspin', etc.)

AS-ping
clasping
 unclasping
gasping
grasping
rasping

AS-pur
Casper
clasper
gasper
grasper
jasper
rasper

A-sted
basted
hasted
pasted
tasted
 untasted
waisted
 short-waisted
wasted

unwasted

AS-ted
blasted
fasted
(gasted)
 flabbergasted
lasted
 outlasted
(trasted)
 contrasted

AST-est
fastest
vastest

A-stful (AIST-ful)
tasteful
 distasteful
wasteful

A-sti
hasty
pasty
tasty

AS-tik
(bastik)
 bombastic
(castik)
 sarcastic
(clastik)
 iconoclastic
drastic
(lastik)
 elastic
  inelastic
 scholastic
mastic
(nastik)
 gymnastic
 monastic
plastic
 neoplastic
 protoplastic
spastic

(tastik)
  fantastic
(yastic)
  ecclesiastic
  enthusiastic
  orgiastic

A-sting
basting
hasting
pasting
tasting
wasting

AST-ing
blasting
casting
  forecasting
fasting
lasting
(trasting)
  contrasting

A-stless (AIST-less)
hasteless
tasteless
waistless
wasteless

AST-li
fastly
  steadfastly
ghastly
lastly
vastly

AST-ness
fastness
vastness

A-stur
chaster
taster
waster

AST-ur
aster
Astor
(bastur)
  alabaster
blaster
caster
  forecaster
castor
faster
(gastur)
  flabbergaster
(lastur)
  pilaster
master
  bandmaster (*i*)
  burgomaster (*i*)
  bushmaster (*i*)
  grand master (*i*)
  past master (*i*)
  postmaster (*i*)
  taskmaster (*i*)
pastor
plaster
  shin-plaster
  sticking plaster
vaster
(yaster)
  piaster
(zaster)
  disaster

AS-turd
bastard
dastard
(lasturd)
  pilastered
mastered
  unmastered
plastered

A-sur
baser
  abaser
  debaser
racer

spacer
tracer
  retracer

AS-ur
(kasur)
  antimacassar
(masur)
  amasser
passer
  surpasser

AT-a
data
(gata)
  regatta
(mata)
  ultimata
(rata)
  errata
  pro rata
strata

AT-a (OT-a)
(brata)
  invertebrata
(gata)
  regatta
(nata)
  serenata
  sonata
(rata)
  inamorata
(tata)
  cantata
  dentata *(Latin)*
(yata)
  riata

A-tal
fatal
natal

A-tan
Satan
(waitin', etc.)

A-tant
blatant
latent
patent

A-ted
baited
bated
  abated
    unabated
  debated
  incubated
  probated
    approbated
(brated)
  celebrated
crated
  consecrated
  desecrated
  execrated
dated
  accommodated
  antedated
  consolidated
  dilapidated
  elucidated
  intimidated
  inundated
  liquidated
  validated
    invalidated
fated
  ill-fated
(flated)
  inflated
  deflated
freighted
gated
  abnegated
  abrogated
    derogated
    interrogated
  castigated
  congregated
  conjugated
  corrugated

delegated
  relegated
fumigated
instigated
irrigated
mitigated
  unmitigated
navigated
  circumnavigated
obligated
propagated
segregated
  desegregated
subjugated
variegated
grated
  integrated
    disintegrated
  migrated
    emigrated
    immigrated
hated
(kated)
  abdicated
  advocated
  authenticated
    unauthenticated
  bifurcated
  communicated
    excommunicated
  complicated
    duplicated
    implicated
    supplicated
  dedicated
  deprecated
  domesticated
  educated
    uneducated
  equivocated
  eradicated
  extricated
  fabricated
    prefabricated
  imprecated
  indicated

intoxicated
located
  allocated
  dislocated
lubricated
masticated
medicated
predicated
prevaricated
prognosticated
reciprocated
rusticated
sophisticated
  unsophisticated
suffocated
syndicated
vacated
vindicated
(lated)
  accumulated
  annihilated
  articulated
  assimilated
  belated
  calculated
  capitulated
    recapitulated
  circulated
  coagulated
  collated
  confabulated
  congratulated
  copulated
  crenellated
  desolated
  dilated
  ejaculated
  elated
  emasculated
  emulated
  expostulated
  flagellated
  formulated
  gesticulated
  granulated
  immolated

inoculated
insulated
interpolated
isolated
legislated
manipulated
matriculated
modulated
mutilated
oscillated
osculated
perambulated
percolated
populated
  depopulated
postulated
regulated
related
  correlated
  unrelated
scintillated
simulated
speculated
stimulated
stipulated
tabulated
tessellated
titillated
translated
triangulated
ululated
vacillated
ventillated
violated
mated
  amalgamated
  approximated
  consummated
  cremated
  decimated
  estimated
  intimated
  sublimated
(nated)
  abominated
  alienated

alternated
assassinated
carbonated
contaminated
  uncontaminated
coordinated
culminated
delineated
designated
detonated
discriminated
disseminated
dominated
  predominated
eliminated
emanated
fascinated
fulminated
germinated
illuminated
  unilluminated
impersonated
incriminated
indoctrinated
marinated
nominated
  denominated
opinionated
originated
peregrinated
predestinated
procrastinated
recriminated
rejuvenated
ruminated
subordinated
terminated
  exterminated
vaccinated
(pated)
  addle-pated
  anticipated
  dissipated
  emancipated
  participated
  syncopated

plaited
plated
  contemplated
  armor-plated
  copperplated
  electroplated
  nickel-plated, etc.
prated
(quated)
  antiquated
  equated
rated
  accelerated
  adulterated
    unadulterated
  ameliorated
  aspirated
  berated
  commemorated
  commiserated
  conglomerated
  corroborated
  decorated
    redecorated
  deteriorated
  elaborated
  enumerated
  evaporated
  exaggerated
  exasperated
  exhilarated
  exonerated
  expectorated
  federated
    confederated
  generated
    degenerated
    regenerated
  inaugurated
  incarcerated
  incinerated
  incorporated
  invigorated
    reinvigorated
  iterated
    reiterated

liberated
  deliberated
moderated
narrated
obliterated
operated
  cooperated
overrated
perforated
recuperated
refrigerated
reverberated
saturated
separated
tolerated
underrated
venerated
vituperated
vociferated
sated
  compensated
  tergiversated
skated
  confiscated
slated
  legislated
stated
  overstated
  reinstated
  understated
  unstated
(strated)
  demonstrated
  frustrated
  illustrated
(tated)
  agitated
  amputated
  capacitated
    incapacitated
  cogitated
  crepitated
  debilitated
  decapitated
  devastated
  dictated

felicitated
gravitated
hesitated
imitated
irritated
meditated
  premeditated
    unpremeditated
militated
necessitated
notated
  annotated
palpitated
precipitated
rehabilitated
resuscitated
vegetated
(trated)
  arbitrated
  concentrated
  penetrated
  perpetrated
(vated)
  aggravated
  captivated
  cultivated
  elevated
  excavated
  innovated
    renovated
  tittivated
waited
  awaited
weighted
  accentuated
  actuated
  attenuated
  eventuated
  extenuated
  fluctuated
  graduated
  habituated
  infatuated
  insinuated
  perpetuated
  punctuated

situated
superannuated
(yated)
  alleviated
  appropriated
    unappropriated
  asphyxiated
  associated
    disassociated
  created
    uncreated
  depreciated
  deviated
  differentiated
    undifferentiated
  emaciated
  enunciated
  expatriated
  expiated
  inebriated
  ingratiated
  initiated
  irradiated
  luxuriated
  negotiated
  obviated
  officiated
  propitiated
  radiated
  repatriated
  repudiated
  substantiated
    unsubstantiated
  vitiated

AT-ed
batted
chatted
dratted
fatted
matted
patted

AT-en
batten
fatten

flatten
(hattan)
  Manhattan
Latin
Patton, George S.
(battin', etc.)

A-test
latest
greatest

AT-est
fattest
flattest

A-tful (AIT-ful)
crateful
fateful
grateful
  ungrateful
hateful
plateful

AT-head
fathead
flathead

ATH-ik
(pathic)
  allopathic
  homeopathic
  osteopathic
  psychopathic
  telepathic, etc.

ATH-ing
bathing
lathing

A-thing (ATHE-ing)
bathing
scathing

ATH-less
bathless
pathless

wrathless

A-thos
bathos
pathos

ATH-ur
blather
gather
  forgather
lather
rather
(see **OTH-ur,** *page 278)*

A-ti
eighty
Haiti
matey
weighty

AT-i
batty
catty
chatty
fatty
natty
  Cincinnati
patty
ratty

AT-ide
bat-eyed
cat-eyed
rat-eyed

AT-ik
attic
(batik)
  acrobatic
(cratik)
  aristocratic
  autocratic
  bureaucratic
  democratic
  idiosyncratic
  plutocratic

Socratic
theocratic
(fatik)
  emphatic
  lymphatic
(matik)
  anagrammatic
  aromatic
  asthmatic
  automatic
  axiomatic
  chromatic
    achromatic
    monochromatic
    polychromatic
  cinematic
  climatic
  diagrammatic
  diaphragmatic
  diplomatic
  dogmatic
  dramatic
    melodramatic
  enigmatic
  grammatic
    epigrammatic
  idiomatic
  mathematic
  miasmatic
  numismatic
  phlegmatic
  pneumatic
  pragmatic
  prismatic
  problematic
  rheumatic
  schematic
  schismatic
  somatic
  stigmatic
  symptomatic
  systematic
    unsystematic
  thematic
  traumatic
(natik)

fanatic
morganatic
(patik)
hepatic
(ratik)
erratic
hieratic
operatic
piratic
quadratic
static
ecstatic
hydrostatic
thermostatic
(watic)
aquatic
subaquatic
(yatic)
Asiatic
Hanseatic
sciatic

AT-iks
(matiks)
mathematics
pneumatics
statics
aerostatics
electrostatics
hydrostatics
(attics, etc.)

A-time
daytime
playtime
May-time
runaway time
(gay time, etc.)

AT-in
Latin
matin
satin
(battin', etc.)
*(see **AT-en,** page 188)*

A-ting
bating
abating
(yating)
abbreviating
*(see **A-ted,** substitute*
A-ting)

AT-ing
batting
chatting
fatting
matting
patting
ratting
tatting

AT-is
gratis
lattice

A-tiv
(bative)
reprobative
dative
consolidative (*i*)
(gative)
investigative (*i*)
mitigative (*i*)
(kative)
communicative (*i*)
incom-
municative (*i*)
deprecative (*i*)
explicative (*i*)
implicative (*i*)
modificative (*i*)
prognosticative (*i*)
replicative (*i*)
significative (*i*)
suffocative (*i*)
supplicative (*i*)
vindicative (*i*)
vivificative (*i*)
(lative)
accumulative (*i*)

assimilative (*i*)
copulative (*i*)
cumulative (*i*)
dilative (*i*)
emulative (*i*)
legislative (*i*)
manipulative (*i*)
speculative (*i*)
stimulative (*i*)
translative (*i*)
undulative (*i*)
(mative)
animative (*i*)
approximative (*i*)
coagulative (*i*)
estimative (*i*)
native
contaminative (*i*)
determinative (*i*)
discriminative (*i*)
emanative (*i*)
germinative (*i*)
illuminative (*i*)
imaginative (*i*)
unimaginative (*i*)
nominative (*i*)
denominative (*i*)
predestinative (*i*)
recriminative (*i*)
subordinative (*i*)
terminative (*i*)
(pative)
anticipative (*i*)
participative (*i*)
(rative)
agglomerative (*i*)
alliterative (*i*)
ameliorative (*i*)
commemorative (*i*)
commiserative (*i*)
confederative (*i*)
corporative (*i*)
incorporative (*i*)
corroborative (*i*)
decorative (*i*)
degenerative (*i*)

deliberative (*i*)
elaborative (*i*)
enumerative (*i*)
exaggerative (*i*)
exonerative (*i*)
generative (*i*)
  degenerative (*i*)
  regenerative (*i*)
operative (*i*)
  inoperative (*i*)
perforative (*i*)
recuperative (*i*)
reiterative (*i*)
remunerative (*i*)
  unremunerative (*i*)
reverberative (*i*)
separative (*i*)
suppurative (*i*)
vituperative (*i*)
(strative)
  ministrative (*i*)
    administrative (*i*)
(tative)
  agitative (*i*)
  authoritative (*i*)
  cogitative (*i*)
  gravitative (*i*)
  hesitative (*i*)
  imitative (*i*)
  interpretative (*i*)
  meditative (*i*)
  qualitative (*i*)
  quantitative (*i*)
  resuscitative (*i*)
  vegetative (*i*)
(trative)
  penetrative (*i*)
(wative)
  insinuative (*i*)
(vative)
  innovative
(yative)
  appreciative (*i*)
  associative (*i*)
  creative
    procreative (*i*)

recreative (*i*)
depreciative (*i*)

AT-l
battle
  embattle
cattle
chattel
prattle
rattle
tattle
(yattle)
  Seattle

A-tless
baitless
dateless
freightless
gateless
hateless
mateless
stateless
weightless
(ate less, etc.)

A-tli (AIT-li)
(dately)
  sedately
greatly
lately
(rately)
  irately
stately
straightly

AT-li (UT-li)
(cutly)
  delicately
(lutly)
  articulately
    inarticulately
  desolately
  disconsolately
(mutly)
  approximately
  consummately

intimately
ultimately
(nutly)
  affectionately
  alternately
  compassionately
  effeminately
  extortionately
  fortunately
(rutly)
  accurately
    inaccurately
  considerately
    inconsiderately
  elaborately
  literately
    illiterately
  moderately
    immoderately
  temperately
    intemperately
(yutly)
  appropriately

AT-ling
battling
Gatling
prattling
rattling
tattling

AT-lur
battler
prattler
rattler
Statler
tattler

A-tment (AIT-ment)
(batement)
  abatement
statement
  instatement
    reinstatement
  overstatement
  understatement

A-tness (AIT-ness)
(dateness)
　sedateness
greatness
lateness
(nateness)
　innateness
　ornateness
straightness

AT-ness
fatness
flatness
patness

A-to
Cato
(mato)
　tomato
Plato
(tato)
　potato

AT-o
bateau (i)
château (i)
(lato)
　mulatto
plateau (i)

AT-o (OT-o)
gato (*Spanish*)
　legato
　obbligato
(koto)
　pizzicato
　staccato
motto
　tomato
(rato)
　enamorato

AT-ra
(matra)
　Sumatra
(patra)

Cleopatra

A-tree
bay tree
May tree

AT-rik
Patrick
(yatrik)
　geriatric
　theatric

A-trun
matron
patron

AT-u (ATCH-oo)
atchoo
statue
(at you, etc.)

AT-um
atom
datum
(latum)
　postulatum
(matum)
　ultimatum
(ratum)
　erratum
stratum
　substratum

A-tur (A-chur)
(clature)
　nomenclature
(lature)
　legislature
nature

A-tur
baiter
　debater
　incubator
cater
　adjudicator

duplicator
fabricator
fornicator
indicator
lubricator
prevaricator
crater
　Crater, Judge
freighter
gator
　alligator
　instigator
　interrogator
　investigator
　litigator
　navigator
greater
hater
later
　annihilator
　calculator
　interpolator
　legislator
　manipulator
　perambulator
　percolator
　regulator
　simulator
　speculator
　stimulator
　translator
　ventilator
　violator
mater
　alma mater
(natur)
　exterminator
　fascinator
　impersonator
　originator
pater
(quater)
　equator
rater
　accelerator
　collaborator

decorator
first-rater, etc.
generator
moderator
narrator
operator
  cooperator
refrigerator
respirator
separator
satyr
skater
straighter
administrator
demonstrator
illustrator
'tater
  agitator
  annotator (i)
  commentator
  computator
  dictator
  hesitater
  imitator
  meditator
  precipitator
  spectator
traitor
  arbitrator
  perpetrator
(vatur)
  captivator
  cultivator
  elevator
  innovator
  renovator
waiter
(yatur)
  appropriator
  aviator
  conciliator
  creator
  delineator
  gladiator
  mediator
  radiator

More **AT-ur** *rhymes*
can be found by
attaching the ending
to the **AT-ed** *verbs.*

AT-ur
batter
chatter
clatter
fatter
flatter
hatter
latter
matter
patter
platter
satyr
scatter
shatter
smatter
spatter
  bespatter
splatter
tatter

AT-urn
pattern
Saturn
slattern

AT-us
(flatus)
  afflatus
hiatus
(ratus)
  apparatus
status

A-twai
gateway
straight way
straitway

A-ur
gayer
grayer

layer
  overlayer
mayor
payer
player
  displayer
prayer
(sayer)
  soothsayer
slayer
sprayer
stayer
(trayer)
  betrayer
  portrayer
(veyor)
  conveyor
  purveyor
  surveyor

AV-a (AH-va)
brava
guava
Java
lava
(sava)
  cassava

AV-e (AH-vai)
ave
(gahvay)
  agave

AV-el
cavil
gavel
gravel
ravel
  unravel
travel

AV-eld
graveled
raveled
traveled
  untraveled

A-ven
craven
graven
haven
maven (*Yiddish*)
raven
ravin'
shaven
  unshaven
(slavin', etc.)

A-vi
gravy
navy
slavey
wavy

AV-id
avid
gravid

AV-ij
lavage
ravage
savage
scavage

A-ving
braving
caving
craving
(graving)
  engraving
'having
  behaving
    misbehaving
laving
paving
raving
saving
shaving
slaving
waiving
waving

AV-ing
calving
halving
having
salving

A-vis
avis
  rara avis
Davis, Jefferson
(gave us, etc.)

AV-ish
lavish
ravish

A-vli (AIV-li)
bravely
gravely

A-vment (AIV-ment)
pavement
slavement
  enslavement

A-vness (AIV-ness)
braveness
graveness

AV-o (AH-vo)
bravo
(tavo)
  octavo

A-vur
braver
(davur)
  cadaver
favor
  disfavor
flavor
graver
quaver
  demiquaver
paver
saver

savor
shaver
slaver
waiver
waver

AV-ur (AH-vur)
(daver)
  cadaver
(laver)
  palaver
slaver
suaver

AV-urn
cavern
tavern

A-vyur
(havior)
  behavior
    misbehavior
savior

A-yo
K.O.
kayo
Mayo
mayo
(away-o, etc.)

AZ-a
Gaza
plaza
(yaza)
  piazza
(has a)

A-zal
hazel
  witch hazel
nasal
(prazel)
  appraisal

AZ-ard
hazzard
mazzard

A-zez
blazes
braises
brazes
crazes
dazes
gazes
glazes
grazes
hazes
mazes
  amazes
phases
phrases
  paraphrases
praises
raises
razes

A-zhun
(brazhun)
  abrasion
(kazhun)
  occasion
(quazhun)
  equation
(razhun)
  erasion
suasion
  dissuasion
  persuasion
(vazhun)

evasion
invasion

A-zi
crazy
daisy
hazy
lazy

A-zing
blazing
braising
brazing
dazing
gazing
  stargazing
glazing
grazing
hazing
lazing
mazing
  amazing
phrasing
  paraphrasing
praising
  upraising

AZ-l
dazzle
  bedazzle
  razzle-dazzle
frazzle

AZ-ling
dazzling
frazzling

AZ-ma
asthma
plasma
  protoplasma
(tasma)
  phantasma
(yasma)
  miasma

A-zon
blazon
  emblazon
brazen
glazen
raisin
(blazin', etc.)

AZ-um
chasm
  sarcasm
plasm
  bioplasm
(yasm)
  enthusiasm

A-zur
blazer
gazer
  stargazer
geyser
laser
maser
phaser
praiser
  appraiser
raiser
razer
razor

202

E

E-a (EE-ya)
(dia)
  idea
  Medea
(kia)
  Latakia
mia *(Italian)*
  Crimea
  mama mia (*Italian*)
Pia
  Cassiopea
  onomatopoeia
  pharmacopoeia
(ria)
  Maria
    Ave Maria
    Santa Maria
(sia)
  panacea
(zia)
  Hosea
(see ya, etc.)

E-al
deal
  ideal
(jeal)
  laryngeal (*i*)
real
  unreal

E-an
(beyun)
  Caribbean
  Maccabean
  plebeian
(deyun)
  Chaldean
(leyun)
  Galilean
(meyun)
  Crimean
peon

European

E-ba
(meba)
  amoeba
Sheba, Queen of

E-bi
freebie
Seabee
C.B.
T.B.

E-biz (EE-beez)
freebies
(jeebies)
  heebie-jeebies
Seabees

EB-ing
ebbing
  Krafft-Ebing,
    Richard von
webbing

EB-l
pebble
rebel
treble

E-bo
(sebo)
  placebo
(zebo)
  gazebo

E-bord
freeboard
keyboard
seaboard

E-born
freeborn
seaborne

ECH-ee
sketchy
tetchy

E-chez
beaches
beeches
bleaches
breaches
breeches
leeches
peaches
  impeaches
preaches
reaches
  overreaches
screeches
(seechez)
  beseeches
speeches
teaches

E-chi
litchi
peachy
preachy
reachy
screechy

E-ching
I Ching (*Chinese*)
beaching
bleaching
breaching
breeching
leaching
leeching
(peaching)

impeaching
preaching
reaching
screeching
(seeching)
  beseeching
teaching

ECH-ing
etching
fetching
retching
sketching
stretching

ECH-up
ketchup
(stretch up, etc.)

E-chur
bleacher
breacher
creature
feature
leacher
(peacher)
  impeacher
preacher
screecher
teacher

ECH-ur
etcher
fetcher
fletcher
lecher
sketcher
stretcher

E-dbed (EED-bed)
reed bed
seedbed
weed bed

ED-beet
deadbeat
(red beet, etc.)

ED-bug
bedbug
dead bug
(red bug, etc.)

E-ded
beaded
deeded
heeded
  unheeded
kneaded
needed
(peded)
  impeded
  stampeded
pleaded
reeded
seeded
ceded
  acceded
  anteceded
  conceded
  exceeded
  interceded
  preceded
  proceeded
  receded
  succeeded
  superseded
weeded
  unweeded

ED-ed
bedded
  embedded
dreaded
headed
  addleheaded
  bareheaded
  beheaded

clearheaded
fatheaded, etc.
leaded
shredded
threaded
wedded
  unwedded

E-den
Eden
Sweden
(needin', etc.)

ED-en
deaden
leaden
redden
(spreadin', etc.)

E-dense
(cedence)
  antecedence
  intercedence
  precedence
credence
(antecedents, etc.)

E-dent
(cedent)
  antecedent
  precedent
credent
needn't

ED-est
reddest
deadest

E-dful (EED-ful)
deedful
heedful
  unheedful
needful
  unneedful

E-dgroan (EED-groan)
reed-grown
seed-grown
weed-grown

ED-hed
deadhead
redhead

ED-heet
dead heat
red heat

E-di
beady
(deedy)
   indeedy
greedy
needy
reedy
seedy
speedy
weedy

ED-i
eddy
heady
ready
   already
   unready
steady
   unsteady
thready

E-dik
(medic)
   comedic
(pedic)
   encyclopedic
Vedic

E-dikt
edict
predict (i)

E-ding
beading
bleeding
   unbleeding
breeding
   inbreeding (i)
   interbreeding
feeding
   overfeeding
   underfeeding
heeding
   unheeding
leading
   misleading
needing
kneading
(peding)
   impeding
   stampeding
pleading
reading
   misreading
reeding
seeding
   reseeding
   superseding
ceding
   acceding
   conceding
   exceeding
   interceding
   preceding
   proceeding
   receding
   seceding
   succeeding
   superceding
speeding
weeding

ED-ing
bedding
   embedding
dreading
heading
   beheading

leading
redding
shedding
sledding
spreading
   bespreading
   overspreading
threading
treading
   retreading
wedding

ED-ish
deadish
reddish

ED-it
credit
   accredit
   discredit
edit
(said it, etc.)

E-dl
needle
tweedle
wheedle

ED-l
medal
meddle
pedal
   bipedal
peddle
treadle

E-dless (EED-less)
creedless
heedless
needless
seedless
steedless
weedless

ED-less
bedless

breadless
headless

ED-li
deadly
medley

ED-line
breadline
deadline
headline

E-dling (EED-ling)
needling
seedling
wheedling

ED-ling
meddling
peddling

ED-lite
headlight
red light

ED-lock
deadlock
wedlock

E-dlur (EED-lur)
needler
wheedler

ED-lur
meddler
medlar
peddler

ED-man
dead man
headman
red man

E-do
credo
Lido

Toledo
(pedo)
  torpedo

ED-rest
bed rest
headrest

E-dtime (EED-time)
feed time
seed time
lead time

E-dur
breeder
cedar
feeder
leader
pleader
reader
speeder
weeder

ED-ur
cheddar
deader
header
redder
shredder
spreader
threader
treader

E-est
freest
weest

E-fdom (EEF-dom)
chiefdom
fiefdom

E-fi
beefy
leafy

E-fur
briefer
reefer

EF-ur
deafer
heifer
zephyr

E-guing
(tiguing)
  fatiguing
(triguing)
  intriguing

EG-ing
egging
begging
legging
pegging

E-gl
eagle
beagle
legal
  illegal
regal
sea gull
(viegle)
  inveigle

EG-nant
pregnant
regnant
  interregnant

E-gress
egress
Negress
regress (i)

E-gur
eager
  overeager
leaguer
  beleaguer

little leaguer
meager
(triguer)
  intriguer

EG-ur
beggar
(legger)
  bootlegger (*i*)

E-ing
being
(creeing)
  decreeing
fleeing
freeing
(greeing)
  agreeing
    disagreeing
seeing
  farseeing
  foreseeing
  overseeing
  unseeing
teeing
  guaranteeing

E-ist
deist
theist

E-izm
deism
(teeism)
  absenteeism
theism
  monotheism (*i*)
  polytheism (*i*)

EJ-ez
edges
dredges
hedges
ledges
  alleges
pledges

sledges
wedges

EJ-ing
edging
dredging
fledging
hedging
ledging
  alleging
pledging
sledging
wedging

E-jun
legion
  collegian
region
(wejun)
  Norwegian

E-ka
(peeka)
  Topeka
(reeka)
  Costa Rica
  eureka
(yeeka)
  Tanganyika

EK-a
(becca)
  Rebecca
Mecca

E-kal
fecal
treacle

E-ken (EE-ken)
weaken
(see **EK-on,** *page 201)*

E-kest
bleakest
meekest

weakest

E-ki
cheeky
cliquey
creaky
leaky
sleeky
sneaky
squeaky
streaky

E-kide
meek-eyed
weak-eyed

E-king
creaking
leaking
peeking
reeking
seeking
shrieking
sneaking
speaking
  bespeaking
  unspeaking
tweaking
wreaking

EK-ing
checking
decking
flecking
pecking
  henpecking (*i*)
recking
wrecking
trekking

E-kish
cliquish
freakish
weakish

EK-l
freckle
heckle
shekel
speckle

EK-less
feckless
necklace
reckless
speckless

E-kli
bleakly
  obliquely
meekly
(neekly)
  uniquely
sleekly
treacly
weakly
weekly

EK-li
freckly
speckly

EK-ling
freckling
heckling
speckling

EK-mate
checkmate
deck mate

E-kness (EEK-ness)
bleakness
  obliqueness
meekness
(neekness)
  uniqueness
sleekness
weakness

EK-ning
beckoning
reckoning

EK-o
echo
deco
  art deco
gecko
secco

E-kok
Leacock, Stephen
peacock
seacock

E-kon
beacon
deacon
weaken
(speakin', etc.)

EK-on
beckon
reckon

EK-ond
beckoned
reckoned
second

E-krab
pea crab
seacrab
treecrab

EK-shun
(fection)
  affection
    disaffection
  confection
  defection
  infection
    disinfection
  perfection
    imperfection

flexion
  deflection
  inflection
  reflection
(jection)
  abjection
  dejection
  ejection
  injection
  interjection
  objection
  projection
  rejection
  subjection
(lection)
  collection
    recollection
  dilection
    predilection
  election
    reelection
  intellection
  selection
(nection)
  connection
(plexion)
  complexion
(rection)
  correction
  direction
    indirection
    misdirection
  erection
  insurrection
  resurrection
section
  bisection
  dissection
  intersection
  vivisection
(spection)
  circumspection
  inspection
  introspection
  retrospection
(tection)

detection
protection
(vection)
  circumvection

EK-sing
flexing
(nexing)
  annexing
(plexing)
  perplexing
vexing

EK-stant
extant
sextant

EK-stile
sextile
textile

EK-sus
nexus
plexus
  solar plexus
sexes (i)
Texas
(wrecks us, vex us, etc.)

EK-tant
(fectant)
  disinfectant
(flectant)
  reflectant
(spectant)
  expectant
  respectant
  suspectant

EK-ted
(fected)
  affected
    disaffected
    unaffected
  confected
  defected

effected
infected
  disinfected
perfected
(flected)
deflected
inflected
reflected
(glected)
  neglected
(rected)
  corrected
  directed
    misdirected
erected
resurrected
(sected)
  bisected
  dissected
  intersected
(spected)
  expected
    unexpected
  inspected
  respected
  suspected
    unsuspected
(tected)
  detected
  objected
  protected

EKT-ful
(glectful)
  neglectful
(spectful)
  respectful
    disrespectful

EK-tik
(clectic)
  eclectic
hectic
(lectic)
  dialectic
(plectic)

apoplectic

EK-ting
(fecting)
  affecting
  effecting
  infecting
    disinfecting
(flecting)
  deflecting
  reflecting
(glecting)
  neglecting
(jecting)
  ejecting
  injecting
  interjecting
  objecting
  projecting
  rejecting
  subjecting
(lecting)
  collecting
    recollecting
  electing
  selecting
(necting)
  connecting
    disconnecting
(recting)
  directing
    misdirecting
  erecting
  resurrecting
(secting)
  dissecting
(specting)
  expecting
  inspecting
  respecting
    self-respecting
  suspecting
    unsuspecting

EK-tive
(fective)

affective
defective
effective
  ineffective
infective
(flective)
  deflective
inflective
reflective
(jective)
  injective
  objective
  subjective
(lective)
  collective
elective
selective
(nective)
  connective
(rective)
  corrective
directive
(spective)
  circumspective
  inspective
  introspective
perspective
prospective
respective
  irrespective
retrospective
(tective)
  detective)
protective

Ek-trum
plectrum
spectrum

Ek-tur (EK-chur)
(fecture)
  confecture
(jecture)
  conjecture
lecture
(tecture)

architecture

EK-tur
(flector)
  deflector
  reflector
(jector)
  injector
  objector
  projector
hectare
hector
(lector)
  collector
  elector
  selector
nectar
  connector
rector
  director
sector
spectre
  inspector
  prospector
  respecter
(tector)
  detector
  protector
vector

EK-tus
prospectus
(expect us, etc.)

E-kur
beaker
bleaker
meeker
peeker
seeker
  self-seeker
sleeker
sneaker
speaker
weaker

EK-ur
checker
chequer
  exchequer
decker
  double-decker
pecker
  woodpecker
wrecker

E-kurz
sneakers
(beakers, etc.)

EK-urz
checkers
(woodpeckers, etc.)

E-kwal
equal
sequel

E-kwense
frequence
sequence

EL-a
(brella)
  umbrella
"fella"
(nella)
  citronella
  prunella
(pella)
  a capella
(tella)
  patella
  tarantella

EL-ant
appellant
propellent
repellent

EL-ba
Elba

Melba

EL-bound
hellbound
spellbound

EL-ching
belching
squelching
welching

EL-chur
belcher
squelcher
welcher

E-lded (EEL-ded)
fielded
shielded
  unshielded
wielded
yielded

E-lding (EEL-ding)
fielding
shielding
wielding
yielding
  unyielding

EL-ding
gelding
melding
welding

EL-dur
elder
gelder
welder
(held 'er, etc.)

EL-fire
hellfire
shellfire

E-li
eely
freely
steely

EL-i
belly
deli
jelly
(sell-e)
  vermicelli
shelly
smelly

EL-ik
(jelic)
  angelic
relic

E-line
beeline
feline
sea-line

E-ling
dealing
  double-dealing
feeling
  unfeeling
healing
(jeeling)
  congealing
  Darjeeling
kneeling
  annealing
pealing
  appealing
  repealing
peeling
reeling
sealing
ceiling
  concealing
squealing
stealing
steeling

(vealing)
  revealing
wheeling

EL-ing
(belling)
  rebelling
dwelling
felling
knelling
(pelling)
  compelling
  impelling
  repelling
quelling
selling
  excelling
  underselling
shelling
smelling
spelling
  dispelling
  expelling
  misspelling
swelling
telling
  foretelling
  fortune-telling
yelling

EL-ish
(bellish)
  embellish
hellish
relish

EL-o
bellow
cello
fellow
hello
mellow
(nello)
  punchinello
(tello)
  Othello

Pocatello
yellow

EL-ot
helot
zealot

EL-ping
helping
yelping

E-lskin (EEL-skin)
eel-skin
real skin
sealskin, etc.

EL-ted
belted
felted
melted
pelted
welted
(*U.S. southern:*
  sheltered, etc.)

EL-thi (EL-thee)
healthy
stealthy
wealthy

EL-ting
belting
felting
melting
pelting
smelting
welting

EL-tur
belter
shelter
smelter
swelter

EL-um
(bellum)

ante-bellum
cerebellum
vellum
(tell 'em, etc.)

E-lur
eeler
dealer
feeler
healer
(jealer)
  congealer
reeler
sealer
squealer
stealer
steeler
wheeler

EL-ur
dweller
feller
  Rockefeller
(peller)
  propeller
seller
cellar
smeller
speller
stellar
  interstellar
sweller
teller
  fortuneteller

EL-us
jealous
zealous
(tell us, etc.)

EL-ving
delving
shelving

E-ma
(dema)

edema
Lima
schema
(tima)
  Fatima
(zema)
  eczema

EM-a
(lema)
  dilemma
je t'aime (*French*)
(*U.S. southern:*
  tremor,etc.)

E-man
bee man
freeman
G-man
he-man
seaman
tea man

EM-bl
(semble)
  assemble
    disassemble
  dissemble
  resemble
tremble

EM-bli
(sembly)
  assembly
trembly

EM-bling
(sembling)
  assembling
  dissembling
  resembling
trembling

EM-bur
ember
member

212

dismember
remember
(sember)
December
(tember)
September
(vember)
November

E-mest
extremest
supremest

E-mi
creamy
dreamy
seamy
(shimi)
sashimi (*Japanese*)
streamy
(see me, etc.)

EM-ik
(demic)
academic
endemic
epidemic
pandemic
(lemic)
polemic
(stemic)
systemic

E-ming
beaming
creaming
deeming
redeeming
dreaming
daydreaming
(feeming)
blaspheming
gleaming
scheming
screaming
seeming

steaming
esteeming
streaming
teeming

EM-ing
(demming)
condemning
Fleming
hemming
lemming
stemming

EM-ish
blemish
Flemish

E-mless (EEM-less)
creamless
dreamless
seamless

E-mli (EEM-lee)
(premely)
supremely
seemly
unseemly
(tremely)
extremely

EM-o
demo
memo

EM-plar
templar
(zemplar)
exemplar

EMP-shun
(demption)
redemption
(yemption)
preemption
(zemption)
exemption

EMP-ted
tempted
attempted
untempted
(yempted)
preempted
(zempted)
exempted

EMP-ting
tempting
attempting
(yempting)
preempting
(zempting)
exempting

EMP-tive
(demptive)
redemptive
(yemptive)
preemptive

E-msong (EEM-song)
dream song
theme song

E-mur
(deemer)
redeemer
dreamer
femur
blasphemer
schemer
screamer
steamer
streamer

E-na
(bena)
verbena
(dena)
Medina
Lena
Messalina

(pena)
  subpoena
(rena)
  arena
  czarina
  farina
  ocarina
  signorina
(thena)
  Athena
Tina
  Argentina
  concertina
(yena)
  hyena
(zena)
  Messina
(*U.S.southern:*
  meaner,etc.)

EN-a
duenna
henna
  Gehenna
senna
(tenna)
  antenna
(venna)
  Ravenna
(yena)
  sienna
  Vienna

E-nal
renal
venal

EN-as
menace
tennis

EN-ching
benching
blenching
clenching
drenching

quenching
trenching
wenching
wrenching

ENCH-man
Frenchman
henchman

EN-chur
bencher
clencher
quencher
trencher

EN-dans
(pendence)
  dependence
    independence
(sendance)
  ascendance
(splendence)
  resplendence
(tendance)
  attendance
(attendants, etc.)

EN-dant
(fendant)
  defendant
pendant
  dependant
    independent
(sendant)
  ascendant
  descendant
  transcendent
(splendant)
  resplendent
(tendant)
  attendant
  superintendent

EN-ded
ended
bended

blended
  unblended
fended
  defended
    undefended
  offended
(friended)
  befriended
    unbefriended
(hended)
  apprehended
    misapprehended
  comprehended
  reprehended
mended
  amended
  commended
  recommended
  emended
pended
  appended
  depended
  impended
(sended)
  ascended
    reascended
  descended
    condescended
  transcended
(spended)
  expended
  suspended
splendid
tended
  attended
    unattended
  contended
  distended
  extended
    unextended
  intended
    superintended
  portended
  pretended
  subtended
wended

EN-di
bendy
(fendi)
  effendi *(Turkish)*
trendy

EN-ding
ending
  unending
bending
  unbending
blending
fending
  defending
  offending
(friending)
  befriending
(hending)
  apprehending
  comprehending
lending
mending
  amending
  commending
    recommending
pending
  appending
  depending
  impending
rending
  heartrending
sending
  ascending
  descending
    condescending
  transcending
spending
  expending
  suspending
(stending)
  distending
tending
  attending
  contending
  extending
  intending

superintending
portending
pretending
  unpretending
trending
vending
wending

E-ndish (EEN-dish)
fiendish
(clean dish, etc.)

END-less
endless
friendless

END-ment
(friendment)
  befriendment
(mendment)
  amendment
(tendment)
  intendment

EN-do
(shendo)
  crescendo
(wendo)
  diminuendo
  innuendo

EN-dum
(dendum)
  addendum
(rendum)
  referendum
(send 'em, etc.)

EN-dur
ender
  tailender
  weekender
bender
blender
fender
  defender

offender
gender
  engender
lender
mender
(pender)
  depender
render
  surrender
sender
slender
spender
  suspender
splendor
tender
  contender
  extender
  pretender
vendor

EN-dus
(mendous)
  tremendous
(pendous)
  stupendous
(rendous)
  horrendous
(send us, etc.)

EN-el
fennel
kennel

E-ness
cleanness
greenness
keenness
leanness
meanness
(reneness)
  sereneness
(sceneness)
  obsceneness

E-nest
cleanest

leanest
meanest

EN-et
senate
tenet

ENG-then
lengthen
strengthen

E-ni
(chini)
  fettucini
genie
(lini)
  Bellini
  Mussolini
meany
(pini)
  scallopini
teeny
weeny

EN-i
any
benny
Jenny
  flying Jenny
  spinning Jenny
many
penny

E-nide
green-eyed
mean-eyed

EN-ik
(genic)
  carcinogenic
  eugenic
  hygienic
  parthenogenic
  photogenic
  pyrogenic, etc.
(lenic)

Hellenic
  Panhellenic
(thenic)
  callisthenic
  neurasthenic

E-ning
cleaning
gleaning
greening
keening
leaning
meaning
  demeaning
preening
screening
(vening)
  convening
weaning
  overweening

EN-ish
(plenish)
  replenish
Rhenish
wennish
(ten-ish, etc.)

E-nli (EEN-lee)
cleanly
greenly
keenly
meanly
queenly
(renely)
  serenely
(scenely)
  obscenely

E-no
(bino)
  bambino
keno
(pino)
  Filipino
Reno

(shino)
  marashino
(sino)
  casino
(tino)
  andantino

EN-on
pennon
tenon

EN-sez
(enses)
  fences
    defenses
    offenses
menses
commences
senses
  incenss
(spences)
  dispenses
tenses
(wenses)
  amanuenses

ENS-forth
henceforth
thenceforth
whenceforth

EN-shal
(dential)
  confidential
  credential
  prudential
  residential
  presidential
  providential
(gential)
  tangential
(lential)
  pestilential
(nential)
  exponential
(quential)

sequential
consequential
(rential)
deferential
differential
inferential
preferential
referential
reverential
torrential
(sential)
essential
inessential
nonessential
quintessential
unessential
(stential)
existential
(tential)
potential
(wential)
influential
(yential)
experiential

EN-shun
(hension)
apprehension
misapprehension
preapprehension
comprehension
incomprehension
mention
dimension
(sension)
ascension
descension
condescension
dissension
(spension)
suspension
(stention)
abstention
extension
tension
attention

inattention
detention
distension
intention
obtention
portention
pretension
retention
(vention)
circumvention
contravention
convention
intervention
invention

EN-shund
mentioned
unmentioned
(tentioned)
well-intentioned

EN-shus
(senshus)
licentious
(tentious)
contentious
pretentious
sententious
(yentious)
conscientious

EN-sil
(hensil)
prehensile
pencil
stencil
(tensil)
utensil

EN-sild
penciled
stenciled

EN-sing
(densing)
condensing

fencing
(mensing)
commencing
(pensing)
recompensing
sensing
incensing
(spencing)
dispensing

EN-sive
(fensive)
defensive
offensive
inoffensive
(hensive)
apprehensive
comprehensive
incomprehensive
pensive
(spensive)
expensive
inexpensive
(stensive)
extensive
(tensive)
intensive

ENS-less
fenceless
defenseless
senseless
(spenseless)
expenseless

ENS-ness
denseness
(menseness)
immenseness
tenseness
intenseness

EN-sur
censer
censor
denser

condenser
fencer
Spencer
dispenser
tensor
extensor

EN-tal
dental
accidental
coincidental
incidental
occidental
gentle
lentil
mental
alimental
complemental
complimental
departmental
detrimental
developmental
elemental
experimental
fundamental
governmental
monumental
parliamental
regimental
rudimental
sacramental
sentimental
unsentimental
supplemental
temperamental
testamental
(nental)
continental
intercontinental
transcontinental
rental
parental
(yental)
Oriental

EN-tans
(pentans)
repentance
unrepentance
sentence

EN-ted
dented
indented
unprecedented
(lented)
relented
(mented)
augmented
battlemented (i)
cemented
commented
complimented
demented
fermented
fomented
lamented
ornamented
unornamented
supplemented
tormented
untormented
(pented)
repented
(quented)
frequented
rented
scented
unscented
absented
accented
assented
consented
dissented
presented
represented
misrepresented
resented
tented
contented
discontented

ill-contented
vented
circumvented
invented
prevented
(zented)
presented
represented
misrepresented
resented

ENT-ful
(ventful)
eventful
uneventful
(zentful)
resentful

En-ti
plenty
twenty

ENT-ing
denting
(lenting)
relenting
unrelenting
(penting)
repenting
(menting)
augmenting
cementing
complimenting
fermenting
fomenting
lamenting
ornamenting
supplementing
tormenting
(quenting)
frequenting
renting
scenting
accenting
assenting
consenting

dissenting
tenting
  contenting
venting
  circumventing
  inventing
  preventing
(zenting)
  presenting
  representing
    misrepresenting
  resenting

EN-tis
(mentis)
  non compos mentis
  (*Latin*)
(prentis)
  apprentice
(lent us, etc.)

EN-tist
dentist
(prentist)
  apprenticed

EN-tive
(sentive)
  incentive
(tentive)
  attentive
    inattentive
  retentive
(ventive)
  inventive

ENT-less
(lentless)
  relentless
(scentless, etc.)

ENT-li
(dently)
  evidently
gently
(lently)

insolently
(nently)
  eminently
(sently)
  innocently
(tently)
  impotently (*i*)
  intently
(ent *plus* ly *adverbial
  endings, all of which
  are awkward)*

ENT-ment
(tentment)
  contentment
(zentment)
  resentment

EN-to
lento
(mento)
  divertimento
  memento
  pimento
  portamento
  pronunciamento
  Sacramento

EN-tor
centaur
mentor
stentor

EN-tri
entry
gentry
sentry

EN-tur
enter
  reenter
center
  dissenter
mentor
  experimenter
  lamenter

tormenter
(quenter)
  frequenter
renter
(venter)
  inventer
  preventer
(zenter)
  presenter

EN-ture
(benture)
  debenture
denture
  indenture
venture
  adventure
    misadventure
    peradventure

EN-tus
(mentous)
  momentous
  tentus
  portentous
*(see **EN-tis**, page 212)*

E-nur
cleaner
gleaner
greener
keener
leaner
meaner
  demeanor
    misdemeanor
(rener)
  serener
(seener)
  obscener
wiener

E-nus
genus
Venus
(seen us, etc.)

EN-za
(denza)
    cadenza
    credenza
(wenza)
    influenza

EN-zes
cleanses
lenses

E-o
Cleo
Leo
Rio
trio

E-on
eon
neon
peon
(be on, etc.)

EP-ard
leopard
peppered
shepherd

E-pen
cheapen
deepen
steepen

E-pi
cheapy
creepy
sleepy
tepee
weepy

EP-id
tepid
trepid
    intrepid

E-pij
seepage
sweepage

E-ping
creeping
heaping
keeping
housekeeping
safekeeping
leaping
peeping
reaping
sleeping
oversleeping
unsleeping
sweeping
weeping
    unweeping

E-pl
people
steeple

E-pness (EEP-ness)
cheapness
deepness

EP-shun
(sepshun)
    conception
        misconception
        preconception
    contraception
    deception
        self-deception
    exception
    inception
    perception
        apperception
    reception

EP-tik
(leptik)
    analeptic
    cataleptic

epileptic
nympholeptic
peptic
    dyspeptic
    eupeptic
septic
    antiseptic
    aseptic
skeptic

E-pur
cheaper
cheeper
creeper
deeper
keeper
    housekeeper
    shopkeeper
leaper
peeper
reaper
sleeper
steeper
sweeper
weaper

EP-ur
hepper
leper
pepper
stepper

ER-as
terrace
(see **ER-is,** *page 215)*

ER-bl
gerbil
herbal
verbal

E-rens (EE-runse)
clearance
(ferense)
    interference
(herense)

adherence
coherence
  incoherence
(perense)
  appearance
    disappearance
    reappearance
(verense)
  perseverance

E-rent
(herent)
  adherent
  coherent
    incoherent
  inherent
(verent)
  perseverant

E-rest
dearest
drearest
merest
nearest
queerest
serest
  sincerest
sheerest
(sterest)
  austerest
(verest)
  severest

E-rful (EER-ful)
earful
cheerful
fearful
  unfearful
tearful

E-ri
eerie
Erie
beery
bleary
cheery

deary
dreary
(keery)
  hara-kiri
leary
query
smeary
teary
weary
  aweary

ER-i (AIR-ee)
berry
  beriberi
bury
cherry
Derry
  Londonderry
ferry
Mary
merry
nary
  millinery
  stationery
(seree)
  lamasery
sherry
skerry
(stery)
  monastery
Terry
  cemetery
  presbytery
very
wherry
(see AR-i, page 171)

ER-id (AIR-eed)
buried
  unburied
(ferried, etc.)

E-rid (EER-eed)
queried
wearied
  unwearied

E-ride
blear-eyed
clear-eyed
tear-eyed

E-rij
peerage
steerage

ER-ik (AIR-ik)
cleric
derrick
(merik)
  Chimeric
  Homeric
  numeric
(nerik)
  generic
spheric
  atmospheric
  hemispheric
(sterik)
  hysteric
(terik)
  enteric
  esoteric

ER-iks (AIR-iks)
hysterics
(clerics, etc.)

E-ring
earring
cheering
clearing
dearing
  endearing
fearing
  interfering
gearing
hearing
  adhering
  cohering
  overhearing
  rehearing
jeering

leering
  gondoliering
nearing
  auctioneering
  cannoneering
  domineering
  electioneering
  engineering
  mountaineering
  pioneering
peering
  appearing
    disappearing
    reappearing
rearing
  careering
searing
shearing
  cashiering
sneering
spearing
(teering)
  privateering
  volunteering
veering
  persevering
  revering

ER-is (AIR-is)
ferrous
terrace
(dare us, etc.)

ER-ish (AIR-ish)
bearish
cherish
perish

ER-it (AIR-it)
herit
  inherit
    disinherit
merit
  demerit
(grin and bear it, etc.)

ER-iz (EE-reez)
dearies
queries
series
wearies

E-riz (AIR-eez)
Ares
berries
buries
cherries
fairies
ferries
sherries

E-rless (EER-less)
earless
cheerless
fearless
peerless
tearless

E-rli (EER-lee)
clearly
dearly
(leerly)
  cavalierly
merely
nearly
queerly
(seerly)
  sincerely
(sterely)
  austerely
(verely)
  severely
yearly

E-rness (EER-ness)
clearness
dearness
nearness
queerness
sereness
  sincereness
(stereness)

austereness
(vereness)
  severness

E-ro
hero
Nero
zero

E-room
sea room
tea room
(free room, etc.)

ER-or (AIR-or)
error
bearer
terror
(wearer, etc.)
*(see **AR-ur,** page 175)*

ER-ub (AIR-ub)
cherub
(dare rub, etc.)

E-rur (EER-ur)
cheerer
clearer
dearer
hearer
jeerer
mirror
nearer
queerer
shearer
sneerer
spearer
steerer
veerer
  severer

E-rzman (EERZ-man)
steersman
(teersman)
  privateersman

ES-chun
(jestion)
  congestion
  digestion
    indigestion
  ingestion
  suggestion
question

E-sel (E-zl)
easel
Diesel
measle
weasel

ES-ens
essence
(cressense)
  excrescence
(dessense)
  incandescence
  iridescence
  recrudescence
(lessense)
  adolescence
  convalescence
  obsolescence
(messense)
  tumescence
    detumescence
    intumescence
(nessense)
  evanescence
  juvenescence
  senescence
quiescence
  acquiescence
(ressense)
  florescence
    reflorescence
  fluorescence
  phosphorescence
  putrescence
(vessense)
  effervescence

E-sent
decent
  indecent
recent

ES-ent
(bessent)
  herbescent
  pubescent
(cessent)
  incessant
crescent
  excrescent
(dessent)
  incandescent
  iridescent
  recrudescent
(jessent)
  turgescent
(lessent)
  adolescent
  coalescent
  convalescent
  obsolescent
  opalescent
  revalescent
(messent)
  tumescent
(nessent)
  evanescent
  juvenescent
    rejuvenescent
  senescent
(pressent)
  depressent
quiescent
  acquiescent
  liquescent
(ressent)
  florescent
    efflorescent
  fluorescent
  phosphorescent
(tressent)
  putrescent
(vessent)

effervescent

E-sez
ceases
creases
  decreases
  increases
fleeces
greases
leases
  releases
nieces
peaces
pieces
  battle-pieces
(presez)
  caprices
(mantelpieces, etc.)

ES-ful
stressful
*(see **ES**, page 90,*
  plus full)

ESH-ing
freshing
  refreshing
meshing
threshing

ESH-li (ESH-lee)
fleshly
freshly

E-shun
(cretion)
  accretion
  secretion
Grecian
(letion)
  deletion
(pletion)
  completion
  depletion
  repletion

ESH-un
(fession)
  confession
  profession
freshen
(gression)
  aggression
  digression
  ingression
  progression
  regression
  retrogression
  transgression
(pression)
  compression
  depression
  expression
  impression
  oppression
  repression
  suppression
session
cession
  concession
  intercession
  obsession
  procession
  recession
  secession
  succession
(scretion)
  discretion
    indiscretion
(zession)
  possession
    dispossession
    prepossession
    repossession
    self-possession

ESH-ur
fresher
  refresher
pressure
thresher

E-shus
(cetious)
  facetious
specious

ES-i
dressy
messy

E-side
B side
lee side
seaside

ES-ij
message
presage

E-sing
ceasing
  unceasing
creasing
  decreasing
  increasing
fleecing
greasing
leasing
  policing
  releasing
piecing

ES-ing
blessing
dressing
  addressing
  redressing
  undressing
'fessing
  confessing
  professing
(gressing)
  digressing
  progressing
  retrogressing
guessing
(lessing)

coalescing
convalescing
messing
pressing
  compressing
  depressing
  impressing
  oppressing
  repressing
  suppressing
quiescing
  acquiescing
(ressing)
  caressing
(sessing)
  assessing
(spressing)
  expressing
stressing
  distressing
(zessing)
  possessing
    dispossessing
    prepossessing
    unprepossessing

E-sis
(jesis)
  exegesis
(mesis)
  mimesis
(tesis)
  erotesis
thesis
  anesthesis

ES-ive
(gressive)
  aggressive
  digressive
  progressive
  regressive
  retrogressive
  transgressive
(pressive)
  compressive

depressive
expressive
  inexpressive
  unexpressive
impressive
oppressive
repressive
suppressive
(sessive)
  accessive
  excessive
  possessive
  recessive
  successive

ESK-ness
(reskness)
  picturesqueness
(teskness)
  grotesqueness

ES-l
nestle
pestle
trestle
vessel
wrestle

E-sless (EES-less)
ceaseless
creaseless

ES-ling
nestling
wrestling

ES-lur
nestler
wrestler

ES-man
chessman
pressman
yesman

ES-ment
(pressment)
  impressment
  repressment
(sessment)
  assessment

ES-ta
(desta)
  podesta
Vesta
(yesta)
  siesta

ES-tal
festal
vestal

ES-ted
bested
breasted
  single-breasted
chested
crested
(fested)
  infested
  manifested
jested
  congested
  digested
    predigested
  ingested
  suggested
(lested)
  molested
    unmolested
nested
quested
  requested
rested
  arrested
  interested (*i*)
    disinterested (*i*)
  unrested
wrested
tested

attested
detested
protested
vested
  divested
  invested

E-sti
beastie
yeasty

ES-ti
chesty
testy

ES-tik
(jestic)
  majestic
(mestic)
  domestic
(pestic)
  anapestic

ES-tin
destine
  clandestine
  predestine
(testine)
  intestine

E-sting
easting
feasting
yeasting
(bee sting)

ES-ting
besting
breasting
(festing)
  infesting
  manifesting
jesting
  congesting
  digesting
  ingesting

suggesting
(lesting)
  molesting
nesting
questing
  requesting
resting
  arresting
  interesting
  unresting
wresting
testing
  attesting
  contesting
  detesting
  protesting
vesting
  divesting
  investing

ES-tive
festive
jestive
  congestive
  digestive
  suggestive
restive

EST-less
crestless
guestless
jestless
questless
restless

E-stli (EAST-lee)
beastly
priestly

ES-to
(festo)
  manifesto
presto

E-stone
freestone

keystone

ES-tral
(cestral)
  ancestral
kestrel
  orchestral
(nestral)
  fenestral

E-stur
Easter
  nor'easter
  sou'easter
feaster

ES-tur
Chester
  Westchester, etc.
fester
jester
Leicester
Lester
  molester
(mester)
  semester
nester
pester
quester
  sequester
tester
  contester
  protester
(vester)
  investor
wester
  nor'wester
  sou'wester

EST-urd
festered
pestered
(questered)
  sequestered
westered

ES-ture
gesture
vesture
  investure

ES-tus
(bestus)
  asbestos
(rest us, etc.)

ES-ur
dresser
(fessor)
  confessor
  professor
(gressor)
  aggressor
  transgressor
guesser
lesser
messer
presser
  oppressor
  suppressor
(sessor)
  assessor
  predecessor
  successor
(zessor)
  possessor

E-ta
cheeta
(*U.S. southern:*
  cheater, etc.)

ET-a
(detta)
  vendetta
(retta)
  operetta

E-ted
bleated
cheated
(creted)

accreted
excreted
secreted
(feeted)
  defeated
greeted
heated
  reheated
(leted)
  deleted
(peted)
  competed
  repeated
pleated
  completed
  depleted
seated
  conceited
  receipted
  unseated
sheeted
sleeted
treated
  entreated
  maltreated
  retreated

ET-ed
(betted)
  abetted
(detted)
  indebted
fetid
fretted
(gretted)
  regretted
jetted
netted
petted
sweated
(vetted)
  brevetted
whetted
  pirouetted

E-ten
eaten
Eton
beaten
  unbeaten
  weather-beaten
Cretan
sweeten
(cheatin', etc.)

E-test
fleetest
neatest
sweetest
(scretest)
  discreetest

ET-ful
fretful
(getful)
  forgetful
(gretful)
  regretful

E-thal
lethal
(queathal)
  bequeathal

ETH-il
ethyl
methyl

E-thing (EETHE-ing)
breathing
(queathing)
  bequeathing
seething
sheathing
teething
wreathing

ETH-less
breathless
deathless

E-thur (EETHE-ur)
either
breather
neither

ETH-ur
feather
(gether)
  together
    altogether
heather
leather
nether
tether
weather
wether
whether

E-ti
meaty
sweety
treaty
  entreaty

ET-i
(breti)
  libretti
(cheti)
  machete
(feti)
  confetti
Getty, John Paul
  spaghetti
jetty
petty
sweaty
yeti

ET-ik
(betic)
  alphabetic
(cretic)
  syncretic
(detic)
  geodetic
(fetic)

prophetic
(jetic)
 apologetic
 energetic
 exegetic
(letic)
 athletic
(metic)
 arithmetic
 cosmetic
 emetic
 hermetic
 mimetic
(netic)
 frenetic
 genetic
  parthenogenetic
 kinetic
 magnetic
  electromagnetic
 phonetic
 splenetic
(retic)
 paretic
 theoretic
(setic)
 ascetic
(tetic)
 dietetic
 peripatetic
(thetic)
 aesthetic
 anesthetic
 antithetic
 bathetic
 epithetic
 parenthetic
 pathetic
  antipathetic
  apathetic
 sympathetic
 synthetic
(wetic)
 noetic
 poetic

ET-iks
(jetics)
 apologetics, etc.
(wetics)
 poetics

E-ting
eating
 overeating
beating
bleating
cheating
(creting)
 secreting
(feeting)
 defeating
fleeting
greeting
heating
meeting
(peeting)
 competing
 repeating
pleating
 completing
seating
 receipting
 unseating
sheeting
treating
 entreating
 maltreating
 retreating

ET-ing
betting
 abetting
fretting
getting
 begetting
 forgetting
(gretting)
 regretting
jetting
letting
netting

petting
setting
 besetting
 upsetting
sweating
wetting
whetting

ET-is
lettuce
(bet us, etc.)

ET-ish
fetish
(ketish)
 coquettish
wettish

E-tl
beetle
betel
fetal

ET-l
fettle
kettle
metal
mettle
nettle
petal
 Popocatepetl
settle
 resettle

E-tli (EET-li)
(cretely)
 concretely
 discreetly
  indiscreetly
fleetly
meetly
neatly
(pletely)
 completely
sweetly

ET-ling
nettling
settling
  unsettling

ET-ment
(betment)
  abetment
(debtment)
  indebtment
(vetment)
  revetment

E-tness (EET-ness)
(creteness)
  concreteness
  discreetness
(feteness)
  effeteness
fleetness
(leteness)
  obsoleteness
neatness
(pleteness)
  completeness
    incompleteness

E-to
neat-o
  bonito *(Spanish)*
(hito)
  Hirohito
Quito
  mosquito
veto

ET-o
(breto)
  libretto
ghetto
(greto)
  allegreto
(leto)
  stiletto
(meto)

palmetto
(reto)
  amoretto
  Tintoretto
(seto)
  falsetto

ET-rik
metric
  barometric
  diametric
  geometric
  isometric
  symmetric
(stetric)
  obstetric

E-tur
eater
  lotus-eater
  overeater
beater
cheater
fleeter
greeter
heater
liter
meter
  centimeter
  kilometer *(i)*
neater
Peter
  repeater
pleater
  completer
skeeter
sweeter
teeter
tweeter

ET-ur
better
  abettor
debtor
fetter
fretter

getter
  begetter
  go-getter
letter
setter
sweater
wetter

ET-wurk
fretwork
network

E-ur
freer
seer
  overseer
*(see **EE**, page 74,*
  and add er)

E-va
diva
(neva)
  Geneva
viva
  aqua viva

E-val
evil
  medieval
(heaval)
  upheaval
(meval)
  primeval
weevil
  coeval

EV-el
bevel
devil
  bedevil
level
revel
(shevel)
  dishevel

E-ven
even
  uneven

EV-en
leaven
  eleven
heaven
seven

EV-enth
'leventh
  eleventh
seventh

EV-i
bevy
Chevy
heavy
levee
Trevi, Fountains of

E-vij
cleavage
leavage

E-vil
(see E-val, page 222)

E-ving
(cheving)
  achieving
cleaving
grieving
  aggrieving
heaving
  upheaving
leaving
  believing
    disbelieving
  relieving
    unrelieving
(preving)
  reprieving
reaving
  bereaving

(seeving)
  conceiving
    misconceiving
    preconceiving
  deceiving
  perceiving
  receiving
sheaving
steeving
thieving
(treving)
  retrieving
weaving
  interweaving
  unweaving

EX-ing
(see EK-sing, page 202)

E-vish
peevish
thievish

E-vment (EEV-ment)
(chievement)
  achievement
(reavement)
  bereavement

E-vur
beaver
(chiever)
  achiever
cleaver
fever
leaver
lever
  believer
    disbeliever
    unbeliever
  cantilever
  reliever
reaver
(seiver)
  deceiver
  receiver

(triever)
  retriever
weaver
(yeaver)
  náiver

EV-ur
ever
  forever
  however
  howsoever
  whatever
  whatsoever
  whencesoever
  whenever
  whensoever
  wheresoever
  wherever
  whichever
  whichsoever
  whithersoever
  whoever
  whomever
  whosoever
clever
(devor)
  endeavor
lever
  cantilever
never
sever
  assever
  dissever

E-wa (EE-wai)
freeway
leeway
seaway

E-zal (E-zl)
easel
bezel
Diesel
measle
weasel

E-zalz (E-zlz)
measles
(easels, etc.)

EZ-ans
peasants
presence
　omnipresence
presents

EZ-ant
peasant
pheasant
pleasant
　unpleasant
present
　omnipresent

E-zhur
leisure
seizure

EZH-ur
leisure
measure
　admeasure
pleasure
　displeasure
treasure

E-zi
easy
　free and easy
　speakeasy
　uneasy
breezy
cheesy
greasy
　(*U.S. southern only*)
queasy
sleazy
sneezy
wheezy

E-zing
easing
breezing
freezing
(peezing)
　appeasing
pleasing
　displeasing
　unpleasing
seizing
sneezing
squeezing
teasing
wheezing

E-zment (EEZ-ment)
easement
(peasement)
　appeasement

E-zon
reason
　unreason
season
treason
(freezin', etc.)

E-zur
Caesar
freezer
geezer
(nezer)
　Ebenezer
(peezer)
　appeaser
pleaser
sneezer
squeezer
teaser
tweezer
wheezer

I

I-a
hiya
Maya
　Jeremiah
(paya)
　papaya
(sia)
　Messiah
(defy ya, etc.)

I-ad
dryad

hamadryad
dyad
(miad)
　Jeremiad
naiad
triad

I-al
dial
(nial)
　denial
　　self-denial

phial
(spial)
　espial
trial
　retrial
viol
　bass viol

I-am
I am
Priam
Siam

I-ans
(fiance)
  defiance
(liance)
  alliance
    misallianc
  reliance
    self-reliance
(pliance)
  appliance
  compliance
  suppliance

I-ant
client
(fiant)
  defiant
giant
(liant)
  reliant
    self-reliant
pliant
  compliant

I-as
bias
(lias)
  Elias
(nias)
  Ananias

I-bing
(bibing)
  imbibing
bribing
gibing
scribing
  ascribing
  circumscribing
  describing
  inscribing
  prescribing
  proscribing
  subscribing
  transcribing

IB-ing
fibbing
jibbing
(libbing)
  ad-libbing
ribbing
squibbing

IB-it
(hibit)
  exhibit
  inhibit
  prohibit

I-bl
Bible
libel
tribal

IB-l
dribble
kibble
nibble
quibble
scribble
sibyl

IB-ld
ribald
(quibbled, etc.)

IB-let
driblet
giblet

IB-li
dribbly
glibly
quibbly
scribbly

IB-ling
dribbling
nibbling
quibbling
scribbling

sibling

IB-lur
dribbler
nibbler
quibbler
scribbler

I-bol
eyeball
highball
my ball

IB-on
gibbon
ribbon

I-born
highborn
skyborne

I-brow
eyebrow
highbrow
my brow

I-bur
(biber)
  imbiber
fiber
giber
scriber
  inscriber
  prescriber
  proscriber
  subscriber
  transcriber
Tiber (*River*)

IB-ur
fibber
jibber

ICH-ez
itches
bitches

breeches
ditches
flitches
hitches
niches
pitches
riches
  enriches
stitches
switches
twitches
witches
  bewitches

ICH-ing
itching
ditching
hitching
pitching
(riching)
  enriching
stitching
switching
twitching
witching
  bewitching

ICH-less
itchless
hitchless
stitchless
switchless

ICH-ment
(richment)
  enrichment
(witchment)
  bewitchment

ICH-ur
pitcher
richer
stitcher
switcher
twitcher
witcher

bewitcher
water witcher

ID-ans
(biddance)
  forbiddance
riddance

I-danse
(bidance)
  abidance
guidance
  misguidance
(sidence)
  subsidence

I-ded
bided
chided
(fided)
  confided
glided
guided
  misguided
  unguided
(lided)
  collided
  elided
prided
(rided)
  derided
sided
  coincided
  decided
    undecided
  lopsided
  many-sided
  one-sided
  subsided
tided
(vided)
  divided
    subdivided
    undivided
  provided
    unprovided

(zided)
  presided
  resided

ID-ed
kidded
lidded
skidded

ID-en
bidden
  forbidden
  unbidden
hidden
midden
  kitchen midden
ridden
  hagridden
  overridden
  priest-ridden

I-dent
strident
trident

I-di
Friday (*i*)
tidy
  untidy

ID-i (ID-ee)
biddy
  chickabiddy
giddy
kiddy
middy

ID-ik
(midic)
  bromidic
  pyramidic
(ridic)
  juridic
(widik)
  druidic

I-ding
biding
  abiding
chiding
(fiding)
  confiding
gliding
guiding
hiding
(liding)
  colliding
  eliding
priding
riding
  deriding
  overriding
siding
  coinciding
  deciding
  subsiding
sliding
  backsliding
striding
  bestriding
(tiding)
  betiding
(viding)
  dividing
  providing
(ziding)
  presiding
  residing

ID-ing
bidding
  forbidding
  outbidding
  overbidding
kidding
ridding
skidding

ID-ingz
tidings
(sidings, etc.)

I-dl
idle
idol
bridal
bridle
sidle
  fratricidal
  homicidal
  infanticidal
  matricidal
  parricidal
  patricidal
  regicidal
  suicidal
  tyrannicidal
tidal

ID-l
diddle
fiddle
griddle
middle
riddle
twiddle

I-dling
idling
bridling
sidling

ID-ling
diddling
fiddling
middling
riddling
twiddling

ID-ni
kidney
Sidney

ID-o
kiddo
widow

I-dur
eider
chider
cider
  decider
  insider
  outsider
glider
rider
  outrider
slider
spider
(vider)
  divider
  provider
wider

ID-ur
kidder
(sidder)
  consider

I-ens
science
(see **I-ans,** *page 225)*

I-et
diet
quiet
  unquiet
riot
(try it, etc.)

I-fen
hyphen
siphon

IF-en
griffon
stiffen

IF-i
iffy
jiffy
sniffy

spiffy
squiffy

IF-ik
(cific)
  pacific
  specific
(glyphic)
  hieroglyphic
(lific)
  prolific
(nific)
  magnific
(rific)
  calorific
  honorific
  horrific
  soporific
  sudorific
  terrific
(tific)
  beatific
  pontific
  scientific

IF-ing
sniffing
tiffing
whiffing

I-fl
Eiffel
eyeful
rifle
stifle
trifle

IF-l
piffle
riffle
sniffle
whiffle

I-fless
knifeless
lifeless

strifeless
wifeless

I-flike
knifelike
lifelike
wifelike

I-fling
rifling
stifling
trifling

IF-ling
piffling
riffling
sniffling
whiffling

I-flur
stifler
trifler

IF-lur
piffler
riffler
sniffler
whiffler

IF-ted
drifted
gifted
  ungifted
lifted
  uplifted
rifted
shifted
sifted

IF-ti
fifty
nifty
shifty
thrifty

IF-ting
drifting
lifting
  shoplifting (*i*)
  uplifting
rifting
shifting
sifting

IFT-less
shiftless
thriftless

IFT-ur
drifter
lifter
  shoplifter (*i*)
  uplifter (*i*)
shifter
sifter
swifter

I-fur
cipher
  decipher
fifer
knifer
lifer
rifer

IF-ur
differ
sniffer
stiffer

IG-fut
bigfoot
pigfoot

IG-i
biggy
piggy
spriggy
twiggy

IG-ing
digging
gigging
jigging
rigging
  thimblerigging
sprigging
swigging
trigging
twigging
wigging

IG-ish
piggish
priggish
whiggish

IG-l
giggle
jiggle
niggle
sniggle
squiggle
wiggle
wriggle

I-glass
eyeglass
spyglass
(my glass, etc.)

IG-li
(giggly, etc.)

IG-ling
(giggling, etc.)

IG-lur
giggler
(higgler, etc.)

IG-ma
(nigma)
  enigma
sigma
stigma

IG-ment
figment
pigment

IG-mi
pygmy
(dig me, etc.)

IG-nant
(dignant)
  indignant
(lignant)
  malignant
(nignant)
  benignant

IG-or
rigor
vigor
(bigger, etc.)

IG-ot
bigot
spigot

IG-ur
bigger
chigger
digger
jigger
prigger
rigger
  thimblerigger
snigger
swigger
trigger

I-ing
eyeing
buying
  alibiing
crying
  decrying
  descrying
drying
dyeing

dying
  undying
frying
(fying)
  acidifying
  amplifying
  beautifying
  candifying
  certifying
  clarifying
  classifying
  codifying
  countrifying
  crucifying
  damnifying
  dandifying
  defying
  deifying
  dignifying
  edifying
  electrifying
  emulsifying
  exemplifying
  falsifying
  fortifying
  fructifying
  glorifying
  gratifying
  horrifying
  identifying
  indemnifying
  intensifying
  justifying
  liquefying
  magnifying
  modifying
  mollifying
  mortifying
  mystifying
  notifying
  nullifying
  pacifying
  personifying
  petrifying
  preachifying
  purifying

putrefying
qualifying
   disqualifying
rarefying
ratifying
rectifying
sanctifying
satisfying
   dissatisfying
   self-satisfying
   unsatisfying
scarifying
signifying
simplifying
solidifying
specifying
stultifying
stupefying
terrifying
testifying
typifying
unifying
verifying
versifying
   diversifying
vilifying
vitrifying
vivifying
   revivifying
hieing
lying
   allying
   belying
   relying
     self-relying
     underlying
(nying)
   denying
     self-denying
plying
   applying
   complying
     uncomplying
   implying
   multiplying
   replying

supplying
prying
(pying)
   occupying
     preoccupying
shying
sighing
   prophesying
spying
   bespying
   espying
tying
   untying
trying
vieing

IJ-id
frigid
rigid

IJ-ing
bridging
   abridging
ridging

IJ-it
digit
fidget
midget

IJ-on
(ligion)
   religion
pigeon
Stygian
widgeon

IJ-us
(digious)
   prodigious
(ligious)
   religious
     irreligious
     sacreligious
(tigious)
   litigious

I-ka
Leica
   balalaika
mica
pica

IK-en
chicken
quicken
sicken
stricken
   horror-stricken
thicken
(stickin', etc.)

IK-et
cricket
picket
thicket
ticket
wicket
(stick it, etc.)

I-ki
dickey
quickie
Ricky
   gin ricky
sticky
tricky

I-king
biking
liking
   disliking
piking
spiking
striking
Viking

IK-ing
bricking
clicking
flicking
kicking
licking

nicking
pricking
slicking
sticking
ticking

IK-li
prickly
quickly
sickly
slickly
stickly
thickly
trickly

IK-ling
pickling
prickling
tickling
trickling

IK-lish
pricklish
ticklish

IK-lur
prickler
stickler
strickler
tickler

IK-ness
quickness
sickness
slickness
thickness

IK-nik
picnic
(sicknik, etc.)

IK-ning
quickening
sickening
thickening

I-kon
icon
Nikon

IK-sen
Nixon, Richard M.
vixen
(fixin', mixin', etc.)

IK-shun
diction
  addiction
  benediction
  contradiction
  interdiction
  jurisdiction
  malediction
  prediction
  valediction
fiction
  crucifixion
(fliction)
  affliction
friction
(liction)
  dereliction
(piction)
  depiction
(striction)
  constriction
  restriction
(viction)
  conviction
  eviction

IK-si (IK-see)
Dixie
nixie
pixie

IK-sing
fixing
  affixing
  prefixing
  transfixing
mixing

admixing
intermixing

IKS-ture (IKS-chur)
fixture
  affixture
mixture
  admixture

IK-sur
fixer
  affixer
(lixer)
  elixir
mixer

IK-ted
(dicted)
  addicted
  contradicted
  interdicted
  predicted
(flicted)
  afflicted
  conflicted
  inflicted
    self-inflicted
(picted)
  depicted
(stricted)
  constricted
  restricted
    unrestricted
(victed)
  convicted
  evicted

IK-ting
(dicting)
  addicting
  contradicting
  interdicting
  predicting
(flicting)
  afflicting
  conflicting

inflicting
(picting)
depicting
(stricting)
constricting
restricting
(victing)
convicting
evicting

IK-tive
(dictive)
addictive
benedictive
contradictive
indictive
interdictive
jurisdictive
predictive
vindictive
fictive
(flictive)
afflictive
conflictive
inflictive
(pictive)
depictive
(strictive)
constrictive
restrictive
(victive)
convictive

IK-tur (IK-chur)
picture
depicture
stricture

IK-tur
(dicter)
contradicter
predicter
(flicter)
afflicter
inflicter
(picter)

depicter
stricter
constrictor
boa constrictor
victor
(kicked 'er, etc.)

I-kur
biker
hiker
piker
spiker
striker

IK-ur
bicker
clicker
dicker
flicker
kicker
knicker
licker
liquor
quicker
sicker
slicker
snicker
sticker
thicker
ticker
tricker
vicar
wicker

IK-urz
knickers
(bickers, etc.)

IL-a
(dilla)
cedilla
(nilla)
Manila
vanilla
(rilla)
gorilla

guerrilla
Scylla
Priscilla
(tilla)
flotilla
villa
(zilla)
maxilla

IL-an
villain
(willin', etc.)

I-land
island
highland
(my land, etc.)

I-ldest (ILE-dest)
mildest
wildest

IL-ding
building
rebuilding
gilding

I-ldli (ILE-dlee)
mildly
wildly

I-ldlike (ILE-dlike)
childlike
wildlike
(styled like, etc.)

I-ldness (ILE-dness)
mildness
wildness

I-ldur (ILE-dur)
milder
wilder

IL-dur
builder

gilder
guilder
wilder
  bewilder

I-lest
vilest
(stylist, etc.)

IL-est
illest
shrillest
stillest

I-let (I-lot)
eyelet
islet
pilot
(defile it, etc.)

IL-et
billet
fillet
millet
skillet

I-lful (ILE-ful)
guileful
wileful

IL-ful
skillful
  unskillful
wilful

I-li (I-lee)
drily
highly
Reilly, the life of
shyly
slily
wily
wryly

IL-i (IL-ee)
billy

hillbilly
Chile
chili
chilly
dilly
  daffy-down-dilly
  Piccadilly
filly
Philly
frilly
hilly
lily
  piccalilli
(nilly)
  willy-nilly
shrilly
silly
stilly

IL-ij
pillage
tillage
village

IL-ik
(dillic)
  idyllic
(krillic)
  acrylic
(tillic)
  dactylic

I-lin
byline
skyline
(high line, etc.)

I-ling
(ciling)
  reconciling
filing
  defiling
guiling
  beguiling
piling
  compiling

riling
smiling
styling
tiling
(viling)
  reviling
whiling

IL-ing
billing
chilling
drilling
filling
  fulfilling
frilling
  befrilling
grilling
killing
milling
shilling
shrilling
spilling
stilling
  distilling
  instilling
swilling
thrilling
tilling
trilling
willing
  unwilling

I-lite
highlight
skylight
twilight
(my light, etc.)

IL-iz
chilies
fillies
lilies
sillies
the willies

IL-ki (IL-kee)
milky
silky

IL-king
bilking
milking

I-lless (ILE-less)
guileless
smileless
wileless

I-lment (ILE-ment)
(filement)
　defilement
(guilement)
　beguilement
(vilement)
　revilement

IL-ment
(filment)
　fulfilment
(stilment)
　instilment

IL-ness
illness
chillness
shrillness
stillness

I-lo
high-low
Milo, Venus de
silo

IL-o
billow
(dillo)
　armadillo
　peccadillo
pillow
willow

IL-ted
hilted
jilted
kilted
lilted
quilted
silted
stilted
tilted
wilted

IL-ti (IL-tee)
guilty
kiltie
silty

IL-ting
jilting
lilting
quilting
silting
tilting
wilting

IL-tur
filter
philter
jilter
quilter

I-lum
phylum
(sylum)
　asylum

I-lur
filer
　defiler
(piler)
　compiler
(siler)
　reconciler
smiler
tiler
viler
　reviler

IL-ur
chiller
driller
filler
　fulfiller
killer
miller
pillar
　caterpillar
Schiller
shriller
spiller
stiller
　distiller
　instiller
swiller
thriller
tiller

IL-yun
billion
(drillion)
　quadrillion
million
　Maximilian
　vermilion
(tillion)
　postillion
　quintillion
　reptilian
　sextillion
trillion
(vilion)
　pavilion
zillion
　Brazilian

IL-yunt
brilliant
(zilient)
　resilient

IL-yunth
billionth
millionth
trillionth

zillionth

I-man
hymen
pieman

I-mat
climate
primate
(time it, etc.)

IM-bal
cymbal
symbol
nimble
thimble

IM-bo
bimbo
(kimbo)
  akimbo
limbo

IM-bur
limber
  unlimber
timber
timbre

IM-en (IM-un)
(simmon)
  persimmon
women
(skimmin', etc.)

IM-est
dimmest
grimmest
primmest
slimmest
trimmest

I-mi
blimey
grimy
limey

rhymy
rimy
slimy
stymie
(try me, etc.)

IM-i (IM-ee)
gimme
jimmy
shimmy

IM-ij
image
scrimmage

IM-ik
mimic
  pantomimic
(nymic)
  patronymic
  synonymic

I-ming
chiming
climbing
griming
  begriming
liming
  beliming
miming
  pantomiming
priming
rhyming
sliming
  besliming
timing

IM-ing
brimming
dimming
  bedimming
skimming
slimming
swimming
trimming

IM-it
limit
(trim it, etc.)

I-mless (IME-less)
chimeless
crimeless
grimeless
rhymeless
rimeless
slimeless
timeless

IM-less
brimless
limbless
rimless
swimless
vimless
whimless

I-mli (IME-li)
(blimely)
  sublimely
timely
  untimely

IM-li
dimly
grimly
primly
slimly
trimly

IM-ness
dimness
grimness
primness
slimness
trimness

I-mon
Simon
Timon
*(see **I-man**, page 235)*

IM-pi
impy
gimpy
limpy
skimpy
wimpy

IM-ping
crimping
limping
primping
scrimping
shrimping
skimping

IM-pit
lime pit
slime pit

IM-pl
dimple
pimple
simple
wimple

IM-pli
dimply
limply
pimply
simply

IM-pling
dimpling
pimpling
wimpling

IM-pur
crimper
limper
scrimper
shrimper
simper
skimper
whimper

IM-stur
mimester
rhymester

I-mur
(blimer)
   sublimer
chimer
climber
primer
rhymer
timer
   old-timer

IM-ur
brimmer
dimmer
glimmer
grimmer
primer
primmer
shimmer
simmer
skimmer
slimmer
swimmer
trimmer

IM-zi (IM-zee)
flimsy
whimsy

I-na
China
(jina)
   angina
   Regina
(lina)
   Carolina
      North Carolina
      South Carolina
(U.S. southern:
   finer, etc.)

I-nal
final

spinal

IN-ching
inching
cinching
clinching
flinching
   unflinching
lynching
pinching
winching

IN-chur
clincher
flincher
lyncher
pincher

I-nded (INE-ded)
blinded
   self-blinded
   snow-blinded
minded
   bloody-minded
   double-minded
   even-minded
   evil-minded
   fair-minded (*i*)
   feebleminded
   like-minded (*i*)
   low-minded (*i*)
   narrow-minded
   public-minded
   reminded
   simpleminded
   single-minded
   sober-minded
   strong-minded, etc.

IN-ded
(scinded)
   abscinded
   rescinded
winded
   broken-winded
   long-winded

I-ndest (INE-dest)
blindest
kindest

IN-di (IN-dee)
shindy
windy

I-nding (INE-ding)
binding
　unbinding
blinding
finding
grinding
minding
　reminding
winding
　unwinding

IN-dl
brindle
dwindle
kindle
　enkindle
　rekindle
spindle
swindle

I-ndli (INE-dli)
blindly
kindly
　unkindly

IND-ling
brindling
dwindling
kindling
　enkindling
　rekindling
swindling

IND-lur
dwindler
kindler
swindler

I-ndness (INED-ness)
blindness
kindness

I-ndur (INE-dur)
binder
　spellbinder
blinder
finder
　faultfinder (*i*)
　pathfinder (*i*)
　water-finder (*i*)
grinder
kinder
minder
　reminder
winder
　sidewinder (*i*)
　stem-winder

IN-dur
cinder
flinder
hinder
Pindar
pinder
tinder

IN-en
linen
(winnin', etc.)

I-ness
dryness
highness
nighness
shyness
slyness
spryness
wryness

I-nest
finest
(linest)
　malignest
(ninest)

benignest
(pinest)
　supinest
(vinest)
　divinest

IN-et
linnet
minute
spinet
(in it, etc.)

IN-ful
bin full
sinful

ING-gl
jingle
Kringle, Kris
mingle
　commingle
　intermingle
shingle
single
tingle

ING-gli
jingly
shingly
singly
tingly

ING-gling
jingling
mingling
　intermingling
singling
tingling

ING-glur
jingler
mingler
　intermingler
shingler
tingler

ING-go
bingo
dingo
gringo
jingo
lingo
(mingo)
   flamingo

ING-gur
finger
linger
   malinger

ING-i
dinghy
dingy
springy
stingy
stringy
swingy
thingy

ING-ing
bringing
   upbringing
clinging
dinging
flinging
ringing
wringing
singing
   psalm singing, etc.
slinging
springing
stinging
stringing
   unstringing
swinging
winging

ING-ket
trinket
(drink it, etc.)

ING-ki (ING-kee)
inky
blinky
dinky
drinky
finky
ginky
hinky
kinky
pinky
slinky
stinky
winky

ING-kide
blink-eyed
pink-eyed

ING-king
inking
blinking
   unblinking
clinking
drinking
finking
linking
pinking
shrinking
   unshrinking
sinking
slinking
stinking
thinking
   far-thinking, etc.
   unthinking
winking
   hoodwinking (i)

ING-kl
crinkle
sprinkle
   besprinkle
tinkle
twinkle
winkle
   periwinkle

wrinkle

ING-kli
crinkly
pinkly
tinkly
twinkly
wrinkly

ING-kling
inkling
crinkling
sprinkling
   besprinkling
tinkling
twinkling
wrinkling

ING-klur
sprinkler
tinkler
twinkler
wrinkler

ING-kon
Lincoln
(winkin', etc.)

ING-kshun
(stinction)
   distinction
     contradistinction
   extinction

ING-ktive
(stinctive)
   distinctive
     contradistinctive
   instinctive

ING-ktness
(cinctness)
   succinctness
(stinctness)
   distinctness
     indistinctness

ING-kur
inker
blinker
clinker
drinker
linker
pinker
shrinker
sinker
stinker
thinker
tinker
winker
  hoodwinker

ING-less
kingless
ringless
springless
stingless
wingless

ING-let
kinglet
ringlet
springlet
winglet

ING-like
flinglike
kinglike
ringlike
springlike
stinglike
winglike

ING-song
singsong
spring song

ING-time
ring time
springtime
swing time

ING-ur
bringer
clinger
dinger
  humdinger
flinger
ringer
singer
  ballad singer
  Meistersinger
  psalm singer, etc.
slinger
springer
stinger
stringer
swinger
winger
wringer
zinger

I-ni (I-nee)
briny
piney
shiny
spiney
tiny
viney
whiney
winy

IN-i (IN-ee)
blinie
finny
Guinea
  New Guinea
Minnie
  ignominy (*i*)
ninny
Pliny
shinny
skinny
tinny
whinny

IN-ik
(binic)

rabbinic
clinic
cynic
(minic)
  Brahminic

I-ning
(bining)
  combining
(clining)
  declining
  inclining
  reclining
dining
fining
  confining
  defining
  refining
lining
  aligning
  maligning
  outlining (*i*)
mining
pining
  opining
  repining
shining
  outshining
shrining
  enshrining
signing
  assigning
  consigning
  countersigning
twining
  entwining
  intertwining
vining
  divining
whining
wining
(zining)
  designing
  resigning

246

IN-ing
inning
chinning
dinning
(ginning)
  beginning
grinning
pinning
  underpinning
  unpinning
shinning
sinning
  unsinning
skinning
spinning
thinning
tinning
winning

IN-ish
finish
Finnish
(minish)
  diminish
thinnish

IN-jent
(tingent)
  contingent
stringent
  astringent

IN-jez
cringes
fringes
  infringes
hinges
  unhinges
(pinges)
  impinges
singes
tinges
twinges

IN-ji
cringy

dingy
stingy
twingy

IN-jing
cringing
fringing
  infringing
hinging
  unhinging
singeing
tingeing
twingeing

INJ-ment
(fringement)
  infringement
(hingement)
  unhingement
(pingement)
  impingement

IN-jur
injure
cringer
fringer
  infringer
ginger

I-nklad (INE-klad)
pine-clad
vine-clad

IN-less
chinless
finless
kinless
pinless
sinless
skinless
winless

I-nli (INE-lee)
finely
(ninely)
  benignly

saturninely
(pinely)
  supinely
(vinely)
  divinely

I-nment (INE-ment)
(finement)
  confinement
  refinement
(linement)
  alignment
(sinement)
  assignment
  consignment
(line meant, etc.)

I-no
I know
(bino)
  albino
rhino
wino

IN-o
minnow
winnow

I-noff
dine off
sign-off

IN-sing
mincing
rinsing
(vincing)
  convincing
    unconvincing
  evincing

INT-ed
dinted
glinted
hinted
minted
printed

imprinted
misprinted
reprinted
sprinted
squinted
stinted
tinted
  rainbow-tinted, etc.
vinted

IN-ti (IN-tee)
flinty
linty
minty
squinty

INT-ide
flint-eyed
squint-eyed

INT-ing
dinting
glinting
hinting
minting
printing
  imprinting
  misprinting
  reprinting
sprinting
squinting
stinting
  unstinting
tinting
  aquatinting

IN-tri
splintrey
wintry

IN-tur
hinter
printer
splinter
sprinter
squinter

tinter
winter

IN-u
in you
been you
pin you
sinew
skin you
(tinue)
  continue
    discontinue
win you

I-nur
diner
finer
  refiner
liner
  eyeliner (*i*)
  maligner
miner
  underminer
minor
shiner
signer
  consigner
  cosigner
(viner)
  diviner
(ziner)
  designer

IN-ur
inner
dinner
(ginner)
  beginner
sinner
skinner
  mule skinner (*i*)
spinner
thinner
winner
  breadwinner (*i*)

I-nus
minus
sinus
(wine and dine
  us, etc.)

IN-yun
minion
  dominion
pinion
  opinion

I-on
ion
lion
  ant lion (*i*)
  dandelion
  mountain lion
  sea lion (*i*)
Ryan
Orion
scion
Zion
(buyin', etc.)

I-or
prior
(see I-ur, page 252)

I-ot
riot
(see I-et, page 227)

I-pend
ripened
stipend

I-pest
ripest
typist

IP-et
snippet
(skip it, etc.)

248

IP-i (IP-ee)
chippy
dippy
drippy
flippy
grippy
hippie
lippy
nippy
nippy
sippy
  Mississippi
slippy
snippy
tippy
yippee
zippy

IP-in
pippin
(sippin', etc.)

I-ping
griping
piping
striping
swiping
typing
  stereotyping
wiping

IP-ing
chipping
dipping
dripping
flipping
gripping
nipping
quipping
  equipping
ripping
shipping
  transshipping
sipping
skipping
slipping

snipping
stripping
  outstripping
tipping
tripping
whipping

IP-l
cripple
nipple
ripple
stipple
tipple
triple

IP-let
ripplet
triplet

IP-li (IP-lee)
fliply
Ripley, Robert L.
ripply
triply

IP-ling
crippling
Kipling, Rudyard
rippling
stippling
stripling
tippling

IP-lur
crippler
tippler

IP-ment
(quipment)
  equipment
shipment
  transshipment

IP-shun
(gyption)
  Egyptian

(niption)
  conniption
(scription)
  circumscription
  conscription
  description
  inscription
  prescription
  subscription
  transcription

IP-si (IP-see)
dipsy
gypsy (i)
(kipsie)
  Poughkeepsie
tipsy

IP-tik
cryptic
(cliptic)
  ecliptic
(liptic)
  apocalyptic
  elliptic
styptic
triptych

IP-tive
(scriptive)
  descriptive
    indescriptive
  inscriptive
  prescriptive
  proscriptive

I-pur
griper
piper
  bagpiper (i)
  pied piper
riper
sniper
striper
swiper
typer

daguerreotyper
electrotyper
linotyper
stereotyper
viper
wiper

IP-ur
chipper
clipper
dipper
dripper
flipper
gripper
hipper
kipper
nipper
ripper
shipper
sipper
skipper
slipper
  lady's slipper
snipper
stripper
tipper
tripper
whipper
zipper
(clip'er, etc.)

IR-ah
hurrah
sirrah

I-rant
spirant
  aspirant
tyrant
  arch-tyrant

I-rat
pirate
(wire it, etc.)

I-rate
irate
gyrate
(high rate, etc.)

IR-el
(ferral)
  deferral
squirrel
(girl, etc.)
(see **U-ral,** *page 295)*

I-reme
bireme
trireme

I-ri
aerie
diary
fiery
(kyrie)
  Valkyrie
(quiry)
  enquiry
  inquiry
wiry

IR-ik
lyric
Pyrrhic
  empiric
(tiric)
  satiric
  satyric

I-ring
firing
hiring
(miring)
  admiring
(quiring)
  acquiring
  enquiring
(spiring)
  aspiring
    unaspiring

conspiring
expiring
inspiring
  uninspiring
perspiring
suspiring
transpiring
tiring
attiring
retiring
untiring
wiring
(ziring)
  desiring
    undesiring

I-rist
direst
(gyrist)
  panegyrist
lyrist

I-rness (IRE-ness)
direness
(tireness)
  entireness

I-ro
Cairo
gyro
  autogyro
tyro

I-rode
byroad
highroad

I-ron
iron
Byron, Lord
(inspirin', etc.)

IR-up
chirrup
stirrup
syrup
(stir up, etc.)

I-rur
direr
hirer
(mirer)
  admirer
(quirer)
  enquirer
  inquirer
(spirer)
  inspirer
wirer

I-rus
Cyrus
(pyrus)
  papyrus
virus
(zirous)
  desirous
(inspire us, etc.)

I-rwurks
fireworks
wire works
(tire works, etc.)

IS-est
(cisest)
  concisest
  precisest
nicest

IS-ez
(bisses)
  abysses
(disses)
  prejudices (*i*)
(fisses)
  artifices (*i*)
  benefices (*i*)
  edifices (*i*)
hisses
kisses
misses
pisses
  precipices (*i*)

ISH-an
(see **ISH-un**, *page 244)*

ISH-al
(dicial)
  judicial
    extrajudicial
    prejudicial
(ficial)
  artificial
  beneficial
  official
  sacrificial
  superficial
(nitial)
  initial

ISH-ense
(niscience)
  omniscience
(ficience)
  proficience

ISH-ent
(ficient)
  deficient
  efficient
    inefficient
  proficient
  sufficient
    insufficient
(niscient)
  omniscient

ISH-ful
dishful
wishful

ISH-i
fishy
squishy
swishy

ISH-ing
dishing
fishing
squishing
swishing
wishing
  ill-wishing
  well-wishing

ISH-un
(bition)
  ambition
  exhibition
  inhibition
  prohibition
(dition)
  addition
  audition
  condition
    precondition
  edition
  erudition
  expedition
  perdition
  rendition
  sedition
  tradition
    extradition
fission
(jician)
  logician
  magician
(lition)
  abolition
  coalition
  demolition
  Galician
  volition
mission
  academician
  admission
    commission
    emission
    intermission
    omission
    permission
    readmission
    remission
    submission

transmission
(nition)
  admonition
  cognition
    precognition
    recognition
  definition
  ignition
  mechanician
  munition
    ammunition
  premonition
  punition
  technician
    pyrotechnician
(rition)
  apparition
  parturition
  rhetorician
(stition)
  statistician
  superstition
(tition)
  arithmetician
  competition
  dialectician
  mathematician
  optician
  partition
  petition
    repetition
  politician
  practician
  tactician
(trition)
  attrition
  contrition
  electrician
  geometrician
  nutrition
  obstetrician
  patrician
(wission)
  tuition
    intuition
(zition)

acquisition
disquisition
inquisition
musician
physician
  metaphysician
position
  composition
  deposition
  disposition
  exposition
  imposition
  juxtaposition
  opposition
  preposition
  proposition
  reposition
  requisition
  supposition
    presupposition
  transposition
  transition
(wishin', etc.)

ISH-ur
disher
fisher
  kingfisher (i)
fissure
wisher
  well-wisher

ISH-us
(bitous)
  ambitious
(ditious)
  expeditious
  judicious
    injudicious
  seditious
(ficious)
  officious
(licious)
  delicious
  malicious
(nicious)

pernicious
(pitious)
  propitious
(pricious)
  capricious
(ricious)
  avaricious
(spicious)
  auspicious
  suspicious
(stitious)
  superstitious
(titious)
  adventitious
  factitious
  ficticious
  supposititious
  surreptitious
(tricious)
  meretricious
  nutritious
vicious

I-si
icy
dicey
spicy

IS-i
hissy
missy
sissy

IS-il (IS-ul)
missile
(*see* **IS-l**, *page 246*)

I-sing
icing
dicing
(ficing)
  sacrificing
  sufficing
pricing
spicing
splicing

(ticing)
  enticing

IS-ing
hissing
kissing
missing
  dismissing
(nissing)
  reminiscing

I-sis
Isis
crisis

IS-it
licit
  elicit
  illicit
  solicit
(plicit)
  explicit
  implicit

I-siv
(cisive)
  decisive
    indecisive
  incisive
(risive)
  derisive
(visive)
  divisive

IS-ive
missive
  admissive
  commissive
  emissive
  omissive
  permissive
  submissive
    unsubmissive

ISK-et (ISK-ut)
biscuit

brisket
(risk it, etc.)

IS-ki
frisky
risky
whiskey

IS-king
frisking
risking
whisking

IS-ko
Cisco
  Francisco
    San Francisco
Crisco
disco

IS-kur
brisker
frisker
risker
whisker
  bewhisker

IS-kus
(biscus)
  hibiscus)
discus
(niscus)
  meniscus
viscous
(frisk us, etc.)

IS-l
bristle
(byssal)
  abyssal
gristle
missal
  dismissal
missel
missile
(pistle)

epistle
sisal
thistle
whistle

I-sless
iceless
diceless
priceless
spiceless
spliceless
viceless

I-sli (I-slee)
(cisely)
  concisely
  precisely
nicely

IS-li (IS-lee)
bristly
gristly
thistly

IS-ling
bristling
whistling

IS-mus
isthmus
Christmas

IS-n
christen
glisten
listen

I-sness
(ciseness)
  conciseness
  preciseness
niceness

IS-ning
christening
glistening

listening

IS-ping
crisping
lisping

ISP-ur
crisper
lisper
whisper

IST-al
crystal
pistol

IS-tanse
distance
  equidistance
(sistance)
  assistance
  consistence
  desistance
  insistence
  persistence
  subsistence
(zistance)
  existence
    coexistence
    nonexistence
    preexistence
  resistance

IS-tant (IS-tunt)
distant
  equidistant
(sistant)
  assistant
  consistent
    inconsistent
  insistent
  persistent
  subsistent
(zistent)
  existent
    coexistent
    nonexistent

  preexistent
  resistant
  nonresistant

IST-ed
cysted
  assisted
    unassisted
  desisted
  encysted
  insisted
  persisted
  subsisted
fisted
listed
  enlisted
misted
twisted
  entwisted
  untwisted
(zisted)
  existed
  resisted
    unresisted

IST-em
system
(missed 'em, etc.)

IST-i
Christie
  Corpus Christi
  Lacrima Christi
misty
twisty

IS-tik
cystic
  solecistic
fistic
  sophistic
(gistic)
  logistic
    eulogistic
    syllogistic
(guistic)

linguistic
(kistic)
  anarchistic
  catechistic
(listic)
  ballistic
  cabalistic
  dualistic
  evangelistic
  fatalistic
  idealistic
  individualistic
  journalistic
  liberalistic
  materialistic
  naturalistic
  nihilistic
  nominalistic
  rationalistic
  realistic
  simplistic
  socialistic
  somnambulistic
  spiritualistic
  stylistic
mystic
  alchemistic
  animistic
  euphemistic
  optimistic
  pessimistic
(nistic)
  anachronistic
  antagonistic
  Calvinistic
  chauvinistic
  communistic
  Hellenistic
  humanistic
(ristic)
  aphoristic
  characteristic
  Eucharistic
  humoristic
  puristic
  touristic

(tistic)
　artistic
　egotistic
　pietistic
　quietistic
(wistic)
　altruistic
　casuistic
　egoistic
(yistic)
　atheistic
　deistic
　　Judaistic
　monotheistic
　pantheistic
　polytheistic

IST-in (IST-een)
pristine
Sistine
(thystine)
　amethystine

IST-ing
listing
　enlisting
misting
(sisting)
　assisting
　consisting
　desisting
　insisting
　persisting
　subsisting
twisting
　untwisting
(zisting)
　existing
　　preexisting
　resisting
　　unresisting

IST-ur
blister
(gister)
　magister

lister
mister
sister
　assister
twister
(zister)
　resister

IS-u (ISH-u)
issue
tissue
(miss you, etc.)

I-sur
dicer
geyser
nicer
slicer
spicer
splicer
(ticer)
　enticer

I-tal
(cital)
　recital
(quital)
　requital
title
　entitle
vital

IT-an
Britain
Briton
(sittin', etc.)
(see IT-en, page 249)

IT-anse
(mittance)
　admittance
　omittance
　pittance
　quittance
　remittance

I-ted
blighted
(dited)
　bedighted
　indicted
　indited
(frighted)
　affrighted
knighted
　beknighted
　benighted
　ignited
lighted
　alighted
　delighted
plighted
　unplighted
(quited)
　requited
　　unrequited
righted
sighted
　cited
　excited
　incited
　recited
　unsighted
spited
united
　reunited
(vited)
　invited

IT-ed
bitted
fitted
　befitted
　benefited (*i*)
　counterfeited (*i*)
　refitted
flitted
gritted
knitted
(mitted)
　admitted

committed
emitted
omitted
permitted
remitted
  unremitted
submitted
transmitted
pitted
quitted
  acquitted
slitted
spitted
twitted
witted
  half-witted
  nit-witted
  outwitted
  quick-witted
  short-witted, etc.

I-tem
item
(bite 'em, etc.)

I-ten
brighten
Brighton
frighten
heighten
lighten
  enlighten
tighten
Titan
triton
whiten
(bitin', etc.)

IT-en
bitten
Briton
kitten
mitten
smitten
written
  underwritten

(flittin', etc.)

I-test
brightest
lightest
  politest
rightest
slightest
tightest
tritest
whitest

I-tful (ITE-ful)
frightful
(lightful)
  delightful
rightful
spiteful

I-thest
blithest
lithest

ITH-i
pithy
smithy

I-thing (ITHE-ing)
scything
tithing
writhing

ITH-m
rhythm
(with 'em, etc.)

I-thness
blitheness
litheness

I-thur
either
blither
lither
neither
tither

writher

ITH-ur
blither
dither
hither
slither
thither
whither
wither

I-ti
Blighty *(English)*
(ditee)
  Aphrodite
flighty
mighty
  almighty
nighty

IT-i
city
ditty
gritty
kitty
(mitty)
  committee
pity
  self-pity
pretty
witty

IT-id
pitied
  unpitied
prettied

IT-ik
critic
  hypocritic
(ditic)
  hermaphroditic
  troglodytic
(lytic)
  analytic
  catalytic

electrolytic
paralytic
(mitic)
  Hamitic
  Semitic
  stalagmitic
(nitic)
  granitic
(ritic)
  arthritic
  sybaritic
(sitic)
  parasitic
(titic)
  stalactitic
(witic)
  Jesuitic

I-ting
biting
  backbiting
blighting
(diting)
  expediting
  indicting
  inditing
fighting
kiting
knighting
  igniting
lighting
  alighting
  delighting
(miting)
  dynamiting
plighting
(quiting)
  requiting
righting
  copyrighting
sighting
citing
  exciting
  inciting
  reciting
slighting

smiting
spiting
uniting
  disuniting
  reuniting
(viting)
  inviting
whiting
writing
  underwriting

IT-ing
fitting
  befitting
    unbefitting
    counterfeiting
  misfitting
  refitting
  unfitting
flitting
gritting
hitting
knitting
(mitting)
  admitting
  committing
  emitting
  omitting
  permitting
  remitting
    unremitting
  submitting
    unsubmitting
  transmitting
pitting
quitting
  acquitting
sitting
  outsitting
slitting
splitting
twitting
witting
  outwitting
  unwitting

I-tis
(ditis)
  carditis
    endocarditis
(jitis)
  laryngitis
  meningitis
(kitis)
  bronchitis
(litis)
  colitis
  tonsilitis
(ritis)
  arthritis
  gastritis
  neuritis
(sitis)
  appendicitis
(yitis)
  tracheitis

IT-ish
British
skittish

IT-l
brittle
little
  belittle
(mittal)
  committal
    noncommittal
  remittal
  transmittal
(quittal)
  acquittal
skittle
spittle
  lickspittle
tittle
vittle
whittle

I-tless (ITE-less)
fightless
frightless

lightless
mightless
sightless
spiteless

I-tli (ITE-lee)
brightly
lightly
 politely
  impolitely
nightly
 knightly
  unknightly
rightly
 uprightly
sightly
 unsightly
slightly
sprightly
tightly
tritely
whitely

IT-lur
brittler
Hitler, Adolf
littler
whittler

IT-lz
skittles
(belittles, etc.)

I-tment (ITE-ment)
(citement)
 excitement
 incitement
(dictment)
 indictment

IT-ment
(mitment)
 commitment
 remitment
(quitment)
 acquitment

I-tness (ITE-ness)
brightness
lightness
 politeness
  impoliteness
rightness
 uprightness
slightness
tightness
triteness
whiteness

IT-ness
fitness
 unfitness
witness

IT-rik
citric
vitric

I-tur
biter
blighter
brighter
citer
 exciter
 inciter
 reciter
(diter)
 indicter
fighter
lighter
 lamplighter
 moonlighter
 politer
miter
 dynamiter
niter
 igniter
 uniter
(quiter)
 requiter
righter
slighter
tighter

triter
(viter)
 inviter
whiter
writer
 typewriter
 underwriter

IT-ur
bitter
 embitter
"critter"
fitter
 counterfeiter
 refitter
flitter
fritter
glitter
hitter
knitter
litter
(mitter)
 admitter
 transmitter
quitter
 acquitter
sitter
spitter
splitter
titter
twitter

IT-urz
bitters
(glitters, etc.)

I-tus
(vitus)
 Vitus, Saint
(unite us, etc.)

I-twait
lightweight
(right weight, etc.)

I-ur
ire
briar
brier
buyer
crier
  towncrier (*i*)
cryer
drier
dryer
(fier)
  amplifier
  beautifier
  clarifier
  classifier
  codifier
  deifier
  electrifier
  fortifier
  glorifier
  horrifier
  identifier
  indemnifier
  intensifier
  justifier
  liquefier
  magnifier
  modifier
  mollifier
  mystifier
  personifier
  petrifier
  purifier
  qualifier
    disqualifier
  rectifier
  satisfier
  scarifier
  simplifier
  stupefier
  terrifier
  testifier
  verifier
  versifier
  vilifier
flier

friar
higher
liar
(pier)
  occupier
(plier)
  multiplier
  replier
  supplier
prior
shyer
sigher
  prophesier
slyer
spryer
(fire, etc.)

I-urz
pliers
(briers, etc.)

I-us
pious
(deny us, etc.)

I-val
rival
  arrival
  outrival
(vival)
  revival
  survival

I-vat
private
(drive it, etc.)

IV-en
driven
  undriven
given
  forgiven
    unforgiven
riven
scriven
thriven

IV-et
civet
privet
rivet
trivet
(give it, etc.)

IV-i
chivvy
divvy
Livy
privy

IV-id
livid
vivid

IV-il
civil
  uncivil
drivel
shrivel
snivel
swivel

I-ving
diving
driving
(niving)
  conniving
(priving)
  depriving
riving
  arriving
  deriving
striving
thriving
(triving)
  contriving
(viving)
  reviving
  surviving

IV-ling
shriveling
sniveling

IV-ot
divot
pivot
(see **IV-et,** *page 252)*

IV-ring
(livering)
  delivering
quivering
shivering
slivering

I-vur
diver
driver
fiver
jiver
liver
(niver)
  conniver
striver
thriver
(triver)
  contriver
(viver)
  surviver

IV-ur
flivver
giver
liver
  deliver
  free-liver
quiver
river
shiver
sliver

I-wai
byway
highway
skyway
(my way, etc.)

IZ-ard
blizzard

gizzard
lizard
scissored
wizard

IZ-en
mizzen
prison
  imprison
risen
  arisen
wizen

IZH-un
(lision)
  collision
  elision
(rision)
  derision
(sision)
  concision
  decision
    indecision
  excision
  incision
  precision
    imprecision
  recision
  rescission
vision
  division
    subdivision
  envision
  provision
  revision
  supervision
  television

IZ-i
busy
dizzy
frizzy
Lizzie
  tin lizzie
tizzy

I-zing
(dizing)
  gormandizing (*i*)
  jeopardizing (*i*)
  standardizing (*i*)
  subsidizing (*i*)
(guising)
  disguising
(jizing)
  apologizing (*i*)
  eulogizing (*i*)
(lyzing)
  analyzing (*i*)
  brutalizing (*i*)
  capitalizing (*i*)
  centralizing (*i*)
  characterizing (*i*)
  civilizing (*i*)
  crystallizing (*i*)
  demoralizing (*i*)
  equalizing (*i*)
  evangelizing (*i*)
  fertilizing (*i*)
  generalizing (*i*)
  idealizing (*i*)
  immortalizing (*i*)
  localizing (*i*)
  mobilizing (*i*)
  monopolizing (*i*)
  neutralizing (*i*)
  paralyzing (*i*)
  rationalizing (*i*)
  realizing (*i*)
  scandalizing (*i*)
  specializing (*i*)
  sterilizing (*i*)
  symbolizing (*i*)
  tantalizing (*i*)
  totalizing (*i*)
  tranquilizing (*i*)
  utilizing (*i*)
  visualizing (*i*)
  vocalizing (*i*)
(mizing)
  compromising (*i*)
  economizing

macadamizing (*i*)
minimizing (*i*)
surmising
(nizing)
  agonizing (*i*)
    antagonizing (*i*)
  canonizing (*i*)
  colonizing (*i*)
  galvanizing (*i*)
  harmonizing (*i*)
  humanizing (*i*)
  modernizing (*i*)
  organizing (*i*)
    disorganizing (*i*)
  patronizing (*i*)
  recognizing (*i*)
  revolutionizing (*i*)
  scrutinizing (*i*)
  solemnizing (*i*)
  tyrannizing (*i*)
prizing
  apprising
  comprising
  enterprising
  surprising
(quizing)
  soliloquizing (*i*)
rising
  arising
  authorizing (*i*)
  cauterizing (*i*)
  deodorizing (*i*)
  familiarizing (*i*)
  memorizing (*i*)
  mesmerizing (*i*)
  pauperizing (*i*)
  plagiarizing (*i*)
  pulverizing (*i*)
  secularizing (*i*)
  summarizing (*i*)
  temporizing (*i*)
  terrorizing (*i*)
  theorizing (*i*)
  uprising
  vaporizing (*i*)
  vulgarizing (*i*)

sizing
  anglicizing (*i*)
  capsizing
  criticizing (*i*)
  emphasizing (*i*)
  exercising (*i*)
  exorcising (*i*)
  italicizing (*i*)
(spising)
  despising
(thizing)
  sympathizing (*i*)
(tising)
  advertising
  appetizing (*i*)
  baptizing
  chastising (*i*)
  dramatizing (*i*)
  hypnotizing (*i*)
  magnetizing (*i*)
  stigmatizing (*i*)
(vising)
  advising (*i*)
  devising
  improvising (*i*)
  revising
  supervising

IZ-ing
fizzing
frizzing
quizzing
whizzing

IZ-it
visit
is it?

IZ-l
drizzle
chisel
fizzle
frizzle
grizzle
sizzle
swizzle

IZ-li
drizzly
frizzly
grisly
grizzly

IZ-ling
chiseling
drizzling
fizzling
frizzling
grizzling
Quisling, Vidkun
sizzling
swizzling

IZ-m
priam
schism
(communism, etc.)

IZ-mal
(bysmal)
  abysmal
(clysmal)
  cataclysmal
dismal
(kismal)
  catechismal
(sizmal)
  paroxysmal
(tismal)
  baptismal
  rheumatismal

I-zur
(dizer)
  gormandizer (*i*)
geyser
  disguiser (*i*)
(jizer)
  apologizer (*i*)
  eulogizer (*i*)
(lyzer)
  analyzer (*i*)
  civilizer (*i*)

equalizer (*i*)
fertilizer (*i*)
generalizer
idolizer (*i*)
moralizer (*i*)
sterilizer (*i*)
tantalizer
tranquilizer (*i*)
tyrannizer (*i*)
miser
  atomizer (*i*)
  economizer (*i*)
  epitomizer (*i*)
  itemizer (*i*)
  surmiser
(nizer)
  agonizer (*i*)
  canonizer (*i*)
  colonizer (*i*)
  galvanizer (*i*)
  harmonizer (*i*)

humanizer (*i*)
lionizer (*i*)
organizer (*i*)
scrutinizer (*i*)
sermonizer (*i*)
synchronizer (*i*)
vulcanizer (*i*)
prizer
  appriser
  surpriser (*i*)
riser
  authorizer (*i*)
  cauterizer (*i*)
  deodorizer (*i*)
  extemporizer (*i*)
  polarizer (*i*)
  pulverizer (*i*)
  temporizer (*i*)
  terrorizer (*i*)
  theorizer (*i*)
  vaporizer (*i*)
  vulgarizer (*i*)

sizer
  assizer (*i*)
  capsizer (*i*)
  exerciser (*i*)
  exorciser (*i*)
  incisor (*i*)
(thizer)
  sympathizer (*i*)
  synthesizer
(tizer)
  advertiser (*i*)
  appetizer (*i*)
  baptizer (*i*)
  chastiser (*i*)
  magnetizer (*i*)
  proselytizer (*i*)
(viser)
  adviser
  improviser (*i*)
  supervisor (*i*)
wiser

O

O-a
boa
(moa)
  Samoa
Noah
  Genoa
(zoa)
  protozoa
  spermatozoa

O-ball
low ball
no ball
snowball

O-bi (O-by)
go by
(know by, etc.)

O-bi (O-bee)
obi
'dobe
  adobe
Kobe

OB-i
bobby
hobby
knobby
lobby
snobby

OB-in
bobbin
dobbin
robin
(sobbin', etc.)

O-bing
probing
robing
  disrobing
  enrobing
  unrobing

OB-ing
bobbing
jobbing
lobbing
mobbing
(nobbing)
  hobnobbing
robbing
sobbing
swabbing
throbbing

OB-l
bauble
bobble
cobble
gobble
hobble
squabble
wabble

OB-ling
gobbling
hobbling
squabbling
wabbling

OB-lur
cobbler
gobbler
hobbler
squabbler
wabbler

O-boi
oh boy
doughboy
lowboy

OB-stur
lobster
mobster

O-bur
prober
rober
 disrober
sober
(tober)
 October

OB-ur
clobber
dauber
jobber
robber
slobber
swabber

O-chez
broaches
brooches
coaches
(croaches)
 encroaches
poaches
(proaches)
 reproaches
roaches

OCH-i
blotchy
splotchy

O-ching
broaching
coaching
(croaching)
 encroaching
poaching
(proaching)
 approaching
 reproaching

OCH-ing
blotching
botching
scotching
splotching
watching

OCH-man
Scotchman
watchman

O-chur
(croacher)
 encroacher
poacher
(proacher)
 reproacher

O-da
coda
(goda)

pagoda
soda

O-dal
modal
nodal
yodel

OD-al
caudle
dawdle

O-ded
boded
 foreboded
coded
goaded
loaded
 overloaded
 unloaded
(moded)
 outmoded
(roded)
 corroded
 eroded
(sploded)
 exploded

OD-ed
nodded
plodded
prodded
sodded
wadded

OD-en
broaden
sodden
trodden
 untrodden

OD-ess
bodice
goddess

OD-est
oddest
modest
  immodest

OD-i
bawdy
body
  busybody (*i*)
  embody
  homebody (*i*)
  nobody (*i*)
  somebody (*i*)
gaudy
"lawdy"
noddy
shoddy
toddy
waddy (*Australian*)
wadi (*Arabic*)

OD-ik
melodic
(modic)
  spasmodic
(sodic)
  episodic
  rhapsodic
(thodic)
  methodic
(yodic)
  periodic

O-ding
boding
  foreboding
goading
loading
  overloading
  unloading
(roding)
  corroding
(sploding)
  exploding

OD-ing
codding
(frauding)
  defrauding
lauding
nodding
(plauding)
  applauding
plodding
prodding
(rauding)
  marauding
wadding

OD-it
audit
plaudit
(sawed it, trod it, etc.)

OD-l
coddle
  mollycoddle
model
  remodel
noddle
swaddle
toddle
twaddle
waddle

OD-li
oddly
godly
  ungodly

OD-ling
coddling
godling
modeling
  remodeling
swaddling
toddling
waddling

OD-lur
coddler

mollycoddler
modeler
toddler
waddler

O-down
hoedown
lowdown
mow down
(go down, etc.)

OD-ule
module
nodule

O-dur
odor
goader
loader

OD-ur
odder
broader
dodder
fodder
(frauder)
  defrauder
plodder
prodder
(rauder)
  marauder
solder

O-em
poem
(know 'em, etc.)

O-est
lowest
slowest
(go west, etc.)

O-et
poet
(know it, etc.)

264

OF-et
profit
prophet
(off it, etc.)

OF-i
coffee
toffy

OF-ik
(sophic)
  philosophic
(strophic)
  catastrophic

OF-ing
offing
coughing
doffing
scoffing

OF-n
often
coffin
soften
(coughin', etc.)

OF-ti
lofty
softy

OF-tur
crofter
softer

OF-ul
awful
lawful
  unlawful

O-fur
chauffeur
gopher
loafer

OF-ur
offer
coffer
cougher
proffer
scoffer

O-ga
(roga)
  Ticonderoga
toga
  Saratoga
yoga

O-gan
brogan
hogan
slogan

OG-an
(boggan)
  toboggan
noggin
(floggin', etc.)

O-gi
bogey
dogie
fogey
stogie
yogi

OG-i
doggy
foggy
froggy
groggy
soggy

OG-ing
clogging
  unclogging
dogging
flogging
fogging
  befogging

jogging
slogging
togging

O-gl
ogle
mogul

OG-l
boggle
(doggle)
  boondoggle
goggle
joggle
toggle

OG-ling
boggling
(doggling)
  boondoggling
joggling

O-gress
ogress
progress (*British pron.*)

OG-ur
auger
augur
dogger
flogger
(fogger)
  pettifogger
hogger
jogger
slogger
togger

O-i
blowy
Bowie, Jim
doughy
showy
snowy

OI-al
loyal
  disloyal
royal
(see **OIL,** *page 112)*

OI-ans
buoyance
(noyance)
  annoyance
(voyance)
  clairvoyance

OI-ant
buoyant
  flamboyant
(voyant)
  clairvoyant

OI-ing
buoying
cloying
(coying)
  decoying (*i*)
(joying)
  enjoying
(ploying)
  deploying
  employing
(stroying)
  destroying
toying

OI-ish
boyish
coyish

O-ij
stowage
towage

O-ik
(roic)
  heroic
stoic
(zoic)

benzoic
Mesozoic
Paleozoic

OI-li
oily
coyly
doily

OIL-ing
oiling
boiling
broiling
  embroiling
coiling
  recoiling
  uncoiling
foiling
moiling
roiling
soiling
spoiling
  despoiling
toiling

OI-lur
oiler
boiler
broiler
foiler
soiler
spoiler
  despoiler
toiler

OI-ment
(joyment)
  enjoyment
(ployment)
  deployment
  employment

O-ing
owing
blowing
bowing

crowing
  overcrowing
flowing
  overflowing
  unflowing
glowing
going
  easygoing
  foregoing
  outgoing
  undergoing
growing
  outgrowing
  overgrowing
hoeing
knowing
  foreknowing
  unknowing
lowing
  helloing
mowing
rowing
sewing
sowing
showing
  foreshowing
slowing
snowing
stowing
  bestowing
throwing
  overthrowing
toeing
towing

O-ing (AH-ing)
awing
cawing
"chawing"
clawing
drawing
  withdrawing
(fawing)
  guffawing
gnawing
(hawing)

hee-hawing
jawing
(lawing)
  outlawing
pawing
sawing
thawing
yawing

OI-ning
coining
joining
  adjoining
  conjoining
  enjoining
  rejoining
(loining)
  purloining

OIN-ted
jointed
  disjointed
  double-jointed
(nointed)
  anointed
pointed
  appointed
    disappointed
    reappointed
    self-appointed

OIN-ting
jointing
(nointing)
  anointing
pointing
  appointing
    disappointing

OINT-less
jointless
pointless

OINT-ment
ointment

(nointment)
  anointment
(pointment)
  appointment
    disappointment

OIN-tur
jointer
(nointer)
  anointer
pointer
  appointer
    disappointer

OI-nur
coiner
joiner
  enjoiner
(loiner)
  purloiner

OI-sing
(joicing)
  rejoicing
    unrejoicing
voicing

OIS-less
choiceless
voiceless

OI-sting
foisting
hoisting
joisting

OI-stur
oyster
cloister
royster

OI-tring
loitering
(noitring)
  reconnoitering

OI-tur
goiter
loiter
(ploiter)
  exploiter

OI-ur
coyer
foyer
(noyer)
  annoyer
(ployer)
  deployer
  employer
(stroyer)
  destroyer

OJ-i
(gogy)
  pedagogy
stodgy

OJ-ik
(gogic)
  anagogic
  pedagogic
logic
  anthropologic
  ethnologic
  horologic, etc.

OJ-ing
dodging
lodging
  dislodging

OJ-ur
codger
dodger
lodger
Roger
  Jolly Roger

O-kal
bocal
focal

local
vocal
yokel

O-ken
oaken
(boken)
  Hoboken
broken
  heartbroken
  unbroken
spoken
  bespoken
  freespoken
  outspoken
  unspoken
  well-spoken
token
  betoken
(jokin', etc.)

OK-et
docket
hocket
locket
pocket
rocket
socket
sprocket
(sock it, etc.)

O-ki
Okie
choky
cokey
croaky
(dokey)
  okey-dokey
Loki
(noki)
  Okefenokee
poky
smoky
(low key, etc.)

OK-i
balky
chalky
cocky
gawky
hockey
jockey
rocky
squawky
stocky
talkie
  walkie-talkie
talky
(waukee)
  jabberwocky
  Milwaukee
(yaki)
  sukiyaki (*Japanese*)
  teriyaki (*Japanese*)

O-king
choking
cloaking
croaking
joking
poking
smoking
soaking
stoking
stroking
toking
(voking)
  convoking
  evoking
  invoking
  provoking
  revoking
yoking

OK-ing
balking
calking
docking
flocking
frocking
  defrocking

hawking
knocking
locking
  unlocking
mocking
rocking
shocking
squawking
stalking
stocking
talking
walking

OK-ish
blockish
hawkish
mawkish

O-kless
cloakless
jokeless
smokeless
yokeless
yolkless

O-ko
coco
  rococo
cocoa
loco

OK-o
(rocco)
  Morocco
  sirocco
socko

OK-shun
auction
(coction)
  concoction
  decoction

OK-si
doxy
  heterodoxy (*i*)

orthodoxy (*i*)
foxy
moxie
proxy

O-ksing
coaxing
hoaxing

OK-sing
boxing
foxing

O-ksur
coaxer
hoaxer
(choke, sir; provokes
  'er; etc.)

OK-tur
doctor
proctor

O-kum
oakum
hokum
(soak 'em, etc.)

O-kur
ocher
broker
choker
cloaker
croaker
joker
poker
smoker
soaker
stoker
stroker
(voker)
  evoker
  invoker
  provoker
  revoker
yoker

mediocre
(woke 'er, etc.)

OK-ur
Acre
balker
blocker
(bocker)
  Knickerbocker
cocker
docker
Fokker
hawker
knocker
locker
mocker
rocker
shocker
soccer
squawker
stalker
  deerstalker (*i*)
talker
walker
(dock 'er, etc.)

O-kus
crocus
focus
(kokus)
  Hohokus
locus
(pocus)
  hocus-pocus
(awoke us, etc.)

OK-us
caucus
glaucous
raucous
(clock us, etc.)

O-kust
focused
locust

OK-ward
awkward
dockward

O-la
bola
cola
(dola)
  gondola
(gola)
  Angola
  plugola
hola! *(Spanish)*
Nola
(tollah)
  ayatollah
(yola)
  payola
  viola
Zola, Emil
  Gorgonzola
(*U.S. southern:
  roller, etc.*)

OL-ar
collar
(see OL-ur, page 265)

OL-ard
bollard
collard
collared
Lollard

OL-ded
folded
  enfolded
  infolded
  manifolded
  refolded
  unfolded
molded
scolded

OL-den
olden

Bolden, Buddy
  embolden
golden
(holden)
  beholden
(holdin', etc.)

OL-dest
oldest
boldest
coldest

OL-ding
folding
  enfolding
  infolding
  unfolding
holding
  beholding
  upholding
  withholding
molding
scolding

OLD-li
boldly
coldly
(foldly)
  manifoldly

OLD-ness
oldness
boldness
coldness

OL-dur
older
bolder
boulder
colder
folder
holder
  beholder
  householder (*i*)
  landholder (*i*)
  leaseholder (*i*)

shareholder (*i*)
molder
scolder
shoulder
smolder

OL-dur (ALL-dur)
alder
balder
Baldur

OL-ej (ALL-ej)
college
knowledge
  acknowledge

O-len
stolen
swollen
(rollin', etc.)

OL-en (ALL-en)
fallen
pollen
(stallin', etc.)

OL-ess
clawless
flawless
lawless
(saw less, etc.)

OL-est
smallest
tallest

OL-fin
dolphin
golfin'

OL-ful
bowlful
doleful
soulful

O-li
drolly
holy
lowly
(poly)
  roly-poly
solely
wholly

OL-i
collie
(dolly, etc.)
*(see **AL-i**, page 155)*

OL-id (ALL-id)
solid
squalid
stolid

O-life
lowlife
(no life, etc.)

OL-ik (ALL-ik)
(bolic)
  carbolic
  diabolic
  hyperbolic
  metabolic
  parabolic
  symbolic
colic
  bucolic
  melancholic
(draulic)
  hydraulic
frolic
(holic)
  alcoholic
rollick
(stolic)
  apostolic
  epistolic
  systolic
(yolic)
  vitriolic

O-ling
bowling
coaling
doling
  condoling
foaling
poling
polling
rolling
  enrolling
  paroling
  unrolling
(soling)
  consoling
strolling
tolling
  extolling
trolling
  controlling
  patrolling

OL-ing (ALL-ing)
balling
  snowballing (i)
bawling
brawling
calling
  recalling
crawling
drawling
falling
  befalling
galling
hauling
  overhauling
lolling
mauling
palling
  appalling
scrawling
sprawling
squalling
stalling
  forestalling
  installing
(thralling)

enthralling
trawling
walling
  caterwauling (i)

OL-ish
(bolish)
  abolish
(molish)
  demolish
polish
smallish
tallish

OL-man
ol' man
coalman
dolman
tollman

OL-ment
(dolement)
  condolement
(jolement)
  cajolement
(rollment)
  enrollment

OL-ment (ALL-ment)
(stallment)
  installment
(thrallment)
  enthrallment
(all meant, etc.)

OL-ness (ALL-ness)
smallness
tallness

O-lo
bolo
polo
solo

OL-o
follow

hollow
(pollo)
  Apollo
swallow
wallow

O-lon
colon
  semicolon
Solon
stolen
*(see **O-len**, page 263)*

OL-op (ALL-op)
collop
dollop
scallop
trollop
(call up, etc.)

OL-stur
bolster
holster
  upholster
pollster

OL-ted
bolted
  unbolted
jolted
molted
(volted)
  revolted

OL-ted (ALL-ted)
faulted
  defaulted
halted
malted
salted
  assaulted
vaulted
(zalted)
  exalted

OL-ti (ALL-ti)
faulty
malty
salty

OL-tik (ALL-tik)
Baltic
(staltic)
  peristaltic

OL-ting
bolting
jolting
molting
(volting)
  revolting

OL-ting (ALL-ting)
faulting
  defaulting
halting
malting
salting
  assaulting
vaulting
(zalting)
  exalting

OL-tish
coltish
doltish

OLT-less (ALL-tless)
faultless
maltless
saltless

OL-tur (ALL-tur)
altar
alter
(bralter)
  Gibraltar
falter
  defaulter
halter
psalter

assaulter
(zalter)
  exalter

OL-um (ALL-um)
column
  whatchamacallum
solemn
(recall 'em, etc.)

O-lur
bowler
coaler
dolor
droller
molar
polar
roller
solar
  consoler
stroller
troller
  controller

OL-ur (ALL-ur)
bawler
  footballer (i)
brawler
caller
choler
collar
crawler
dollar
hauler
Mahler, Gustav
mauler
scrawler
smaller
sprawler
squalor
taller
trawler
(call 'er, etc.)

OL-ving (ALL-ving)
solving

(volving)
  devolving
  evolving
  involving
  revolving
(zolving)
  absolving
  dissolving
  resolving

OL-vur (ALL-vur)
solver
(volver)
  revolver

OL-waiz (ALL-waiz)
always
hallways
(small ways, Paul
weighs, etc.)

O-ma
coma
  sarcoma
  Tacoma
(loma)
  Alta Loma
  Casa Loma
(noma)
  carcinoma
  Sonoma
(ploma)
  diploma
Roma
  aroma
soma

OM-a
comma
momma
(see AM-a, page 157)

O-mad
nomad
(so mad, etc.)

O-man
bowman
foeman
Roman
showman
snowman
yeoman

OM-bat
combat
wombat

OM-bur
omber
somber

O-men
omen
bowmen
(domen)
  abdomen
foemen
(nomen)
  cognomen
showmen
snowmen
yeomen
(roamin', etc.)

OM-et
comet
grommet
vomit
(bomb it, etc.)

O-mi
oh me
foamy
homey
loamy
(yomi)
  Naomi, Ruth and
(know me, etc.)

OM-ik
comic

(nomic)
  agronomic
  astronomic
  economic
  gastromonic
  metronomic
  physiognomic
  taxonomic
(tomic)
  atomic
    anatomic

O-ming
coaming
combing
foaming
gloaming
homing
roaming
(yoming)
  Wyoming

OMP-us
pompous
stomp us

O-mur
comber
  beachcomber (*i*)
homer
Homer
(nomer)
  misnomer
roamer

OM-ur
bomber
calmer

O-mward (OME-ward)
homeward
Nome-ward
Rome-ward

O-na
Jonah

(lona)
  Barcelona
Mona
  Cremona
Rona
  corona
(zona)
  Arizona
(*U.S. southern:
  owner, etc.*)

ON-a
donna
  belladonna
  madonna
  prima donna
(wanna)
  iguana
  (don't wanna)

O-nal
(ronal)
  coronal
tonal
  atonal
  bitonal
  polytonal
zonal

ON-da
(conda)
  anaconda
  La Giaconda
fond o'
Honda
(*U.S. southern:
  yonder, etc.*)

ON-ded
bonded
(sconded)
  absconded
(sponded)
  responded
    corresponded

O-ndef (OAN-def)
stone-deaf
tone-deaf

ON-dij
bondage
  vagabondage
frondage

ON-ding
(sconding)
  absconding
(sponding)
  responding
    corresponding

OND-ness
blondness
fondness

ON-dur
blonder
condor
fonder
launder
ponder
(sconder)
  absconder
squander
wander
yonder
(conned 'er, etc.)

O-nent
(ponent)
  component
  deponent
  exponent
  opponent
  proponent

ON-est
honest
  dishonest
wannest

ON-et
bonnet
sonnet
(pawn it, etc.)

ONG-ing
longing
  belonging
  prolonging
thronging
wronging

ONG-kur
conker
conquer
honker

ONG-kurz
bonkers
conkers
conquers
honkers
Yonkers

ONG-guest
longest
strongest

ONG-gur
conger
longer
stronger

O-nhed (OAN-hed)
own head
bonehead
clonehead

O-ni
bony
crony
(loney)
  baloney
    abalone
(mony)
  acrimony

alimony (i)
matrimony (i)
parsimony (i)
patrimony
sanctimony (i)
testimony (i)
phony
pony
(roni)
  macaroni
stony
tony

ON-i
bonny
brawny
scrawny
tawny
  mulligatawny

ON-ik
(bonic)
  bubonic
  carbonic
chronic
(clonic)
  cyclonic
conic
  draconic
  laconic
(donic)
  Chalcedonic
  hedonic
(Ionic)
  colonic
(monic)
  harmonic
    enharmonic
    philharmonic
  mnemonic
  pneumonic
  pulmonic
(nonic)
  canonic
phonic
  antiphonic

homophonic
monophonic
polyphonic
symphonic
telephonic
(ronic)
  ironic
  Pharaonic
sonic
  masonic
tonic
  architectonic
  diatonic
  isotonic
  Platonic
  Plutonic
  Teutonic
(vonic)
  Slavonic
(yonic)
  embryonic
  histrionic
  Ionic

ON-lks (AH-niks)
onyx
(donics)
  hedonics
(monics)
  mnemonics
(yonics)
  histrionics
(tonics, etc.)

O-ning
owning
  disowning
boning
droning
groaning
moaning
  bemoaning
(poning)
  postponing
stoning
throning

dethroning
enthroning
toning
  atoning
  intoning

ON-ing
awning
conning
dawning
donning
lawning
pawning
spawning
yawning

ON-ish
(monish)
  admonish
(stonish)
  astonish

O-nless
boneless
moanless
throneless
toneless
zoneless
(known less, etc.)

O-nli
only
lonely

O-nment (OAN-ment)
(donement)
  condonement
(ownment)
  disownment
(thronement)
  enthronement
(tonement)
  atonement

ON-sor
sponsor

tonsor

ON-tal
(dontal)
  peridontal
frontal
(zontal)
  horizontal

ON-ted
daunted
  undaunted
flaunted
haunted
taunted
vaunted
wanted

ON-ting
daunting
flaunting
haunting
jaunting
taunting
vaunting
wanting

ON-to
(ronto)
  Esperanto
  Toronto
Tonto

ON-tur
daunter
flaunter
gaunter
haunter
saunter
taunter

O-nur
owner
boner
donor
  condoner

droaner
groaner
honer
kronor (*Swedish*)
loaner
loner
moaner
  bemoaner
toner
  atoner
(known 'er, etc.)

ON-ur
goner
honor
  dishonor
wanner

O-nus
onus
bonus
tonus
(known us, etc.)

OOD-ed
hooded
wooded

OOD-i
goody
  goody-goody
woody
(should 'e, etc.)

OOK-i
bookie
cooky
hookey
lookee
rookie
rooky

OOK-ing
booking
brooking
cooking

crooking
hooking
looking
rooking

OOK-ur
booker
cooker
  pressure cooker
hooker
looker
snooker
(shook 'er, etc.)

OOL-en
woolen
(pullin', etc.)

OOL-et
bullet
pullet

OOL-i
bully
fully
pulley
wooly

OOL-ish
bullish
fullish

OOL-ur
fuller
puller
  wire-puller (*i*)

OOT-ed
booted
mooted
tooted
(see **U-ted***, page 304)*

OOT-ing
footing
putting

OP-et
moppet
poppet
(stop it, etc.)

O-pi
dopey
mopy
ropy
soapy

OP-i
choppy
copy
floppy
hoppy
poppy
sloppy
soppy

OP-ik
(scopic)
  horoscopic
  kaleidoscopic
  periscopic
  spectroscopic
  stereoscopic
  telescopic, etc.
(thropic)
  anthropic
    misanthropic
    philanthropic, etc.
topic
tropic
(yopic)
  myopic

OP-iks
topics
tropics

O-ping
coping
doping
groping
hoping

loping
  eloping
  interloping
moping
roping
sloping
soaping
toping

OP-ing
chopping
(clopping)
  clip-clopping
cropping
dropping
  eavesdropping (*i*)
flopping
gawping
hopping
lopping
mopping
plopping
popping
propping
shopping
slopping
sopping
stopping
stropping
swapping
topping
wapping
whopping

OP-l
hopple
stopple
topple

O-pless
hopeless
ropeless
soapless
(cope less, etc.)

OP-shun
option
(doption)
  adoption

OP-sis
(nopsis)
  synopsis
(topsis)
  thanatopsis
(yopsis)
  coreopsis

OP-ted
opted
  co-opted
(dopted)
  adopted

OP-tik
optic
Coptic
(noptic)
  synoptic

O-pur
coper
doper
groper
loper
  eloper
  interloper
moper
roper
soaper
toper

OP-ur
bopper
  bebopper
  teenybopper
chopper
copper
cropper
  sharecropper (*i*)
dropper

eavesdropper (*i*)
eyedropper (*i*)
hopper
  clodhopper (*i*)
  grasshopper (*i*)
pauper
popper
proper
  improper
shopper
stopper
swapper
topper
whopper
(stop 'er, etc.)

O-pus
opus
  magnum opus
(nopus)
  Canopus
(rope us, etc.)

OR-a
aura
flora
(gora)
  angora
Nora
  signora
(rora)
  aurora
Torah

OR-aks
borax
thorax

OR-al
oral
aural
chloral
choral
floral
laurel
moral

immoral
(naural)
  binaural
  monaural
sorrel

OR-bel
corbel
doorbell

OR-bl
corbel
warble

OR-chur
scorcher
torcher

OR-churd
orchard
tortured

OR-dant
(cordant)
  concordant
  discordant
mordant

OR-ded
boarded
chorded
corded
  accorded
  recorded
    unrecorded
forded
  afforded
hoarded
lorded
sordid
warded
  awarded
  rewarded
    unrewarded
(more dead, etc.)

OR-ding
boarding
chording
cording
  according
  recording
fording
  affording
hoarding
lording
warding
  awarding
  rewarding
    unrewarding

ORD-ship
boardship
lordship
wardship

OR-dur
order
  disorder
  money order (*i*)
  reorder
boarder
border
(corder)
  recorder
hoarder
warder

OR-el
laurel
(*see* **OR-al**, *page 270)*

OR-ens
Florence
(horrence)
  abhorrence
Lawrence
  St. Lawrence
torrents
warrants

OR-ent
(horrent)
  abhorrent
torrent
warrant

OR-fik
Orphic
morphic
  anthropomorphic
  endomorphic, etc.

OR-gan
organ
gorgon
Morgan

OR-hed
forehead
sorehead
warhead

OR-house
"porehouse"
shore house
storehouse
whorehouse

OR-i
dory
  hunky-dory (*i*)
glory
gory
  allegory
  category
hoary
Lorre, Peter
lorry
(priori)
  a priori
quarry
sorry
story
Tory
  accusatory
  adulatory

amatory
ambulatory
auditory
circulatory
commendatory
compensatory
conciliatory
confiscatory
congratulatory
conservatory
contributory
corroboratory
crematory
defamatory
denunciatory
depilatory
depository
derogatory
designatory
dictatory
dilatory
discriminatory
dormitory
exclamatory
explanatory
gesticulatory
gustatory
hallucinatory
improvisatory
incantatory
incriminatory
inflammatory
interrogatory
inventory
laboratory
laudatory
mandatory
migratory
obligatory
observatory
oratory
predatory
premonitory
preparatory
probatory
promontory

purgatory
reformatory
repertory
repository
respiratory
restoratory
retaliatory
territory
transitory
vibratory
*There are many
more words in this
group. Those un-
listed are useless to
the lyricist, and, for
that matter, most of
those listed are al-
most so.*

OR-id (OR-eed)
gloried
storied

OR-id
florid
horrid
torrid

OR-ij
forage
storage

OR-ik
Doric
(goric)
   allegoric
   paregoric
   phantasmagoric
(loric)
   caloric
(moric)
   sophomoric
(phoric)
   amphoric
   camphoric
   metaphoric

phosphoric
semaphoric
(storic)
   historic
      prehistoric
(thoric)
   plethoric
Yorick
   meteoric
   theoric

OR-ing
boring
coring
   encoring
(doring)
   adoring
flooring
goring
(horing)
   abhoring
(noring)
   ignoring
(ploring)
   deploring
   exploring
   imploring
poring
pouring
roaring
scoring
shoring
snoring
soaring
storing
   restoring
warring

OR-ja
Borgia, Lucrezia
   & Cesare
Georgia

OR-ji
orgy
(porgie)

Georgie Porgie

OR-jun
Borgian
Georgian
(gorgin', etc.)

OR-king
corking
forking

OR-less
oarless
oreless
coreless
doorless
shoreless

OR-lok
oarlock
forelock
warlock

OR-mal
formal
  informal
normal
  abnormal
  anormal

OR-man
corpsman
doorman
floorman
foreman
Norman
shoreman
  longshoreman (*i*)

OR-mant
dormant
(formant)
  conformant
  informant

OR-mi
stormy
swarmy
(before me, etc.)

OR-ming
forming
  conforming
    nonconforming
  deforming
  informing
  performing
  reforming
  transforming
storming
swarming
warming

ORM-less
formless
gormless (*North
  English*)
stormless

ORM-li
(formly)
  uniformly
warmly

OR-mur
dormer
former
  conformer
  informer
  performer
  reformer
  transformer
stormer
  barnstormer
swarmer
warmer
  foot warmer (*i*)

OR-net
cornet
hornet (*i*)

(worn it, etc.)

ORN-ful
mournful
scornful

OR-ni
corny
horny
thorny

OR-ning
borning
  suborning
(dorning)
  adorning
morning
  good morning
mourning
scorning
warning
  forewarning

ORN-less
hornless
scornless
thornless

OR-nur
(borner)
  suborner
corner
(dorner)
  adorner
mourner
scorner
warner

OR-o
borrow
morrow
  tomorrow
sorrow
toro (*Spanish*)

OR-or
horror
(see **OR-ur,** *page 275)*

OR-sal
dorsal
morsel

OR-sen
coarsen
hoarsen
(endorsin', etc.)

OR-sest
coarsest
hoarsest

ORS-ful
forceful
(morseful)
  remorseful
(zorceful)
  resourceful

OR-shun
(bortion)
  abortion
portion
  apportion
  proportion
    disproportion
(stortion)
  distortion
  extortion
torsion
  contortion

OR-sing
coursing
  discoursing
(dorsing)
  endorsing
forcing
  enforcing
horsing
(vorcing)

divorcing

OR-sless
forceless
horseless
(morseless)
  remorseless
sourceless
  resourceless

OR-sman
horseman
Norseman

OR-sment
(dorsement)
  endorsement
(forcement)
  enforcement
    reinforcement
(vorcement)
  divorcement

OR-sness
coarseness
hoarseness

OR-some
boresome
foursome
(pour some, etc.)

OR-sur
coarser
courser
(dorser)
  endorser
(forcer)
  enforcer
    reinforcer
hoarser

OR-tal
chortle
mortal
  immortal

portal

OR-ted
(borted)
  aborted
courted
(ported)
  deported
  imported
  reported
  supported
snorted
sported
  disported
  exported
sorted
  assorted
  consorted
  unsorted
(storted)
  distorted
  extorted
thwarted
(torted)
  contorted
  retorted
(zorted)
  exhorted
  resorted

OR-teks
cortex
vortex

OR-ti
forty
sortie
warty

OR-ting
(borting)
  aborting
courting
(porting)
  deporting
  importing

reporting
supporting
(scorting)
escorting
snorting
sorting
assorting
consorting
sporting
exporting
transporting
(storting)
distorting
extorting
thwarting
(torting)
contorting
retorting
(zorting)
exhorting
resorting

OR-tiv
(bortive)
abortive
sportive

ORT-li
courtly
portly
shortly

ORT-ment
(portment)
comportment
deportment
(sortment)
assortment

ORT-nite
fortnight
(sport night, etc.)

OR-tune
fortune
misfortune

(portune)
importune

OR-tur
mortar
porter
exporter
importer
reporter
supporter
transporter
quarter
shorter
snorter
sorter

OR-tured (OR-chard)
orchard
tortured

OR-um
(corum)
decorum
forum
(lorem)
ad valorem
quorum
(adore 'em, etc.)

OR-ur
borer
corn borer
corer
(dorer)
adorer
gorer
horror
(norer)
ignorer
(plorer)
implorer
pourer
roarer
scorer
shnorrer (*Yiddish*)
snorer

soarer
(splorer)
explorer
storer
restorer

OR-us
chorus
(norus)
sonorous (*i*)
porous
(saurous)
Brontosaurus
Ichthyosaurus
thesaurus
Tyrannosaurus
Taurus
(bore us, etc.)

OR-ward
foreword
forward
henceforward
straightforward
thenceforward
shoreward

O-sest
closest
grossest

OS-et
cosset
faucet
posset
(toss it, etc.)

OSH-i
sloshy
squashy
(washy)
wishy-washy

OSH-ing
coshing (*British*)
joshing

noshing (*Yiddish*)
quashing
squashing
washing

O-shur
gaucher
kosher
(oh sure, etc.)

OSH-ur
cosher (*British*)
nosher (*Yiddish*)
squasher
washer

O-shun
ocean
Goshen
　Land o' Goshen
lotion
motion
　commotion
　emotion
　locomotion
　promotion
notion
potion

O-shus
(cocious)
　precocious
(rocious)
　ferocious
(trocious)
　atrocious

OS-i
bossy
flossy
glossy
mossy
posse
saucy

OS-il
docile
dossal
fossil
jostle
(lossal)
　colossal
(postle)
　apostle
wassail

OS-ing
bossing
　embossing
crossing
　double-crossing
　railway crossing
dossing
glossing
tossing

O-sis
(kosis)
　narcosis
　psychosis
　　metempsychosis
(losis)
　tuberculosis
(nosis)
　diagnosis
　hypnosis
　prognosis
(rosis)
　cirrhosis
　neurosis
(yosis)
　apotheosis

O-siv
plosive
　implosive
(splosive)
　explosive
(rosive)
　corrosive
　erosive

O-sness
(boseness)
　verboseness
closeness
grossness
(roseness)
　moroseness

O-so
oh so
(roso)
　amoroso
　doloroso
so-so
(woso)
　virtuoso
(know so, etc.)

OS-om
awesome
blossom
possum
　opossum
(saw some, etc.)

O-stal
coastal
postal

O-sted
boasted
coasted
hosted
posted
　unposted
roasted
toasted

OST-ed
costed
　accosted
frosted
(zausted)
　exhausted

OST-ik
caustic
(crostic)
  acrostic
gnostic
  agnostic
    diagnostic

O-sting
boasting
coasting
posting
roasting
toasting

OST-ing
costing
  accosting
frosting
(zausting)
  exhausting

O-stli
ghostly
mostly

OST-rum
nostrum
rostrum

O-stur
boaster
coaster
poster
  four-poster
roaster
  Zoroaster
toaster

OST-ur
(coster)
  accoster
Gloucester
(noster)
  paternoster
(poster)

imposter
roster

O-sur
closer
grocer
(no, sir; go, sir;
  etc.)

OS-ur
(bosser)
  embosser
Chaucer
crosser
  double-crosser
saucer
  flying saucer
(law, sir, etc.)

O-ta
(dota)
  Kadota
(kota)
  Dakota
quota
(sota)
  Minnesota
(yota)
  iota
(*U.S. southern
  motor, etc.*)

O-tait
notate
rotate

O-tal
(dotal)
  anecdotal
  antidotal
(rotal)
  sclerotal
total
  teetotal

O-ted
bloated
boated
coated
  petticoated (*i*)
doted
floated
  refloated
gloated
moated
  demoted
  promoted
noted
  denoted
  unnoted
quoted
  misquoted
throated
voted
  devoted

OT-ed
blotted
clotted
dotted
jotted
knotted
lotted
  allotted
plotted
potted
rotted
  garroted (*i*)
slotted
sotted
  besotted
potted
  bespotted
squatted
totted
trotted

OT-en
cotton
gotten
  begotten

misbegotten
forgotten
unforgotten
ill-gotten
misgotten
rotten

O-thing (OTHE-ing)
clothing
loathing

OT-hook (OAT-hook)
boathook
coathook

OTH-ur
bother
father
pother
rather (*British*)

O-ti
(roaty)
throaty
(yote)
coyote

OT-i
(cotty)
manicotti
dotty
haughty
knotty
naughty
spotty

OT-ij
cottage
frottage
wattage

OT-ik
(cotic)
narcotic
(notic)
hypnotic

(potic)
nepotic
(rotic)
cirrhotic
erotic
neurotic
(spotic)
despotic
(yotic)
chaotic
idiotic
macrobiotic
(zotic)
exotic
quixotic

O-ting
bloating
boating
coating
doting
floating
gloating
(moating)
demoting
promoting
noting
denoting
quoting
misquoting
voting
devoting

OT-ing
blotting
clotting
dotting
jotting
knotting
lotting
allotting
plotting
potting
rotting
sotting
besotting

spotting
squatting
totting
trotting
yachting

OT-ish
clottish
hottish
schottische
Scottish
sottish

O-tist
(dotist)
anecdotist
noticed
unnoticed

O-tive
motive
emotive
locomotive
votive

OT-l
bottle
dottle
glottal
mottle
throttle
wattle

OT-less
clotless
cotless
dotless
knotless
potless
rotless
spotless
thoughtless

OT-li
hotly
motley

(rotly)
  overwroughtly
squatly
tautly

O-to
koto (*Japanese*)
photo
roto
(soto)
  De Soto
(toto)
  in toto

OT-o
blotto
(coto)
  staccato
(gato)
  legato
grotto
motto
(sotto)
  risotto

OTS-man
Scotsman
yachtsman

OT-um
autumn
bottom
(got 'em, etc.)

O-tur
oater
bloater
boater
floater
gloater
motor
  promoter
quoter
rotor
voter

OT-ur
otter
blotter
daughter
hotter
plotter
potter
rotter
slaughter
spotter
squatter
totter
trotter
water
(caught 'er, etc.)

OUCH-ing
couching
crouching
grouching
slouching
vouching

OUCH-ur
groucher
sloucher
voucher

OUD-ed
clouded
  beclouded
  unclouded
crowded
  overcrowded
shrouded
  enshrouded
  unshrouded

OUD-est
loudest
proudest

OUD-i
cloudy
dowdy
  pandowdy

howdy
(laude)
  cum laude
rowdy

OUD-ing
clouding
crowding
  overcrowding
shrouding
  enshrouding

OUD-li
loudly
proudly

OUD-ness
loudness
proudness

OUD-ur
chowder
louder
powder
prouder
(crowd 'er, etc.)

OU-el
bowel
dowel
rowel
towel
trowel
vowel
  avowal
  disavowal

OU-ing
bowing
cowing
(dowing)
  endowing
(lowing)
  allowing
  disallowing
ploughing

rowing
vowing
  avowing

OUL-ing
fouling
fowling
growling
howling
prowling
scowling

OUL-ur
fouler
growler
howler
prowler
scowler
yowler

OUN-ded
bounded
  abounded
  rebounded
  unbounded
(dounded)
  redounded
founded
  confounded
  dumfounded
  unfounded
grounded
  ungrounded
hounded
mounded
pounded
  compounded
  expounded
  impounded
rounded
  surrounded
sounded
  resounded
(stounded)
  astounded

OUN-dest
(foundest)
  profoundest
roundest

OUN-ding
bounding
  abounding
  rebounding
(dounding)
  redounding
founding
  confounding
  dumfounding
grounding
hounding
pounding
  compounding
  expounding
  impounding
  propounding
rounding
  surrounding
sounding
  resounding
(stounding)
  astounding

OUND-less
boundless
groundless
soundless

OUND-li
(foundly)
  profoundly
roundly
soundly

OUND-ling
foundling
groundling

OUND-ness
roundness
soundness

OUN-dri
boundary
foundry

OUN-dur
bounder
flounder
founder
  profounder
pounder
rounder
sounder
(surround 'er, gowned
  'er, etc.)

OUN-i
brownie
downy

OUN-ing
browning
clowning
crowning
downing
drowning
frowning
gowning

OUN-ish
brownish
clownish
downish

OUN-jing
lounging
scrounging

OUN-less
crownless
frownless
gownless

OUN-sez
ounces
bounces
flounces

(nounces)
  announces
  denounces
  pronounces
  renounces
pounces
trounces

OUN-sing
bouncing
flouncing
(nouncing)
  announcing
  denouncing
  pronouncing
  renouncing
pouncing
trouncing

OUN-sur
bouncer
flouncer
(nouncer)
  announcer
  denouncer

OUN-ted
counted
  accounted
  discounted
  miscounted
  recounted
  uncounted
mounted
  amounted
  dismounted
  remounted
  surmounted
  unmounted

OUN-ti
bounty
county
mountie

OUN-tin
fountain
mountain
(countin', etc.)

OUN-ting
counting
  accounting
  discounting
mounting
  amounting
  dismounting
  remounting
  surmounting

OUN-ward
downward
townward

O-ur
blower
goer
grower
hoer
knower
lower
mower
rower
sewer
(stower)
  bestower
thrower

O-ur (AH-ur)
clawer
drawer
gnawer
rawer

OUR-i
Bowery
dowry
floury
flowery
showery

OUR-ing
flowering
  deflowering
scouring
souring
(vouring)
  devouring

OUR-ur
(flowerer)
  deflowerer
scourer
sourer
  devourer

OUT-ed
clouted
doubted
  undoubted
flouted
grouted
pouted
routed
scouted
shouted
spouted
sprouted
touted

OUT-est
stoutest
(voutest)
  devoutest

OUT-i
doughty
gouty
grouty
pouty

OUT-ing
outing
clouting
doubting
  undoubting
flouting

grouting
louting
pouting
routing
scouting
shouting
spouting
sprouting
touting

OUT-li (OUT-lee)
stoutly
(voutly)
    devoutly

OUT-ness
stoutness
(voutness)
    devoutness

OUT-ur
outer
doubter
pouter
router
scouter
shouter
spouter
stouter

OU-ur
bower
    embower
cower
flower
    cauliflower (*i*)
    deflower
glower
plougher
plower
power
    empower
    horsepower (*i*)
    overpower
    sea power
shower

tower
vower
(see **OUR,** *page 124)*

OU-wow
bow-wow
pow-wow

OU-zal
(rousal)
    arousal
    carousal
(spousal)
    espousal

OUZ-zez
blouses
browses
houses
rouses
    arouses
    carouses
(spouses)
    espouses

OU-zi (OU-zee)
drowzy
frowzy
lousy

OUZ-zing
browsing
housing
rousing
    arousing
    carousing

OUZ-ur
browser
rouser
    carouser
trouser

OU-zurz
trousers
(carousers, etc.)

OV-el
grovel
hovel
novel

O-ven
cloven
(toven)
    Beethoven,
        Ludwig van
woven
    interwoven

OV-en
oven
coven

O-vine
ovine
bovine

O-vur
over
    moreover
clover
Dover
drover
plover
rover
trover

O-wair
nowhere
(go where, etc.)

O-yur (AH-yur)
lawyer
sawyer
    Sawyer, Tom

O-zen
chosen
frozen
"squozen"
(posin', etc.)

289

O-zez
Moses
(roses, etc.)

OZ-ez
causes
clauses
gauzes
pauses
vases (*British*)

O-zhun
(plosion)
  implosion
(rosion)
  corrosion
  erosion
(splosion)
  explosion

O-zi
cozy
dozy
nosy
posy
prosy
rosy

O-zing
closing
  disclosing
  enclosing

inclosing
unclosing
dozing
nosing
posing
  composing
    decomposing
  deposing
  imposing
    unimposing
  interposing
  juxtaposing
  opposing
  proposing
  supposing
    presupposing
  reposing
(sposing)
  disposing
    predisposing
  exposing
  transposing

OZ-ing
causing
pausing

OZ-it
closet
posit
  deposit
(claws it, etc.)

OZ-l
mazel (*Hebrew*)
nozzle
schnozzle (*Yiddish*)
sozzle

O-zur
closer
  discloser
  encloser
dozer
  bulldozer
poser
  composer
  disposer
  opposer
  proposer
  supposer

O-zyur
closure
  disclosure
  foreclosure
  inclosure
crosier
hosier
(posure)
  composure
(sposure)
  exposure

U

U-al
dual
fuel
(newal)
  renewal
(sual)
  pursual

U-ant
fluent
  affluent
  confluent
(suant)
  pursuant

U-ba
Cuba
scuba
tuba

U-bi (OO-bi)
booby
ruby

UB-i
chubby
grubby
hubby
nubby
stubby
tubby

U-bik
cubic
pubic
(rubic)
  cherubic

U-bing
cubing
tubing

UB-ing
blubbing
clubbing
drubbing
dubbing
grubbing
nubbing
rubbing
scrubbing
snubbing
stubbing
subbing

UB-ish
clubbish
rubbish

U-bit
cubit
two-bit
(you bit, etc.)

UB-l
bubble
double
  redouble

rubble
stubble
trouble

UB-li
bubbly
doubly
stubbly

UB-ling
bubbling
doubling
troubling

UB-lur
bubbler
doubler
troubler

U-brik (OO-brik)
lubric
rubric
(new brick)

U-bur (OO-bur)
goober
tuber

UB-ur
blubber
dubber
grubber
lubber
  landlubber (i)
rubber
scrubber

UCH-ez
clutches
crutches
hutches
touches
  retouches

UCH-i
duchy

touchy

UCH-ing
clutching
touching
  retouching

U-da (OO-du)
Buddha
(cuda)
  barracuda
(myuda)
  Bermuda

U-ded (OO-ded)
brooded
duded
(cluded)
  concluded
  excluded
  included
  occluded
  precluded
  secluded
(luded)
  alluded
  colluded
  deluded
  eluded
(nuded)
  denuded
(truded)
  extruded
  obtruded
  protruded
(zuded)
  exuded

UD-ed
blooded
budded
flooded
scudded
studded
thudded

U-dent (OO-dent)
prudent
  imprudent
student

U-dest (OO-dest)
crudest
nudest
rudest
shrewdest

U-di (OO-dee)
broody
moody

UD-i
bloody
buddy
ruddy
study

UD-id (UD-eed)
bloodied
muddied
studied
  unstudied

U-ding (OO-ding)
brooding
(cluding)
  concluding
  excluding
  including
  occluding
  precluding
  recluding
  secluding
(luding)
  alluding
  deluding
  eluding
(nuding)
  denuding
(truding)
  intruding
  obtruding

(zuding)
  exuding

UD-ing
budding
flooding
scudding
studding

U-dl (OO-dl)
boodle
  caboodle
doodle
  flapdoodle
  Yankee Doodle
feudal
noodle
poodle

UD-l
cuddle
fuddle
huddle
muddle
puddle

U-dli (OOD-lee)
crudely
lewdly
rudely
shrewdly

UD-ling
cuddling
fuddling
  befuddling
huddling
puddling

UD-lur
cuddler
fuddler
huddler
muddler
puddler

UD-ness (OO-dness)
crudeness
lewdness
nudeness
rudeness
shrewdness

U-dur (OO-dur)
brooder
cruder
ruder
shrewder
(truder)
  intruder
Tudor

UD-ur
udder
rudder
shudder

U-e (OO-ee)
buoy
  Drambuie
chewy
dewy
fluey
gluey
gooey
hooey
Louis
  St. Louis
phooey
screwy

U-el (OO-el)
crewel
cruel
duel
fuel
jewel

U-est (OO-est)
bluest
newest
truest

292

U-et (OO-et)
cruet
suet
(do it, etc.)

UF-en
roughen
toughen
(bluffin', etc.)

UF-est
bluffest
roughest
toughest

UF-i
fluffy
huffy
puffy
stuffy

UF-in
muffin
  ragamuffin
puffin
(stuffin', etc.)

U-fing (OO-fing)
goofing
hoofing
proofing
roofing
spoofing
woofing

UF-ing
bluffing
cuffing
fluffing
huffing
luffing
puffing
roughing
stuffing

UF-l
duffel
muffle
ruffle
scuffle
shuffle
snuffle
truffle

UF-li
bluffly
gruffly
roughly
snuffly
toughly

UF-ling
muffling
scuffling
shuffling
snuffling

UF-lur
muffler
scuffler
snuffler

UF-ness
bluffness
gruffness
roughness
toughness

U-fur (OO-fur)
goofer
hoofer
roofer
spoofer
twofer

UF-ur
bluffer
buffer
duffer
gruffer
puffer

rougher
suffer
tougher

U-gar
cougar
Luger

UG-est
druggist
smuggest
snuggest

UG-i
buggy
muggy

UG-ing
drugging
hugging
mugging
plugging
shrugging
slugging
tugging

U-gl (OO-gl)
bugle
frugal
fugal

UG-l
juggle
smuggle
snuggle
truggle

UG-li (UG-lee)
ugly
smugly
snuggly

UG-ling
juggling
smuggling
struggling

UG-lur
juggler
smuggler
snuggler
struggler

UG-ness
smugness
snugness

UG-ur
lugger
mugger
　hugger-mugger
plugger
　songplugger
rugger
snugger

U-id
Druid
fluid

U-in
bruin
ruin
shoo-in
(do in, stewin', etc.)

U-ing (OO-ing)
*This group of words
rhymes correctly with
the one immediately
following it.*
blueing
brewing
cooing
(cruing)
　accruing
doing
　overdoing
　undoing
　wrongdoing
gluing

(looing)
　hallooing
mooing
(nooing)
　canoeing
poohing
　pooh-poohing
　shampooing
　screwing
strewing
　construing
　　misconstruing
(tooing)
　tattooing
wooing

U-ing (YOO-ing)
(buing)
　imbuing
chewing
cueing
　barbecuing
(duing)
　subduing
hewing
mewing
(newing)
　renewing
(shewing)
　eschewing
spewing
stewing
suing
　ensuing
　pursuing
viewing
　interviewing
　reviewing

UJ-ez
budges
drudges
fudges
grudges
　begrudges
judges

adjudges
misjudges
nudges
smudges
trudges

UJ-ing
budging
drudging
fudging
grudging
　begrudging
judging
nudging
smudging
trudging

UJ-on
bludgeon
dudgeon
gudgeon
(mudgeon)
　curmudgeon
(grudgin', etc.)

UK-et
bucket
ducat
(tucket)
　Nantucket
　Pawtucket
(duck it, etc.)

U-ki (OO-kee)
fluky
kooky
pooky
spooky

UK-i
ducky
lucky
　unlucky
mucky
plucky
(tucky)
　Kentucky

UK-ing
ducking
plucking
shucking
sucking
trucking
tucking

UK-l
buckle
  unbuckle
chuckle
knuckle
muckle
suckle
  honeysuckle (*i*)
truckle

UK-ld
cuckold
(buckled, etc.)

UK-ling
buckling
  unbuckling
chuckling
duckling
suckling
truckling

UK-lur
buckler
  swashbuckler
truckler

UK-shun
duction
  abduction
  induction
  production
    reproduction
  reduction
  seduction
  traduction

ruction
(struction)
  construction
  destruction
  instruction
  obstruction

UK-ted
(ducted)
  abducted
conducted
  deducted
  inducted
(structed)
  constructed
  instructed
  obstructed
    unobstructed

UK-ting
(ducting)
  abducting
  conducting
  deducting
  inducting
(structing)
  constructing
  instructing
  obstructing

UK-tive
(ductive)
  conductive
  deductive
  inductive
  productive
    reproductive
  seductive
(structive)
  constructive
  instructive
  obstructive

UK-tress
(ductress)
  conductress

seductress
(structress)
  instructress

UK-tur
ductor
  abductor
  conductor
    non-conductor
  inductor
(structor)
  destructor
  instructor
  obstructor

U-kr (OO-kr)
euchre
lucre

UK-ur
bucker
chucker
chukker
clucker
mucker
pucker
succor
sucker
  sapsucker
  seersucker, etc.
trucker

U-la (OO-luh)
(bula)
  Ashtabula
  "Boola Boola"
hula
  hula-hula
moola
(zoola)
  Missoula
(*U.S. southern:
  ruler, etc.*)

U-lep
julep
tulip

U-less
clueless
dewless
screwless
viewless
(do less, etc.)

UL-et
gullet
mullet

UL-gait
(mulgate)
  promulgate (*i*)
Vulgate

UL-i (OO-li)
coolie
coolly
drooly
duly
  unduly
newly
ruly
  unruly
Thule
truly

U-ling (OO-ling)
cooling
drooling
fooling
mewling
ruling
schooling
tooling

UL-ing
culling
dulling
gulling
lulling

mulling
(nulling)
  annulling

U-lip
julep
tulip

U-lish (OO-lish)
coolish
foolish
ghoulish
mulish

UL-jense
(dulgence)
  indulgence
(fulgence)
  effulgence
  refulgence

UL-jent
(dulgent)
  indulgent
fulgent
  effulgent

UL-jez
bulges
(dulges)
  indulges
(fulges)
  effulges
(vulges)
  divulges

ULK-i
bulky
hulky
sulky

ULK-ing
bulking
hulking
skulking
sulking

ULK-ur
skulker
sulker

UL-shun
(mulsion)
  emulsion
(pulsion)
  compulsion
  expulsion
  impulsion
  propulsion
  repulsion
(vulsion)
  convulsion
  revulsion

UL-sing
pulsing
  repulsing
(vulsing)
  convulsing

UL-sive
(mulsive)
  emulsive
(pulsive)
  compulsive
  impulsive
  propulsive
  repulsive
(spulsive)
  expulsive
(vulsive)
  convulsive

UL-tant
(sultant)
  consultant
(zultant)
  exultant
  resultant

UL-ted
(sulted)
  consulted

insulted
(zulted)
  exulted
  resulted

UL-ting
(culting)
  occulting
(sulting)
  consulting
  insulting
(zulting)
  exulting
  resulting

UL-ture (UL-chur)
culture
  agriculture
vulture
(arboriculture, etc.)

U-lu (OO-loo)
Lulu
  Honolulu
Zulu

U-lur (OO-lur)
cooler
drooler
mewler
ruler

Ul-ur
color
  discolor
  Technicolor
  tricolor
cruller
duller
sculler

Ul-urd
colored
  discolored
dullard

UL-yun
mullion
scullion

U-ma
duma
Dumas, Alexandre
puma
Yuma
(zuma)
  mazuma
  Montezuma

Uman
human
(new man, etc.)
Truman, Harry S

UM-ba
rumba
"numbah"
(*U.S. southern:*
  slumber, etc.)

UM-bl
bumble
crumble
fumble
grumble
humble
jumble
mumble
rumble
stumble
tumble

UM-bli
crumbly
humbly
stumbly

UM-bling
crumbling
fumbling
grumbling
humbling

jumbling
mumbling
rumbling
stumbling
tumbling

UM-blur
fumbler
grumbler
humbler
jumbler
mumbler
rumbler
stumbler
tumbler

UM-bo
gumbo
jumbo
  mumbo-jumbo

UM-brus
cumbrous
(numbrous)
  penumbrous
slumbrous

UM-bur
umber
cumber
  cucumber
  encumber
    disencumber
lumbar
lumber
number
slumber

UM-drum
humdrum
(some drum, etc.)

U-men
(bumen)
  albumen
(cumen)

acumen
(tumen)
  bitumen

UM-est
dumbest
glummest
numbest

UM-et
grummet
plummet
summit
(from it, etc.)

UM-ful (OOM-ful)
doomful
roomful

UM-i
gloomy
rheumy
(sue me, to me, etc.)

UM-i
crumby
dummy
gummy
mummy
rummy
tummy
yummy

U-mid
humid
tumid

U-ming (OO-ming)
blooming
booming
dooming
fuming
  perfuming
grooming
looming
  illuming

(suming)
  assuming
    unassuming
  consuming
(tombing)
  entombing
(zuming)
  exhuming
  presuming
  resuming

UM-ing
coming
  becoming
    unbecoming
  forthcoming
  overcoming
  shortcoming
drumming
gumming
humming
numbing
  benumbing
plumbing
slumming
strumming
summing
thumbing

UM-it
grummet
summit
(from it, etc.)

UM-li
comely
dumbly
glumly
numbly

UM-ok
hummock
stomach

UM-pass
compass

encompass
rumpus
(stump us, etc.)

UM-pet
crumpet
strumpet
trumpet
(bump it, etc.)

UM-pi
bumpy
dumpy
frumpy
grumpy
humpy
jumpy
lumpy
stumpy

UMP-ing
bumping
dumping
jumping
lumping
plumping
pumping
slumping
stumping
thumping
trumping

UM-pish
grumpish
lumpish

UMP-kin
bumpkin
pumpkin

UM-pl
crumple
rumple

UM-pling
crumpling

dumpling
rumpling

UMP-shun
gumption
(sumption)
  assumption
  consumption
  subsumption
(zumption)
  presumption
  resumption

UMP-shus
bumptious
scrumptious

UM-pur
bumper
dumper
jumper
lumper
plumper
pumper
stumper
thumper
trumper

U-mur (OO-mur)
bloomer
boomer
(fumer)
  perfumer
humor
roomer
rumor
(sumer)
  consumer
tumor

UM-ur
comer
  newcomer
drummer
dumber
glummer

hummer
mummer
number
plumber
strummer
summer
  midsummer

U-murd
humored
  good-humored
  ill-humored
rumored

U-murs
bloomers
(rumors, etc.)

UN-chez
brunches
bunches
crunches
hunches
lunches
munches
punches
scrunches

UN-chi
crunchy
punchy

UN-ching
bunching
crunching
lunching
munching
punching
scrunching

UN-chun
luncheon
truncheon

UN-chur
buncher
cruncher
luncher
muncher
puncher

UN-dai
Monday
Sunday
(one day, etc.)

UN-dans
(bundance)
  abundance
(dundance)
  redundance

UN-dant
(bundant)
  abundant
(dundant)
  redundant

UN-dl
bundle
trundle

UN-don
undone
London
(none done etc.)

UN-dur
under
  thereunder
blunder
plunder
sunder
  asunder
thunder
wonder

UN-el
funnel
gunwale

runnel
tunnel

U-ness
blueness
newness
trueness

UN-ful
spoonful
tuneful

UNG-gl
bungle
jungle

UNG-gur
hunger
(monger)
  costmonger
  fishmonger (*i*)
  ironmonger
  rumormonger, etc.
younger

UNG-ki
chunky
flunky
funky
monkey
spunky

UNG-kl
uncle
(buncle)
  carbuncle
(duncle)
  peduncle

UNG-kn
drunken
shrunken
sunken

UNG-kshun
unction

junction
  conjunction
  injunction
  subjunction
(punction)
  compunction
  expunction

UNG-kshus
unctious
(bunctious)
  rambunctious

UNG-ktur (UNG-chur)
juncture
  conjuncture
puncture
  acupuncture

UNG-kur
bunker
drunker
dunker
hunker

UNG-kurd
bunkered
drunkard

U-ni (OO-ni)
loony
moony
puny

UN-i
bunny
funny
honey
money
sunny
tunny

U-nik
Munich
Punic
runic

tunic

U-ning (OO-ning)
crooning
(looning)
  ballooning
mooning
  communing
(pooning)
  harpooning
pruning
(puning)
  impugning
spooning
swooning
tuning

UN-ing
cunning
dunning
punning
running
  outrunning
  overrunning
shunning
stunning
sunning

U-nish (OO-nish)
(foonish)
  buffoonish
(troonish)
  poltroonish

UN-ish
one-ish
punish

U-nist (OO-nist)
(loonist)
  balloonist
(poonist)
  harpoonist
(soonist)
  bassoonist
(tunist)

opportunist

UN-jez
lunges
plunges
sponges
  expunges

UN-jing
lunging
plunging
sponging
  expunging

UN-jun
dungeon
(lungin', etc.)

UN-jur
lunger
sponger

U-nless (OON-less)
moonless
tuneless

U-nlite (OON-lite)
moonlight
noon light

U-no
uno (*Spanish*)
  numero uno (*Spanish*)
Juno
(you know, do know,
etc.)

UN-tal
frontal
(puntal)
  contrapuntal

UN-ted
blunted
bunted
fronted

affronted
confronted
grunted
hunted
punted
shunted
stunted

UN-ting
bunting
fronting
  affronting
  confronting
grunting
hunting
punting
shunting
stunting

Un-tur
blunter
bunter
grunter
hunter
punter
shunter

U-nur (OO-num)
crooner
lunar
(muner)
  communer
(pooner)
  harpooner
  lampooner
pruner
schooner
sooner
spooner
tuner

UN-ur
gunner
  machine gunner (*i*)
runner
stunner

U-nyon
union
  disunion
  reunion
(munion)
  communion

UN-yon
onion
bunion
grunion

U-pi (OO-pi)
croupy
droopy
soupy

UP-i
guppy
puppy

U-pid
Cupid
stupid

U-ping (OO-ping)
cooping
  recouping
grouping
looping
scooping
stooping
swooping
trooping
whooping

U-pl (OO-pl)
pupil
scruple
(tuple)
  (octuple, etc.)

UP-l
couple
supple

UP-let
couplet
(tuplet)
 (octuplet, etc.)

UP-shun
(ruption)
 corruption
 disruption
 eruption
 interruption

UPT-li
(bruptly)
 abruptly
(ruptly)
 corruptly

UPT-ness
(bruptness)
 abruptness
(ruptness)
 corruptness

U-pur (OO-pur)
cooper
hooper
looper
snooper
stupor
super
trooper
whooper

UP-ur
upper
crupper
scupper
supper

UR-a
pleura
(tura)
 coloratura
(vura)
 bravura

U-ral
mural
 extramural
 intramural
neural
pleural
plural
rural

UR-ans
durance
 endurance
(surance)
 assurance
 reassurance
 insurance

UR-ban
bourbon
 suburban
turban

UR-bing
curbing
(sturbing)
 disturbing
(turbing)
 perturbing

UR-bl
gerbil
herbal
verbal

UR-chez
birches
churches
lurches
perches
searches
 researches
smirches
 besmirches

UR-chur
nurture

searcher
 researcher

UR-ded
girded
 begirded
 engirded
herded
worded
 reworded

UR-di
birdie
(gurdy)
 hurdy-gurdy
sturdy
wordy

UR-ding
girding
 begirding
 engirding
herding
wording

UR-dl
curdle
girdle
hurdle

UR-dur
verdure
(see UR-jur, page 297)

UR-dur
girder
herder
murder

UR-ens
(currence)
 concurrence
 occurrence
 recurrence
(ference)
 transference

(terrence)
  deterrence

UR-ent
currant
current
  concurrent
  recurrent

U-rest
(curest)
  securest
(murest)
  demurest
purest
(scurest)
  obscurest
surest

UR-est (OOR-est)
dourest
poorest

UR-gl
burgle
gurgle

U-ri
fury
houri
jury
  de jure
(zouri)
  Missouri

UR-i
curry
furry
flurry
hurry
scurry
slurry
Surrey
surrey
worry

U-ring
curing
  procuring
  securing
during
  enduring
(juring)
  abjuring
  adjuring
  non-juring
luring
  alluring
(scuring)
  obscuring
(suring)
  assuring
    reassuring
  ensuring
  insuring
(turing)
  maturing

UR-ing (OOR-ing)
mooring
touring

UR-ing
erring
  unerring
blurring
(curring)
  concurring
  incurring
  occurring
    reoccurring
  recurring
furring
  conferring
  deferring
  inferring
  preferring
  referring
  transferring
(murring)
  demurring
purring

shirring
spurring
(terring)
  deterring
  interring
    disinterring
whirring

UR-ish (OOR-ish)
boorish
poorish
Moorish

UR-ish
flourish
nourish
(turish)
  amateurish

U-rist
jurist
purist
(turist)
  caricaturist

UR-jent
urgent
(mergent)
  emergent
(surgent)
  insurgent
  resurgent
(tergent)
  detergent
(vergent)
  convergent
  divergent

UR-jez
urges
dirges
merges
  emerges
  submerges
purges
scourges

surges
verges
  converges
  diverges

UR-ji
clergy
(lurgy)
  metallurgy
(turgy)
  thaumaturgy, etc.

UR-jik
(lurgic)
  metallurgic
(rurgic)
  chirurgic
(turgic)
  dramaturgic
  liturgic
  thaumaturgic

UR-jing
urging
dirging
merging
  emerging
  submerging
purging
scourging
splurging
surging
verging
  converging
  diverging

UR-jun
burgeon
sturgeon
surgeon
virgin
(urgin', etc.)

UR-jur
merger
purger

verdure
verger

UR-ki
jerky
(kurky)
  Albuquerque
murky
perky
quirky
smirky
turkey

UR-kin
firkin
gherkin
jerkin
(smirkin', etc.)

UR-king
clerking
jerking
lurking
shirking
smirking
working

UR-kur
lurker
shirker
smirker
worker

UR-li (YUR-li)
(curely)
  securely
(murely)
  demurely
purely
(scurely)
  obscurely
surely
(turely)
  maturely

UR-li (OOR-li)
dourly
poorly

UR-li
burly
curly
girlie
pearly
surly
swirly

UR-ling
curling
hurling
pearling
sterling
swirling
twirling

UR-lish
churlish
girlish

UR-loin
purloin
sirloin

UR-lu
curlew
purlieu

UR-lur
curler
hurler
twirler
whirler

UR-mal
dermal
  epidermal
thermal
  geothermal

UR-man
ermine

firman
German
merman
sermon
(termine)
　determine
vermin

UR-ment
(furment)
　deferment
　preferment
　referment
(lurement)
　allurement
(scurement)
　obscurement
(terment)
　interment

UR-mi (UR-mee)
(dermy)
　taxidermy
germy
squirmy
wormy

UR-mik
dermic
　epidermic
　hypodermic
　taxidermic
thermic
　geothermic

UR-ming
firming
　affirming
　confirming
squirming
worming

UR-mit
hermit
permit (*n*)
(affirm it, etc.)

UR-mite
termite
thermite

UR-moil
turmoil
sperm oil

UR-mur
firmer
　affirmer
murmur
squirmer

UR-nal
(bernal)
　hibernal
(fernal)
　infernal
journal
kernel
colonel
(sternal)
　external
(ternal)
　eternal
　fraternal
　internal
　maternal
　nocturnal
　paternal
vernal
(yurnal)
　diurnal

UR-ness (YUR-ness)
(cureness)
　secureness
(mureness)
　demureness
pureness
　impureness
(scureness)
　obscureness
sureness
(tureness)

matureness

UR-ness (OOR-ness)
dourness
poorness

UR-ni
ferny
journey
tourney
　attorney

UR-ning
earning
burning
churning
(journing)
　adjourning
　sojourning
learning
spurning
(surning)
　concerning
　discerning
　　undiscerning
turning
　overturning
　returning
yearning

UR-nish
burnish
furnish

URN-ment
(surnment)
　concernment
　discernment

UR-no
(ferno)
　inferno
Sterno

UR-nur
earner
burner
(journer)
　sojourner
learner
sterner
turner
yearner

UR-o
borrough
burrow
furrow
thorough

U-ror
furor
juror
(see **UR-ur,** *page 301)*

UR-ping
burping
chirping
slurping
(surping)
　usurping

UR-sa
bursa
(versa)
　vice versa

UR-sal
(hearsal)
　rehearsal
(versal)
　reversal
　universal

UR-sez
burses
　disburses
　imburses
　　reimburses
curses

accurses
hearses
　rehearses
(merses)
　immerses
nurses
purses
(sperses)
　disperses
　intersperses
verses
　converses
　reverses
　traverses
(werses)
　coerces

UR-shal
(mercial)
　commercial
(versial)
　controversial

UR-shun
(mersion)
　immersion
(sertion)
　assertion
　insertion
(spersion)
　aspersion
(wercion)
　coercion
(zurtion)
　desertion
　exertion

UR-si (UR-see)
mercy
nursie
(versy)
　controversy

UR-sing
(bursing)
　disbursing

imbursing
　reimbursing
cursing
(hearsing)
　rehearsing
(mersing)
　immersing
nursing
(spersing)
　dispersing
(versing)
　conversing
　reversing
　traversing
(wersing)
　coercing

UR-sive
cursive
　incursive
(scursive)
　discursive
　excursive
(spersive)
　dispersive
(versive)
　conversive
　perversive
　subversive
(wersive)
　coercive

URS-ness
terseness
(verseness)
　averseness
　perverseness

UR-sted
thirsted
worsted

UR-sting
bursting
thirsting

UR-sur
bursar
curser
  precursor
mercer
purser
(verser)
  converser
"worser"

UR-sus
Ursus
versus

UR-tan
certain
  uncertain
curtain
(hurtin', etc.)

UR-ted
blurted
flirted
(serted)
  asserted
  concerted
    disconcerted
  inserted
spurted
squirted
(verted)
  averted
  converted
  diverted
  inverted
  perverted
  reverted
  subverted
(zerted)
  deserted
  exerted

URTH-less
mirthless
worthless

UR-ti
dirty
flirty
thirty

UR-ting
blurting
flirting
hurting
(serting)
  asserting
  concerting
    disconcerting
  inserting
skirting
spurting
squirting
(verting)
  averting
  converting
  diverting
  inverting
  perverting
  reverting
  subverting
(zerting)
  deserting
  exerting

UR-tive
furtive
(sertive)
  assertive

UR-tl
fertile
girtle
kirtle
myrtle
turtle

URT-less
shirtless
skirtless

URT-li
curtly
(lertly)
  alertly
(nertly)
  inertly
pertly
(spertly)
  expertly

URT-ness
curtness
(lertness)
  alertness
(nertness)
  inertness

UR-tu
"kerchoo"
virtue
(alert you, hurt you,
etc.)

UR-tur
curter
squirter
(verter)
  converter
  perverter
  subverter

U-rur
curer
  procurer
  securer
juror
(murer)
  demurer
purer
(scurer)
  obscurer
surer
  ensurer
  insurer
(turer)
  maturer

UR-ur (OOR-ur)
dourer
poorer

UR-ur
(currer)
  incurrer
(ferrer)
  deferrer
(murrer)
  demurrer
stirrer

UR-vent
fervent
servent
  conservant
  observant
    unobservant

UR-vi
nervy
scurvy
(turvy)
  topsy-turvy

UR-ving
Irving, Washington
curving
nerving
  unnerving
serving
  conserving
swerving
  unswerving
(zerving)
  deserving
    undeserving
  observing
    unobserving
  preserving
  reserving
    unreserving

UR-vur
fervor
server
  observer
  preserver
    life preserver

UR-zhun
(cursion)
  incursion
Persian
(scursion)
  excursion
(spersion)
  aspersion
  dispersion
version
  aversion
  conversion
  diversion
  introversion
  inversion
  perversion
  subversion

U-sez
uses
deuces
  deduces
  induces
  introduces
  produces
    reproduces
  reduces
  seduces
  traduces
juices
(scuses)
  excuses

U-sez (OO-sez)
(booses)

cabooses
looses
nooses
  burnooses
sluices
spruces
truces

US-ez
buses
busses
"cusses"
fusses
(scusses)
  discusses
trusses

USH-ez
blushes
brushes
crushes
flushes
gushes
hushes
lushes
mushes
rushes
thrushes

USH-i
gushy
mushy
slushy

USH-ing
blushing
  unblushing
brushing
crushing
flushing
gushing
hushing
lushing
rushing

U-shun (OO-shun)
(blution)
  ablution
(bution)
  attribution
  contribution
  distribution
  retribution
(cution)
  electrocution
  elocution
  execution
  locution
    circumlocution
  prosecution
(lution)
  convolution
  dilution
  evolution
  involution
  pollution
  revolution
  solution
    absolution
    dissolution
    resolution
      irresolution
(nution)
  diminution
(putian)
  Lilliputian
(tution)
  constitution
  destitution
  institution
  prostitution
  restitution
  substitution

USH-un
(cussion)
  concussion
  percussion
Prussian
Russian
(scussion)

discussion
(rushin', etc.)

USH-ur
usher
blusher
crusher
gusher
plusher

U-si (OO-si)
goosey
juicy

US-i
fussy
hussy
mussy

U-sing
(ducing)
  adducing
  deducing
  inducing
  introducing
  producing
    reproducing
  reducing
  seducing
  traducing

U-sing (OO-sing)
goosing
loosing
sprucing

US-ing
busing
bussing
"cussing"
fussing
mussing
(scussing)
  discussing
  trussing

U-siv
(busive)
  abusive
(clusive)
  conclusive
    inconclusive
  exclusive
  reclusive
  seclusive
(ducive)
  conducive
(fusive)
  diffusive
  effusive
(lusive)
  allusive
  collusive
  dilusive
  elusive
  illusive
(trusive)
  intrusive
  obtrusive
    unobtrusive
(tusive)
  contusive

US-iv
(cussive)
  concussive
  percussive

US-ki
dusky
husky
musky

US-king
busking
dusking
husking

US-kur
busker
husker
tusker

US-l
bustle
hustle
muscle
mussel
(puscle)
  corpuscle (*i*)
rustle
tussle

US-ling
bustling
hustling
muscling
rustling
tussling

US-lur
bustler
hustler
rustler
tussler

U-sness
(fuseness)
  diffuseness
  profuseness
loosensess
(struseness)
  abstruseness
(tuseness)
  obtuseness

U-som (OO-sum)
gruesome
twosome
(do some, etc.)

US-ted
busted
crusted
  encrusted
dusted
(gusted)
  disgusted
(justed)

adjusted
lusted
rusted
trusted
  distrusted
  entrusted
  mistrusted

UST-ful
lustful
trustful
  distrustful
  mistrustful

US-ti
crusty
dusty
fusty
gusty
lusty
musty
rusty
trusty

US-ting
busting
crusting
  encrusting
dusting
gusting
  disgusting
(justing)
  adjusting
lusting
rusting
thrusting
trusting
  distrusting
  entrusting

US-tingz
hustings
(dustings, etc.)

UST-li
(bustly)

robustly
(gustly)
augustly
justly
unjustly

UST-ness
(bustness)
robustness
(gustness)
augustness
justness
unjustness

US-trus
blustrous
lustrous

U-stur (OO-stur)
booster
rooster
(loosed 'er, etc.)

US-tur
bluster
Buster
  filibuster
  sodbuster (*i*)
  trustbuster (*i*)
cluster
Custer, George A.
duster
  feather duster
  knuckle-duster
fluster
juster
  adjuster
luster
  lackluster
muster
(trust 'er, etc.)

US-turd
bustard
custard
mustard

(blustered, etc.)

U-sur
(ducer)
  producer
  reducer
  seducer
  traducer
  transducer
(you, sir; etc.)

U-sur (OO-sur)
gooser
looser
sprucer

U-tal (OO-tl)
brutal
tootle

U-tant
mutant
nutant
(sputant)
  disputant

U-ted
*This group of words
rhymes correctly with
the one immediately
following it.*
(cuted)
  electrocuted
  executed
  persecuted
(futed)
  confuted
  refuted
(luted)
  convoluted
  diluted
    undiluted
  involuted
  polluted
    unpolluted
  saluted

muted
  commuted
  transmuted
(puted)
  computed
  disputed
    undisputed
  imputed
  reputed
suited
  unsuited
(tuted)
  constituted
  instituted
  prostituted
  substituted

U-ted (OO-ted)
booted
bruited
(crooted)
  recruited
fluted
fruited
looted
rooted
  uprooted
routed
  rerouted
tooted

U-test
cutest
  acutest
mutest
(nutest)
  minutest
(stutest)
  astutest

UTH-ful (OOTH-ful)
toothful
truthful
youthful

**UTH-ing
(OOTHE-ing)**
smoothing
soothing

UTH-less(OOTH-less)
ruthless
toothless
truthless

UTH-ur (OOTHE-ur)
smoother
soother

UTH-ur
other
brother
mother
(nother)
  another
smother

U-ti
*This group of words
rhymes correctly with
the one immediately
following it.*
beauty
cutie
  on the Q.T.
duty

U-ti (OO-ti)
booty
cootie
fruity
  tutti-frutti
snooty

UT-i
nutty
putty
smutty

U-tik
(ceutic)

pharmaceutic
(peutic)
  therapeutic

U-til
utile
futile
rutile

U-ting
*This group of words
rhymes correctly with
the one immediately
following it.*
(cuting)
  electrocuting
  executing
  persecuting
  prosecuting
(futing)
  confuting
  refuting
(luting)
  diluting
  polluting
  saluting
muting
  commuting
  transmuting
(puting)
  computing
  deputing
  imputing
suiting
(tuting)
  constituting
    reconstituting
  instituting
  prostituting
  substituting

U-ting (OO-ting)
booting
bruiting
(crooting)
  recruiting

looting
mooting
rooting
  uprooting
routing
  rerouting
tooting

UT-ing
butting
  abutting
  rebutting
cutting
glutting
gutting
jutting
putting (*golf*)
rutting
shutting
strutting

UT-ish
ruttish
sluttish

U-tist
flutist
lutist
(cutest, etc.)

UT-l
(buttal)
  rebuttal
cuttle
scuttle
shuttle
subtle

UT-less (OOT-less)
bootless
fruitless
rootless

UT-lur
butler
scuttler

subtler
sutler

U-ness
cuteness
  acuteness
(luteless)
  absoluteness
muteness
(nuteness)
  minuteness
(stuteness)
  stuteness

UT-un
button
glutton
mutton
(cuttin,' etc.)

U-tur
*This group of words
rhymes correctly with
the one immediately
following it.*
cuter
  persecutor
  prosecutor
(luter)
  polluter
muter
  commuter
neuter
  minuter
pewter
  computer
(stuter)
  astuter
suitor
tutor

U-tur (OO-tur)
(booter)
  freebooter
hooter
(kooter)

accouter
looter
rooter
scooter
shooter
  sharpshooter

UT-ur
utter
butter
clutter
cutter
flutter
gutter
mutter
putter (*golf*)
shutter
splutter
sputter
strutter
stutter

U-ture (YOO-chure)
future
suture

U-ur
*This group of words
rhymes correctly with
the one immediately
following it.*
ewer
fewer
newer
sewer
  pursuer
skewer
stewer
viewer
  interviewer
  reviewer

U-ur (OO-ur)
bluer
brewer
doer

evildoer
wrongdoer, etc.
truer
wooer

U-urd
skewered
steward

U-val (OO-val)
(moval)
  removal
(proval)
  approval
    disapproval

UV-en
oven
coven
sloven
(lovin', shovin', etc.)

U-vi (OO-vi)
groovy
movie

U-ving (OO-ving)
grooving
(hooving)
  behooving
moving
  removing
  unmoving
proving
  approving
    disapproving
  disproving
  improving
  reproving

UV-ing
loving
  unloving
shoving

U-vur (OO-vur)
(couver)
  Vancouver
Hoover
mover
  remover
(noover)
  maneuver
prover

UV-ur
cover
  discover
    rediscover
  recover
  uncover
  undercover
hover
lover
shover

U-zez
*This group of words
rhymes correctly with
the one immediately
following it.*
uses
  disuses
  misuses
bruises
(buses)
  abuses
    disabuses
(cuses)
  accuses
fuses
  confuses
  diffuses
  infuses
  refuses
  suffuses
  transfuses
muses
  amuses
  bemuses
(ruses)

peruses
(scuses)
  excuses

UZ-ez (OOZ-ez)
oozes
chooses
cruises
loses
snoozes

Uz-ez
buzzes
fuzzes

U-zhun
(clusion)
  conclusion
  inclusion
  occlusion
  seclusion
fusion
  confusion
  diffusion
  effusion
  infusion
  profusion
  transfusion
(lusion)
  allusion
  collusion
  delusion
  illusion
    disillusion
(trusion)
  intrusion
  protrusion
(tusion)
  contusion

U-zi (OOZ-i)
boozy
choosey
floozie
newsy
woozy

UZ-in
cousin
cozen
dozen
(buzzin' etc.)

U-zing
*This group of words
rhymes correctly with
the one immediately
following it.*
using
  misusing
(busing)
  abusing
(cusing)
  accusing
fusing
  confusing
  diffusing
  infusing
  refusing
  suffusing
musing
  amusing
(rusing)
  perusing
(scusing)
  excusing

UZ-ing
oozing
boozing
bruising
choosing
cruising
losing
snoozing

U-zl
(fusil)
  refusal

UZ-l (OOZ-l)
(boozle)
  bamboozle

(rusal)
  perusal

UZ-l
guzzle
muzzle
nuzzle
puzzle

UZ-ling
guzzling
nuzzling
puzzling

UZ-lur (OOZ-lur)
(boozler)
  bamboozler
foozler

UZ-lur
guzzler
muzzler
puzzler

U-zom (OOZ-um)
bosom
(lose 'em, etc.)

U-zur
*This group of words
rhymes correctly with
the one immediately
following it.*
user
(cuser)
  accuser
(fuser)
  refuser
muser
(refus 'er, etc.)

UZ-ur (OO-zur)
oozer
boozer
cruiser
loser
snoozer
(lose 'er, etc.)

Three Syllable Rhymes

A

A-a-bl
frayable
  defrayable
payable
  repayable
swayable
  unswayable

A-bi-a
labia
(rabia)
  Arabia

AB-i-est
blabbiest
crabbiest
flabbiest
gabbiest
grabbiest
scabbiest
shabbiest

AB-i-li
blabbily
crabbily
flabbily
gabbily
grabbily
shabbily

AB-i-ness
blabbiness
crabbiness
flabbiness
gabbiness
grabbiness
scabbiness
shabbiness

AB-i-ur
blabbier
crabbier
flabbier

gabbier
scabbier
shabbier

AB-u-lait
(fabulate)
  confabulate
tabulate

A-bur-ing
laboring
  belaboring
neighboring

ACH-a-ble
catchable
latchable
  unlatchable
matchable
  unmatchable
patchable
  repatchable
  unpatchable
scratchable
  unscratchable
(tachable)
  attachable
  detachable

A-da-bl
aidable
  unaidable
braidable
fadable
  unfadable
gradable
  degradable
    biodegradable
  ungradable
(suadable)
  dissuadable
  persuadable
tradable

retradable
untradable

A-ded-ness
fadedness
gradedness
  degradedness
jadedness
shadedness

A-di-an
'Cadian
  Acadian
(nadian)
  Canadian

A-di-ant
radiant
gradient

A-di-um
(ladium)
  palladium
(nadium)
  vanadium
radium
stadium

AF-i-kl
graphical
  biographical
    autobiographical
    cartographical, etc.
(raphical)
  seraphical
*(see **AF-ik,** page 148,
  add al)*

AF-ti-ness
craftiness
draftiness

AG-ed-li
jaggedly
raggedly

AG-ed-mess
jaggedness
raggedness

AG-i-ness
bagginess
cragginess
nagginess
ragginess
sagginess
scragginess
shagginess

A-gran-si
flagrancy
fragrancy
vagrancy

AG-ur-ing
staggering
swaggering

A-i-kl
(braical)
   algebraical
   Hebraical
laical
(saical)
   pharisaical

A-i-ti
gaity
laity

AJ-i-kl
magical
tragical

AJ-il-ness
agileness
fragileness

A-jus-ness
(rageousness)
   courageousness
   outrageousness
(pageousness)
   rampageousness
(tageousness)
   advantageousness

A-ka-bl
breakable
   unbreakable
fakable
   unfakable
makable
   unmakable
placable
   implacable
shakable
   unshakable
takable
   overtakable
   partakable
   retakable
      unretakable
   untakable

AK-a-bl
backable
crackable
   uncrackable
smackable
trackable
   untrackable

AK-et-ed
bracketed
jacketed
packeted
racketed

AK-et-ing
bracketing
jacketing
packeting
racketing

A-ki-ness
achiness
cakiness
flakiness
quakiness
shakiness
snakiness

AK-sa-bl
axable
(laxable)
   relaxable
taxable
   untaxable

AK-shun-l
factional
fractional

AK-shus-ness
factiousness
fractiousness

AK-ta-bl
actable
   unactable
(pactible)
   compactible
(stractible)
   abstractible
   distractible
   extractible
tractable
   attractable
   detractible
   intractable
   protractible
   retractible
   subtractible

AK-ti-kl
(dactical)
   didactical
practical
tactical

AK-to-ri
factory
  olfactory
  satisfactory
    dissatisfactory
(fractory)
  refractory
(lactery)
  phylactery

AK-tu-al
actual
factual
tactual
(tractual)
  contractual

AK-tur-ing
(facturing)
  manufacturing
fracturing

AK-u-lait
(jaculate)
  ejaculate
(maculate)
  immaculate

AK-u-lar
(nacular)
  vernacular
(racular)
  oracular
(tacular)
  spectacular

A-kur-i
bakery
fakery

AK-ur-i
quackery

A-la-ble
bailable
mailable

sailable
  assailable
    unassailable
  unsailable
saleable
(vailable)
  available
    unavailable

A-li-a
(dalia)
  Sedalia
(galia)
  regalia
(lalia)
  echolalia
(stralia)
  Australia
Thalia
(tralia)
  Centralia
(fail ya, jail ya, etc.)

AL-i-ing
dallying
rallying
sallying
tallying

AL-is-is
(nalysis)
  analysis
(ralysis)
  paralysis
(talysis)
  catalysis
(yalysis)
  dialysis

AL-i-ti
(bality)
  verbality
(cality)
  classicality
  comicality
  fantasticality

locality
magicality
practicality
  impracticality
rascality
technicality
theatricality
tragicality
verticality
vocality
whimsicality
(dality)
  modality
  sodality
(gality)
  conjugality
  egality
  frugality
  legality
  illegality
  prodigality
  regality
(mality)
  formality
    informality
  normality
    abnormality
(nality)
  banality
  carnality
  constitutionality
    unconstitutionality
  conventionality
    unconventionality
  criminality
  finality
  nationality
  originality
    unoriginality
  personality
    impersonality
  rationality
    irrationality
  tonality
    atonality
(pality)

municipality
principality
(rality)
  corporality
  generality
  liberality
    illiberality
  morality
    immorality
  plurality
(tality)
  brutality
  hospitality
    inhospitality
  mentality
    fundamentality
    instrumentality
    sentimentality
      unsentimentality
  mortality
    immortality
  vitality
(wality)
  actuality
  duality
  effectuality
    ineffectuality
  eventuality
  graduality
  individuality
  mutuality
  punctuality
  sensuality
  sexuality
  spirituality
(yality)
  artificiality
  bestiality
  confidentiality
  congeniality
  connubiality
  consequentiality
    inconsequentiality
  conviviality
  cordiality
  geniality

joviality
officiality
partiality
  impartiality
provinciality
reality
  unreality
sociality
speciality
substantiality
  transubstantiality
  unsubstantiality
superficiality
territoriality
  extraterritoriality
triviality
(zality)
  causality

AL-i-um
pallium
thallium
Valium

AL-ji-a
(ralgia)
  neuralgia
(stalgia)
  nostalgia

AL-o-est
callowest
fallowest
hallowest
sallowest
shallowest

AL-o-gi
(nalogy)
  analogy
(yalogy)
  genealogy
(see **OL-o-ji**, *page 348*)

AL-o-gist
(nalogist)
  analogist
(yalogist)
  genealogist
(*see* **OL-o-jist,** *page 349)*

AL-o-ness
callowness
fallowness
sallowness
shallowness

AL-o-ur
callower
sallower
shallower

AL-ur-i
calorie
gallery
salary

A-ma-bl
aimable
blameable
claimable
  proclaimable
  reclaimable
framable
namable
  unnameable
shamable
  unshamable
tamable
  untamable

AM-a-tiv
amative
(sclamative)
  exclamative

AM-a-tize
dramatize
(grammatize)

anagrammatize
diagrammatize
epigrammatize

AM-bu-lait
ambulate
  perambulate
  somnambulate

AM-bu-lism
ambulism
(nambulism)
  somnambulism
(tambulism)
  noctambulism

AM-bu-list
(nambulist)
  somnambulist
(rambulist)
  perambulist
(tambulist)
  noctambulatist

AM-et-ur
amateur
(rameter)
  parameter
(tameter)
  pentameter
  voltameter
(yameter)
  diameter
(zameter)
  hexameter

AM-in-nait
laminate
(taminate)
  contaminate

AM-i-ti
amity
(lamity)
  calamity

A-mless-ness
aimlessness
blamelessness
namelessness
shamelessness

AM-or-ing
clamoring
hammering
stammering
yammering

AM-or-ur
clamorer
hammerer
stammerer

AM-or-us
amorous
clamorous
glamorous
(enamor us, hammer
  us, etc.)

AM-pur-ing
hampering
pampering
scampering
tampering

AM-pur-ur
hamperer
pamperer
scamperer
tamperer

A-na-bl
drainable
gainable
  ungainable
(splainable)
  explainable
    inexplainable
stainable
  sustainable
    unsustainable

strainable
  restrainable
    irrestrainable
(tainable)
  ascertainable
    inascertainable
  attainable
    unattainable
  containable
    uncontainable
  detainable
  maintainable
    unmaintainable
  obtainable
    unobtainable
trainable
  retrainable
  untrainable

AN-da-bl
mandible
  commandable
  demandable
  reprimandable
(spandable)
  expandable
standable
  understandable

AN-di-ness
handiness
randiness
sandiness

AN-du-ring
(landering)
  philandering
pandering
slandering
(yandering)
  meandering

AN-dur-ur
ganderer
(landerer)
  philanderer

panderer
slanderer
(yanderer)
  meanderer

AN-dur-ur
wanderer
(*see* **ON-dur-ur,** *page 350)*

A-ne-us
(laneous)
  miscellaneous
(raneous)
  subterraneous
  temporaneous
    contemporaneous
    extemporaneous
(straneous)
  extraneous
(taneous)
  cutaneous
    subcutaneous
  instantaneous
  simultaneous
  spontaneous

A-nful-i
banefully
(dainfully)
  disdainfully
painfully

ANG-kur-ing
anchoring
hankering

ANG-kur-us
cankerous
rancorous
(tankerous)
  cantankerous

A-ni-a
(bania)
  Albania

(lania)
  miscellanea
mania
  Anglomania
  bibliomania
  decalcomania
  dipsomania
  discomania
  egomania
  erotomania
  Francomania
  kleptomania
  megalomania
  nymphomania
  pyromania, etc.
  Rumania
  Tasmania
(tania)
  Aquitania
  Lusitania
  Mauretania
(vania)
  Pennsylvania
  Transylvania
(wania)
  Lithuania

A-ni-ak
maniac
  bibliomaniac, etc.

A-ni-an
(banian)
  Albanian
(kranian)
  Ukranian
(manian)
  Rumanian
  Tasmanian
(ranian)
  Iranian
  Mediterranean
  subterranean
  Ukranian
(tanian)
  Mauretanian

(wanian)
  Lithuanian
(vanian)
  Pennsylvanian
  Transylvanian

AN-i-bl
cannibal
Hannibal
plannable
  unplannable

AN-i-kl
(kanical)
  mechanical
manacle
(rannical)
  tyrannical
(tanical)
  botanical

AN-i-mus
animus
(lanimus)
  pusillanimous
(nanimus)
  magnanimus
  unanimous

AN-ish-ing
banishing
vanishing

AN-is-tur
banister
canister

AN-i-ti
(banity)
  urbanity
(fanity)
  profanity
(manity)
  humanity
    inhumanity
(nanity)

inanity
sanity
  insanity
vanity
(yanity)
  Christianity

AN-ji-bl
frangible
  infrangible
tangible
  intangible

AN-shi-ait
(stantiate)
  circumstantiate
  substantiate
    transubstantiate

AN-ti-side
(fanticide)
  infanticide

AN-tur-ing
bantering
cantering

AN-u-al
annual
manual

AN-u-lait
annulate
granulate

AN-ur-i
cannery
granary
tannery

A-pa-bl
capable
  incapable
(scapable)
    escapable
      inescapable

AP-i-est
flappiest
happiest
sappiest
scrappiest
snappiest

AP-id-li
rapidly
vapidly

AP-i-li
flappily
happily
Napoli
sappily
scrappily
snappily

AP-i-ness
happiness
sappiness
scrappiness
snappiness

AP-i-ur
happier
sappier
scrappier
snappier

A-pur-i
drapery
papery

A-pur-ing
capering
papering
tapering

AR-a-bl (AIR-a-bl)
bearable
  unbearable
(clairable)
  declarable
    undeclarable

pairable
  repairable
tearable
  untearable
wearable
  unwearable

AR-a-bl
arable
  inarable
parable

AR-a-tiv
(clarative)
  declarative
narrative
(parative)
  comparative
  preparative

AR-bur-ing
barbering
harboring

AR-di-ness
hardiness
  foolhardiness
tardiness

AR-ful-i (AIR-ful-i)
carefully
prayerfully

AR-i-a (AIR-i-a)
area
(garia)
  Bulgaria
(laria)
  malaria
(staria)
  wisteria

AR-i-al (AIR-i-al)
aerial
burial

(larial)
  malarial
(warial)
  actuarial

AR-i-an
Arian
(barian)
  barbarian
(brarian)
  librarian
Darien
(garian)
  Bulgarian
  Hungarian
  vulgarian
(grarian)
  agrarian
Marian
  grammarian
(narian)
  disciplinarian
  doctrinarian
  nonegenarian
  octagenarian
  septuagenarian
  sexagenarian
  veterinarian
(parian)
  riparian
(quarian)
  antiquarian
  Aquarian
(tarian)
  egalitarian
  equalitarian
  establishmentarian
   disestablishment-
    arian
    antidisestablish-
     mentarian
  humanitarian
  libertarian
  proletarian
  Sagittarian
  sectarian

  unitarian
  utilitarian
  vegetarian
(varian)
  Bavarian
  ovarian
(zarian)
  Caesarean
(ferryin', buryin')

AR-i-at
lariat
(sariat)
  commissariat
(tariat)
  proletariat
  secretariat

AR-i-fi
clarify
scarify

AR-i-ing
carrying
harrying
marrying
tarrying

AR-i-ness (AIR-i-ness)
airiness
hairiness
(tariness)
  solitariness
(trariness)
  arbitrariness
  contrariness
wariness

AR-ing-li (AIR-ing-li)
erringly
  unerringly
blaringly
caringly

  uncaringly
daringly
glaringly
sparingly
  unsparingly

AR-i-ti
(barity)
  barbarity
charity
clarity
(darity)
  solidarity
(larity)
  angularity
   triangularity
  circularity
  hilarity
  insularity
  jocularity
  muscularity
  particularity
  polarity
  popularity
   unpopularity
  regularity
   irregularity
  secularity
  similarity
   dissimilarity
  singularity
parity
  imparity
(sparity)
  disparity
(yarity)
  familiarity
  peculiarity

AR-i-um
barium
(quarium)
  aquarium
(rarium)
  honorarium

(tarium)
  sanitarium

AR-i-ur
barrier
carrier
tarrier

AR-i-us (AIR-i-us)
(carious)
  precarious
  vicarious
(farious)
  multifarious
  nefarious
(garious)
  gregarious
(larious)
  hilarious
(quarious)
  Aquarius
(tarious)
  Sagittarius
various
(marry us, etc.,
or bury us, etc.,
depending on
pronunciation)

AR-ki-kl
(narchical)
  Monarchical
(rarchical)
  hierarchical

AR-ming-li
charmingly
(larmingly)
  alarmingly

AR-nish-ing
garnishing
tarnishing
varnishing

AR-o-ing
harrowing

narrowing

AR-shal-izm
martialism
partialism
  impartialism

AR-ti-kl
article
particle
  atomic particle

AR-ti-zan
artisan
partisan

ART-less-li
artlessly
heartlessly

AR-tur-ing
bartering
chartering
martyring

A-shi-ait
(gratiate)
  ingratiate
(maciate)
  emaciate
satiate
(spatiate)
  expatiate

ASH-i-ness
ashiness
flashiness
splashiness
trashiness

A-shun-al
(cational)
  educational
(gational)
  congregational
(national)

nominational
  denominational
(rational)
  inspirational
(sational)
  sensational
  unsensational
(yational)
  creational
  recreational

ASH-un-al
national
  international
passional
rational
irrational

A-shun-less
(brationless)
  celebrationless
  vibrationless
(cationless)
  vocationless
(dationless)
  foundationless
(lationless)
  relationless
(mationless)
  formationless
nationless
(rationless)
  inspirationless
(sationless)
  conversationless
stationless

A-shun-ur
(bationer)
  probationer
(cationer)
  vacationer
stationer

A-shus-ness
(caciousness)

efficaciousness
(daciousness)
  audaciousness
  mendaciousness
graciousness
  ungraciousness
(laciousness)
  fallaciousness
  salaciousness
(naciousness)
  tenaciousness
(paciousness)
  capaciousness
  rapaciousness
(quaciousness)
  loquaciousness
  spaciousness

A-si-bl
chaseable
braceable
  embraceable
faceable
  unfaceable
  effaceable
    ineffaceable
placeable
  replaceable
    irreplaceable
(rasible)
  erasible
  inerasible
traceable
  retraceable
    irretraceable
(vasible)
  evasible

AS-i-bl
passable
  surpassable
    insurpassable
passible
  impassible
(rascible)
  irascible

AS-i-nait
fascinate
(racinate)
  deracinate
(sassinate)
  assassinate

A-si-ness
laciness
raciness
spaciness

AS-i-ness
brassiness
classiness
gassiness
glassiness
grassiness
sassiness

AS-i-tee
(dacity)
  audacity
  mendacity
(gacity)
  sagacity
(lacity)
  salacity
(nacity)
  pertinacity
  pugnacity
  tenacity
(pacity)
  capacity
    incapacity
  opacity
  rapacity
(quacity)
  loquacity
(racity)
  veracity
  voracity
(spicacity)
  perspicacity
(vacity)
  vivacity

AS-iv-li
massively
passively
  impassively

A-siv-ness
suasiveness
  dissuasiveness
  persuasiveness
(vasiveness)
  evasiveness
  pervasiveness

AS-iv-ness
massiveness
passiveness
  impassiveness

A-stful-i (AIST-ful-i)
tastefully
  distastefully
wastefully

AS-ti-kul
(tastical)
  fantastical
(yastical)
  ecclesiastical

A-stil-i
hastily
pastily
tastily

AS-ti-sizm
(lasticism)
  elasticism
  scholasticism
(nasticism)
  monasticism
(tasticism)
  fantasticism

AS-tur-ing
mastering
  remastering

pastoring
plastering
  replastering

AS-ur-ait
lacerate
macerate
  emacerate

A-ta-bl
baitable
  debatable
    undebatable
(flatable)
  inflatable
    reinflatable
(slatable)
  translatable
    untranslatable
(see **AT (AIT),** *page 70,*
  and add able*)*

A-tful-i (AIT-ful-i)
fatefully
gratefully
hatefully

AT-ful-ness
  (AIT-ful-ness)
fatefulness
gratefulness
hatefulness

ATH-ur-ing
blathering
gathering
lathering
slathering

ATH-ur-ur
blatherer
gatherer
latherer
slatherer

AT-i-bl
(batable)
  combatable
    uncombatable
(patible)
  compatible
    incompatible

AT-i-fi
gratify
ratify
stratify
(yatify)
  beatify

AT-i-fide
gratified
ratified
stratified
  unstratified
(yatified)
  beatified

AT-i-ka
Attica
(patica)
  hepatica
(yatica)
  sciatica

AT-i-kul
(batical)
  sabbatical
(matical)
  enigmatical
  grammatical
    epigrammatical
    ungrammatical
  mathematical
(ratical)
  piratical

AT-i-ness
cattiness
chattiness
fattiness

nattiness
tattiness

AT-i-sizm
(maticism)
  grammaticism
(naticism)
  fanaticism

AT-i-tude
attitude
gratitude
  ingratitude
latitude
platitude
(yatitude)
  beatitude

AT-om-ist
atomist
(natomist)
  anatomist

AT-ri-side
fratricide
matricide
patricide

AT-ur-ait (ACH-ur-ait)
maturate
saturate

AT-ural
lateral
  bilateral
  collateral
  equilateral
  quadrilateral
  trilateral
  unilateral
(all identities are
  useless as rhyme,
  excepting bilateral
  and trilateral, *which*
  function as a four-
  rhyme)

AT-ur-i
battery
flattery

AT-ur-ing
battering
chattering
clattering
flattering
　unflattering
mattering
nattering (*British
　and Canadian*)
pattering
scattering
shattering
smattering
spattering
　bespattering
splattering
tattering

AT-ur-ur
batterer
chatterer
flatterer
scatterer
shatterer
spatterer
splatterer

AV-el-ing
caviling
gaveling
graveling
raveling
　unraveling

traveling

AV-el-ur
caviler
raveler
traveler

A-vi-an
avian
(navian)
　Scandinavian
(ravian)
　Moravian
Shavian

AV-ij-ing
ravaging
savaging

AV-ish-ing
lavishing
ravishing
　enravishing

AV-ish-ment
lavishment
ravishment
　enravishment

A-vish-ness
knavishness
slavishness

AV-i-ti
cavity
　concavity
gravity
(pravity)

depravity

A-vur-i
bravery
savory
　unsavory
slavery

A-vur-ing
favoring
flavoring
quavering
savoring
wavering
　unwavering

A-vur-us
(daverous)
　cadaverous
flavorous
savorous
(favor us, etc.)

A-zi-a
(fasia)
　aphasia
(nasia)
　athanasia
　euthanasia
(tasia)
　fantasia

A-zi-ness
craziness
haziness
laziness

E

E-a-bl
(greeable)
  agreeable
    disagreeable
seeable
  foreseeable
    unforeseeable

E-al-ist
(dealist)
  idealist
realist
  surrealist

E-a-lize
(dealize)
  idealize
realize

E-al-izm
(dealism)
  idealism
realism
  surrealism

E-al-ti
fealty
realty

E-an-dur
Leander (i)
  oleander (i)
meander (i)

E-cha-bl
bleachable
breachable
  unbreachable
(peachable)
  impeachable
    unimpeachable
reachable

unreachable
teachable
  unteachable

ECH-i-ness
catchiness
sketchiness
stretchiness

ECH-u-ri
lechery
treachery

ECH-u-rus
lecherous
treacherous

E-da-bl
feedable
heedable
leadable
  unleadable
pleadable
readable
  unreadable
seedable
  concedeable
  exceedable

E-dful-ness
  (EED-ful-ness)
heedfulness
needfulness

E-di-al
medial
  remedial

E-di-an
(jedian)
  tragedian
median
  comedian

ED-i-bl
edible
  inedible
credible
  incredible
dreadable
threadable
  unthreadable

E-di-ense
(bedience)
  obedience
    disobedience
(gredients)
  ingredients
(spedience)
  expedience

E-di-ent
(bedient)
  obedient
    disobedient
(gredient)
  ingredient
(spedient)
  expedient
    inexpedient

E-di-est
beadiest
greediest
neediest
seediest
speediest

ED-iest
headiest
readiest
steadiest

ED-i-kait
dedicate

rededicate
medicate
  overmedicate
predicate

E-di-li
greedily
needily
seedily
speedily

ED-i-li
headily
readily
steadily
  unsteadily

ED-i-ment
pediment
  impediment
sediment

E-di-ness
greediness
neediness
seediness
speediness

ED-i-ness
headiness
readiness
  unreadiness
steadiness
  unsteadiness
threadiness

ED-i-ted
edited
  reedited
  unedited
credited
  accredited
    unaccredited
  discredited

ED-i-ting
editing
  reediting
crediting
  accrediting
  discrediting

ED-i-tor
editor
creditor
predator

E-di-um
medium
tedium

E-di-ur
beadier
greedier
needier
reedier
seedier
speedier

ED-i-ur
headier
readier
steadier
  unsteadier
threadier
(steady 'er, etc.)

E-dless-li (EED-less-li)
heedlessly
needlessly

**E-dless-ness
(EED-less-ness)**
heedlessness
needlessness
seedlessness

ED-u-lus
credulous
  incredulous
sedulous

E-dur-ship
leadership
readership

E-fi-ness
beefiness
leafiness

EF-i-sense
(neficence)
  beneficence
(leficence)
  maleficence

EF-ur-ense
deference
preference
reference

E-gal-izm
legalism
regalism

EG-nan-si
pregnancy
regnancy
  interregnancy

E-gur-li
eagerly
  overeagerly
meagerly

E-gur-ness
eagerness
  overeagerness
meagerness

E-i-ti
deity
(neity)
  contemporaneity
  heterogeneity
  homogeneity
  simultaneity
  spontaneity

E-ji-an
collegian
Norwegian
(see **E-jun,** *page 200)*

EJ-i-bl
dredgeable
legible
    allegeable
    illegible

E-ki-li
cheekily
creakily
leakily
sneakily
squeakily

E-ki-ness
cheekiness
creakiness
leakiness
sneakiness
squeakiness

EK-on-ing
beckoning
reckoning
    dead reckoning

EK-shun-al
(rectional)
    correctional
    insurrectional
sectional

EK-shun-ism
(fectionism)
    perfectionism
(rectionism)
    insurrectionism
(tectionism)
    protectionism

EK-shun-ist
(fectionist)

perfectionist
(rectionist)
    insurrectionist
(tectionist)
    protectionist

EK-si-ti
(plexity)
    complexity
    perplexity
vexity
    convexity

EK-ted-ness
(fectedness)
    affectedness
(jectedness)
    abjectedness
    dejectedness
(spectedness)
    expectedness
        respectedness
        unexpectedness

Ek-ti-bl
(fectible)
    perfectible
        imperfectible
(jectable)
    rejectable
(lectible)
    collectible
        uncollectible
    delectable
(rectible)
    correctible
        uncorrectible
(spectable)
    expectable
        unexpectable
    respectable
        unrespectable
    suspectable
        unsuspectable
(tectible)
    detectible

undetectible

EK-ti-fi
(jectify)
    objectify
rectify

EK-ti-kal
(lectical)
    dialectical
(plectical)
    apoplectical

EK-tiv-li
(fectively)
    defectively
    effectively
        ineffectively
(flectively)
    reflectively
(jectively)
    objectively
    subjectively
(lectively)
    collectively
    electively
    selectively
(nectively)
    connectively
(rectively)
    correctively
(spectively)
    circumspectively
    introspectively
    prospectively
    respectively
        irrespectively
    retrospectively
(tectively)
    protectively

EK-tiv-ness
(fectiveness)
    effectiveness, etc.
(see **EK-tiv-li,** *above)*

EK-to-rait
(lectorate)
  electorate
rectorate
  directorate
(spectorate)
  expectorate
(tectorate)
  protectorate

EK-to-ral
(lectoral)
  electoral
pectoral

EK-to-ri
(fectory)
  refectory
rectory
  directory

EK-tu-al
(fectual)
  effectual
    ineffectual
(lectual)
  intellectual

EK-tur-al
(jectural)
  conjectural
(tectural)
  architectural

EK-u-lait
peculate
speculate

EK-u-lar
(lecular)
  molecular
    orthomolecular
    submolecular
secular

EK-u-tive
(secutive)
  consecutive
    unconsecutive
(zecutive)
  executive

E-la-bl
feelable
  unfeelable
healable
  unhealable
(jealable)
  congealable
pealable
  appealable
    unappealable
  repealable
sealable
  concealable
    unconcealable
  unsealable
(vealable)
  revealable

EL-e-gait
delegate
relegate

EL-fish-ness
elfishness
selfishness

EL-i-bl
(delible)
  indelible
(pellable)
  compellable
spellable
  expellable
  unspellable
tellable
  untellable

EL-ish-ing
(bellishing)

embellishing
relishing

EL-o-est
mellowest
yellowest

EL-thi-est
healthiest
stealthiest
wealthiest

EL-thi-li
healthily
stealthily
wealthily

EL-thi-ur
healthier
stealthier
wealthier

EL-tur-ing
sheltering
sweltering
weltering

EL-tur-ur
shelterer
swelterer
welterer

EL-ur-i
celery

EL-us-li
jealously
zealously

EM-bur-ing
embering
membering
  dismembering
  remembering

E-mi-ness
creaminess
dreaminess
seaminess
steaminess

E-mi-ur
creamier
dreamier
premier
seamier
steamier

Em-ni-ti
(demnity)
  indemnity
(lemnity)
  solemnity

EM-ur-i
emery
memory

EN-a-tor
genitor
  primogenitor
  progenitor
senator

END-a-bl
endable
  unendable
bendable
  unbendable
blendable
(fendable)
  defendable
lendable
mendable
  amendable
  commendable
    recommendable
    uncommendable
  unmendable
sendable
  ascendible

descendible
(stendible)
  extendible

ED-den-si
(pendency)
  dependency
  impendency
(sendancy)
  ascendancy
  transcendancy
(splendency)
  resplendency
tendency
  intendency

END-less-li
endlessly
friendlessly

END-less-ness
endlessness
friendlessness

EN-dur-est
slenderest
tenderest

EN-dur-ing
gendering
  engendering
rendering
  surrendering
tendering

EN-dur-li
slenderly
tenderly

EN-dur-ness
slenderness
tenderness

EN-dur-ur
renderer
slenderer

tenderer

EN-dur-us
splendorous
(render us, etc.)

EN-dus-li
(mendously)
  tremendously
(pendously)
  stupendously
(rendously)
  horrendously

E-ni-a
(denia)
  gardenia
(menia)
  Armenia
(thenia)
  neurasthenia
  Parthenia
(zenia)
  Xenia

E-ni-al
genial
  congenial
    uncongenial
menial
venial

EN-i-al
(lenial)
  millennial
(renial)
  perennial
(tenial)
  centennial
    bicentennial
    tricentennial
(yenial)
  biennial

E-ni-ense
lenience

(venience)
  convenience
    inconvenience

E-ni-ent
lenient
(venient)
  convenient
    inconvenient

EN-i-son
benison
venison

EN-i-ti
lenity
(menity)
  amenity
(renity)
  serenity
(senity)
  obscenity

EN-i-tive
genitive
lenitive
splenitive

EN-i-tude
lenitude
splenitude
(renitude)
  serenitude

E-ni-um
(lenium)
  selenium
(scenium)
  proscenium

E-ni-us
genius
  heterogeneous
  homogeneous
  ingenious

EN-sa-tiv
(pensative)
  compensative
sensitive
  insensitive

EN-shi-ait
(sensiate)
  licenciate
(tentiate)
  potentiate

EN-shun-al
(stentional)
  extensional
(tentional)
  intentional
    unintentional
(ventional)
  conventional
  preventional

EN-shus-ness
(sentiousness)
  licentiousness
(tentiousness)
  contentiousness
  pretentiousness
(yentiousness)
  conscientiousness

EN-sl-bl
(densable)
  condensable
fencible
  defensible
    indefensible
(hensible)
  prehensible
    comprehensible
      incomprehensible
    reprehensible
sensible
  insensible
(spensable)
  dispensable

indispensable
(stensible)
  extensible
  ostensible

EN-si-kl
(rensical)
  forensical
(sensical)
  nonsensical

EN-si-ti
density
(mensity)
  immensity
(pensity)
  propensity
(tensity)
  intensity

EN-siv-ness
(fensiveness)
  offensiveness
    inoffensiveness
(hensiveness)
  comprehensiveness
pensiveness
(stensiveness)
  extensiveness

ENS-less-li
(fenselessly)
  defenselessly
senselessly

ENS-less-ness
(fenselessness)
  defenselessness
senselessness

EN-su-ri
(spensary)
  dispensary
sensory
  extrasensory

EN-ta-bl
dentable
  undentable
(mentable)
  documentable
  fermentable
  lamentable (*i*)
  tormentable
(sentable)
  accentable
ventable
  circumventable
  inventible
  preventable
    unpreventable
(zentable)
  presentable
    representable
    unpresentable
  resentable

EN-ta-kl
pentacle
tentacle

EN-ta-li
dentally
  accidentally
  incidentally
  transcendentally
mentally
  experimentally
  instrumentally
  sentimentally
    unsentimentally

EN-ta-list
(dentalist)
  transcendentalist
mentalist
  experimentalist
  fundamentalist
  instrumentalist
  sentimentalist
(yentalist)
  Orientalist

EN-tal-izm
(dentalism)
  transcendentalism
mentalism
  elementalism
  sentimentalism
(yentalism)
  Orientalism

EN-tal-ness
gentleness
(mentalness)
  sentimentalness

EN-ta-ri
dentary
  sedentary
(mentary)
  alimentary
  complementary
  complimentary
    uncomplimentary
  elementary
  parliamentary
  rudimentary
  sedimentary

EN-ta-tiv
(mentative)
  argumentative
tentative
(zentative)
  representative
    unrepresentative

EN-ti-kl
denticle
  identical
pentacle
tentacle
(thentical)
  authentical

EN-ti-ti (EN-ti-tee)
entity
  nonentity

(dentity)
  identity

EN-tive-ness
(tentiveness)
  attentiveness
    inattentiveness
  retentiveness
(ventiveness)
  inventiveness

EN-tu-ait (EN-chu-ait)
(sentuate)
  accentuate
(ventuate)
  eventuate

EN-tus-li
(mentously)
  momentously
(tentously)
  portentously

EN-tus-ness
(mentousness)
  momentousness
(tentousness)
  portentousness

EN-ur-ait
generate
  degenerate
  regenerate
venerate

E-nur-i
beanery
deanery
greenery
scenery
(sheenery)
  machinery

EN-u-us
(jenuous)
  ingenuous

336

disingenuous
strenuous
tenuous

E-nyen-si
leniency
(veniency)
  conveniency
    inconveniency

E-o-la
(riola)
  variola
viola
  movieola

E-pi-li
creepily
sleepily
weepily

E-pi-ness
creepiness
sleepiness
weepiness

EP-ta-bl
(septable)
  acceptable
    unacceptable
  perceptible
    imperceptible
  susceptible
    insusceptible

EP-ti-kl
(septacle)
  receptacle
skeptical

EP-ur-us
leperous
(streperous)
  obstreperous

ER-fu-li (EER-fu-li)
cheerfully
fearfully
tearfully

E-rful-ness
  (EER-ful-ness)
cheerfulness
fearfulness
tearfulness

E-ri-al
(derial)
  sidereal
(jerial)
  managerial
(nereal)
  funereal
(perial)
  imperial
serial
cereal
(sterial)
  ministerial
(terial)
  material
    immaterial
(thereal)
  ethereal

E-ri-est
eeriest
beeriest
bleariest
cheeriest
dreariest
weariest

ER-i-ing (AIR-i-ing)
berrying
burying
ferrying

ER-i-kl (AIR-i-kl)
clerical
(merical)

chimerical
numerical
spherical
  atmospherical
  stratospherical
  tropospherical, etc.
(sterical)
  hysterical
(terical)
  esoterical

E-ri-li
eerily
beerily
cheerily
drearily
wearily

ER-i-li (AIR-i-li)
airily
merrily
verily

E-ri-ness
eeriness
beeriness
bleariness
cheeriness
dreariness
weariness

ER-i-on (AIR-i-un)
(perion)
  Hyperion
(terion)
  criterion
(buryin', etc.)

E-ri-or
(ferior)
  inferior
(perior)
  superior
(sterior)
  exterior
  posterior

(terior)
  anterior
  interior
  ulterior
(see E-ri-ur, page 331)

ER-ish-ing
  (AIR-ish-ing)
cherishing
perishing

ER-i-ted (AIR-i-ted)
ferreted
(herited)
  inherited
    disinherited
merited
  unmerited

ER-i-ti (AIR-i-ti)
(lerity)
  celerity
(merity)
  temerity
(serity)
  sincerity
    insincerity
(sperity)
  asperity
  prosperity
(sterity)
  austerity
    dexterity
      ambidexterity
  posterity
verity
  severity

ER-it-ing (AIR-i-ting)
ferreting
(heriting)
  inheriting
    disinheriting
meriting
  unmeriting

E-ri-ur
eerier
beerier
blearier
cheerier
drearier
wearier
(see E-ri-or, page 330)

ER-i-ur (AIR-i-ur)
airier
burier
merrier
terrier
warier

E-ri-us
cereous
(lerious)
  delirious
(perious)
  imperious
serious
Sirius
(sterious)
  mysterious
(weary us, etc.)

E-rless-ness
cheerlessness
fearlessness

E-ryal-ist (EER-yal-ist)
(perialist)
  imperialist
(terialist)
  materialist

E-ryal-izm
  (EER-yal-izm)
(perialism)
  imperialism
    anti-imperialsim
(terialism)
  materialism

ES-a-ri
(fessory)
  confessory
pessary
(sessory)
  accessory
  intercessory

ES-en-si
(bescency)
  pubescency
(descency)
  incandescency
(lescency)
  convalescency
(screscency)
  excrescency
(vescency)
  effervescency

E-sent-li
decently
  indecently
recently

ESH-un-al
(fessional)
  confessional
(gressional)
  congressional
  digressional
  regressional
(scretional)
  discretional
sessional
  accessional
  processional
  recessional
(spressional)
  expressional
(zessional)
  possessional

ESH-un-ist
(gressionist)
  progressionist

(pressionist)
impressionist
neoimpressionist
postimpressionist
sessionist
secessionist
successionist
(spressionist)
expressionist

E-shus-ness
(setiousness)
facetiousness
speciousness

ES-i-bl
(dressible)
redressible
(gressible)
transgressible
(pressible)
compressible
incompressible
impressible
repressible
irrepressible
suppressible
unsuppressible
(sessible)
accessible
inaccessible
(spressible)
expressible
inexpressible

ES-i-mal
decimal
(tesimal)
centesimal
infinitesimal

ES-iv-ness
(gressiveness)
aggressiveness
progressiveness
(pressiveness)

depressiveness
impressiveness
oppressiveness
(sessiveness)
excessiveness
(spressiveness)
expressiveness
inexpressiveness

ES-ti-al
bestial
(lestial)
celestial

ES-ti-bl
comestible
(jestible)
digestible
indigestible
testable
contestable
incontestable
detestable
(vestible)
divestible

ES-tri-an
(destrian)
pedestrian
(questrian)
equestrian

ES-tur-ing
festering
pestering
westering

ES-tu-us
(pestuous)
tempestuous
(sestuous)
incestuous

E-ta-bl
eatable
uneatable

beatable
unbeatable
cheatable
(featable)
defeatable
undefeatable
treatable
untreatable

ET-a-bl
getable
forgettable
unforgettable
(gretable)
regrettable

ET-fu-li
fretfully
(getfully)
forgetfully
(gretfully)
regretfully

ET-ful-ness
fretfulness
(getfulness)
forgetfulness
(gretfulness)
regretfulness

ETH-less-li
breathlessly
deathlessly

ETH-less-ness
breathlessness
deathlessness

ETH-u-ri
feathery
heathery
leathery

ETH-u-ring
feathering
tethering

weathering

ET-i-kl
(betical)
  alphabetical
(metical)
  arithmetical
  hermetical
(retical)
  heretical
  theoretical
(tetical)
  dietetical
(thetical)
  antipathetical
  antithetical
(wetical)
  poetical

ET-i-ness
pettiness
sweatiness

ET-ish-li
pettishly
(kettishly)
  coquettishly

ET-ish-ness
pettishness
(kettishness)
  coquettishness

ET-i-sizm
(leticism)
  athleticism
(seticism)
  asceticism
(theticism)
  estheticism

ET-ri-kl
metrical
  barometrical
  diametrical
  geometrical

symmetrical
  asymmetrical
(stetrical)
  obstetrical

ET-ur-ing
bettering
fettering
lettering

E-va-bl
(ceivable)
  conceivable
    inconceivable
  deceivable
    undeceivable
  perceivable
  receivable
(chievable)
  achievable
(leavable)
  believable
    unbelievable

EV-el-ing
bevelling
deviling
  bedeviling
leveling
reveling
(sheveling)
  disheveling

EV-el-ur
leveler
reveler

E-vi-ait
(breviate)
  abbreviate
deviate
(leviate)
  alleviate

EV-i-li
heavily
levelly
reveille

EV-il-ri
devilry
revelry

E-vish-li
peevishly
thievishly

E-vish-ness
peevishness
thievishness

EV-i-ti
brevity
(jevity)
  longevity
levity

E-vi-us
devious
previous

EV-o-lense
(levolence)
  malevolence
(nevolence)
  benevolence

EV-o-lent
(levolent)
  malevolent
(nevolent)
  benevolent

EV-ur-mor
evermore
nevermore

EV-ur-ur
cleverer
(deavorer)

endeavorer
severer

E-za-bl
feasible
  infeasible
freezable
  refreezable
  unfreezable
(peasable)
  appeasable
    unappeasable
seizable
squeezable

EZ-an-tri
peasantry
pleasantry

E-zi-a
(desia)
  Rhodesia
(nesia)
  amnesia
  magnesia
(sees ya, etc.)

E-zi-an
(nesian)
  Polynesian
(tesian)
  artesian
  Cartesian

EZ-i-dent
president
resident

E-zi-li
easily
  uneasily
breezily
queasily
sleazily
weaselly
wheezily

E-zi-ness
easiness
  uneasiness
breeziness
cheesiness
queasiness
sleaziness

wheeziness

E-zing-li
freezingly
(peasingly)
  appeasingly
pleasingly
teasingly
wheezingly

E-zun-ing
reasoning
  unreasoning
seasoning
  overseasoning
  underseasoning

EZ-yur-ing
measuring
pleasuring
treasuring

EZ-yur-ur
measurer
pleasurer
treasurer

I

I-a-bl
buyable
dyable
  undyable
(fiable)
  classifiable
    unclassifiable
  electrifiable
  justifiable
  modifiable
  pacifiable
  satisfiable

  unsatisfiable
  verifiable
    unverifiable
flyable
friable
fryable
liable
  reliable
(niable)
  deniable
    undeniable
pliable

appliable
viable

I-a-bli
(fiably)
  justifiably
(liably)
  (reliably, etc.)
(see **I-a-bl,** above)

I-a-kl
(diacal)

zodiacal
(niacal)
  maniacal
    egomaniacal
    erotomaniacal, etc.
(see "mania", *page 316,*
  add cal*)*

I-ant-li
(fiantly)
  defiantly
(liantly)
  reliantly
pliantly
  compliantly

I-ba-bl
(bibable)
  imbibable
bribable
  unbribable
scribable
  describable
    indescribable
  inscribable
  prescribable
  proscribable
  subscribable
  transcribable
    untranscribable

IB-i-a
fibia
  amphibia
Libya
tibia

ICH-i-ness
itchiness
bitchiness
twitchiness
witchiness

ICH-u-ri
stitchery
witchery

ID-en-ness
(biddenness)
  forbiddenness
hiddenness

ID-i-an
Gideon
Lydian
(ridian)
  meridian
(sidian)
  obsidian
(tidian)
  quotidian

ID-i-fi
(cidify)
  acidify
(lidify)
  solidify

ID-i-kl
(midical)
  pyramidical
(ridical)
  juridical
  veridical
(widical)
  druidical

ID-i-ti
(bidity)
  morbidity
(cidity)
  acidity
  lucidity
  viscidity
(cridity)
  acridity
(jidity)
  frigidity
  rigidity
  turgidity
(lidity)
  gelidity
  solidity

insolidity
stolidity
validity
  invalidity
(midity)
  humidity
  timidity
  tumidity
(pidity)
  cupidity
quiddity
  liquidity
(vidity)
  avidity
  lividity

ID-i-um
idiom
(ridium)
  iridium

ID-i-us
(fidious)
  perfidious
hideous
(sidious)
  insidious
(stidious)
  fastidious
    unfastidious
(vidious)
  invidious

ID-u-al
(vidual)
  individual
(zidual)
  residual

I-et-al
dietal
(rietal)
  varietal

I-et-ed
dieted

quieted
  disquieted
rioted

I-e-ti
(briety)
  sobriety
    insobriety
piety
(priety)
  propriety
    impropriety
(riety)
  notoriety
  variety
(siety)
  society
(ziety)
  anxiety

I-et-ing
dieting
quieting
  disquieting
rioting

I-et-ist
pietist
quietist

I-et-izm
pietism
quietism

I-et-ur
dieter
(prietor)
  proprietor
quieter
rioter

IF-i-kait
(nificate)
  significate
(tificate)
  pontificate

IF-ti-li
niftily
shiftily
thriftily

IF-ti-ness
niftiness
shiftiness
thriftiness

IFT-less-ness
shiftlessness
thriftlessness

IF-ur-us
(biferous)
  herbiferous
(ciferous)
  calciferous
  vociferus
(niferous)
  carboniferous
  coniferous
(stiferous)
  pestiferous

IG-a-mi
bigamy
(lygamy)
  polygmy
trigamy

IG-am-ist
bigamist
(lygamist)
  polygamist
trigamist

IG-a-mus
bigamous
(lygamous)
  polygamous
trigamous

IG-ma-tist
(nigmatist)

enigmatist
stigmatist

IG-ni-fi
dignify
lignify
signify

IG-ni-ti
dignity
  indignity
(lignity)
  malignity
(nignity)
  benignity

IG-ni-us
igneous
ligneous

IG-or-us
rigorous
vigorous

IG-u-wus
(biguous)
  ambiguous
(tiguous)
  contiguous
(ziguous)
  exiguous

IJ-en-us
(digenous)
  indigenous
(lygenous)
  polygenous
(tigenus)
  vertigenous

IJ-i-an
Phrygian
Stygian

IJ-id-li
frigidly
rigidly

IJ-id-ness
frigidness
rigidness

IJ-ur-ent
(frigerant)
   refrigerant
(ligerent)
   belligerent

IJ-us-ness
(ligiousness)
   religiousness
(tigiousness)
   litigiousness

IK-a-tiv
(dicative)
   indicative
fricative

IK-en-ing
quickening
sickening
thickening

IK-e-ti
rickety
(snickety)
   persnickety

IK-e-ting
cricketing
picketing
ticketing

IK-e-tur
cricketer
picketer
ticketer

IK-i-li
stickily
trickily

IK-i-ness
pickiness
stickiness
trickiness

IK-li-ness
prickliness
sickliness

IK-sa-ble
fixable
mixable

IK-shun-al
dictional
   addictional
fictional
frictional

IK-si-ti
fixity
(lixity)
   prolixity

IK-tiv-li
(dictively)
   addictively
   vindictively
fictively
(strictively)
   constrictively
   restrictively

IK-tiv-ness
(dictiveness)
   addictiveness
   vindictiveness
(strictiveness)
   constrictiveness
   restrictiveness

IK-to-ri
(dictory)
   contradictory
   interdictory
   valedictory

victory

IK-u-lait
(sticulate)
   gesticulate
(ticulate)
   articulate
   reticulate
(triculate)
   matriculate

IK-u-lar
(hicular)
   vehicular
(licular)
   pellicular
(nicular)
   funicular
(ricular)
   auricular
(ticular)
   cuticular
   particular

IK-wi-ti
(biquity)
   ubiquity
(niquity)
   iniquity
(tiquity)
   antiquity

IK-wi-tus
(biquitous)
   ubiquitous
(niquitous)
   iniquitous

IL-a-bl
fillable
   refillable
(stillable)
   distillable
syllable
   monosyllable
tillable
   untillable

IL-a-jur
pillager
villager

I-lan-dur
highlander
islander
   Long Islander

IL-et-ed
billeted
filleted

IL-et-ing
billeting
filleting

IL-fu-li
skillfully
willfully

IL-ful-ness
skillfulness
willfulness

IL-i-ait
(filiate)
  affiliate
(miliate)
  humiliate
(siliate)
   concilate

IL-i-est
chilliest
frilliest
hilliest
silliest

IL-i-ness
chilliness
frilliness
hilliness
silliness

IL-ing-li
chillingly
killingly
thrillingly
trillingly
willingly

IL-i-tait
(bilitate)
  debilitate
  habilitate
   rehabilitate
militate
(silitate)
  facilitate

IL-i-ti
(bility)
  ability
   disability
   inability
  acceptability
   unacceptability
  accessibility
   inaccessibility
  accountability
   unaccountability
  adaptability
   inadaptability
  admissibility
   inadmissibility
  adorability
  advisability
   inadvisability
  affability
  agreeability
   disagreeability
  amenability
  amicability
   inamicability
  applicability
   inapplicability
  assimilability
   unassimilability
  attainability
   unattainability

audibility
  inaudibility
availability
  unavailability
capability
  incapability
changeability
  unchangeability
  interchangeability
communicability
  incommunicability
compatibility
  incompatibility
comprehensibility
  incomprehensibility
conceivability
  inconceivability
convertibility
  inconvertibility
corruptibility
  incorruptibility
credibility
  incredibility
culpability
curability
  incurability
deceptibility
deductibility
demonstrability
deplorability
desirability
  undesirability
destructibility
  indestructibility
detestability
digestibility
  indigestibility
dispensability
  indispensability
divisibility
  indivisibility
ductability
durability
  endurability
   unendurability
edibility

inedibility
eligibility
  ineligibility
excitability
  unexcitability
exhaustibility
  inexhaustibility
explicability
  inexplicability
fallibility
  infallibility
flammability
  inflammability
flexibility
  inflexibility
formidability
frangibility
  infrangibility
gullibility
ineffability
inevitability
intelligibility
  unintelligibility
inexorability
invincibility
inviolability
irascibility
irritability
legibility
  illegibility
liability
measurability
  immeasurability
mobility
  immobility
movability
  immovability
mutability
  immutability
navigability
negotiability
  nonnegotiability
nobility
notability
passibility
  impassibility

penetrability
  impenetrability
perceptibility
  imperceptibility
perfectibility
  imperfectibility
permissibility
  impermissibility
placability
  implacability
plausibility
  implausibility
pliability
portability
possibility
  impossibility
practicability
  impracticability
preferability
pregnability
  impregnability
preventability
  unpreventability
probability
  improbability
readability
  unreadability
reliability
  unreliability
respectability
responsibility
  irresponsibility
reversibility
  irreversibility
risibility
satiability
  insatiability
sensibility
  insensibility
separability
  inseparability
solubility
  insolubility
stability
  instability
suitability

unsuitability
surmountability
  insurmountability
susceptibility
  insusceptibility
tangibility
  intangibility
tolerability
  intolerability
tractability
  intractability
viability
visibility
  invisibility
volubility
vulnerability
  invulnerability
(jility)
  agility
  fragility
(mility)
  humility
(nility)
  juvenility
  senility
(quility)
  tranquility
(rility)
  puerility
  sterility
  virility
(sility)
  docility
  facility
  imbecility
(stility)
  hostility
(tility)
  fertility
    infertility
  gentility
  subtility
  utility
    inutility
  volatility
(vility)

civility
  incivility
servility

IL-ki-est
milkiest
silkiest

IL-ki-ur
milkier
silkier

IL-o-i
billowy
pillowy
willowy

IL-o-ing
billowing
pillowing

IL-o-kwense
(diloquence)
  grandiloquence
(niloquence)
  magniloquence

IL-o-kwent
(diloquent)
  grandiloquent
(niloquent)
  magniloquent

IL-o-kwi
(liloquy)
  soliloquy
(triloquy)
  ventriloquy

IL-u-ri
pillory
  capillary
(sillary)
  ancillary
(stillery)
  distillery

(tillery)
  artillery

IL-yan-si
brilliancy
(zilliency)
  resiliency

IM-e-tur
dimeter
limiter
(rimeter)
  perimeter
scimitar
(timeter)
  altimeter
trimeter

IM-in-ait
criminate
  discriminate
    indiscriminate
  incriminate
  recriminate
(liminate)
  eliminate

IM-i-nal
(bliminal)
  subliminal
criminal

I-mi-ness
griminess
sliminess

IM-i-ti
(blimity)
  sublimity
(nimity)
  anonymity
  equanimity
  magnanimity
  unanimity
(simity)
  proximity

IM-pu-ring
simpering
whimpering

IM-pu-rur
simperer
whimperer

IM-u-lait
simulate
  dissimulate
stimulate

I-na-bl
(binable)
  combinable
    uncombinable
(clinable)
  declinable
  inclinable
finable
  definable
    indefinable
  refinable
signable
  assignable

IN-di-kait
indicate
syndicate
vindicate

IN-e-al
lineal
pineal

ING-gu-ring
fingering
lingering
  malingering

ING-gu-rur
fingerer
lingerer
  malingerer

ING-i-ness
springiness
stringiness

ING-ka-bl
drinkable
  undrinkable
shrinkable
  unshrinkable
sinkable
  unsinkable
thinkable
  unthinkable

ING-ki-ness
inkiness
finkiness
ginkiness
kinkiness
slinkiness
stinkiness

IN-i-a
(dinia)
  Sardinia
Virginia
  West Virginia
zinnia

I-ni-est
briniest
shiniest
spiniest
tiniest
whiniest

IN-i-kl
binnacle
  rabbinical
clinical
cynical
pinnacle

IN-ish-ing
finishing
(minishing)

diminishing

IN-is-tur
minister
  administer
sinister

IN-i-ti
(finity)
  affinity
  infinity
(jinity)
  virginity
(linity)
  alkalinity
  masculinity
  salinity
(ninity)
  assininity
  femininity
(sinity)
  vicinity
trinity
(vinity)
  divinity

I-ni-ur
brinier
shinier
spinier
tinier
whinier

IN-jen-si
stringency
  astringency
(tingency)
  contingency

IN-jil-i
dingily
stingily

IN-ji-ness
dinginess
stinginess

IN-tur-i
splintery
wintery

I-nur-i
binary
finery
  refinery

IN-u-us
sinuous
(tinuous)
  continuous
    discontinuous

I-o-la (E-o-la)
(riola)
  variola
viola
  movieola

I-o-let
triolet
violet

I-o-tur
rioter
(see **I-et-ur,** *page 336)*

IP-ti-kl
(clipitcal)
  ecliptical
cryptical
(liptical)
  apocalyptical
  elliptical

IP-u-lait
(nipulate)
  manipulate
stipulate

IP-u-li
flippily
nippily
Tripoli

zippily

IP-u-ri
frippery
slippery

I-ra-bl
fireable
(quirable)
   requirable
(spirable)
   expirable
   transpirable
tirable
   untirable
wireable
(zirable)
   desirable

IR-i-kl
lyrical
miracle
(pirical)
   empirical
(tiracle)
   satirical

I-ri-us
Sirius
(see **E-ri-us,** *page 331)*

IS-en-ing
christening
glistening
listening

ISH-a-li
(dicially)
   judicially
      prejudicially
fishily
   artificially
officially
   superficially

ISH-en-si
(ficiency)
   deficiency
   efficiency
      inefficiency
   proficiency
   sufficiency
      insufficiency
      self-sufficiency

ISH-i-ait
(ficiate)
   officate
(nitiate)
   initiate
(pitiate)
   propitiate
vitiate
   novitiate

ISH-un-al
(ditional)
   additional
   conditional
      unconditional
   traditional
      untraditional
(litional)
   volitional
(witional)
   tuitional
      intuitional
(zitional)
   inquisitional
   positional
      depositional
      prepositional
      propositional
      transpositional

ISH-un-ist
(bitionist)
   exhibitionist
   prohibitionist
(ditionist)
   traditionist

(litionist)
   abolitionist
   coalitionist

ISH-un-ur
(missioner)
   commissioner
(titioner)
   practitioner

ISH-u-ri
(diciary)
   judiciary
fishery

ISH-us-ness
(diciousness)
   judiciousness
   seditiousness
(liciousness)
   deliciousness
(niciousness)
   perniciousness
(pitiousness)
   propitiousness
(priciousness)
   capriciousness
(riciousness)
   avariciousness
(spiciousness)
   auspiciousness
      inauspiciousness
   suspiciousness
(titiousness)
   fictitiousness
viciousness

IS-i-bl
hissable
kissable
missable
   admissible
      inadmissible
   dismissible
      undismissible
   omissible

349

permissible
  impermissible

I-si-est
iciest
diciest
spiciest

I-si-kl
icicle
bicycle
tricycle

I-sil-i
icily
spicily

IS-im-o
(lissimo)
  generalissimo
(nissimo)
  pianissimo
(stissimo)
  prestissimo
(tissimo)
  fortissimo
(vissimo)
  bravissimo

I-si-ness
iciness
diciness
spiciness

IS-i-ti
(bricity)
  lubricity
(dicity)
  periodicity
  pudicity
    impudicity
(licity)
  catholicity
  felicity
    infelicity
  publicity

(plicity)
  complicity
  duplicity
  multiplicity
  simplicity
(ricity)
  historicity
(ticity)
  authenticity
  elasticity
    inelasticity
  plasticity
  rusticity
(tricity)
  eccentricity
  electricity

IS-it-ness
licitness
  illicitness
(plicitness)
  implicitness
(splicitness)
  explicitness

IS-i-tude
(cissitude)
  vicissitude
(licitude)
  solicitude

I-siv-li
(cisively)
  decisively
    indecisively
  incisively
(risively)
  derisively
(visively)
  divisively

I-siv-ness
(cisiveness)
  decisiveness
    indecisiveness
  incisiveness

(risiveness)
  derisiveness
(visiveness)
  divisiveness

ISK-i-est
friskiest
riskiest

I-so-ri (I-zo-ri)
(cisory)
  incisory
(risory)
  derisory

IS-ti-kl
(guistical)
  linguistical
mystical
(tistical)
  artistical
  egotistical
  pietistical
  statistical

IS-to-ri
history
mystery
(sistory)
  consistory

I-ta-bl
(sitable)
  excitable
    unexcitable
  incitable
(dictable)
  indictable
(nitible)
  ignitable
(quitable)
  requitable

IT-a-bl
fittable
(mittable)

admittable
transmittable

I-ten-ing
brightening
frightening
heightening
lightening
tightening
whitening

I-ten-ur
brightener
frightener
heightener
lightener
whitener

I-tful-i
frightfully
(lightfully)
  delightfully
rightfully
spitefully

IT-i-gait
litigate
mitigate

IT-i-kl
critical
  diacritical
  hypercritical
  hypocritical
(litical)
  analytical
  political
(mitical)
  hermitical
(ritical)
  anchoritical
(witical)
  Jesuitical

IT-i-li
Italy

grittily
prettily
wittily

I-ti-ness
flightiness
mightiness
  almightiness

I-tli-ness
knightliness
sightliness
  unsightliness
spriteliness

IT-l-ness
brittleness
littleness

IT-u-ait (ICH-u-ait)
(bituate)
  habituate
situate

IT-u-al
(bitual)
  habitual
ritual

IT-ur-ait
(bliterate)
  obliterate
iterate
  reiterate
literate (i)
  illiterate (i)

IT-ur-ing
bittering
  embittering
frittering
glittering
tittering
twittering

I-ur-i
diary
fiery
friary
priory
wiry

I-va-bl
(privable)
  deprivable
(rivable)
  derivable
(trivable)
  contrivable
(vivable)
  revivable

IV-a-bl
givable
  forgivable
    unforgivable
livable

IV-el-ur
civiler
driveler
sniveler

IV-i-a
Livia
  Bolivia
trivia

IV-i-al
trivial
(vivial)
  convivial

IV-id-ness
lividness
vividness

IV-i-ti
(clivity)
  declivity
  proclivity

(sivity)
  passivity
    impassivity
(tivity)
  activity
  captivity
  festivity
  motivity
  nativity
  objectivity
  productivity
  receptivity
  relativity
  sensitivity
  subjectivity

IV-i-us
(blivious)
  oblivious
(civious)
  lascivious

IV-or-us
(bivorous)
  herbivorous
(nivorous)
  carnivorous
  omnivorous

IV-ur-i
chivari
livery
  delivery
quivery
shivery
slivery

IV-ur-ing
(livering)

delivering
quivering
shivering
slivering

IV-ur-ur
(liverer)
  deliverer
quiverer
shiverer

I-za-bl
(lysable)
  analysable
(nizable)
  reconizable
prizable
sizable
(spisable)
  despisable
(tizable)
  magnetizable
(visable)
  advisable
  devisable

IZ-a-bl
risible
visible
  divisible
    indivisible
  invisible

IZH-on-al
visional
  divisional
  provisional
  revisional

IZ-i-est
busiest
dizziest
fizziest
frizziest

IZ-i-kal
(disical)
  paradisical
physical
  metaphysical
quizzical

IZ-i-li
busily
dizzily
fizzily
frizzily

IZ-i-tor
(quisitor)
  acquistor
  inquisitor
visitor

IZ-i-ur
busier
dizzier
fizzier
frizzier

I-zor-i
(risory)
  derisory
(visory)
  advisory
  provisory
  supervisory

O

O-bi-a
phobia
  Anglophobia
  Francophobia
  hydrophobia
  xenophobia, etc.

OB-ur-i
robbery
slobbery
snobbery

OB-ur-ing
clobbering
slobbering

OD-i-fi
codify
modify

OD-i-kl
(modical)
  spasmodical
(sodical)
  episodical
  rhapsodical
(thodical)
  methodical
(yodical)
  periodical
(zodical)
  prosodical

OD-i-ness
bawdiness
gaudiness

OD-i-ti
oddity
(modity)
  commodity
    incommodity

O-di-um
odium
rhodium
sodium

O-di-us
odious
(lodious)
  melodious
(modious)
  commodious
    incommodious

OD-u-lar
modular
nodular

OD-ur-ing
doddering
foddering

OF-a-gus
(cophagus)
  sarcophagus
(crophagous)
  necrophagous
(sophagus)
  esophagus
(zoophagous, etc.)

OF-ul-i
awfully
lawfully
  unlawfully

OF-ul-ness
awfulness
lawfulness
  unlawfulness

OF-ur-ing
offering
coffering
proffering

OG-a-mi
(nogamy)
  monogamy
(sogamy)
  misogamy
(zogamy)
  exogamy

OG-a-mist
(nogamist)
  monogamist
(sogamist)
  misogamist

OG-am-us
(nogamous)
  monogamous
(sogamous)
  exogamous

OG-a-tive
rogative
  derogative
  interrogative
  prerogative

OG-ra-fi
(cography)
  lexicography
(mography)
  demography
  seismography
    thermography
(nography)
  iconography
  pornography
  stenography
(pography)
  topography
(thography)
  lithography
  orthography
(tography)

cryptography
photography
(yographiy)
bibliography
biography
  autobiography
choreography
geography
hagiography
ideography

OG-ra-fur
(cographer)
  lexicographer
(nographer)
  stenographer
(thographer)
  lithographer
(tographer)
  cartographer
  cryptographer
  photographer
(yographer)
  biographer
  choreographer
  geographer
  hagiographer, etc.

OI-a-bl
(joyable)
  enjoyable
(ployable)
  employable

OI-al-ist
loyalist
royalist

OI-al-izm
loyalism
royalism

OI-al-ti
loyalty
royalty
  viceroyalty

O-i-kal
(roical)
  heroical
stoical

OIN-ted-li
(jointedly)
  disjointedly
pointedly

OIS-tur-ing
cloistering
roistering

OJ-en-i
(mogeny)
  homogeny
progeny
(zogeny)
  misogyny

OJ-i-kal
(gojical)
  anagogical
  pedagogical
logical
  analogical
  anthological
  anthropological
  archaeological
  astrological
  biological
  chronological
  cosmological
  demonological
  etymological
  genealogical
  geological
  ideological
  illogical
  meteorological
  mythological
  neurological
  ornithological
  penological
  psychological

seismological
sociological
symbological
technological
theological

O-ka-liz
focalize
localize
vocalize

O-kal-izm
localism
vocalism

OK-a-tive
vocative
  invocative
  provocative

O-ken-li
brokenly
(spokenly)
  outspokenly

OK-i-li
chalkily
cockily
gawkily
rockily
stockily

OK-i-ness
chalkiness
cockiness
gawkiness
rockiness
squawkiness
stockiness
talkiness

OK-ra-si
(mocracy)
  democracy
(pocrisy)
  hypocrisy

(rocracy)
  bureaucracy
(tocracy)
  aristocracy
  autocracy
  plutocracy
(yokrasy)
  theocracy

OK-u-lar
ocular
jocular
(nocular)
  binocular
  monocular

OK-ur-i
crockery
mockery
rockery

O-la-bl
(solable)
  consolable
    inconsolable
    unconsolable
(trollable)
  controllable
    uncontrollable

O-lar-ize
polarize
solarize

O-lful-ness
dolefulness
soulfulness

O-li-a
(cholia)
  melancholia
(golia)
  Mongolia
(nolia)
  magnolia

O-li-ait
foliate
  defoliate
  infoliate
spoliate

OL-id-li
solidly
squalidly
stolidly

OL-id-ness
solidness
squalidness
stolidness

OL-i-fi (ALL-i-fi)
mollify
qualify
  disqualify

OL-i-fide (ALL-i-fide)
mollifed
qualifed
  disqualified
  unqualified

OL-i-kl (ALL-i-kl)
(bolical)
  diabolical
  hyperbolical
  symbolical
follicle
(tolical)
  apostolical

**OL-ik-som
(ALL-ik-sum)**
frolicsome
rollicksome

O-li-o
oleo
folio
  portfolio
polio

**OL-ish-ing
(ALL-ish-ing)**
(bolishing)
  abolishing
(molishing)
  demolishing
polishing

OL-i-ti (ALL-i-ti)
jollity
polity
quality
  equality
    inequality
(volity)
  frivolity

O-li-um
(noleum)
  linoleum
(troleum)
  petroleum

OL-o-ing (ALL-o-ing)
following
hollowing
swallowing
wallowing

OL-o-ji (ALL-o-ji)
(bology)
  symbology
(crology)
  necrology
(kology)
  pharmacology
  psychology
  toxicology
(lology)
  philology
(mology)
  cosmology
  entomology
  epistemology
  etymology
  homology

ophthalmology
seismology
thermology
(nology)
chronology
demonology
ethnology
hymnology
hypnology
iconology
penology
phenomenology
phrenology
sinology
technology
terminology
(pology)
anthropology
apology
(rology)
horology
meteorology
nephrology
neurology
urology
(sology)
glossology
(strology)
astrology
(thology)
anthology
ornithology
pathology
(tology)
climatology
cryptology
dermatology
Egyptology
eschatology
histology
parasitology
sitology
tautology
(trology)
gastrology
(wology)

zoology
(yology)
archaeology
biology
craniology
embryology
geology
hagiology
ideology
neology
phraseology
physiology
sociology
theology
(zology)
doxology
toxology

OL-o-jist (ALL-o-jist)
(bologist)
symbologist
(kologist)
lexicologist
pharmacologist
psychologist
(lologist)
philologist
(mologist)
cosmologist
entomologist
etymologist
seismologist
(nologist)
humanologist
hypnologist
phrenologist
sinologist
(rologist)
horologist
meteorologist
neurologist
(thologist)
ornithologist
pathologist
(tologist)
histologist

numismatologist
ontologist
(wologist)
zoologist
(yologist)
biologist
embryologist
geologist
ideologist
physiologist
sociologist

OL-o-jize (ALL-o-jize)
(pologize)
apologize
(thologize)
mythologize

OL-o-jur (ALL-o-jur)
(lologer)
philologer
(strologer)
astrologer

OL-o-ur (ALL-o-ur)
follower
hollower
swallower
wallower

OL-ti-est (ALL-ti-est)
faultiest
maltiest
saltiest

OL-ti-ness (ALL-ti-ness)
faultiness
maltiness
saltiness

**OL-tur-ing
(ALL-tur-ing)**
altering
unaltering
faltering
unfaltering

OL-u-bl (ALL-u-bl)
soluble
  insoluble
voluble

OL-va-bl (ALL-va-bl)
solvable
  absolvable
  dissolvable
    indissolvable
  insovable
  resolvable

OM-e-tri
(crometry)
  micrometry
(grometry)
  hygrometry
(nometry)
  chronometry
  galvanometry
  trigonometry
(yometry)
  geometry

OM-e-tur
crometer)
  micrometer
(dometer)
  odometer
  speedometer
(grometer)
  hygrometer
(kometer)
  tachometer
(mometer)
  dynamometer
  seismometer
  thermometer
(nometer)
  chronometer
  declinometer
  galvanometer
(rometer)
  barometer
(tometer)

magnetometer
(trometer)
  spectrometer
(yometer)
  audiometer

OM-i-kl
comical
(nomical)
  astronomical
  economial
(tomical)
  atomical
    anatomical

OM-i-nait
(bominate)
  abominate
dominate
  predominate
nominate
  denominate

OM-in-al
(dominal)
  abdominal
nominal

OM-in-ans
dominance
prominence

OM-in-ant
dominant
  predominant
prominent

OM-in-i
dominie
hominy

ON-dur-ing
pondering
squandering
wandering

ON-dur-ur
ponderer
squanderer
wanderer

O-ni-a
(gonia)
  begonia
  Patagonia
(monia)
  ammonia
  pneumonia
(phonia)
  aphonia
(yonia)
  Ionia

O-ni-al
(Ionial)
  colonial
(monial)
  ceremonial
  matrimonial
  patrimonial
  testimonial
(ronial)
  baronial

O-ni-an
(conian)
  Draconian
(donian)
  Caledonian
  Macedonian
(gonian)
  Patagonian
(sonian)
  Johnsonian
(tonian)
  Etonian
  Miltonian
  Newtonian
(yonian)
  Amazonian
  Ionian
  Oxonian

ON-i-est
bonniest
brawniest
tawniest

ON-ika
Monica
　harmonica
　Santa Monica
(ronica)
　Veronica

ON-i-kal
chronical
conical
　iconical
(nonical)
　canonical
(ronical)
　ironical

ON-i-mus
(nonymous)
　anonymous
(tonomous)
　autonomous

ON-ish-ing
(monishing)
　admonishing
(stonishing)
　astonishing

ON-ish-ment
(monishment)
　admonishment
(stonishment)
　astonishment

O-ni-um
(conium)
　zirconium
(monium)
　harmonium
　pandemonium
(phonium)

euphonium
(tonium)
　plutomium

O-ni-us
(lonious)
　felonious
(monious)
　acrimonious
　ceremonius
　harmonious
　　inharmonious
　parsimonious
　sanctimonious
(phonious)
　euphonious
(roneous)
　erroneous

ON-o-graf
chronograph
monograph

ON-o-mi
(conomy)
　economy
(gronomy)
　agronomy
(stronomy)
　astronomy
　gastronomy
(tonomy)
　autonomy

ON-o-mist
(conomist)
　economist
(gronomist)
　agronomist
(stronomist)
　gastronomist
(tonomist)
　autonomist

ON-o-mize
(conomize)

:conomize
(stronomize)
　astronomize

OOK-ur-i
cookery
rookery

O-pi-a
(topia)
　Utopia
(yopia)
　Ethiopia
　myopia

O-pi-an
(lopian)
　Fallopian
(topian)
　Utopian
(yopian)
　Ethiopian

OP-i-kal
(thropical)
　anthropical
　　misanthropical
topical
tropical

O-pi-ness
dopiness
ropiness
soapiness

OP-i-ness
choppiness
sloppiness
soppiness

OP-o-lis
(cropolis)
　Acropolis
　necropolis
(mopolis)
　cosmopolis

(tropolis)
  metropolis
(yopolis)
  Heliopolis

OP-si-kal
dropsical
popsicle

OP-u-lait
copulate
populate

OR-a-bl
(dorable)
  adorable
(norable)
  ignorable
(plorable)
  deplorable
  explorable
storable
  restorable

OR-a-li
orally
morally

OR-di-al
cordial
(mordial)
  primordial

OR-di-nait
ordinate
  coordinate
  subordinate (v)
    insubordinate (i)

OR-dur-ing
ordering
bordering

O-ri-a
(goria)
  phantasmagoria

(phoria)
  dysphoria
  euphoria
(storia)
  Astoria
(toria)
  Victoria
(yoria)
  Peoria

O-ri-al
boreal
  arboreal
(dorial)
  ambassadorial
(morial)
  armorial
  memorial
    immemorial
(norial)
  manorial
(poreal)
  corporeal
    incorporeal
(sorial)
  censorial
  professorial
  sensorial
  tonsorial
(storial)
  ancestorial
  consistorial
(torial)
  dictatorial
  directorial
  editorial
  electorial
  equatorial
  executorial
  factorial
  gladiatorial
  gubernatorial
  inquisitorial
  pictorial
  piscatorial
  proctorial

procuratorial
proprietorial
purgatorial
senatorial
territorial
  extraterritorial
tutorial

O-ri-an
(borean)
  hyperborean
Dorian
(gorian)
  Gregorian
(sorian)
  censorian
(storian)
  consistorian
  historian
(torian)
  stentorian
  valedictorian
  Victorian

OR-id-li
floridly
horridly
torridly

OR-i-fi
glorify
horrify

OR-i-kal
oracle
(gorical)
  allegorical
  categorical
(phorical)
  metaphorical
(storical)
  historical
(torical)
  oratorical
  rhetorical

OR-i-ness
goriness
hoariness
(toriness)
  dilatoriness

OR-i-ti
(jority)
  majority
(nority)
  minority
(rority)
  sorority
(thority)
  authority
(yority)
  inferiority
  juniority
  seniority
  superiority

OR-i-um
(porium)
  emporium
(sorium)
  sensorium
thorium
(torium)
  auditorium
  crematorium
  moratorium
  sanatorium
  sudatorium

OR-i-us
(boreous)
  arboreous
  laborious
glorious
  inglorious
  vainglorious
(roarious)
  uproarious
(sorious)
  censorious
(torious)

meritorious
notorious
stentorious
victorious
(zorious)
  uxorious

ORM-a-tive
formative
  informative
  reformative

ORM-i-ti
(formity)
  conformity
    nonconformity
  deformity
  uniformity
(normity)
  enormity

OR-o-ing
borrowing
sorrowing

OR-o-ur
borrower
sorrower

OR-sa-bl
forcible
  enforceable

OR-ti-fi
fortify
mortify

ORT-li-ness
courtliness
portliness

OR-tu-nate
fortunate
(portunate)
  importunate

OR-us-li
(corously)
  decorously
(norously)
  sonorously
porously

OR-yus-li
(boriously)
  laboriously
gloriously
  ingloriously
  vaingloriously
(roariously)
  uproariously
(toriously)
  meritoriously
  notoriously
  stentoriously
  victoriously
(zoriously)
  uxoriously

O-shun-al
(motional)
  emotional
(votional)
  devotional

O-shus-ness
(cociousness)
  precociousness
(rociousness)
  ferociousness
(trociousness)
  atrociousness

OS-i-ness
glossiness
mossiness

OS-i-ti
(bosity)
  verbosity
(cosity)
  precocity

(losity)
  velocity
(mosity)
  animosity
(nosity)
  luminosity
(posity)
  pomposity
(prosity)
  reciprocity
(rosity)
  ferocity
  generosity
  porosity
(scosity)
  viscosity
(strosity)
  monstrosity
(trosity)
  atrocity
(vosity)
  nervosity
(wosity)
  impetuosity
  virtuosity
(yosity)
  curiosity
  religiousity

O-siv-ness
(plosiveness)
  explosiveness
(rosiveness)
  corrosiveness

O-ta-bl
floatable
notable
potable
quotable
votable

OT-an-i
botany
(notony)
  monotony

(yotony)
  neotony

O-ta-ri
notary
rotary
votary

O-ted-li
bloatedly
(votedly)
  devotedly

OT-i-est
dottiest
haughtiest
naughtiest

OT-i-li
haughtily
naughtily

OT-i-ness
dottiness
haughtiness
naughtiness
spottiness

OT-i-ur
dottier
haughtier
naughtier

OT-om-i
(botomy)
  lobotomy
  phlebotomy
(kotomy)
  dichotomy
(yotomy)
  tracheotomy

OT-ur-i
lottery
pottery
tottery

watery

OT-ur-ing
slaughtering
tottering
watering

OUD-i-ness
cloudiness
dowdiness
rowdiness

OUND-less-li
boundlessly
groundlessly
soundlessly

OUND-less-ness
boundlessness
groundlessness
soundlessness

OUNT-a-bl
countable
  accountable
    unaccountable
  discountable
mountable
  surmountable
    insurmountable

OUT-i-ness
doughtiness
goutiness

OU-ur-i
bowery
flowery
showery

OU-ur-ing
cowering
flowering
glowering
powering
  overpowering

showering
towering

OU-zi-ness
drowsiness
frowziness

O-zi-est
coziest
nosiest
prosiest
rosiest

O-zi-li
cozily
nosily
prosily
rosily

O-zi-ness
coziness
doziness
nosiness

prosiness
rosiness

O-zi-ur
cozier
crosier
hosier
nosier
prosier
rosier

U

U-a-bl
(duable)
  subduable
(newable)
  renewable
suable
  pursuable
viewable
  reviewable

UB-i-ness
chubbiness
grubbiness
stubbiness

U-bri-us
(gubrious)
  lugubrious
(lubrious)
  salubrious
    insalubrious

U-bur-us
tuberous
  protuberous

UD-i-li
bloodily
ruddily

U-di-nal
(tudinal)
  attitudinal
  longitudinal

UD-i-ness
bloodiness
muddiness
ruddiness

U-di-nus
(tudinous)
  fortitudinous
  multitudinous
  platitudinous
  vicissitudinous

U-di-ti
crudity
nudity

U-el-ur
crueler
jeweler

UF-i-ness
fluffiness
huffiness
puffiness

stuffiness

UG-ur-i
snuggery
thuggery

U-i-ti
(cuity)
  perspicuity
  vacuity
(duity)
  assiduity
(fluity)
  superfluity
(guity)
  ambiguity
  contiguity
(nuity)
  annuity
  continuity
    discontinuity
  ingenuity
(scuity)
  promiscuity
(tuity)
  fatuity
  gratuity
  perpetuity

362

U-i-tus
(cuitous)
  circuitous
(tuitous)
  fatuitous
  fortuitous
  gratuitous

UK-i-li
luckily
pluckily

UK-shun-al
(ductional)
  inductional
(structional)
  constructional
  instructional

UK-ti-bl
(ductible)
  conductible
  deductible
(structible)
  destructible
    indestructible

UK-tiv-li
(ductively)
  productively
(structively)
  constructively
  destructively
  instructively

UK-tiv-ness
(ductiveness)
  productiveness
(structiveness)
  constructiveness
  destructiveness
  instructiveness

UK-to-ri
(ductory)
  introductory

reproductory

UK-ur-ing
puckering
succoring
suckering

U-lish-ness
  (OOL-ish-ness)
foolishness
ghoulishness
mulishness

U-li-ti
(dulity)
  credulity
  incredulity
(rulity)
  garrulity

UL-ki-ness
bulkiness
sulkiness

UL-mi-nait
culminate
fulminate

UL-siv-li
(pulsively)
  impulsively
  repulsively
(vulsively)
  convulsively

UL-siv-ness
(pulsiveness)
  compulsiveness
  impulsiveness
  repulsiveness
(vulsiveness)
  convulsiveness

UM-bur-ing
cumbering
  encumbering

lumbering
numbering
  outnumbering
slumbering

U-mi-nait (OO-mi-nait)
luminate
  illuminate
ruminate

U-mi-nant
  (OO-mi-nant)
luminant
  illuminant
ruminant

UM-i-ness
  (OOM-i-ness)
gloominess
roominess

UM-ing-li
(comingly)
  becomingly
    unbecomingly
hummingly
numbingly
  benumbingly

U-mi-nus
luminous
  voluminous
(tuminous)
  bituminous

UMP-shus-li
bumptiously
scrumptiously

U-mur-al
humeral
numeral

UM-ur-i
flummery
mummery

summary
summery

U-mur-us
humerus
humorous
numerous

UN-di-ti
(cundity)
    fecundity
    jocundity
(fundity)
    profundity
(tundity)
    rotundity

UN-dur-ing
blundering
plundering
sundering
thundering
wondering

UN-dur-ur
blunderer
plunderer
sunderer
thunderer
wonderer

UN-dur-us
blunderous
thunderous
wonderous

UNGK-u-lar
(buncular)
    carbuncular
(vuncular)
    avuncular

U-ni-form
uniform
cuneiform
luniform

UN-i-li
funnily
sunnily

U-ni-ti
unity
(munity)
    community
    immunity
(punity)
    impunity
(tunity)
    importunity
    opportunity

UN-ur-i (OON-ur-i)
(foonery)
    buffoonery
(troonery)
    poltroonery

UN-ur-i
gunnery
nunnery

U-pur-ait
(cuperate)
    recuperate
(tuperate)
    vituperate

U-ra-bl
curable
    incurable
    procurable
    securable
durable
    endurable
(surable)
    assurable
    insurable

UR-a-bl
(ferable)
    inferable
    referable

transferable
(terable)
    deterable
    undeterable

U-ral-ist
muralist
pluralist
ruralist

UR-bal-ist
herbalist
verbalist

UR-bal-izm
herbalism
verbalism

UR-di-li
sturdily
wordily

U-ri-ait
(furiate)
    infuriate
(zuriate)
    luxuriate

U-ri-al
(curial)
    mercurial
(neurial)
    seigneurial

UR-i-ing
currying
flurrying
hurrying
scurrying
worrying

UR-ish-ing
flourishing
nourishing

U-ri-ti
(curity)
  security
    insecurity
purity
  impurity
(scurity)
  obscurity
(turity)
  maturity
    immaturity

UR-i-ur
currier
furrier
hurrier
worrier

U-ri-us
curious
furious
(jurious)
  injurious
(nurious)
  penurious
spurious
(zurious)
  luxurious

UR-jen-si
urgency
(mergency)
  emergency
(surgency)
  insurgency
(vergency)
  divergency

UR-ji-kal
(rurgical)
  chirurgical
surgical
(turgical)
  liturgical

UR-jur-i
perjury
surgery

UR-ku-lar
(bercular)
  tubercular
circular

UR-li-est
earliest
burliest
curliest
surliest

UR-li-ness
earliness
burliness
curliness
surliness

UR-lish-li
churlishly
girlishly

UR-lish-ness
churlishness
girlishness

UR-mi-nait
germinate
terminate
  exterminate
  indeterminate

UR-mi-nal
germinal
terminal

UR-mi-nus
terminus
verminous

UR-na-bl
(cernible)

discernible
  indiscernible
learnable
turnable
  returnable

UR-nal-izm
journalism
(ternalism)
  externalism

UR-nish-ing
burnishing
furnishing

UR-nish-ur
burnisher
furnisher

UR-ni-ti
(dernity)
  modernity
(ternity)
  eternity
  fraternity
  maternity
  paternity
  taciturnity

UR-pen-tine
serpentine
turpentine

UR-sa-ri
bursary
cursory
  precursory
nursery
(versary)
  anniversary

UR-si-bl
(bursable)
  reimbursable
(mersible)
  immersible

(versible)
  conversible
  reversible
    irreversible
(wursible)
  coercible

UR-siv-ness
(scursiveness)
  discursiveness
(wursiveness)
  coerciveness

URTH-less-ness
mirthlessness
worthlessness

UR-va-tive
(servative)
  conservative
  observative
  preservative

UR-zhun-ist
(cursionist)
  excursionist
(mersionist)
  immersionist
versionist

U-shun-al
(cutional)
  elocutional
(lutional)
  evolutional
(tutional)
  constitutional
  institutional

U-shun-ur
(cutioner)
  executioner
(lutioner)
  revolutioner

U-si-bl
crucible
(ducible)
  deducible
  educible
  inducible
  producible
  reducible
    irreducible
  seducible
  traducible

U-sid-li
deucedly
lucidly
  pellucidly

U-siv-ness
(busiveness)
  abusiveness
(clusiveness)
  conclusiveness
  exclusiveness
(duciveness)
  conduciveness
(fusiveness)
  diffusiveness
  effusiveness
(lusiveness)
  allusiveness
  delusiveness
(trusiveness)
  intrusiveness
  obtrusiveness
    unobtrusiveness

US-ki-li
duskily
huskily
muskily

US-ku-lar
muscular
(puscular)
  corpuscular
  crepuscular

U-so-ri
(clusory)
  conclusory
(lusory)
  delusory
  elusory
  illusory

UST-ful-i
lustfully
trustfully
  distrustfully

UST-i-bl
(bustible)
  combustible
    incombustible
(justible)
  adjustable

US-ti-est
crustiest
dustiest
gustiest
lustiest
mustiest
rustiest
trustiest

US-ti-ness
crustiness
dustiness
gustiness
lustiness
mustiness
rustiness

US-tri-us
(dustrious)
  industrious
(lustrious)
  illustrious

US-tur-ing
blustering
clustering

flustering
mustering

U-ta-bl
(futable)
  confutable
mutable
  commutable
    incommutable
  immutable
(putable)
  computable
  disputable
  imputable
scrutable
  inscrutable
suitable

UTH-ful-li
truthfully
youthfully

UTH-ful-ness
truthfulness
youthfulness

UTH-less-li
ruthlessly
truthlessly

UTH-ur-hood
brotherhood
motherhood

UTH-ur-ing
brothering
mothering
smothering

UTH-ur-li
brotherly
motherly
southerly

U-ti-ful
beautiful
dutiful

U-ti-kl
cuticle
(peutical)
  therapeutical
(seutical)
  pharmaceutical

U-ti-neer
mutineer
scrutineer

U-ti-nus
glutinous
mutinous

U-ti-us
beauteous
duteous

UT-ur-ing
uttering
buttering
fluttering
guttering
muttering
spluttering
sputtering
stuttering

UT-ur-ur
mutterer
splutterer
sputterer
stutterer

UV-a-bl (OOV-a-bl)
movable
  immovable
  removable
    irremovable
provable
  improvable
  reprovable

U-vi-al (OOV-ee-al)
fluvial
  effluvial
(luvial)
  alluvial
  antediluvial
pluvial

U-vi-an (OOV-ee-an)
(luvian)
  antediluvian
(ruvian)
  Peruvian

U-za-bl (YOO-za-bl)
usable
(cuseable)
  excusable
    inexcusable
(fusible)
  diffusible
  transfusible